Visual Basic® 3.0
Programming
with
Windows™ Applications,
Second Edition

Visual Basic® 3.0 Programming

with
Windows™ Applications,
Second Edition

Douglas A. Hergert

RANDOM HOUSE
ELECTRONIC PUBLISHING

Visual Basic® 3.0 Programming with Windows™ Applications, Second Edition

Copyright © 1993 by Douglas A. Hergert

Produced by MicroText Productions
Composed by Context Publishing Services

Published in the United States by Random House, Inc., New York, and simultaneously in Canada by Random House of Canada, Limited.

Manufactured in the United States of America.

0 9 8 7 6 5 4 3 2

First edition

ISBN 0-679-79149-3

New York   Toronto   London   Sydney   Auckland

Contents

PART II

Visual Basic 3 Applications   151

Acknowledgments

My thanks to Claudette Moore, Jono Hardjowirogo, and Ron Petrusha for advice and encouragement. Special thanks also go to Elaine Andersson, Andrew Hergert, Audrey Hergert, and Boubacar Diatta for inspiration and support.

D.A.H.

Introduction

Visual Basic 3.0 is Microsoft's creative programming environment for Windows. It gives you an accessible and dynamic collection of tools for developing applications within the Windows graphical interface. Using Visual Basic you can create powerful programs that have the same look and feel as other Windows applications that you already use.

In **Versions 2.0 and 3.0**, Standard Edition, Microsoft has introduced a variety of innovations into the Visual Basic environment and language. The programming environment has some important new tools designed to streamline the process of developing applications, including the Properties window, the Toolbar, and an enhanced set of debugging commands. In addition, Visual Basic provides several new controls that you can now add to your applications. The Visual Basic language is more powerful than ever, with a number of new commands, functions, and structures—notably, a flexible new **Variant** data type, and complete programming support for creating *multiple-document interface* applications. Furthermore, in Version 3.0 you can use the new data control to establish connections between Visual Basic applications and databases you have created in other software environments—such as Microsoft Access, dBASE, FoxPro, or Paradox. This remarkable new feature gives your applications access to data from existing databases. (Visual Basic is also available in a Professional Edition, which provides additional new features. You can run the program examples in this book in either the Standard or Professional Edition of Version 2.0 or 3.0. The screen illustrations presented in this book are from the Standard Edition.)

This book introduces you to the steps of application development in Visual Basic, and presents a library of practical Visual Basic programs for you to work with. If you are already familiar with the Basic language, this book will help you broaden your programming knowledge and adapt your

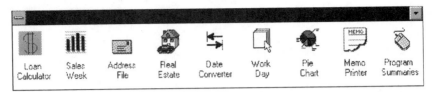

Figure I.1 The Visual Basic applications presented in this book

skills to the unique features of Visual Basic. If you are an active Windows user but not a programmer, you can use the applications in this book with Visual Basic to expand your current library of Windows programs.

Part I of this book is a tutorial-style introduction to the tools of the Visual Basic environment. You'll learn how to develop Windows-style interfaces for new applications you design, selecting from Visual Basic's ready-made controls: graphical objects such as command buttons, text boxes, icons, lists, labels, check boxes, and grids. Then you'll find out how to complete your application by setting properties and writing procedures in this object-oriented version of the Basic language. You'll also discover the significance of the Visual Basic's *event-driven* programming model, and you'll begin experimenting with a vast library of new programming tools.

Part II presents a collection of complete and working programming projects that you can examine, run, and customize for your own use. For your convenience, all the applications are also included on the exercise disk packaged with this book. Each chapter begins with a description of the application itself, along with instructions for running and using the program. You'll load each project into Visual Basic, examine its components, and then run it. Finally, you can use a Visual Basic command named **Make EXE File** to create executable application files, which you can then run directly from the Windows environment.

The chapters in Part II serve as self-contained tutorials on selected programming topics and techniques. You can read these chapters in any order that suits your own interests. Figure I.1 shows the icons for the applications presented in these chapters. The programs are designed to perform a wide variety of useful tasks at home or at work, and the examples will also help you to begin formulating your own imaginative ideas for additional Visual Basic applications.

The appendix introduces the design procedures for connecting an Access database to a Visual Basic 3.0 application. Using the new data control and its associated properties, you'll learn to create an application in which you can view and revise records from an existing database and add records to the database.

INSTALLING VISUAL BASIC

Visual Basic comes with a **Setup** utility that makes installation a simple process of following instructions that appear on the screen. Here is an overview of the steps for installing Visual Basic on your hard disk:

1. Start Windows on your computer and insert disk 1 of the Visual Basic product in your floppy disk drive. In the Windows Program Manager, choose the **Run** command from the **File** menu. Enter **A:SETUP** or **B:SETUP** in the **Command Line** box, as shown in Figure I.2, and click **OK**.

2. Setup performs some of its own initialization tasks, and then presents a dialog box that asks you for your name. After you enter and confirm your name, another dialog box gives you the opportunity to select the drive and directory location for Visual Basic. As you can see in Figure I.3, the default directory for the program is **C:\VB**. Whether you accept this default or enter a different path name, the Setup program creates the necessary directory and subdirectories on your disk. Click the **Continue** button to proceed with the installation.

3. In the next dialog box, shown in Figure I.4, you choose between a complete or partial installation of the components of Visual Basic. This box tells you how much memory is needed on your hard disk for the full installation. If you have enough space, you should click the **Complete Installation** button. If not, click **Custom Installation**; the resulting dialog box allows you to choose which components you want to install. The Setup utility subsequently begins copying files to your disk. As the process continues, Setup charts the progress of the installation, and notifies you when it is time to swap disks. Installation takes several minutes.

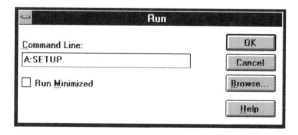

Figure I.2 Running the Setup utility

Figure I.3 Selecting a drive and directory for the Visual Basic installation

4.   When installation is complete, you will find a program group named **Visual Basic 3.0** in the Windows Program Manager, as shown in Figure I.5. To start Visual Basic, double-click the program icon.

5.   To prepare for the exercises in this book, create a new directory for the applications provided on the exercise disk. Give the directory a name such as **\VB3APPS**. Then copy all the files with **MAK, FRM, BAS**, and **ICO** extension names from the exercise disk to the directory location. Here is the significance of these extensions:

   •   The **MAK** extension identifies a *project* file, which contains a list of all the file components of a particular Visual Basic application.

   •   The **FRM** extension identifies a *form* file, which defines the appearance and behavior of a window or dialog box in an application. (A **FRM** file may also contain *code*—that is, Basic declarations, procedures, and functions.)

Figure I.4 Choosing between a complete or partial installation

- The **BAS** extension identifies a *module* file, containing additional code for the application.
- An **ICO** file identifies a graphic icon that may appear as part of an application.

Figure I.5 The Visual Basic application icon

About the Exercise Disk

The projects on the exercise disk are saved in the Visual Basic 2.0 format, allowing you to open and run the projects in *either* Visual Basic 2.0 or 3.0. When you open a project into Visual Basic 3.0, a message like the following appears on the screen for *each* form in the project:

```
'FORMNAME.FRM' has old file format. When
saved it will be saved in newer format.
```

Click OK on the message box to open the form. When the entire project is open, immediately choose the **Save Project** command from the **File** menu to save the project in the Visual Basic 3.0 format.

PART I

The Visual Basic 3 Programming Environment

1

A First Look at Visual Basic

Microsoft Visual Basic is a dramatic new approach to creating applications for Microsoft Windows. More than a traditional programming language, it is an elaborate development environment that helps you build sophisticated Windows-style programs. Using the tools provided in Visual Basic, you will design programs that match the visual and conceptual elegance of professionally developed Windows applications. Your programs can include any of the familiar elements of the Windows user-interface, such as pull-down menus, dialog boxes, icons, toolbars, and mouse control—features that could require enormous amounts of time and effort to create in a traditional programming language.

Visual Basic is a multifaceted programming environment, rich in individual tools and features. The purpose of the environment is to streamline the development process by providing the visual elements of a Windows user-interface as ready-made *controls* that you can incorporate into your application almost instantly. In the initial steps of creating an application, you use these controls to plan and build your program's interface, *directly on the screen*. In most cases, you'll begin writing Basic instructions and procedures—the activity traditionally known as *programming*—at the point when your application's visual interface is already complete. You can then modify the interface—adding or removing controls, or reorganizing your program's visual presentation—at any time during the development process.

You typically use Visual Basic's controls to depict the operations and choices you are planning to offer in an application. Conveniently, the appearance and behavior of these controls are predefined. Consider a couple of examples:

- A Visual Basic *command button* control looks and acts like any other command button in the Windows environment; clicking the button with the mouse produces the familiar push-button effect on the screen. You might provide a command button to depict a calculation or other operation that your program can perform.

- A *text box* control accepts an input value from the keyboard. A Visual Basic text box possesses the same keyboard editing functions provided by other Windows text boxes.

Along with command buttons and text boxes, Visual Basic provides a complete set of ready-made controls, including *lists, labels, check boxes, option buttons, scroll bars, frames, picture boxes,* and other features used in the Windows environment. These controls vastly simplify your job as a programmer. You can concentrate your efforts on the important computational and data processing procedures of your program; the elements of your user-interface—including screen graphics, keyboard functions, and mouse operations—are provided automatically by Visual Basic.

In this chapter you'll begin exploring the tools and resources available in Visual Basic. The chapter is divided into three main parts:

1. A brief survey of the Visual Basic development environment.

2. A look at a sample Visual Basic project, a database program named the *Real Estate* program. You will load the program from the exercise disk included with this book. After running *Real Estate* to see how it works, you'll begin examining the parts of the application.

3. A preview of the steps required for developing an application in Visual Basic. You'll learn much more about these steps in the remaining chapters of Part I.

Begin now by starting up Visual Basic on your computer. (If you haven't yet installed Visual Basic, do so now by following the steps outlined in the Introduction to this book.) In Windows, double-click the Microsoft Visual Basic 3.0 icon. After a few seconds, the Visual Basic development environment appears on your screen, as shown in Figure 1.1.

THE VISUAL BASIC DEVELOPMENT ENVIRONMENT

As you can see by looking at the program title at the top of the screen, Visual Basic starts out in the *design* mode. This means that the environment

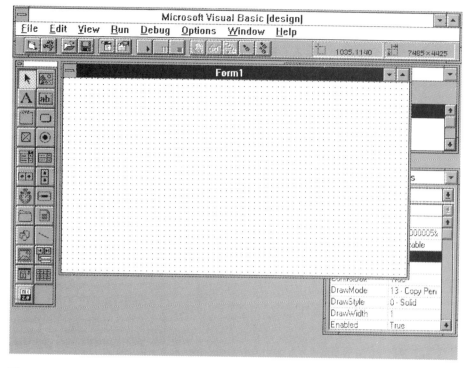

Figure 1.1 *Visual Basic's* opening screen

is ready for you to begin designing the user interface for a new application.
At first glance, the screen seems crowded with a bewildering assortment of
windows and menus, but you will quickly become as comfortable with this
environment as you are with your favorite word processor or spreadsheet
program.

Forms and Projects

In the middle of the screen, taking up most of the space, is a window named
Form1. In a given session with Visual Basic this empty window can become
the starting point for your work on a new application.

The windows in which you build a Visual Basic application are called
forms. You can use a form for any number of different purposes, depending
on the needs of your application. For example, a form can become a dialog
box. You design a dialog box by selecting controls and placing them inside
a form. Alternatively, your program can use a form as an area to display
text output, tables of numeric data, or graphics. Initially, there is one form
for every new application that you begin, but you can add as many forms
as are required in the plan of your program.

In Visual Basic 2.0 and 3.0 you can also add a special type of form called the MDI form, which allows you to develop a multiple-document interface for an application. An MDI form serves as the controlling application window in a program that allows the user to create and open multiple document windows simultaneously. You'll study the details of this feature in Chapter 9.

You design one application at a time in Visual Basic. Each form that you add to your application is stored on disk as a separate file. During development time a given application can therefore consist of many different files on disk. (For example, the program you'll be examining later in this chapter is made up of six disk files.) The file components of an application are together called a *project*. Visual Basic keeps track of the files of a given project and can open them all in a single operation.

In this first chapter, you'll focus on the general characteristics of several major tools that are part of the Visual Basic environment:

- The *Toolbox*, initially located at the left side of the screen, contains the assortment of visual controls that you can select for use in your application.

- The *Properties* window gives you tools for identifying and changing the initial characteristics of the forms and controls that you add to your application.

- The *Project window*, initially at the right side of the screen (partially hidden by **Form1**), lists the components of the application that you are currently creating.

- The Visual Basic menu system and toolbar together provide a variety of commands and shortcuts for use during program development.

As you examine these tools you'll also perform a few introductory hands-on exercises in the Visual Basic environment.

The Toolbox and the Properties Box

As you can see in Figure 1.2, the Toolbox contains two columns of icons. These icons represent the controls you put in an application. You can insert any number of controls into a form, and arrange those controls in whatever way suits your application design.

Each of the controls represented in the Toolbox has its own special characteristics. Learning how to use controls successfully is one of the major tasks ahead of you as you begin developing applications. For now, take a brief look at each of the icons in the Toolbox and review the purpose of the corresponding control. If you have spent any time working in the Windows environment, these controls will be familiar: Examples of most

Figure 1.2 The Toolbox

of them are likely to appear on the screen at some point during any typical
Windows session.

Here are brief descriptions of the controls as they are represented in the
Toolbox, by rows from top to bottom:

- The *pointer* icon at the upper-left corner of the Toolbox is actually
  not a control at all, but rather represents the mouse pointer you use
  to manipulate controls in a form.

- The *picture box* control to the right of the pointer can be an icon or
  other graphical display element in an application.

- The *label* control (represented by the **A** icon in the Toolbox) is
  typically a short text label that identifies an element of a dialog box.
  You can also use the label control to display longer blocks of text.

- The *text box* control (represented by the bold letters **ab** and a vertical
  bar cursor inside a small box) is an input box that accepts text entered
  from the keyboard.

- The *frame* control (represented by a small box with the letters **XYZ** in
  the title position) can be used to group together a collection of other
  controls in a form.

- The *command button* (depicted in the Toolbox as a small rectangular button with a shadow) is a control that the user can click to perform a specific operation or select an option in an application.

- The *check box* (represented by a square filled with an X) depicts an option that can be turned on or off. A dialog box might contain a list of check boxes; each of the options in the list can be switched on or off independently of the other options.

- The *option button* (a circle filled with a bold dot) is another control that represents an *on/off* option. A list of option buttons always represents a group of *mutually exclusive* options: Only one of the options in the list can be switched on at a time; the other options in the list are off.

- The *combo box* control is a text box with an attached list that can drop down beneath the input area. To make an entry into such a box, the user can either type text directly from the keyboard or select a text entry from the drop-down list.

- The *list box* control is a list of text options, any one of which can be selected as an input item.

- The *horizontal scroll bar* is a control that depicts a physical position or a numeric quantity in relation to minimum and maximum values. Arrows appear on the left and right ends of the bar, and a scroll box moves back and forth across the bar. One typical use of this control is to scroll text inside an input box.

- The *vertical scroll bar* contains arrows at the top and bottom of the bar and a scroll box that moves up and down.

- The *timer* control (a stopwatch icon) represents timed events in an application.

- The *drive list box* control (a disk drive icon) allows the user to view the valid disk drives in the system and to activate a new drive.

- The *directory list box* control (a folder icon) displays the hierarchy of directories on a disk.

- The *file list box* control (a sheet of paper with lines of text on it) displays file names from a directory.

- The *shape* control (represented in the Toolbox by a collection of overlapping geometric shapes) appears as a filled or unfilled shape on a form. You can choose among a variety of shapes for this control, including squares, rectangles, ovals, and circles.

- The *line* control (represented as a diagonal line) appears as a vertical, horzontal, or diagonal line on a form. This control is useful for dividing a form into sections or for separating one set of controls from another.

- The *image* control (represented as a framed picture) functions much like the picture box control, but can provide better performance and memory usage.

- The *data* control allows you to use an existing database in a Visual Basic application. (The appendix shows you how to use this control.)

- The *common dialog* control provides standard dialog boxes for common operations such as opening, saving, and printing files, and accessing colors and fonts.

- The *grid* control (the last icon in the second column of the Toolbox) appears as a two-dimensional group of cells arranged in rows and columns, similar to a worksheet in a program like Microsoft Excel. You can use this control to display tables of data in a form or to accept data input from the user.

- The *OLE* control (the last icon in the first column) allows you to use *object linking and embedding* in a Visual Basic application. OLE is a Windows technique for sharing information and graphics between different applications.

You'll be seeing examples of some of these controls in the sample application presented later in this chapter. Meanwhile, the following brief exercise will show you how simple it is to put a control on a form.

Hands-On Exercise: Placing a Control on a Form

As you have seen, the *active* form in the opening Visual Basic screen is initially named **Form1**. You can practice placing controls on this form as though you were planning to create a dialog box for an application. Start now by performing the following steps:

1. Move the mouse pointer to the *command button* icon in the Toolbox (the third icon from the top in the right-hand column).

2. Double-click the left mouse button. A button named **Command1** immediately appears in the center of **Form1**, as shown in Figure 1.3. Visually, the command button has a three-dimensional quality. Notice also that the command button is surrounded by small bold squares, which are called *sizing handles*. Their presence indicates that this control is currently selected for some subsequent action.

3. Drag the command button to a new position in the upper-left corner of **Form1**: Position the mouse pointer over the control, and hold

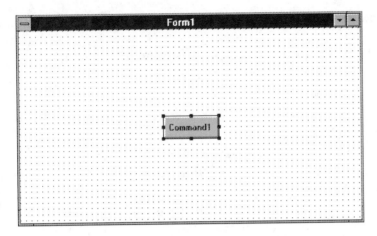

Figure 1.3 Placing a command button on the form

down the left mouse button while you drag the control to its new position. As you drag the icon, you will see an outline of the control move to the new position. If you watch closely, you'll notice that the movement occurs in small vertical and horizontal jumps within the dotted grid background of the form. While you drag the control, take note of the rapid changes occurring in the boxed pair of numbers located above the form just to the right of the Toolbar. These numbers give the current position of the control in relation to the upper-left corner of the form. When you release the mouse button, the repositioning is complete.

4. Decrease the size of the command button: Position the mouse pointer over the sizing handle located at the lower-right corner of the command button; the mouse pointer becomes a two-headed diagonal arrow. Hold down the left mouse button and carefully move the arrow one notch to the left and one notch up within the background grid of the form. (Notice the resulting change that occurs in the pair of numbers located to the right of the position coordinates near the upper-right corner of the screen; these two numbers give the width and height of the control.) Release the mouse button, and the sizing operation is complete.

5. Click the mouse button anywhere inside **Form1** to deactivate the command button control.

You have just placed your first control on a form. If you were actually planning an application, this command button might ultimately represent a particular operation that your program would perform on demand—for example, saving a record, calculating a mathematical value, clearing values from the screen, displaying a new dialog box of options, or exiting from the current program. You'll see buttons that represent operations like these in this chapter's sample application. To perform one of these operations during a run of the program, the user simply clicks the appropriate command button.

As you begin adding controls to an application, you'll want to be able to specify the characteristics of each control—its appearance and location, its name, and its behavior. These and other characteristics are called *properties* in Visual Basic. Each property has a name and a *default setting.* Interestingly enough, you have just changed four of the properties of the command button control in **Form1**: the **Width** and **Height** properties, representing the size of the control; and the **Left** and **Top** properties, representing the position of the control. You have used the mouse to change these particular properties directly on the screen. Other properties are controlled via an important Visual Basic feature called the *Properties window.*

Controls and Their Properties

Each of the controls depicted in the Toolbox has its own set of properties; in addition, the forms of an application also have properties. To modify the appearance, position, or behavior of a given control or form, you have to change the setting of the appropriate property. Some properties—such as the ones named **Top** and **Left**—are common to most or all controls; others are special purpose properties that are relevant only to specific controls. The Properties window gives you simple techniques for working with properties. You use the Properties window to perform any of these actions:

- View the list of properties that apply to a given control or form.

- Determine the current setting of a particular property for a selected control or form.

- View the list of available settings for a property.

- Change the setting of a property for a selected control or form.

The Properties window initially is located at the lower-right corner of the Visual Basic screen. To make it the active window, you can simply press the F4 function key. Then you can use the mouse to reposition and resize it, just as you would any other window. Figure 1.4 shows the Properties window, with a list of properties that apply to **Form1**.

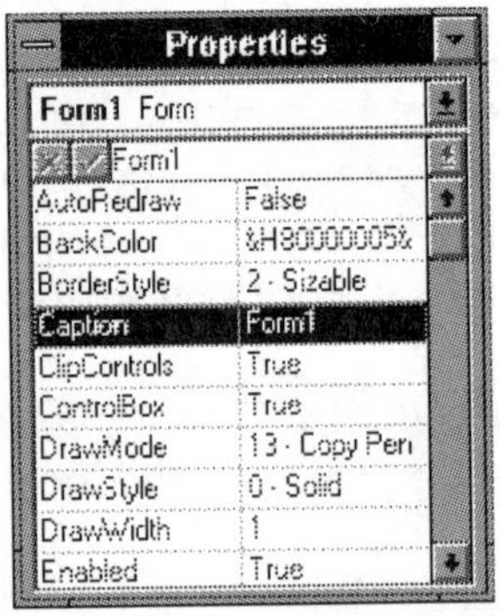

Figure 1.4 The Properties window

The Properties window displays a two-column grid of properties. The left column lists the properties that apply to the currently selected form or control, and the right column shows the current setting for each property. Just above the grid is the *Settings box,* which currently displays the name **Form1**. For a property that has a fixed group of settings, the drop-down list attached to this box displays those settings; otherwise, the Settings box accepts a setting as input from the keyboard. Above the settings box is the *Object box,* the drop-down list attached to this box displays all the controls on the current form. After you select a control and a property, you use the Settings box to change the setting of that property. Every property for a given control has a default setting—that is, a setting that remains in effect unless you explicitly change it.

As you've seen already, the four property settings that determine the position and size of a form or a control are displayed just beneath Visual Basic's menu bar to the right of the Toolbar. Appropriately enough, these four properties are named **Left**, **Top**, **Width**, and **Height**. The two boxes that display the properties for these settings, shown in Figure 1.5, are called the *Position box* and the *Size box:*

- The *Position box* displays the position coordinates of the selected control or form—that is, the **Left** and **Top** property settings. For a control, the coordinates represent the position in relation to the upper-left corner of the containing form. For a form, the coordinates are in relation to the upper-left corner of the screen. In both cases, the first coordinate is the horizontal position and the second is the vertical position.

- The *Size box* contains the dimensions of the selected control or form—that is, the **Width** and **Height** settings. The first dimension is the width and the second is the height.

Position   Size

Figure 1.5 The Position box and the Size box

Hands-On Exercise: Using the Properties Window

For a quick introduction to the Properties window, you'll now change two properties of the command button control that you have already placed on **Form1**. First, you'll display a new description inside the button. (Recall that the button currently displays the default text **Command1**.) The property that defines this name is called **Caption**. Second, you'll change the display style of this name to italics. The property that controls this display characteristic is called **FontItalic**. Changing the **Caption** property requires you to enter the new text for the caption. In contrast, the **FontItalic** property has a fixed list of available settings; to choose a setting, you pull down the list attached to the Settings box.

Follow these steps to make these two changes:

1. Click the **Command1** command button to select the control. The sizing handles appear around the perimeter of the button.

2. Press the F4 function key to activate the Properties window. The **Caption** property is initially selected. The Settings box displays the default caption of the command button, **Command1**. To change this caption you can simply begin typing new text from the keyboard while the control is selected.

3. Type the caption **Start** for the command button, then press the Enter key to complete the change. The new name appears both inside the Settings box and inside the command button itself.

4. Now use the vertical scroll bar to move up and down the property grid, and take a thorough look at the properties defined for a command button. Then click the **FontItalic** property. At this point in your work, your screen looks something like Figure 1.6.

5. Click the down arrow icon located at the right of the Settings box, pulling down the list of available settings for the **FontItalic** property. The list contains two settings, **False** and **True**. The current setting is **False**. Click **True**. The display style of the button caption immediately changes to italic.

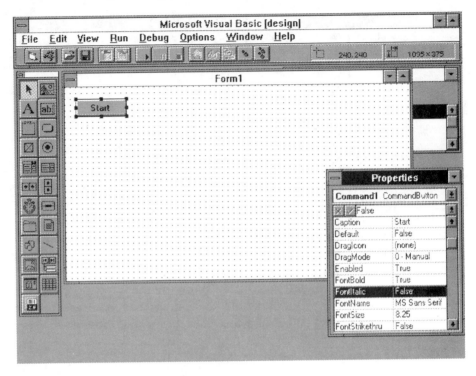

Figure 1.6 Using the Properties window

For most new controls that you add to an application, you will typically need to change only a few of the default property settings during your work in the design mode. Later on you'll see that properties can be also changed by the program itself, in response to events that take place during *run time*.

So far you have worked with several elements of the Visual Basic environment: the Toolbox, the Properties window, a form, and a control. Next, you'll examine the window that has so far been partially hidden behind **Form1**, the *Project window*.

The Project Window

The Project window lists all the files of the application you are currently creating. To view the Project window on the screen, you can take the following steps:

1. Click **Window** in Visual Basic's menu bar. The resulting drop-down menu lists the variety of windows you can work with in the Visual Basic environment.

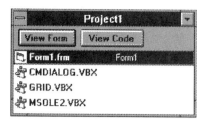

Figure 1.7 The Project window

2. Click **Project** to view the Project window.

3. Drag the bottom border of the window down a little so you can see the entire list of files that the window contains.

After this action, the Project window appears on the screen as shown in Figure 1.7. As you can see, the current project has the default name **Project1** and contains four files, named **Form1.frm**, **CMDIALOG.VBX**, **GRID.VBX**, and **MSOLE2.VBX**. The window has three columns for displaying information about the files in its list: First, an icon represents the file type. To the right of the icon is the file name under which the file is saved, or the default file name if the file has not yet been saved to disk. The third column shows the setting of a property called **Name** for all forms in the project list.

Projects contain forms, *modules,* and *custom controls*:

• As you've already seen, a form is a visual part of an application—a dialog box or a window in which the application displays text, data, or graphics.

• A module is one place to store *code*—the declarations, instructions, and procedures of a Visual Basic program.

• A custom control file defines a Toolbox control that is not built into the default Visual Basic environment. In Visual Basic 3.0 (Standard Edition) the common dialog control, the grid control, and the OLE control are implemented as custom controls. The characteristics of these controls are defined in the files CMDIALOG.VBX, GRID.VBX, and MSOLE2.VBX, which the Visual Basic Setup program copies to the directory named \WINDOWS\SYSTEM. If an application uses these custom controls, the VBX files must be included in the application's project window. As you'll see later, however, you can delete these VBX files from the Project list for an application that does not use them.

Forms and Modules

There are two locations in which you can write and store code for an application:

- A form generally contains the procedures that apply to its own controls. Two windows are therefore available for viewing the contents of a form: As you've already seen, the Form window displays the visual controls that you have placed in the form. The Code window displays the declarations and procedures you write for the form, and operates as a full-function text editor for developing procedures.

- A module contains procedures that you write for use by more than one form. Like the Code window for a form, a module window serves as an editor for entering and modifying code.

You'll find out more about these code areas later. For now, concentrate on the tools that the Project window gives you for working with forms and modules. Notice first that there are two command buttons at the top of the Project window: **View Form** and **View Code**. These two buttons give you instant access to the parts of a file, as you'll learn in the following exercise.

Hands-On Exercise: Using the Project Window

The **View Form** and **View Code** buttons apply to the currently selected file in the Project window. You select a file in the list by clicking the file with the mouse or by pressing the up or down arrow key. For now, make sure that **Form1** is selected, and then perform the following steps:

1. Click the **View Code** button to display the Code window for this form. The window appears as shown in Figure 1.8. Because you have not written any code for this form, the Code window is empty. But notice the boxes labeled **Object** and **Proc** beneath the title bar of the window; these are designed to help you locate different portions of your code as you begin developing a program.

2. Press Alt+F4 to close the Code window.

3. Pull down the **File** menu and choose the **New Module** command. In response, Visual Basic adds a module file to the current project and opens the module's code window, which looks about the same as the code window for a form.

4. Press Alt+F4 to close the code window for the module.

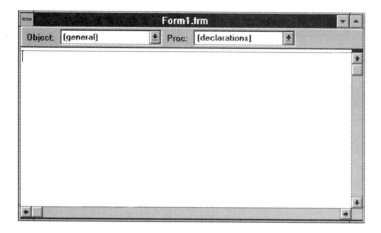

Figure 1.8 The Code window for **Form1**

Visual Basic uses several different extensions for the names of the files in your project:

- The **FRM** extension identifies a form file.
- The **BAS** extension identifies a module file.
- The **MAK** extension is for a special *project file*. This file keeps track of the various parts of your application.
- The **VBX** extension identifies a custom control.

As you can see, the list of file names increases in length as you add new forms and modules to your application. (The module you just added to the project is now listed in the Project window as **Module1.bas**.) You use commands listed in the **File** menu to change the number of files in your program.

The Visual Basic Menus and the Toolbar

The Visual Basic menu system provides many tools that you'll use during the process of developing an application. There are eight pull-down menus in the system: **File**, **Edit**, **View**, **Run**, **Debug**, **Options**, **Window**, and **Help**, shown in Figures 1.9 to 1.16.

As in other Windows applications, you can pull down a menu by clicking the menu name with the mouse or by pressing the Alt key and then striking the first letter of the menu name. For example, pressing Alt and then F displays the **File** menu. Once a menu is displayed, you select a command by clicking the command name with the mouse or by striking the appro-

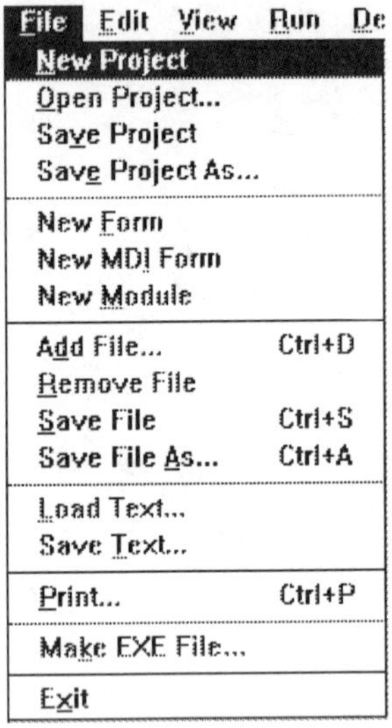

Figure 1.9 The **File** menu

priate *access* key on the keyboard. In addition, some of the menu commands have keyboard shortcuts that you can use to invoke a command without pulling down a menu.

Here are brief summaries of the commands and tools provided in each menu:

* The **File** menu contains commands for working individually or collectively with the files of a project. For example, the **New Project** command starts you out fresh with the file components of a new project. The **Open Project** command opens all the files of an existing project in one efficient operation; likewise, the **Save Project** command saves all the files of the current project to disk. (**Save Project As** gives you the opportunity to provide a new file name for the current project.) The **File** menu also contains commands that add new forms and modules to your current application (**New Form**, **New MDI Form**, and **New Module**). You'll work with some of these commands in an upcoming exercise. You can also remove files from a project (**Remove File**), save forms and modules individually to disk (**Save File** or **Save File As**), and load text files into a project or save part of a project as a text file (**Load Text** or **Save Text**). The **Print** command allows you to print the form and the code of an open file. The **Make EXE File** command creates a single compiled EXE file from the parts of the current application. As you begin opening existing projects from MAK files stored on disk, the **File** menu displays a *most-recently-used* list,

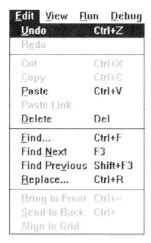

Figure 1.10 The **Edit** menu

containing the names of the last four projects you have opened. To reopen one of these files quickly, you simply select the file's name in the list. Finally, the **Exit** command closes the Visual Basic window, ending your current session with the program.

- The **Edit** menu contains an assortment of tools that are useful during the process of writing the text of a Basic program. The **Undo** command allows you to restore the original text after a mistaken editing operation. The **Cut**, **Copy**, and **Paste** commands together provide the cut-and-paste and copy-and-paste operations. You can also establish dynamic links between Visual Basic forms and documents created in other applications using the **Paste Link** command. The **Find** and **Replace** commands are efficient tools for locating a specific text item or for performing search-and-replace operations.

- The **View** menu provides commands for viewing code, creating new procedures, and scrolling from one procedure to the next. There is also a toggle (**Toolbar**) for displaying or hiding Visual Basic's Toolbar.

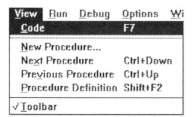

Figure 1.11 The **View** menu

Figure 1.12 The **Run** menu

- The **Run** menu contains the **Start** command, which you use when you are ready to try running an application that you have developed. **Start** begins a performance of the current application. Once the performance is underway, you can use other commands that appear in the **Run** menu to pause and restart a performance if you need to perform *debugging* operations.

- The **Debug** menu provides a variety of debugging tools, including *watch* expressions, which you can use to examine the value of a variable or expression while your program is running; *single-step* performance, which is a way of stepping through your program one command at a time; and *breakpoints*, which give you a precise way of interrupting your program at an anticipated trouble spot. You'll learn more about these tools in Chapter 5.

- The two commands of the **Options** menu give you ways to customize Visual Basic's working environment and to specify certain essential characteristics of the current project.

- The **Window** menu gives you quick access to the major window elements of Visual Basic, including the Project window, the Properties window, and the Toolbox. In addition, the **Menu Design** command displays a special dialog box in which you can design a customized menu system for an application. You'll start working with menu designs in Chapter 2. (The **Data Manager** command opens a separate application that comes with Visual Basic; you can use this application to create, open, or examine a database stored in any of several formats.)

- The **Help** menu provides a variety of entry points into the Visual Basic help system. The commands in this menu are similar to the Help commands in other Windows applications. The **Learning Microsoft Visual Basic** command starts the on-line Visual Basic tutorial, which you should take the time to go through sometime near the beginning of your work with Visual Basic.

Visual Basic's Toolbar, the row of icons located immediately beneath the menu bar, contains an assortment of shortcuts for performing selected menu commands. As you can see in Figure 1.17, the Toolbar contains

Debug	Options	Window	Help
Add Watch...			
Instant Watch...	Shift+F9		
Edit Watch...	Ctrl+W		
Calls...	Ctrl+L		
Single Step	F8		
Procedure Step	Shift+F8		
Toggle Breakpoint	F9		
Clear All Breakpoints			
Set Next Statement			
Show Next Statement			

Figure 1.13 The **Debug** menu

Figure 1.14 The **Options** menu

Window	Help
Color Palette	
Debug	Ctrl+B
Menu Design	Ctrl+M
Procedures	F2
Project	
Properties	F4
Toolbox	
Data Manager	

Figure 1.15 The **Window** menu

Help
Contents
Search For Help On...
Obtaining Technical Support...
Learning Microsoft Visual Basic
About Microsoft Visual Basic...

Figure 1.16 The **Help** menu

Figure 1.17 Visual Basic's Toolbar

fourteen icons. Clicking an icon with the mouse produces the same results as choosing the corresponding menu command. Here is a summary of the features available in the Toolbar:

- The first two icons open new files for the current project. They are the same as the **New Form** and **New Module** commands in the **File** menu.

- The third and fourth icons also perform commands from the **File** menu. You can use these tools to open a new project from disk (**Open Project**) and save changes in the current project to disk (**Save Project** or **Save Project As**).

- The next two icons open and activate important windows that are available for use in the Visual Basic environment: The Menu Design window and the Properties window. Both icons are equivalent to commands in the **Window** menu.

- The next group of three icons perform commands from the **Run** menu. You use these icons to begin a performance of the current project (the same as choosing the **Start** command from the **Run** menu or pressing the F5 function key), create a break in the performance of a project, or stop the performance.

- The final group of five icons in the Toolbar perform operations from the **Debug** menu. You can use these icons to create a breakpoint and a watch expression; to investigate the sequence of procedure calls that have taken place before the current point in a program performance; and to initiate two types of single-step program execution. You'll practice these operations in Chapter 5.

Hands-On Exercise: Using Commands from the File Menu

Imagine that you have been building a dialog box in **Form1**, which is currently the only form in your application. You have decided that you need an additional form for a second dialog box and a second module in which to write general purpose procedures that will be used in both forms. Here are the steps for adding these two files to your application:

1. Pull down the **File** menu and select the **New Form** command (or click the New Form icon in the Toolbar). This command adds a form named **Form2** to your application.

2. Pull down the **File** menu again and select **New Module** (or click the New Module icon). The new module has the default name **Module2**.

3. Click the Project window with the mouse (or choose the **Project** command from the **Window** menu) to view the current list of files

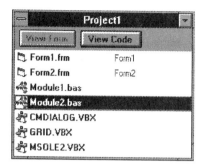

Figure 1.18 The Project window with additional files

in your application. Enlarge the window so you can view the entire list of files in the project, as shown in Figure 1.18.

4. Now close this project without saving it. (Normally, you would save each file of your project, supplying a new file name for each; but this project was an exercise that you don't need to save.) Pull down the **File** menu and select the **New Project** command. Visual Basic displays a series of message boxes on the screen, asking you if you wish to save the files of your project. Respond by clicking the **No** button in each case.

5. Finally, to prepare for the next section of this chapter, open a sample application from disk. Pull down the **File** command and choose **Open Project** (or click the Open Project icon on the Toolbar). In the **Directories** box, select the directory in which you have stored the sample programs from the exercise disk that came with this book. In the file list box, double-click the file named **REALEST.MAK.**

A FIRST APPLICATION EXAMPLE

In response to the final step in the previous exercise, Visual Basic opens the various files of the application you have selected. The application's file names are displayed in the Project window, as shown in Figure 1.19. This sample application, called the *Real Estate* program, will be the focus of your attention throughout most of the remainder of this chapter.

The program consists of six files on disk:

- REALEST.MAK is the main project file.

- HOMEGLOB.BAS is a code module that contains global declarations for the program.

Figure 1.19 The Project Window for the *Real Estate* Application

- HOMEINPT.FRM, MORTINPT.FRM, and HLOANOPT.FRM are the three forms that the program uses as dialog boxes.

- HLOANTBL.FRM is a form that the program uses to display a table of calculated data.

You'll try running this program shortly; when you do so, you'll see each of the program's four forms appear on the screen at least once during the performance. These forms contain examples of the Visual Basic controls that you've been learning about in this chapter.

The *Real Estate* Application

Real Estate is a database application, designed for a user who is in the process of searching for a house to buy. Imagine that you are selling your current home and looking for a new one to buy. It might take you weeks or even months to find the right house, and along the way you might walk through dozens of houses that are available on the market. At some point in this process, the houses you've already seen may become a mental blur of remodeled kitchens, garden decks with built-in hot tubs, and panoramic views of the city.

The *Real Estate* application gives you a quick way to keep track of essential information about all the homes you've seen, along with your own evaluative notes. You can also use the program to review the information about a given house at any time. The program maintains a database on disk, storing the house records as you enter them into the program's main dialog box. Each time you run the *Real Estate* application, the program provides you with a list of all the addresses you have stored in the database so far. To look at the description of a given home, you simply select an address from the list. Alternatively, you can enter new addresses into the database or revise existing records.

In addition, the program can quickly give you an idea of the monthly mortgage payment you would have to make after the purchase of a particular house. The program has a payment calculator that produces tables of loan payments within a range of principal amounts and interest rates. Because you may not be certain of the exact details of the loan or mortgage until the purchase is actually complete, you may want to look at a range of payment calculations while you are anticipating the transaction. The *Mortgage Calculator* component of this program supplies this information.

Running the Application

The best way to start examining this sample application is to run it. As you do, keep in mind that all of the program's three dialog boxes—with their input boxes and labels, their command buttons and options, and all the other elements of this application's user-interface—were designed and built inside the Visual Basic development environment. (In Chapter 2 you'll work through the steps of creating dialog boxes like these, and in Chapter 3 you'll explore the techniques for establishing the appropriate control properties.)

The following steps will guide you through a sample run of the *RealEstate* application:

1. Use any of the following techniques to begin the performance: Choose the **Start** command from the **Run** menu; press the F5 function key; or click the Run icon in the Toolbar. Whichever technique you use, the application title at the top of the screen changes to **Microsoft Visual Basic [run]**, indicating that you are now in the *run mode*. The program's opening input dialog appears in Figure 1.20; as you can see, there are about a dozen controls that you will use to enter the information about a recently viewed house:

   • A combo box labeled **Address** is for the address of the house. As you begin entering records into the database, the drop-down list attached to this box provides the complete list of addresses that you have visited so far. You can select an address from this list to view the corresponding house record.

   • Text boxes labeled **Asking Price**, **Sq. Feet**, **Bedrooms**, and **Bathrooms** are for entering basic information about the house. In addition, there is a scrollable text box labeled **Comments** for you to enter a line of descriptive information and impressions; and a text box labeled **Date Viewed**, which initially displays the current date. (You can change the date entry if you wish.)

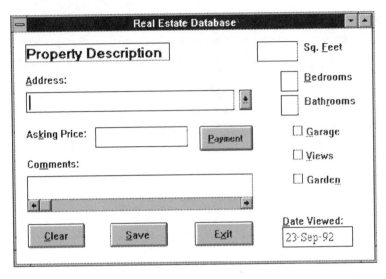

Figure 1.20 The opening dialog box of the *Real Estate* application

- There are three check boxes labeled **Garage**, **Views**, and **Garden**. Initially these boxes are unchecked; you click them individually with the mouse if the current house includes any of these features.

2. Enter the following imaginary home record into the dialog box:

> **Address:** 980 Orange Drive, Berkeley
> **Asking Price:** 195500
> **Sq. Feet:** 2250
> **Bedrooms:** 3
> **Bathrooms:** 2
> **Garage:** (checked)
> **Views:** (unchecked)
> **Garden:** (checked)
> **Comments:** Built in the 1920s; nicely renovated; big kitchen.

You can use the Tab key or the mouse to select the correct text box for each data entry. You can also press the Alt key in combination with any one of the indicated access keys; for example, press Alt+B to activate the text box labeled **Bedrooms**, or Alt+V to check the **Views** box. Check your work after you complete the entries. Use standard Windows editing functions to correct any errors.

3. Click the **Save** button (or press Alt+S) to save this record in the database. Then click the **Clear** button (or press Alt+C) to clear the

current record from the dialog box so you can begin entering a new record.

4. Enter the following two additional records into the database, one at a time. (Click **Save** and then **Clear** after entering each record.)

> **Address:** 50 Main Street, Albany
> **Asking Price:** 237000
> **Sq. Feet:** 2650
> **Bedrooms:** 4
> **Bathrooms:** 2
> **Garage:** (checked)
> **Views:** (checked)
> **Garden:** (checked)
> **Comments:** Comfortable ranch house; large yard; bay views.

> **Address:** 1350 32nd Avenue, El Cerrito
> **Asking Price:** 259000
> **Sq. Feet:** 2425
> **Bedrooms:** 3
> **Bathrooms:** 1
> **Garage:** (checked)
> **Views:** (unchecked)
> **Garden:** (unchecked)
> **Comments:** Overpriced; small bedrooms; needs major repairs.

5. Click the arrow at the right side of the **Address** box to view the drop-down list of existing address records. The list is shown in Figure 1.21. Click the third address in the list (980 Orange Drive). The program reads the corresponding home record from the database on disk and displays its data in the dialog box.

6. Click the **Payment** button to calculate the anticipated monthly mortgage payment for this home. A new dialog box named *Mortgage Calculator* appears on the screen. The asking price from the current home record has been copied to a text box labeled **Selling Price**. The dialog box, which is displayed in Figure 1.22, requires additional entries before a mortgage table can be calculated.

7. Enter a rate of **9.75** into the text box labeled **Rate**, and a value of **20** into the box labeled **Down Payment**. Click the down arrow at the right side of the combo box labeled **Term**, and select the final entry in the drop-down list, **30 years**.

8. Click the command button labeled **Table values...** Another dialog box appears on the screen, with two lists of option buttons. Your

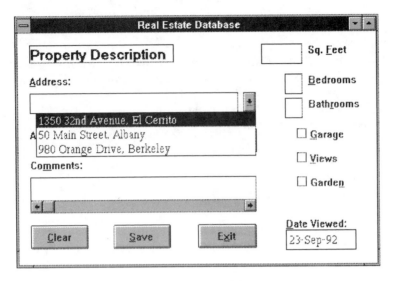

Figure 1.21 The drop-down list of addresses

selections on this dialog box will determine the increments between consecutive rows and adjacent columns of values in the resulting mortgage table. Select **$10,000** in the first column of options and **0.25%** in the second column, as shown in Figure 1.23. Click the **OK** button to return to the **Mortgage Calculator** dialog box.

9. Click the **Calc** button to produce the mortgage table from your current loan parameters. The resulting table appears in Figure 1.24. The mortgage payment for the loan parameters that you entered into the **Mortgage Calculator** dialog box is displayed in bold face

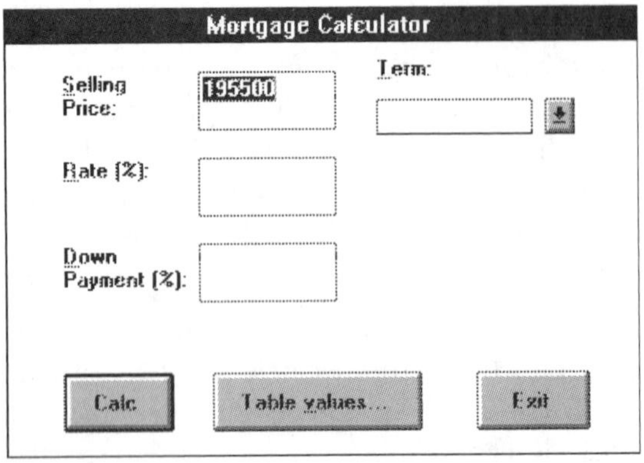

Figure 1.22 The *Mortgage Calculator* Dialog Box

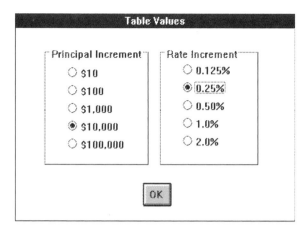

Figure 1.23 The *Table Values* dialog box

type in the center of the table. The rest of the table contains payment calculations for a nearby range of principal amounts and interest rates.

10. Click the **Exit** button to return to the main dialog box of the *Real Estate* application. Finally, click **Exit** in the main dialog box to end the program performance.

Examining the Elements of the Application

The dialog boxes included in the *Real Estate* application illustrate eight of the controls from the Visual Basic Toolbox: labels, text boxes, frames, command buttons, check boxes, option buttons, combo boxes, and a horizontal scroll bar. (Review Figures 1.20 to 1.24 to find the examples of each of these controls.) Now that you are back in the design mode, you can examine the three forms that represent the application's three dialog

Loan Table

	9.250%	9.500%	9.750%	10.000%	10.250%
$136,400	$1,122.13	$1,146.93	$1,171.89	$1,197.01	$1,222.28
$146,400	$1,204.40	$1,231.01	$1,257.80	$1,284.76	$1,311.89
$156,400	$1,286.66	$1,315.10	$1,343.72	$1,372.52	$1,401.50
$166,400	$1,368.93	$1,399.18	$1,429.63	$1,460.28	$1,491.11
$176,400	$1,451.20	$1,483.27	$1,515.55	$1,548.04	$1,580.72

Figure 1.24 The mortgage table

boxes. As you can see in the Project window, the program uses the following names to identify these forms:

- **HomeInpt** (stored on disk as HOMEINPT.FRM) is the main dialog box for the *Real Estate* application.

- **MortInpt** (MORTINPT.FRM) is the main dialog box for the *Mortgage Calculator* feature.

- **LoanOpts** (HLOANOPT.FRM) is the secondary dialog box for specifying increments on the resulting mortgage table.

You can open each of these forms in turn by selecting a form name in the project list and then clicking the **View Form** button at the top of the Project window. The forms look almost the same as they did during the program performance. One difference you'll notice is the presence of the background grid that Visual Basic supplies for forms in the design mode.

An interesting exercise at this point is to examine the property settings for controls used in this application. You could choose almost any control in any of the three dialog box forms for this exercise. A good control to start with is the comment text box, near the lower-left corner of the **HomeInpt** form. Select this form in the Project window and click **View Form**. Then activate the comment text box by clicking it once with the mouse. Then press F4 to view the Properties window and use the scroll bar to examine the settings of the properties. As you'll recall, the second column of the Properties window shows the current setting for each property in the list. Several properties have been explicitly reset from their default values for this text box control:

- The **Name** property assigns a name to the control; this name serves to identify the control in the application's code. The **Name** setting for this text box is **Comments**. **Name** is an important property that you will set for most of the controls that you add to a form.

- The **FontSize** property specifies the size of the display font. The setting for the comments box is **12**.

- The **FontBold** property determines whether the text in the box will be displayed in bold. The setting is **False** for this control.

- The **ScrollBars** property determines whether the text box will have a scroll bar. The setting is **1-Horizontal**. (An associated property named **Multiline** has a setting of **True**.)

- The **Text** property gives the initial text value displayed inside the box. The setting for this property is empty, meaning that no text appears inside the box when the program begins.

You'll learn more about the settings for these and other properties in Chapter 3. For now, keep in mind that these particular property settings apply to only one control, the **Comments** text box. As you develop the interface for an application, you'll establish property settings individually for each control in your program.

Viewing the Code behind the Application

Before leaving the *Real Estate* application, you should take a first look at some of the code that lies behind the application's visible forms. Think of the major tasks that the program must perform in response to your input and selections during run time:

- As you enter the information about a given house, the program organizes all of the data together as a complete record.

- When you click the **Save** button, the program stores the current house record in the database on disk and adds the home's address to the list attached to the **Address** combo box.

- If you select an existing address from the **Address** list, the program searches for that address in the database, reads the corresponding record from the file, and displays the record's data in the main dialog box.

- If you click the **Payment** button, the program temporarily transfers control to the *Mortgage Calculator*. This component, in turn, computes and displays the mortgage payment table when you click the **Calc** button. The calculations are based on the numeric loan parameters that you enter into the dialog box and the settings you select on the **LoanOpts** form. When you click the **Exit** button, control returns to the main dialog box of the *Real Estate* application.

- When you click the **Clear** button, the program erases the information for the current home record from the main dialog box, thus preparing for a new record input.

- Finally, the program performance ends when you click the **Exit** button on the main dialog box.

Notice that all these operations and calculations occur *in response to* your actions during run time. You enter a value into a text box, you select an entry from a list, or you click a command button—and the application produces an appropriate programmed response to your activity. Visual Basic is an *event-driven* language. Each programmed action that takes place during a performance is in response to an anticipated event—usually an event that is initiated by the user.

This event-driven language model determines to a great extent how you organize your programs in Visual Basic. A program consists largely of *event procedures* that define the action of the application in response to specific events that are anticipated during run time. When you place a control in a form, you have to think about the associated events that might take place around the control. If you want your program to respond to a potential event, you write an event procedure that defines the response.

The *Real Estate* application is full of interesting event procedures, and you'll investigate many such procedures in later chapters. For now, take a look at one fairly simple example—the procedure that takes control when you click the **Payment** button during run time. In the design mode, you can examine this procedure simply by double-clicking the **Payment** button on the main dialog box. When you do, Visual Basic opens a Code window displaying an event procedure named **PmtButton_Click**. This Code window appears in Figure 1.25. Your goal in looking at this procedure now is not to master the details of the code, but rather to begin understanding the significance of Visual Basic's event-driven programming model. This procedure's name, **PmtButton_Click**, describes its purpose in the program: Quite simply, it is performed when the **Payment** button is clicked by the user. **PmtButton** is the **Name** setting for this button.

The procedure performs three main actions: It displays the main dialog box for the *Mortgage Calculator*, a form named **MortInpt**; then it copies the asking price entry from the main dialog box to the payment dialog box; finally, it temporarily closes the main dialog box window of the *Real Estate*

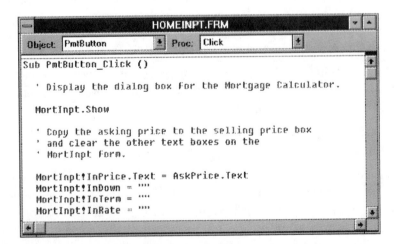

Figure 1.25 The **PmtButton_Click** procedure

application, so the user can concentrate on the mortgage payment calculation. By scrolling down the text of the procedure, you can see the code for all of these actions. (The procedure also includes *comments* that briefly describe these three actions. As in other versions of Basic, a comment in a Visual Basic program begins with a single-quote character.) When these actions are complete, the program performance pauses, waiting for the next event that requires a response.

To close the Code window, press Alt+F4 from the keyboard, or double-click the control menu box located at the upper-left corner of the window. You can now look at the code behind other controls if you want to. Just double-click any control that you want to investigate. In particular, you may be interested in looking at the event procedures behind the other command buttons in the main dialog box form.

When you are finished looking at the *Real Estate* application, pull down the **File** menu and select the **Exit** command to leave Visual Basic. You'll return to this application in Chapter 8, where you'll have the opportunity to examine the program's code in detail.

SUMMARY: THE STEPS OF APPLICATION DEVELOPMENT IN VISUAL BASIC

Application development in Visual Basic is essentially a three-step process. In the first two steps you design an interface, using the major tools provided in the Visual Basic environment—the Toolbox, the Properties window, the Project window, and the forms that you add to your project. The third step is writing code. Here is a brief summary of these steps:

1. Open one or more forms and select visual controls (command buttons, text boxes, lists, and so on) to represent the options and requirements of your application.

2. Establish the initial properties of these controls; in other words, specify how the elements of your application will appear on the screen and how they will behave while your program is running.

3. Finally, write sequences of instructions—event procedures—for some or all of the controls that you have built into your application. These procedures will ultimately determine how your program will respond to events that take place while the program is running. Events include a wide range of user-initiated actions, such as clicking a button with the mouse, selecting a menu option, or entering a data value into a text box from the keyboard.

Only the last of these three steps involves the process traditionally called *programming*. The first two steps take place completely within the menu-driven, interactive environment of Visual Basic.

In the upcoming chapters of this book you'll learn about these three essential steps in detail. Take a moment now to reflect on the learning process that you are about to begin. There are many tools to master, some of them simple and mechanical, others conceptual and subtle. But because these tools are all interrelated, the process of learning to use them may sometimes seem remarkably circular. At the outset you'll want to become familiar with the controls that Visual Basic offers for your applications, and you'll want to understand the significance of their properties. Then you'll begin writing code to respond to events in your applications; you'll expand what you know about programming at the same time that you master the elements of the Visual Basic environment.

As you develop your own understanding of the relationships among the various elements of a Visual Basic application—controls, properties, and code—you will eventually go back to learn more about each one of these features individually. In short, the process of learning about Visual Basic is much like the process of developing and fine-tuning an application: You alternately focus your attention on individual controls, the properties and events that relate to those controls, and the procedures that govern your program's response to events.

2

Building an Application,
Step 1: Selecting Forms and
Controls

INTRODUCTION

In the first phase of Visual Basic application development you select the
tools and design the windows for your program's on-screen presentation.
During this process, you are also laying the structural foundation for the
event-driven program that will define your program's behavior. This step
takes place directly on the screen in an interactive, dynamic, and efficient
process. As you create the forms that will eventually become your program's
dialog boxes and windows—and you place appropriate controls on these
forms—you can see your application taking shape in front of you.

The results of this step are impressive, but neither complete nor final.
When you move on to the subsequent steps of application development,
you can go back and make changes in the visual interface at any point,
fine-tuning the initial concept of your program as you proceed. But by the
end of this stage, you already have a very satisfying sense that your programming project is underway. You also have a clear plan for organizing the
work remaining ahead of you.

As a hands-on introduction to the process of building a visual interface,
this chapter guides you through the initial development of a financial
application called the *Loan Calculator*. Similar in format to the *Mortgage
Calculator* component of the larger application you examined in Chapter
1, this program is designed to compute the monthly payment for a bank
loan of any size and produce a payment comparison table for a range of
nearby principal amounts and interest rates. You'll work with a variety of

controls in the application, including labels, text boxes, image controls, command buttons, frames, option buttons, a combo box, and a grid. You'll begin planning the use of these controls to depict the application's input requirements, options, operations, and output displays.

The variety of tools available in Visual Basic gives you great flexibility in planning the style of your application's interface. To explore this idea, you'll also begin developing a second version of the *Loan Calculator* application, presenting the program's options in a rather different way from the first version. You'll combine several of the program's original controls in a pull-down menu located at the top of the main dialog box. To build this menu system, you'll work with Visual Basic's menu planning tool, called the *Menu Design Window.* In the end result, you'll be able to compare the two different approaches and decide which interface you prefer.

Although the focus of this chapter is on forms and controls, you'll occasionally find yourself looking ahead at properties and code as well. The three steps of program development in Visual Basic are not always independent, neatly sequential processes. More typically, you will find yourself focusing your attention alternately on different levels of your application, or even concentrating on multiple elements of the program at once.

In Chapters 3, 4, and 5 you'll continue working on both versions of this application. You'll define properties for most of the program's forms and controls, and you'll continue writing code to define the program's reactions to events. Finally, you'll work on some Visual Basic debugging techniques. At various stages in your work you'll load parts of the *Loan Calculator* application from files on the exercise disk that came with this book. As you complete this program, you'll develop the essential skills you need to build applications in Visual Basic.

The *Loan Calculator* Application

Before you begin developing the application, here is a brief preview of the finished project. If you want to follow along through the steps of this preview, choose the **Open Project** command from the **File** menu, and open the project named **LOANCALC.MAK** from the directory where you have copied files from the exercise disk. Then press F5 to run the program. The *Loan Calculator* includes three forms—two dialog boxes and a form for displaying a table of monthly payments. The main dialog box has controls for the expected input parameters of a loan: the principal amount, the interest rate, and the term of the loan. As in the *Mortgage Calculator*, the **Term** control is a combo box with a list of likely loan periods, expressed in years.

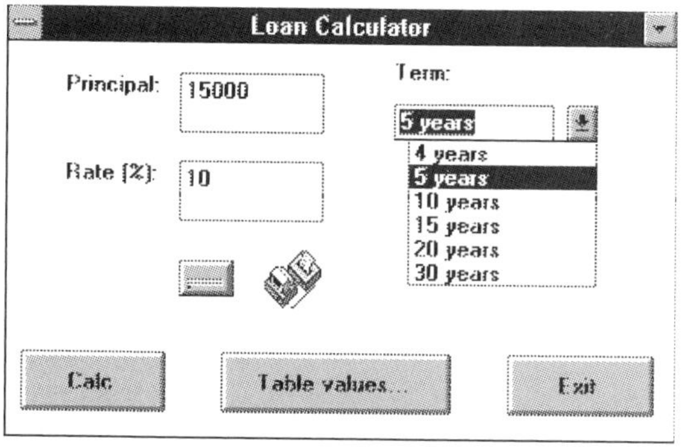

Figure 2.1 The main dialog box of the *Loan Calculator*

To use this application, you begin by entering the three major input values that describe your anticipated loan. For example, imagine that you are buying a new car and you are planning to finance about $15,000 of the purchase price as a five-year loan from your bank. You expect the interest rate to be about 10 percent. Figure 2.1 shows the *Loan Calculator* dialog box with this information already entered into the appropriate input controls.

Before clicking the **Calc** button, you now have the option of selecting appropriate increments for the payment comparison table that the program will produce. To view the program's second dialog box, you click the **Table values...** button. As you saw in Chapter 1, the resulting dialog box has two sets of option buttons, representing table increments for the principal and the interest rate. You select **$100** for the principal increment and **0.25%** as the interest increment (Figure 2.2). When you click the **OK** button, the second dialog box disappears from the screen and you are ready to produce the output table.

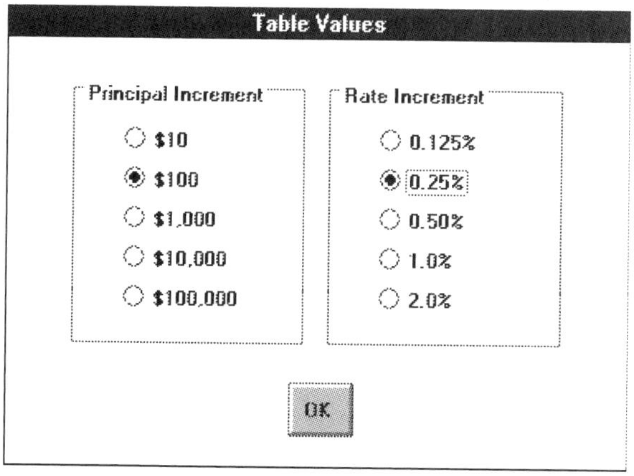

Figure 2.2 The *Table Values* dialog box

Loan Table					
	9.50%	9.75%	10.00%	10.25%	10.50%
$14,800	$310.83	$312.64	$314.46	$316.28	$318.11
$14,900	$312.93	$314.75	$316.58	$318.42	$320.26
$15,000	$315.03	$316.86	[$318.71]	$320.55	$322.41
$15,100	$317.13	$318.98	$320.83	$322.69	$324.56
$15,200	$319.23	$321.09	$322.96	$324.83	$326.71

Figure 2.3 The payment table

The main dialog box has three options for output destinations. Clicking the **Calc** button displays the payment table on the screen in a new window located beneath the dialog box. As you can see in Figure 2.3, the monthly payment for a five-year $15,000 loan at a 10 percent interest rate is $318.71. The table also shows a nearby range of other calculated monthly payments, varying by the amount of the principal and the interest rate.

Once you have produced the table that you want, you can select one or both of the other output destinations, represented by icons in the dialog box: Clicking the disk-drive icon produces a text file on disk for your payment table. Alternatively, clicking the printer icon sends the output to your printer. During a run of the program you can produce as many different output tables as you want. When you are finished, click the **Exit** button to terminate the program performance.

The job ahead of you in this chapter is to create the three forms of this application and place the appropriate controls on the two dialog boxes and the output form. You'll find that several of the controls—labels, input boxes, and control buttons—are very simple to create and put in place. Others—icons, option buttons, the combo box, and the grid—require some extra steps.

You'll create temporary files for the forms you design in this chapter's first exercise. (The forms for the final version of *Loan Calculator* appear on the exercise disk as LOANINPT.FRM, LOANOPTS.FRM, and LOAN-TABL.FRM. In this chapter you'll save your work instead as TEMP-INPT.FRM, TEMPOPTS.FRM, and TEMPTABL.FRM.) Then, in Chapters 3, 4, and 5, you'll load the same project—progressively closer to completion—from the files provided on the exercise disk. In this way you avoid having to perform repetitive steps that may not be central to the learning process at hand.

Start up Visual Basic now if you have not already done so. If you've already been working in the Visual Basic environment, pull down the **File** menu and select the **New** command to begin a new project.

PLANNING AN APPLICATION

Because you already know how many forms you need for the *Loan Calculator*, you'll begin this exercise by preparing the forms for your project. For each of the project's three forms you'll work through these tasks:

- Add the form to the project.

- Use the mouse to move the form to its correct position and adjust its size.

- Save the form to disk under an appropriate file name.

After saving the three forms individually on disk as FRM files, you'll save the project's MAK file.

Use **Form1**, the form already provided in the new project, for the application's main dialog box. Here are the steps for preparing this form:

1. Use the mouse to size the form: Position the mouse pointer over the right border of the form. The pointer becomes a two-headed horizontal arrow. Hold down the left mouse button and drag the border to the left, decreasing the width of the frame. Likewise, to decrease the height of the frame, use the mouse to drag the bottom border up. The correct dimensions for the main dialog box are **5700 x 3615**. These dimensions will appear in the Size box, located at the far right of the Toolbar. By the way, screen dimensions in Visual Basic are expressed in units named *twips*. A measurement of 1140 twips is equal to about one inch in a printed form.

2. Next, try moving the frame to a new location on the screen. To drag a frame, you position the mouse pointer over the frame's title bar and hold down the left mouse button as you move the frame. Drag the frame to the position **1035, 1170**. The location measurements—representing the distance from the upper-left corner of the screen—appear in the Position box, just to the left of the Size box in the Properties bar.

3. Pull down the **File** menu and select the **Save File As** command. Type the name **TEMPINPT** in the **File Name** box. The form is saved on disk under the file name TEMPINPT.FRM.

The Project window now displays the new file name for your first form. Your job now is to add the other two forms to the project.

Adding Forms

In Chapter 1 you learned how to use the **New Form** command to add a form to a project. Pull down the **File** menu now and select **New Form**. (Alternatively, click the New Form icon, the first tool in the Toolbar.) When you do so, a new form appears on the screen with the default name **Form2**. You'll use this new form for the project's second dialog box, which eventually will be named **Table Values**. Continue your work by following these steps:

1. Resize the new form, giving it the dimensions **5910x4290**.

2. Move the form to the position **1320, 1470**.

3. Choose the **Save File As** command from the **File** menu and save the form as TEMPOPTS.FRM.

4. Select the **New Form** command again to add a third form to the project. This form has the default name **Form3**. It will become the output window for the payment table that the program generates.

5. Resize the form, giving it the dimensions **8070x2295**.

6. Move the form to the position **240, 4845**.

7. Save the form as TEMPTABL.FRM.

After you complete all these steps your screen will be a jumble of windows and forms, as shown in Figure 2.4. You can temporarily close all three forms by double-clicking the small control menu boxes at the upper-left corner of each form or by selecting each form in turn and pressing Alt+F4.

If you accidentally close the Project window, pull down the **Window** menu and select the **Project** command to reopen it. Likewise, the **Toolbox** command in the **Window** menu reopens the Toolbox if you inadvertently close it. Sometimes you may close the Project window and the Toolbox intentionally, just to clear up your work-space on the screen. If you do so, the commands in the **Window** menu allow you to open these windows again.

There are two more changes to make in the list of files in this project. Part of the plan for the project is a code module that will supply some essential global variable declarations. You'll add this module to the project in the upcoming exercise. In addition, you'll remove two VBX files representing custom controls that will not be used in the application. (The GRID.VBX file remains in the project, because you'll eventually be adding a grid to display the application's output table.) Here are the steps for these changes:

1. Choose the **New Module** command from the **File** menu or click the New Module tool, the second icon on the Toolbar. In response,

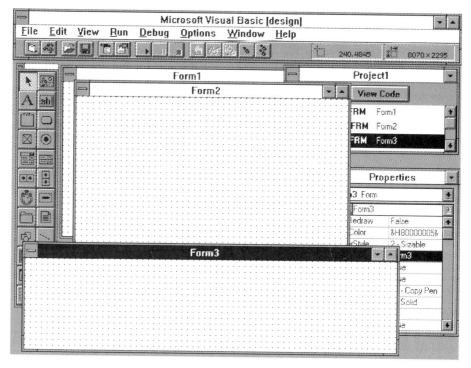

Figure 2.4 The three forms of the *Loan Calculator* application

Visual Basic adds a new module to the current project and opens a code window for the module. Press Alt+F4 or double-click the control menu box at the upper-left corner of the code window. This action closes the window, but **Module1.bas** remains the current selection in the Project window.

2. Select the **Save File As** command in the **File** menu. Enter the name **TEMPGLOB** as the file name. On disk, the file is saved as TEM-PGLOB.BAS. Resize the Project window so you can see the entire list of files in the application you are building. (You can use the mouse to change the size and the position of the Project window, just as you have done for the forms in this application.)

3. Now select the custom control file CMDIALOG.VBX in the Project window. Pull down the **File** menu and choose the **Remove File** command. CMDIALOG.VBX disappears from the list of project files. In addition, the OLE icon is removed from Visual Basic's Toolbox.

4. Select MSOLE2.VBX at the bottom of the Project window, and choose **Remove File** from the **File** menu to remove this custom control as well.

Figure 2.5 The Project window for the *Loan Calculator* application

Saving the Project

At this point the project itself still has the default name **Project1**. To save the project for the first time, use Visual Basic's **Save Project As** command:

1. Pull down the **File** menu and select **Save Project As**.

2. Type the name **TEMPCALC** in the **File Name** text box and click the **OK** button.

The project is now saved on disk under the name TEMPCALC.MAK. When you have completed these save operations, the Project window lists all the files in the application, as shown in Figure 2.5. The entire application consists of six files on disk: the three FRM files, one BAS file, one VBX file for the grid control, and one MAK file.

Now that you have taken the trouble to save each form individually on disk, subsequent save operations will be much simpler when you make new changes in this application. Once each part of a project has a file name, you can save the entire project quickly by selecting the **Save Project** command. To avoid losing any work, you should periodically pull down the **File** menu and select **Save Project** as you proceed through the steps of application development.

WORKING WITH CONTROLS

You are now ready to begin placing controls on the two forms that will become the application's dialog boxes. Visual Basic gives you two techniques for adding a control to a selected form:

- The simpler technique is the one you have already practiced in Chapter 1: Double-click the appropriate control icon in the Toolbox. The corresponding control appears immediately in the center of the active form.

- Another technique is to select a control in the Toolbox and then drag the mouse over the area where you want to place the control. This technique is required in some special situations, as you'll see later in this chapter.

Using the first of these two techniques, you can quickly place several controls on a form in succession by double-clicking the control icons in the Toolbox. Then when you have added all the controls you want, you can start moving and sizing the controls inside the form. However, this approach calls for a little advance planning. When you eventually run your program, the order in which controls are activated by the Tab key matches the order in which you originally placed the controls on the form. You can change the Tab order during design time by changing the setting of a property named **TabIndex** for each of the controls on your form. But it is easier to anticipate this order when you are first adding controls to your application. Keep this property in mind as you begin adding controls to the *Loan Calculator* application.

Placing Controls on a Form

Select the TEMPINPT form in the Project window and click the **View Form** button. This empty form, still called **Form1**, will be the main dialog box of your application. When your work is complete, the form will contain eleven controls in all: three labels, two text boxes, one combo box, three command buttons, and two image controls. You'll begin this exercise by double-clicking an icon in the Toolbox for each of these controls. Each time you do so, the newest control will appear in the center of the form, superimposed over the previous control. In effect, Visual Basic piles all eleven controls, one in front of another, in the middle of the form. Here are the steps for placing controls on the form:

1. Double-click the label icon (represented by a bold **A** in the Toolbox) three times. As you do so, the controls named **Label1**, **Label2**, and **Label3** appear in succession in the middle of the form.

2. Double-click the text box icon (represented by **ab|** inside a box) two times. **Text1** and **Text2** appear in the form.

3. Double-click the combo box icon (the fifth icon down the left column of the Toolbox). **Combo1** appears.

4. Double-click the command button icon (the third icon down the right-hand column of the Toolbox) three times. The controls named **Command1**, **Command2**, and **Command3** appear in the form.

5. Double-click the image control (the second-to-last icon in the left-hand column) twice. Nothing appears to happen in the form itself, but the Properties window identifies the two new controls as **Image1** and **Image2**.

6. Use the mouse to drag the eleven controls from the center of the form to their *approximate* positions inside the form. Use Figure 2.7 as your guide, but don't spend too much time on this task; you'll adjust the controls to their exact sizes and locations in the next step. (When you move the image controls, you'll find that they are represented as broken rectangular borders, initially the same size as a command button.)

7. Select each control in turn, and drag the control to its correct location, as shown in Table 2.1. Then drag the sizing handles to give the control its correct size, also specified in Table 2.1.

You've already seen that controls align themselves in location and size to the increments marked off by the grid in the background of the form. This grid simplifies the task of positioning controls in line with one another. However, you might occasionally want to assign a position or size that does not conform to the grid increments. In this case, you can follow these steps to deactivate grid alignment:

1. Choose the **Environment** command in the **Options** menu.

2. In the resulting **Environment Options** dialog box, scroll to the bottom of the **Setting** list.

3. Select the last option in the list, **Align to Grid**, and press the N key. This switches the option setting to **No**, as shown in Figure 2.6. Then click **OK** to confirm the new setting.

Normally, you'll want to keep the **Align to Grid** option in its active status (the **Yes** setting), but occasionally you may find yourself turning this option off for positioning or sizing a particular control inside a form.

When you finish moving and resizing all the controls, **Form1** appears as in Figure 2.7. An interesting exercise at this point is to try running the application, just to examine some of the features that Visual Basic builds into your dialog box before you write any of your own code. However, there is one additional feature you must take into account before running a program for the first time. When an application consists of multiple forms, you may need to select and identify a *startup form*—that is, the form that appears on the screen at the beginning of the program performance and determines the program's initial appearance and behavior.

Table 2.1 Positions and sizes of controls in the main dialog box.

Control	Position	Size
Label1	480, 240	855x495
Label2	480, 960	855x495
Label3	3240, 120	1215x255
Text1	1440, 240	1215x495
Text2	1440, 960	1215x495
Combo1	3240, 480	1695x300
Command1	120, 2520	1215x495
Command2	1800, 2520	1935x495
Command3	4200, 2520	1215x495
Image1	1440, 1680	495x495
Image2	2160, 1680	495x495

By default, Visual Basic designates the first form you add to your project as the startup form. In the application you are currently creating, this means that **Form1** has been correctly identified as the startup; no change in the startup setting is required. All the same, you should learn how to change this designation in the event that you need to specify the startup

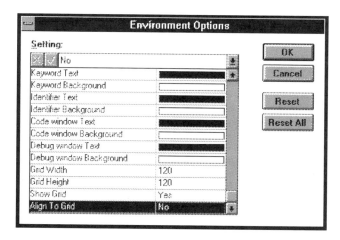

Figure 2.6 The *Environment Options* dialog box

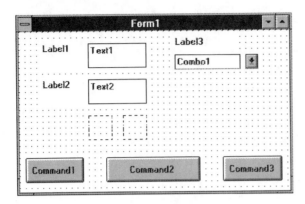

Figure 2.7 Form1 with its controls in place

form in some other project. You use the **Project** command in the **Options** menu for this purpose:

1. Pull down the **Options** menu and select **Project**. The dialog box shown in Figure 2.8 appears on the screen. This box displays a selection of options that apply to the current project. Notice that **Form1** is displayed as the setting for the **Start Up Form** option.

2. Select the **Start Up Form** option, and then click the down arrow icon displayed at the right side of the settings box. In the resulting list, you'll see that you can select any of the project's forms as the startup form. For now, click the **Cancel** button or press Escape to close the dialog box without changing the startup.

3. Now pull down the **Run** menu and select the **Start** command, or simply press the F5 shortcut key. When the main dialog box appears on the screen, you are in Visual Basic's run mode. (You'll see the title **Microsoft Visual Basic [run]** at the top of the screen.) Try the following experiments on the controls in **Form1**:

    *   Press the Tab key several times to see the order in which controls are activated. An active control is said to have the *focus* of the program. Notice how each type of control changes in appearance when it receives the focus. Also note that the label controls do not receive the focus at all.

    *   Try entering, editing, inserting, and deleting text inside either of the two text boxes. (You can even try a cut-and-paste operation.) These boxes have all the editing functions of any Windows text box.

    *   Click a command button and notice the graphic push-button effect on the screen.

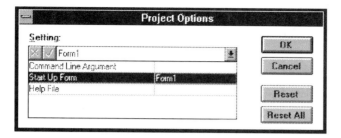

Figure 2.8 The **Project Options** dialog box

- Click the small down arrow icon at the right side of the combo box. This is the arrow that you normally click to view the drop-down list attached to a combo box control. (Alternatively, you can activate the combo box and press F4 to view the drop-down list.) At this point in the development of the application, the list is still empty, but you will nonetheless see part of a frame drop down from the box.

Because the application does not yet have an exit routine, you have to use one of Visual Basic's three techniques for terminating the program performance. They are:

- Pull down the **Run** menu and choose the **End** command.
- Click the End tool, the ninth icon in Visual Basic's Toolbar.
- Double-click the control menu box at the upper-left corner of the frame.

When you return to the design mode, **Form1** reappears with its original contents (Figure 2.7), regardless of any changes you may have made in text boxes during run mode. Run time activities never affect the original design time definition of an application.

Defining the Appearance of Controls

The dialog box you've been working on contains three individual controls that are still vaguely defined, even for this stage of the development process; these controls are the combo box and the two image controls. The drop-down list attached to the combo box is still empty. The two image controls, which you have created for displaying icons, are also empty. Further development of these controls requires you to work with properties and code, topics introduced in later chapters. But taking the time to define these controls now, at this early point in your work, will give you a preview of skills you'll master later.

In the following two exercises you'll define the combo box list and select icons for the picture boxes.

Combo Boxes

The drop-down list for a combo box is created at run time rather than at development time. The list in the *Loan Calculator* application is a simple case, because the entries in the drop-down list remain fixed during the entire program performance. (Contrast this with the drop-down list that you saw in the *Real Estate* application: The **Address** combo box in that program has a list that gets longer each time you add a new home record to the database.)

The simplest way to define a fixed list for a combo box is at the time the startup form is first "loaded" onto the screen, at the beginning of the program performance. In many applications, this action—opening the form and displaying it on the screen—is the first event the program recognizes. It is called the **Load** event for the form. As with other events that occur during a program performance, Visual Basic always looks for a corresponding event procedure when the **Load** event takes place. The event procedure in this case is named **Form_Load**.

In other words, the **Load** event triggers a performance of the **Form_Load** procedure at the time a form is first displayed on the screen. Any instructions that you include in the **Form_Load** procedure of the startup form are therefore performed at the beginning of the program run. This procedure is a perfect place in which to put instructions that initialize conditions in your program—including the instructions that build a fixed list for a combo box.

Follow these steps to create the **Form_Load** procedure in **Form1**:

1.   If the form is closed, select **Form1** in the Project window and click the **View Form** button.

2.   Position the mouse pointer in any empty area of the form—that is, an area that does not contain a control. Double-click the left mouse button to open the Code window for the form. As shown in Figure 2.9, Visual Basic automatically prepares a template for the **Form_Load** procedure, consisting of the first and last lines of code.

3.   Between the **Sub** and **End Sub** lines, type the following six lines of Visual Basic code:

```
Combo1.AddItem "4 years"
Combo1.AddItem "5 years"
Combo1.AddItem "10 years"
```

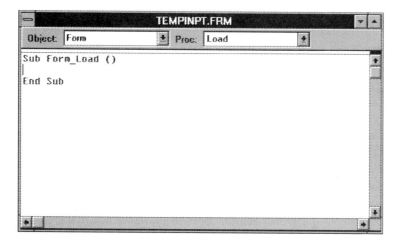

Figure 2.9 The **Form_Load** procedure in the Code window

```
Combo1.AddItem "15 years"
Combo1.AddItem "20 years"
Combo1.AddItem "30 years"
```

5. Check your typing carefully for errors. When you are sure the six lines are correct (Figure 2.10), press Alt+F4 to close the Code window.

6. Press F5 to try running the program again. When the dialog box appears on the screen, click the down arrow icon at the right of the **Combo1** control. You'll see the drop-down list that you have just

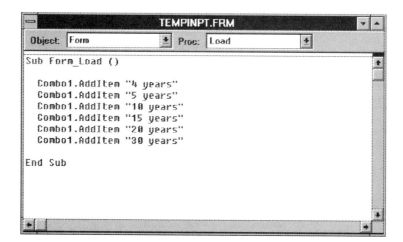

Figure 2.10 Entering code into the **Form_Load** procedure

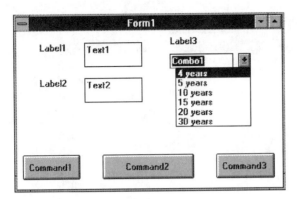

Figure 2.11 The drop-down list defined for the **Combo1** control

defined (Figure 2.11). Click any one of the entries in the list. Your selection becomes the new text displayed inside the combo box.

7. Pull down the **Run** menu and select the **End** command to terminate the program run. (Alternatively, click the End icon, the ninth icon in the Toolbar.)

You've now written your first event procedure. As you've guessed, each of the **Combo1.AddItem** statements in the *Form_Load* procedure appends a text item to the drop-down list of the **Combo1** control. **AddItem** is known as a *method*, a built-in Visual Basic procedure whose action applies to a specific object. In this case, the relevant object is the **Combo1** control. The usual syntax for calling a Visual Basic method is:

```
ObjectName.MethodName
```

where *ObjectName* identifies the object to which the method applies. The name of the object and the name of the method are separated by a period.

You'll learn much more about methods and event procedures in later chapters. After this brief detour into Visual Basic code, you can now return to the dialog box that you are building. Your next task is to place icons inside the two image controls in **Form1**.

Image Controls and Icons

One of the uses of a Visual Basic image control is to display an icon that you select at design time. An icon is actually defined as a property of the image control. The property name in this case is **Picture**. Visual Basic comes with a large library of icons that you can display in picture boxes. These icons are stored as files with the extension ICO in a directory named \VB\ICONS. This directory is in turn divided into several subdirectories that contain the ICO files, organized by subject. For example, the subdirectory named \VB\ICONS\COMPUTER contains icons that depict the hardware elements of a computer system, such as disk drives, keyboards, mouse devices, and so on.

Take another look at the two icons that are to become part of the main *Loan Calculator* dialog box, back in Figure 2.1. You'll recall that these icons represent two output operations that the program can perform: storing the current payment table in a text file on disk and sending the table to the printer. Here are the file descriptions of these two icons:

- The disk drive icon is defined in a file named DRIVE01.ICO. The path location of this file is \VB\ICONS\COMPUTER.

- The computer and printer icon is defined in a file named NET06.ICO. The file's location is \VB\ICONS\COMM.

In the following steps you'll add these icons to the **Form1** dialog box:

1. Select **Form1** in the Project window and click the **View Form** button, if the form is not already displayed on the screen.

2. Click the first of the two image controls, which currently has the default name **Image1**. Size handles appear around the perimeter of the box when you select the control.

3. Press F4 to activate the Properties window. The default selection in the list is a property named **Picture**. The Settings box displays the text **(none)** as the setting for this property, as shown in Figure 2.12.

4. Now click the small button containing an ellipsis (**...**), just to the right of the Settings box. When you do so, a new dialog box named **Load Picture** appears on the screen. Use the **Directories** box to

Figure 2.12 Selecting the **Picture** property on the Properties bar

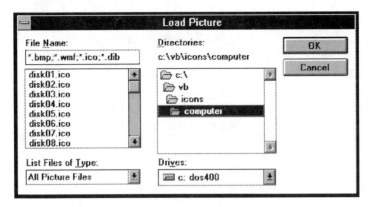

Figure 2.13 The **Load Picture** dialog box

navigate to the directory path named \VB\ICONS\COMPUTER. A list of ICO files appears in the **Files** box, as shown in Figure 2.13.

5.   In the **Files** box, scroll down to the file named DRIVE01.ICO. Double-click the file name. The **Load Picture** dialog box is closed and the disk-drive icon appears in the **Image1** control, as shown in Figure 2.14.

6.   Repeat the process (steps 2 to 5) for the second image control, named **Image2**. This time navigate to the subdirectory named \VB\ICONS\COMM and select the file named NET06.ICO. The computer and printer icon appears in the **Image2** picture box.

At this point in your work, the **Form1** dialog box contains all the controls you have planned for it (Figure 2.14). But for the most part, the controls all still have their default properties. Most glaringly, none of the labels, captions, or initial text values have been set in ways that are relevant to this application. You'll work on these and other properties in Chapter 3. For now, pull down the **File** menu and select the **Save Project** command to save your work, or simply click the Save icon in Visual Basic's Toolbar. (Recall that **Save Project** saves changes you have made in any of the project's forms and modules.)

Frames and Option Buttons

Your next job is to prepare the application's second dialog box, currently called **Form2** (TEMPOPTS.FRM on disk). Looking back at Figure 2.2, you'll recall that this form is to contain two groups of option buttons, each group enclosed in a frame. In addition, there is a command button at the bottom of the form.

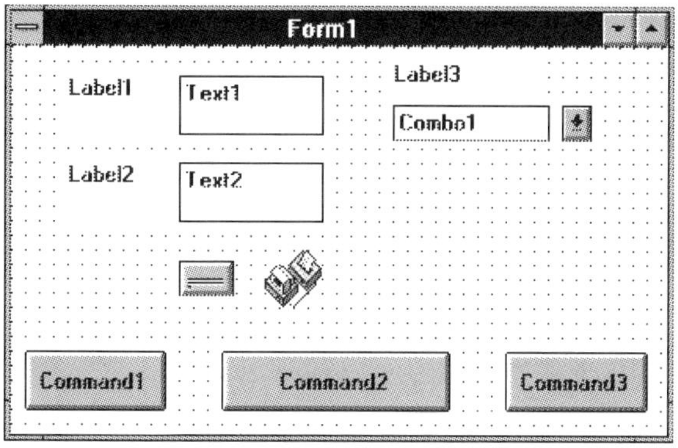

Figure 2.14 The dialog box with all of its controls in place

Option buttons are always defined in groups. One option in a group may be *on* at a given time; all the other buttons are switched off. The active option button contains a solid black bullet; inactive option buttons are represented by empty circles. Because only one option may be active at a time, these controls are sometimes called "radio buttons."

Any option buttons inside a form are automatically defined as a group. But when you want to include more than one group of options in a given dialog box, you need a way to separate the groups from one another. One way is to enclose each group of options inside a frame. This is the approach you'll use in the *Loan Calculator* application.

The frame control is represented by the third icon down the left-hand column of the Toolbox. You'll begin the following exercise by placing two frames and a command button on **Form2**:

1. Select **Form2** in the Project window, and then click the **View Form** button. The form becomes the active window on the screen.

2. Move the mouse pointer to the Toolbox. Double-click the frame icon twice. Then double-click the command button icon once. Move the three controls from their original positions at the center of the form to their approximate new positions: Place the command button, **Command1**, at the bottom of the form. The two frames, **Frame1** and **Frame2**, belong at the upper-left and upper-right sides of the form.

3. Size and position the three controls according to the measurements provided in Table 2.2.

Now you are ready to place the option buttons inside each of the frames. But this is where the double-clicking technique fails for adding Toolbox controls to the form. If you double-click the option button icon now, the resulting control will be located inside the *form*, but not inside a *frame*. Even

**Table 2.2 Positions and sizes of the controls in
the second dialog box**

Control	Position	Size
Frame1	600, 360	2175x2415
Frame2	3000, 360	2175x2415
Command1	2640, 3120	615x495

if you later move the control to a position that *appears* to be inside one of
the two frames, the control will still belong to the form, not the frame. For
this reason, you must manually drag each option button to its position
inside a frame in order to create the two groups of options in the correct
way.

Here are the steps for placing the first option button, initially named
Option1, inside **Frame1**:

1. Inside the Toolbox, click the option button icon once with the
   mouse.

2. Without pressing the mouse button, move the pointer to a position
   near the upper-left corner of **Frame1**. The pointer takes on a
   cross-hair shape.

3. To create the option button control, hold down the left mouse
   button and gradually move the mouse pointer down and to the right.
   A shadow of the control appears inside **Frame1**. When the control
   is approximately the correct size (see Figure 2.15), release the mouse
   button. **Option1** appears inside the frame.

You now need to repeat these three steps for each of the remaining four
option buttons in **Frame1**, and then for the five option buttons in **Frame2**.
Start out by creating the option buttons in their approximate positions and
sizes. Then, when all ten buttons are in place, adjust the positions and sizes
according to the measurements in Table 2.3. Note that all ten option
buttons have the same size. The positions are measured in relation to the
upper-left corner of the *containing frame*, not the form. For this reason,
corresponding option buttons in each of the two frames have the same
position measurements.

As you work on positioning these option buttons inside their frames, you
might want to use a special Visual Basic technique for selecting multiple
controls. If you hold down the Ctrl key when you select a series of controls,
the controls become a multiple selection. You can then move all of the

Table 2.3 Positions and sizes of the option buttons in the second dialog box

Frame1	Frame2	Position	Size
Option1	Option6	480, 360	1095x375
Option2	Option7	480, 720	1095x375
Option3	Option8	480, 1080	1095x375
Option4	Option9	480, 1440	1095x375
Option5	Option10	480, 1800	1095x375

controls in the selection at once by dragging them with the mouse. To deactivate the multiple selection, click the mouse anywhere inside the form. By the way, inside a *form* you can select multiple controls simply by dragging the mouse in a border around the controls you want to select.

When you finish your work, **Form2** appears as shown in Figure 2.15. You'll return to this form in Chapter 3 to define the properties of its controls. For now, select the **Save Project** command to save your work.

Now turn to the final form in this application, the form in which the program will ultimately display its output table.

The Grid Control

To display a two-dimensional table of numbers in a form, your program can print the numbers directly to the form, or you can organize the output

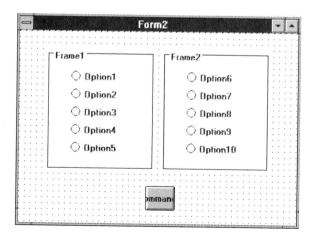

Figure 2.15 The second dialog box with all its controls in place

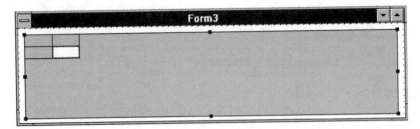

Figure 2.16 Adding a grid control to a form

in a grid control. You'll see both of these approaches illustrated in the various versions of the *Loan Calculator* application. In this first version, follow these steps to add a grid control to **Form3**:

1. Select **Form3** in the Project window and click the **View Form** button.

2. Activate the Toolbox and double-click the grid icon at the bottom of the left-hand column of controls.

3. Move the grid control to the position **120, 120**, and then resize the control to the dimensions **7695x1695**. By default, the grid has only two columns and two rows, as shown in Figure 2.16. You'll learn how to change these and other grid properties in Chapter 3.

4. For now, press Alt+F4 to close **Form3** and then click the Save icon in Visual Basic's Toolbar to save the project to disk.

In this chapter's final exercise, you'll begin developing the interface for a new version of the *Loan Calculator* application. In the new interface, several of the options from the original version will be reorganized as commands in a pull-down menu. To create this menu you'll use Visual Basic's Menu Design Window.

To enable you to focus on creating the menu for this new version, the beginning stage of the application is available as a project on the exercise disk. Follow these steps to open this project and prepare for the work ahead:

1. Pull down the **File** menu and select the **Open Project** command.

2. In the **Directories** box select the directory in which you have copied the files from the exercise disk that came with this book.

3. In the **Files** box, double-click the file named CH2EX2.MAK.

4. When the project is loaded into memory, select the form CH2EX2A.FRM in the Project window and click the **View Form** button. This form is the starting point for your work in the upcoming exercise.

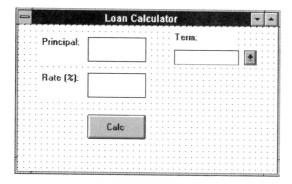

Figure 2.17 Starting point for the second version of the *Loan Calculator* application

As you can see in Figure 2.17, the form is a simplified version of the *Loan Calculator* application. The two icons and two of the command buttons have been removed.

ALTERNATIVE PROGRAM DESIGN

There are always many different ways to design dialog boxes in Visual Basic. For example, you've already seen several controls and groups of controls that represent options in a dialog box, including:

- Command buttons
- Groups of option buttons or check boxes
- Combo boxes with their attached drop-down lists

Your own style of designing dialog boxes will depend on what you judge to be the most efficient and visually pleasing presentation for a given application and on your familiarity with the needs and abilities of the people who will ultimately be using your program. In some instances you might find yourself designing a dialog box in one way, only to change the organization altogether after you've worked with the application for a while. For example, you might decide to reorganize a control-crowded interface into a menu-driven application. This sort of change is illustrated in the upcoming exercise.

Working with the Menu Design Window

If you compare Figures 2.1 and 2.17, you'll find that several features are missing from the second version of *Loan Calculator*: the **Table values** button, the **Exit** button, and the two output options formerly represented by icons. The output options and the **Exit** command all can be placed conveniently in a single pull-down menu. In most Windows applications, a menu that offers a variety of output options—along with a command that exits from the application itself—is typically called the **File** menu. Here are the commands the **File** menu will include in *Loan Calculator*:

File
   Print Table
   Save Table
   Exit

You create menus for Visual Basic applications in the Menu Design Window. To open this window, begin by activating the main dialog box for the new version of the application. Then pull down the **Window** menu and choose the **Menu Design** command. The window that appears on the screen is shown in Figure 2.18.

This window contains options for defining the commands, properties, and characteristics of an entire menu bar with one or more pull-down menus. The resulting menu bar becomes part of the active form in your application. The top half of the Menu Design Window contains text boxes and check boxes for command names and a variety of properties. For

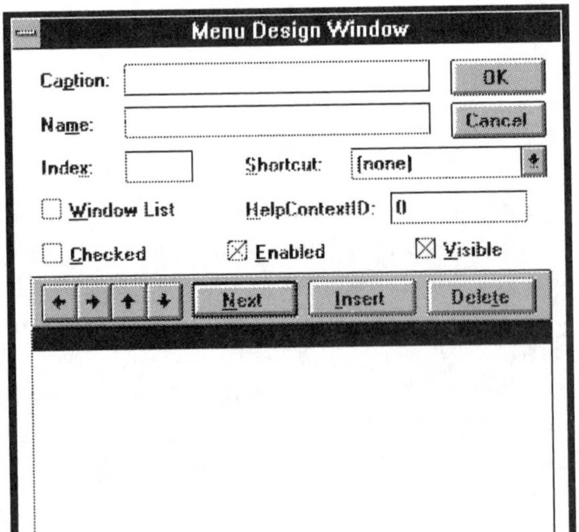

Figure 2.18 The Menu Design Window

example, the **Caption** box is for the name of a menu as it appears in the menu bar, or the name of one of the commands that appears in a menu list. The **Name** box is for the corresponding *control name*, which is a special identifier that you assign to each menu entry for programming purposes. The bottom half of the Menu Design Window contains a large list box, which displays the hierarchy of your menu system as you begin designing it.

In this introductory exercise, you'll supply only two items of information for each menu entry: the **Caption** and **Name** values. Here are the steps for defining the **File** menu for the *Loan Calculator*:

1. Enter **&File** into the **Caption** box. The ampersand character indicates that the *next* character will be the *access key* for the menu and will be underlined in the menu name. This means that the user can press Alt+F to pull down the **File** menu that you are creating. The menu name appears at the top of the menu list box in the Menu Design Window (Figure 2.19).

2. Enter **FileMenu** into the **Name** box.

3. Click the **Next** button to begin defining the next entry in the menu.

4. Click the right arrow icon above the list box. A string of four hyphens appears at the beginning of the new caption in the menu list box, indicating that this entry is a command within the **File** menu.

5. Enter **&Print Table** as the caption of the new entry. Then enter **PrintTableCommand** as the control name.

6. Click the **Next** button or simply press the Enter key. You don't need to press the right arrow icon again; the new entry is assumed to be at the same menu level as the previous entry.

7. Enter **&Save Table** as the new caption and **SaveTableCommand** as the new control name.

8. Click the **Next** button or press Enter.

9. Enter **E&xit** as the final caption and **ExitCommand** as the control name. Figure 2.19 shows the Menu Design Window at this point in your work.

10. Click the **OK** button to complete your work in the Menu Design Window.

11. Save this version of the application.

After these steps, you can pull down the new **File** menu that now appears in your dialog box. You'll see the three commands that you included in the menu, as shown in Figure 2.20.

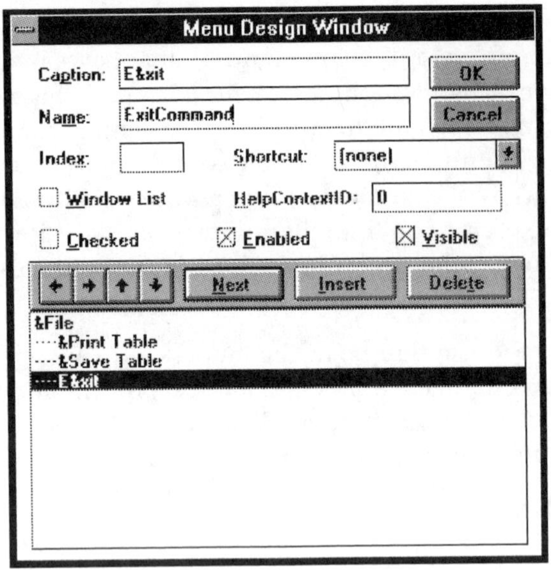

Figure 2.19 A menu definition in the Menu Design Window

There is much more to learn about menus and the Menu Design Window. You'll work more with this particular menu later. But for now, you can already see that the application's pull-down **File** menu is a reasonable alternative to the original design of the *Loan Calculator* application.

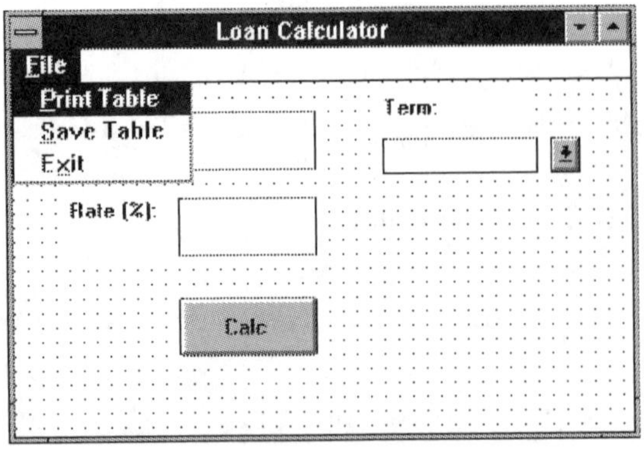

Figure 2.20 The new **File** menu, as created in the Menu Design Window

SUMMARY: FORMS AND CONTROLS

The first stage of application development moves quickly and produces satisfying results. You open the forms for your application and you begin placing controls on those forms to represent the features of your program. You use the mouse to move each form and control to its initial position and to adjust the size of each object that will appear on the screen. As you do so, Visual Basic assigns numeric settings to the corresponding properties: **Top** and **Left** for the position measurements, and **Width** and **Height** for the size dimensions. An additional property, **TabIndex**, is determined by the order in which you place controls on a form.

But many other important properties still need to be defined. The command buttons and labels on your forms need text captions. Text boxes require appropriate initial values. The appropriate number of rows and columns need to be defined for the grid control. The forms themselves need titles and possibly background textures or colors. Along with these visual characteristics, you need to set other properties to prepare the way for the programming tasks that lie ahead. All these changes take place in the Properties window, which is the focus of Chapter 3.

3

Building an Application,
Step 2: Assigning Properties

INTRODUCTION

The objects of a Visual Basic application—forms and controls—have properties that you can change during either design time or run time. These
properties determine an object's characteristics—its visual appearance on
the screen, its functional elements, its *value*, and its treatment during run
time. In this chapter you'll continue exploring the properties available for
a variety of forms and controls. You'll learn to recognize the range of
appropriate settings for a given property, and you'll practice the mechanical steps for selecting settings at design time.

Begin by reviewing the features of the Properties window. You can view
and activate the Properties window during design time by pressing the F4
function key. You also can move the window to any convenient position on
the screen and resize it to view any portion of its contents. You've seen that
the window contains a scrollable two-column property list, where the
column on the left shows the properties available for a selected object and
the column on the right shows the current settings for those properties.
For example, Figure 3.1 shows the scrollable list of properties for a form.

At the top of the Properties window, just beneath the title bar, is the
Object box, a pull-down list from which you can select the name of any
control contained in the active form. This list gives you a convenient way
of selecting the object whose properties you want to view or change.
Beneath the Object box is the Settings box. For a property that has a fixed
group of settings, this box has an attached list of those settings. An active

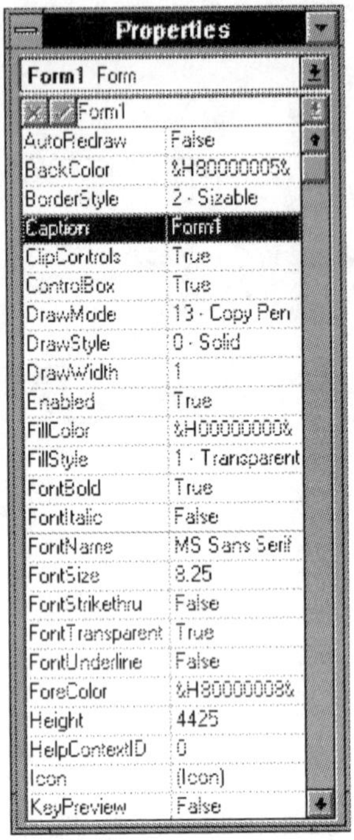

Figure 3.1 The properties list for a form

down arrow button at the right of the Settings box indicates that a settings list exists for the current property. To view the list, you click the down arrow. In Figure 3.2, for example, you can see the settings list for a form property named **BorderStyle**. This property determines the appearance and function of the form's border during run time. The default setting is **Sizable**, which means that the user can drag the border to change the size and shape of the form.

Sometimes there are no fixed settings for a given property. In this case, no settings list is available and the down arrow button at the right of the

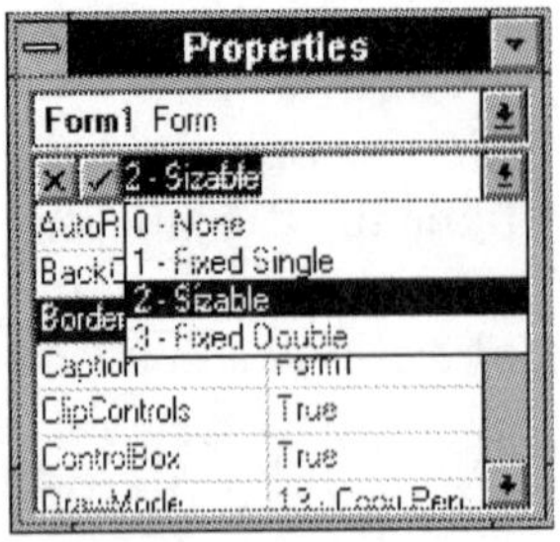

Figure 3.2 The drop-down list attached to the Settings box

Figure 3.3 A property that has no fixed settings

Settings box is dimmed. For example, Figure 3.3 shows the Settings box for the **Name** property. To set this property, you enter a text value directly into the Settings box. Notice the Cancel button (labeled X) and the Enter button (labeled with a check mark) that appear at the left of the Settings box. When you first type a new setting into the box, you can click the Enter button to confirm your entry or the Cancel button to restore the previous entry.

These are the two main ways to establish the setting of a property during design time: Select a value from the drop-down list attached to the Settings box, or enter a value directly into the box. Sometimes, however, Visual Basic presents other techniques for selecting a property setting. In Chapter 2, for example, you learned to set the **Picture** property of an image control by selecting an icon file from the **Load Picture** dialog box. In this chapter you'll see an example of another special technique—this time for setting the display colors of a form or control.

As you've learned, Visual Basic displays the position coordinates and the dimensions (expressed in *twips*) of the selected form or control in the two boxes located just to the right of the Toolbar, near the top of the screen. These boxes tell you the current settings of the properties named **Left**, **Top**, **Width**, and **Height**.

In the hands-on exercises for this chapter you will continue developing the *Loan Calculator* application that you began in Chapter 2. As your starting point in this chapter, you can load the application into memory from files supplied on the exercise disk. The project named CH3EX1.MAK contains the first version of the *Loan Calculator* application as you left it in Chapter 2. To load this file, pull down the **File** menu and select the **Open Project** command. Select the directory where you have copied the files of the exercise disk and open CH3EX1.MAK. The three forms in the project are stored in disk files named CH3EX1A.FRM, CH3EX1B.FRM, and CH3EX1C.FRM. They are the same as the forms you created in Chapter 2, except that they are saved under different file names.

This chapter is merely an introduction to the subject of properties. You'll continue to discover new properties as you proceed in your work with Visual Basic. Keep in mind that all properties have default settings—that is, settings that remain in effect unless they are changed during either design time or run time. In a typical application, you'll leave many properties—for both forms and controls—unchanged from their default settings.

ASSIGNING PROPERTIES TO FORMS

To work with the properties of a form, you begin by activating the form itself. If a control inside the form is selected, click the mouse over an empty area inside the form; this action deselects the control and selects the form for subsequent property definitions.

One of the first form properties you normally think of setting is **Name**. This property defines the name by which a form can be identified in an application's code. The name also appears in the Project window, next to the file name for a form. Default **Name** settings are **Form1**, **Form2**, **Form3**, and so on, up to the number of forms in your application.

Follow these steps to change the **Name** setting for the form currently identified as **Form1**:

1. Select **Form1** in the Project window and click the **View Form** button.

2. Press F4 to activate the Properties window. Inside the window, scroll down the property list and click the **Name** property.

3. Enter the text **LoanInpt** as the new **Name** setting. Press the Enter key or click the Enter button to complete the entry.

Notice that **LoanInpt** appears in the Project window list, next to the file name CH3EX1A.FRM. Now perform these same three steps for the remaining two forms in the project. Change the name of **Form2** to **LoanOpts**, and the name of **Form3** to **LoanTabl**. Figure 3.4 shows the Project window at this point in your work.

In Chapter 4, you'll begin to see some of the programming situations in which the **Name** property is important. In general, an operation that involves an entire form is performed via a reference to the form's **Name** setting. For example, operations that hide or display a form, or send text or graphics to a form, identify the form by its **Name**.

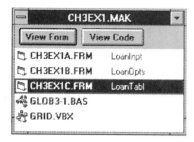

Figure 3.4 The Project window with new **Name** settings

Visual Properties of Forms

One important property that changes the visual appearance of a form is **Caption**. The text you enter for this property appears in the title bar at the top of the selected form; in other words, the **Caption** setting provides the title that will describe or identify the purpose of the form to the user. Here are the steps for changing the caption of the **LoanInpt** form:

1. Select **LoanInpt** in the Project window and click the **View Form** button if the form is not already displayed on the screen.

2. Scroll to the **Caption** property in the Properties window. Click **Caption** to make it the current property.

3. Enter **Loan Calculator** as the new caption setting for this form. (This title indicates to the user that **LoanInpt** is the main dialog box for the application.) Notice that the characters of this text appear in the title bar of the form even as you type them into the Settings box. Press the Enter key or click the Enter button to complete the entry. The newly titled form is shown in Figure 3.5.

Now change the **Caption** entries for the other two forms in the project: The new setting for the **LoanOpts** form is **Table Values**, because this is the dialog box in which the user specifies the increments for the principal and interest rates in the resulting payment table. The new **Caption** setting for the **LoanTabl** form is simply **Loan Table**. This is of course the form in which the output table will appear.

A property that can result in rather dramatic changes in the appearance of a form is **BackColor**. As its name suggests, this property controls the background color displayed inside a form—that is, the surface surrounding any controls contained in the form. A specific color in Visual Basic is represented by a long integer value. The value of the integer specifies the

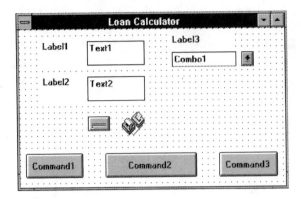

Figure 3.5 The **LoanInpt** form with a new **Caption** setting

mix of red, green, and blue that goes into the corresponding color. Visual Basic supplies several convenient ways to represent colors in the code of a program. But during design time, the best way to introduce color (or black-and-white patterns) into a form or control is by using the Color Palette.

Using the Color Palette

The **LoanOpts** form is a convenient object in which to experiment with the Color Palette:

1. In the Project window, select **LoanOpts** and click the **View Form** button. Press F4 to activate the Properties window.

2. Scroll to the **BackColor** property in the Properties window. Click this property name in the list. An integer representing the current setting appears in the Settings box.

3. Click the ellipsis in the small button located at the right of the Settings box. In response, Visual Basic opens the Color Palette box, which shows the range of colors from which you can choose for the background and foreground of an object (Figure 3.6).

4. Click the second box in the first row of colors. This selection gives the **LoanOpts** form a light gray background, as in Figure 3.7. (Experiment with other colors or shades if you wish.)

There is another way to work with color settings: Pull down the **Window** menu and select the **Color Palette** command. In response, Visual Basic opens a color palette dialog box in which you can select and customize colors for use in your applications.

Figure 3.6 The Color Palette box

Functional Properties of Forms

Several properties specify how a Visual Basic form will function as a window: The **BorderStyle** property determines whether the user can drag borders to change the size and shape of the window. The **MaxButton** and **MinButton** properties specify whether the maximize and minimize icons will appear at the upper-right corner of the frame; and the **ControlBox** property determines whether there will be a control menu box at the upper-left corner of the frame. These latter three properties have fixed setting lists consisting of two possible values: **True** or **False**. The default setting is **True** for all three.

In the *Loan Calculator* application, you have carefully defined appropriate sizes for each dialog box and for the form that displays the output table. You can therefore disable the properties that would allow the user to drag borders or maximize the window size. Furthermore, you can safely eliminate the control menu box in all but the main dialog box.

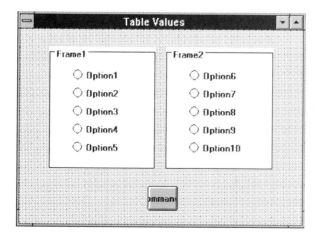

Figure 3.7 The **LoanOpts** form with background color

In the following steps you change the functional elements of the three forms:

1. Activate the **LoanInpt** form. Select **BorderStyle** in the Properties window. Pull down the settings list and select **1-Fixed Single**.

2. While **BorderStyle** remains the current property, activate each of the other two forms in turn and select the **1-Fixed Single** setting for them as well.

3. Activate **LoanInpt** again. Select **MaxButton** in the properties list and change its setting to **False**. Do the same for the other two forms in the project.

4. Change the **MinButton** property to **False** for the **LoanOpts** and **LoanTabl** forms.

5. Change the **ControlBox** property to **False** for the **LoanOpts** and **LoanTabl** forms.

The **BorderStyle**, **MaxButton**, **MinButton**, and **ControlBox** properties affect only the run-time characteristics of a form, not the design-time characteristics. While you are designing your application, you always have full control over the size, shape, and status of each form. Notice that the changes you have made in these properties have not affected the appearance of the forms in the design mode. But when you later start running the completed application, you'll see the changes that have taken place in the three forms:

- The mouse pointer does not change to a two-headed arrow when you position it along the border of a form.

- The maximize icon does not appear at the upper-right corners of the forms.

- The **LoanOpts** and **LoanTabl** forms are missing their minimize icons and control menu boxes.

ASSIGNING PROPERTIES TO CONTROLS

The exercise you've just completed illustrates an important shortcut technique for setting properties. Once you select a property in the properties list, you can activate any number of forms or controls in sequence to change their individual settings for the current property. This is a good way to organize your work when there are many properties to set: Select a property, then change the setting for each control to which that property applies. You'll use this technique in the upcoming exercise as you change the settings for two important control properties: **Caption** and **Text**.

Visual Properties of Controls

The **Caption** property applies to several different types of controls in the *Loan Calculator*. This property defines the text of a label, the name of a command button, the title of a frame, and the description attached to an option button. **Caption** is therefore a good property to start with as you turn your attention to the controls in the application's two dialog boxes.

Table 3.1 shows the new **Caption** settings for controls on both the **LoanInpt** form and the **LoanOpts** form. You can quickly establish all of these settings in sequence, beginning with the following steps:

1. Select the **Label1** control on the **LoanInpt** form.

2. Select **Caption** in the Properties window if it is not already the current property.

3. Type **Principal:**, the new text for the label, and press Enter.

4. Select the next control, **Label2**, and enter **Rate (%):** as its new text.

5. Repeat Step 4 for each of the controls listed in Table 3.1.

Next you should set the initial text values to be displayed in the three text boxes in the **LoanInpt** form. The setting of the **Text** property specifies the value displayed inside these boxes.

In some applications there may be a reasonable default input value for a particular text box; when you design such an application, you might decide to assign this value as the initial **Text** setting for the box. This is not the case in the *Loan Calculator*. The application does not try to suggest values for the principal, interest rate, and term of the loan—the actual input values for these parameters could fall within wide ranges of numbers. For this reason, you'll supply blank values for the two text boxes and the combo box. Here are the steps for changing the **Text** setting for the three text boxes:

1. Select the first text box, for the principal of the loan. Visual Basic's default text value inside this box is **Text1**.

2. Select **Text** in the Properties window if it is not already the selected property.

3. Double-click inside the Settings box to highlight the current text. Press the Delete key on your keyboard to erase the text. Then press Enter to confirm the revision.

Table 3.1 The new Caption settings for the LoanInpt and LoanOpts controls

Default Caption setting	New Caption setting
Label1	Principal:
Label2	Rate (%):
Label3	Term:
Command1 (LoanInpt)	Calc
Command2	Table values...
Command3	Exit
Option1	$10
Option2	$100
Option3	$1,000
Option4	$10,000
Option5	$100,000
Option6	0.125%
Option7	0.25%
Option8	0.50%
Option9	1.0%
Option10	2.0%
Frame1	Principal Increment
Frame2	Rate Increment
Command1 (LoanOpts)	OK

4. Select the second text box, **Text2**. Repeat Step 3 to clear the text from this box.

5. Select the combo box, which displays the text **Combo1**. Repeat Step 3 to clear the text.

After completing these steps, you've specified values for the properties that determine the *appearance* of the two dialog boxes. The main dialog box now appears as shown in Figure 3.8. However, several properties remain to be set.

Functional Properties of Controls

Think back to the steps you originally took to place controls on the main dialog box (Chapter 2): You took care to add controls in a specific order.

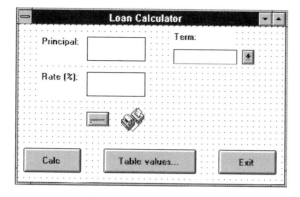

Figure 3.8 The main dialog box with appropriate property settings

You learned that the order of placement during design time determines the run-time *tab order*—that is, the order in which controls are activated when the user repeatedly presses the Tab key. Here is the current Tab order for the controls of the **LoanInpt** form: First the two text boxes, then the combo box, then the three command buttons **Calc**, **Table values**, and **Exit**. (The image controls are not activated by pressing Tab.)

Suppose you decide to change this tab order so that the **Table values** button will be activated before the **Calc** button. You make this change by resetting the values of the **TabIndex** property. **TabIndex** has an integer value for the relevant controls in a form. The sequence of integers represents the tab order.

Before you try to change the **TabIndex** sequence, you have to make sure you know what the current sequence is. You'll begin the following exercise by examining the current **TabIndex** value for the combo box:

1. Activate the combo box in the **LoanInpt** form.

2. Activate the Properties window and select the **TabIndex** property. The setting for the combo box is 5. To make the **Table values** button next in the sequence, you have to set the **TabIndex** property to 6 for the command button.

3. Activate the **Table values** button and enter **6** as the new **TabIndex** setting for this control.

4. Activate **Calc** command button next. Notice that Visual Basic has adjusted its **TabIndex** setting to **7**.

The next time you run the program, you'll see that this change in the **TabIndex** property has produced the tab order that you wanted.

Now turn back to the **LoanOpts** form. Recall the main functional characteristic of a group of option buttons: Only one option in the group is selected at a given time. If the user makes a new selection, the previously selected option is deactivated. To conform to this rule, you should select one of the options in each group as the default selection.

Option buttons have a **Value** property that determines whether an option is on or off. As you might guess, the available settings of the **Value** property are **True** and **False**. The default setting is **False** for all option buttons. During design time, Visual Basic allows you to set the **Value** property to **True** for one option in a group. (If you then set **Value** to **True** for another option in the same group, Visual Basic automatically resets the original option back to **False**.)

For the *Loan Calculator* application, you will set the middle option in each group to **True**. This means that the selected principal increment will be **$1,000** and the selected rate increment will be **0.50%**. To change these settings, follow these steps:

1. Select the middle option in the first group, **$1,000**.

2. Select the **Value** property in the Properties window. The current setting is **False**.

3. Pull down the settings list and select the **True** setting.

4. Perform the same steps to change the **Value** setting of the middle option in the second group.

The **LoanOpts** form now appears as in Figure 3.9.

Code-Related Properties for Controls

Some control properties are designed to help you prepare for the code that you will eventually write for your program. Just as with forms, one of the most important control properties in this regard is **Name**. This property supplies the name that you will use to identify a particular control inside your code. You'll work with the **Name** property in the upcoming exercise.

Assigning Control Names

You should assign a meaningful **Name** setting to every control that will appear in the code of your program. In the *Loan Calculator* application, this includes all the controls that supply input values to your program—the text boxes, the combo box, and the option buttons—along with the command buttons and image controls that represent procedures that your program can perform. Of course, it would be legal to use Visual Basic's default **Name** settings (such as **Text1**, **Combo1**, **Option1**, and **Command1**), but default names are not at all descriptive of the roles these

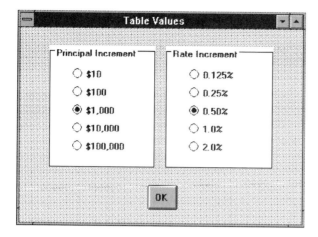

Figure 3.9 The **LoanOpts** form with option buttons activated

controls play in your application. Supplying your own **Name** settings gives
you the opportunity to devise meaningful names for the elements of your
program, making your code more readable and easier to understand.

Table 3.2 provides a list of the new **Name** settings you'll assign to the
controls of the **LoanInpt** and **LoanOpts** forms. Missing from this list are
the few controls that have no role in the code of the program—the three
labels, and the two frames. These controls can keep their default names,
such as **Label1** and **Frame1**. Also missing from Table 3.2 are the option
buttons, **Option1** to **Option10**. You'll deal specially with these controls later
in this chapter.

**Table 3.2 The new Name settings for the *Loan Calculator*
controls**

Default Name setting	New Name setting
Text1	**InPrinc**
Text2	**InRate**
Combo1	**InTerm**
Image1	**SaveTabl**
Image2	**PrntTabl**
Command1 (LoanInpt)	**Calc**
Command2	**Options**
Command3	**ExitButton**
Command1 (LoanOpts)	**OkOpts**

Here are the steps for assigning these control names:

1. Select the **Text1** control in the **LoanInpt** form.

2. Select **Name** in the Properties window.

3. Type **InPrinc** as the setting for this control, then press the Enter key.

4. Select the next control, **Text2**. Enter the new **Name** setting, **InRate**, for this control.

5. Repeat Step 4 for the remaining controls in Table 3.2.

As an example of the use of a control name in code, you should now turn back to the **Form_Load** procedure that you wrote in Chapter 2. You'll recall that you entered code into this procedure to create the drop-down list for the combo box in the **LoanInpt** form. This is how the procedure looks at the moment:

```
Sub Form_Load ()
   Combo1.AddItem "4 years"
   Combo1.AddItem "5 years"
   Combo1.AddItem "10 years"
   Combo1.AddItem "15 years"
   Combo1.AddItem "20 years"
   Combo1.AddItem "30 years"
End Sub
```

The default control name **Combo1** no longer has meaning in your application because you have changed the name of the combo box to **InTerm**. Normally, you do not write code for an application until you have already assigned names to your controls. But in this special case the code already exists, and therefore has to be modified to adjust to the new control name.

You can use Visual Basic's search-and-replace feature to change all the instances of the name **Combo1** to **InTerm** in this procedure. Here are the steps:

1. Select the **LoanInpt** form in the project box and click the **View Code** button. Pull down the **Object** list and select **Form**. The **Form_Load** procedure appears inside the Code window.

2. Pull down the **Edit** menu and choose the **Replace** command. In the resulting dialog box (Figure 3.10) enter **Combo1** in the **Find What** box and **InTerm** in the **Replace With** box.

3. Leaving all the other settings unchanged, click the **Replace All** button.

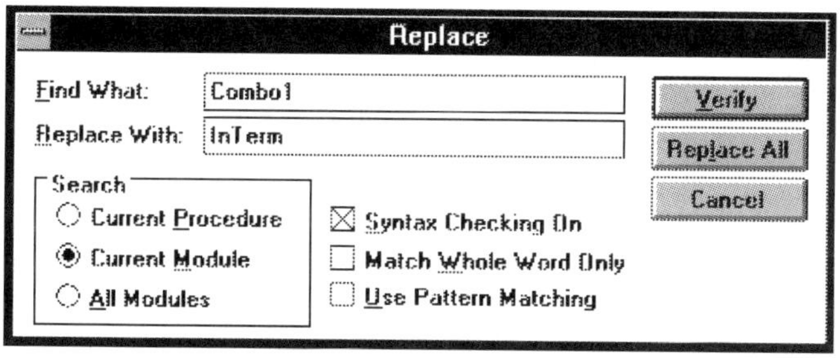

Figure 3.10 The dialog box for the **Replace** command

When you complete this operation, the **Form_Load** procedure appears as follows:

```
Sub Form_Load ()
   InTerm.AddItem "4 years"
   InTerm.AddItem "5 years"
   InTerm.AddItem "10 years"
   InTerm.AddItem "15 years"
   InTerm.AddItem "20 years"
   InTerm.AddItem "30 years"
End Sub
```

The statements in the procedure now refer correctly to **InTerm**, which is the new name for the combo box control. Try running the program again, and you will find that the combo box list appears just as it did when you first created this code.

Creating Control Arrays

For some event procedures, it is convenient to assign a single name to an entire group of controls. Individual controls in the group are then identified by the common name plus an *index* number. For example, in the upcoming exercise, you'll assign the control name **PInc** to five option buttons. In your code, the names of the five individual buttons will be:

```
PInc(0)
PInc(1)
PInc(2)
PInc(3)
PInc(4)
```

A group of controls identified in this way—with an indexed name—is called a *control array*. You may find a great variety of reasons for creating control arrays; in general, they simplify operations with controls that have a common function. For example, structuring a group of option buttons as a control array makes it very easy to identify and react to the option that the user selects at run time.

The following exercise will help you master the mechanical details of setting up a control array during design time. You'll establish both groups of option buttons in the **LoanOpts** form as control arrays. The common name for the first array is **PInc** (for "principal increment"), and the name of the second array is **RInc** (for "rate increment").

Here are the steps for creating these two control arrays:

1. Select the **LoanOpts** form in the Project window and click the **View Form** button.

2. Select the first option button (**Option1**) in the frame on the left side of the form.

3. Select the **Name** property in the Properties window.

4. Enter the name **PInc** as the **Name** setting.

5. Select the next option button down the same frame and again enter **PInc** as the control name. Visual Basic displays a question box on the screen (Figure 3.11) asking you to confirm that you intend to create a control array. Click the **Yes** button to confirm.

6. Continue assigning the same **Name** setting—**PInc**—to the remaining option buttons in the current frame.

7. Repeat Steps 2 through 6 for the option buttons in the other frame, but this time assign the name **RInc** to all five of the option buttons in the frame.

When you create a control array, Visual Basic automatically assigns appropriate settings to a property named **Index**. To examine this property, select the first of the controls in the **RInc** array; then select **Index** in the Properties window. The setting is **0**. If you now look at each of the next

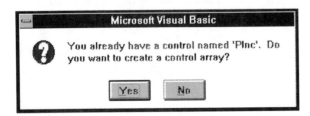

Figure 3.11 Confirmation for creating a control array

RInc controls in turn, you'll see that they have **Index** values of **1**, **2**, **3**, and **4**. In other words, the controls in this group have the following names:

```
RInc(0)
RInc(1)
RInc(2)
RInc(3)
RInc(4)
```

Likewise, the controls in the **PInc** array have the same sequence of **Index** settings. This confirms that your control arrays have been created success-fully. As you'll learn later in this chapter, you can define control arrays in menus as well. You'll see code examples illustrating the use of control arrays in Chapter 4.

Before leaving this first version of the *Loan Calculator* application, turn your attention now to the properties of the grid control that you have placed on the **LoanTabl** form.

The Properties of a Grid Control

A grid control has some properties that you can conveniently set at design time, and others that can be set only during run time by the code in your application. Among the properties that you can set at design time are those that determine the column and row dimensions of the grid itself (**Cols** and **Rows**), the number of fixed columns and rows at the top and left sides of the grid (**FixedCols** and **FixedRows**), and of course the control name (**Name**).

In Chapter 2 you placed a grid control inside the **LoanTabl** form and you adjusted the position and size of the grid. Now, follow these steps to change a few of the grid's most important property settings:

1. Select the **LoanTabl** form in the Project window and click the **View Form** button. Then click the grid control to select it, and take a few moments to scroll through the property list for the grid. This list includes some special properties that apply to no other control but the grid. Notice in particular that the default setting for both **Cols** and **Rows** is 2, meaning that the grid initially has two columns by two rows of cells.

2. Select the **Name** property and enter **LoanGrid** as the control name setting.

3. Select the **Cols** property and enter a value of **7** as the new setting. Likewise, select **Rows** and enter **7** as the setting. The grid now

contains seven rows by seven columns, for a total of 49 cells. Initially, the first column and row in the grid are *fixed* and displayed in gray. In a spreadsheet-type application these cells do not scroll. But the *Loan Calculator* application uses the grid exclusively for table output, so the fixed column and row are unnecessary.

4. Select the **FixedCols** property and enter **0** as its new setting. Do the same for the **FixedRows** property.

5. Change three other properties that affect the appearance and function of the grid: Select the **ScrollBars** property and change the setting to **O-None**. As a result, the vertical scroll bar disappears from the grid. Then select the **HighLight** property and change its setting to **False**. This property determines whether the selected cell will be displayed in a highlight color. Select the **Enabled** property and switch its setting to **False**. This property specifies whether a control can respond to mouse clicks or other events that the user initiates; because this grid is designed only to display data, no events need to take place around it in the *Loan Calculator* application.

6. Finally, try selecting a new font and point size for the text that the program will display in the grid. Change the **FontName** setting to **Times New Roman** if this font is available in your Windows configuration. (If not, select some other proportionally spaced serif font.) Then select **9.75** as the new setting the **FontSize** property.

The grid control now appears as shown in Figure 3.12. You'll notice that the columns are not wide enough to fill up the full size of the grid control. Column widths are established individually in a grid, and the **ColWidth** property can be used only in code, not at design time. You'll see how to set this property in Chapter 4.

In Chapter 2 you began building an alternative menu-driven version of the *Loan Calculator* application. Now you'll continue developing this example by adding menus that represent the options currently appearing on

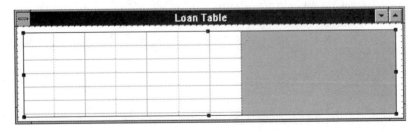

Figure 3.12 New properties for the grid control

the **LoanOpts** form. To prepare for the exercise ahead, save the work you've done on the current application and then load the new project from the files supplied on the exercise disk. CH3EX2.MAK is the name of the alternative *Loan Calculator* program. It includes two forms: CH3-EX2A.FRM, named **LoanInpt**; and CH3EX2B.FRM, named **LoanTabl**. Using these files you can continue working with menus, starting from the point where you left off at the end of Chapter 2.

PROPERTIES IN MENUS

During a performance of the first version of the *Loan Calculator*, the user can call up a separate dialog box to select increment values for the payment table. To view the dialog box, the user clicks the **Table Values...** command button. The window has two groups of option buttons for setting the principal increment and the rate increment.

An alternative design is to place these two groups of options in two pull-down menus on the main dialog box. In the second version of the application the dialog box already has one pull-down menu, named **File**. The additional two menus could be named **Principal Increment** and **Rate Increment**. This expanded menu system eliminates the need for a second dialog box and places the options closer at hand.

In Chapter 2, you used Visual Basic's Menu Design Window to create the **File** menu. Now you'll return to this window to expand the menu hierarchy by adding the two new menus. In designing the **File** menu, you dealt with only two of the property options in the Menu Design Window—**Caption** and **Name**. For these new menus, you'll work with two additional properties named **Index** and **Checked**. In the Menu Design Window, **Index** is represented as a text box and **Checked** is a check box:

- The **Index** text box is for specifying the index of each element in a control array that you create for a menu. In the context of a menu, a control array is a group of commands that have the same control name.

- The **Checked** property specifies whether a given command will have a check mark displayed next to it in the menu list. In the *Loan Calculator* you'll use this property to indicate the default selection in each of the new menu lists.

Select the **LoanInpt** form in the Project window and click the **View Form** button. Then pull down Visual Basic's **Window** menu and select the **Menu**

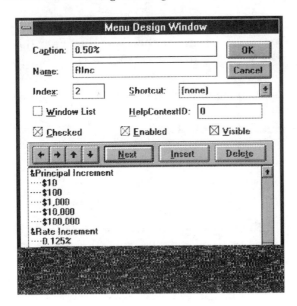

Figure 3.13 The Menu Design Window with new menu entries

Design command. When the window appears on the screen, you'll see the definition for the **File** menu that you created in Chapter 2. Notice the locations of the **Index** text box and the **Checked** check box, beneath the **Name** box (Figure 3.13).

The new menu entries for this application are described in Table 3.3. Here is an outline of the steps for defining these new menus:

1. Click the **Next** button four times, placing the menu list highlight just after the last of the existing entries.

2. Click the left arrow icon to start again at the highest menu level.

3. Activate the **Caption** box and enter the name of the first of the two new menus: **&Principal Increment**.

4. Activate the **Name** box and enter the menu's control name, **PrincMenu**. Leave the **Index** box blank for this entry and leave the **Checked** box unchecked.

5. Click the **Next** button to start a new entry and then click the right arrow icon to indicate that this entry is to appear as a command inside the **Principal Increment** menu.

6. Enter the text **$10** into the **Caption** box, and the name **PInc** into the **Name** box. Because this entry is to be the first element of a control array, enter the number **0** into the **Index** box. The **Checked** box remains unchecked. Click **Next** to begin the next entry.

Table 3.3 New menu entries for the second version of the *Loan Calculator* application.

Level	Caption	Name	Index	Checked
menu	**&Principal Increment**	**PrincMenu**	—	no
----command	**$10**	**PInc**	0	no
----command	**$100**	**PInc**	1	no
----command	**$1,000**	**PInc**	2	yes
----command	**$10,000**	**PInc**	3	no
----command	**$100,000**	**PInc**	4	no
menu	**&Rate Increment**	**RateMenu**	—	no
----command	**0.125%**	**RInc**	0	no
----command	**0.25%**	**RInc**	1	no
----command	**0.50%**	**RInc**	2	yes
----command	**1.0%**	**RInc**	3	no
----command	**2.0%**	**RInc**	4	no

7. Continue creating the remaining entries described in Table 3.3. Remember to check the **Checked** box for the third entries (with **Index** values of **2**) in the **PInc** and **RInc** arrays. Also, take care to place each entry at its correct level in the menu hierarchy.

When you finish your work in this exercise, the Menu Design Window will appear as shown in Figure 3.13. The two new menus are outlined in the menu list shown in the lower half of the window. In effect, you have created two control arrays for this menu. The array named **PInc** represents the five entries in the **Principal Increment** menu, and the array named **RInc** represents the five entries in the **Rate Increment** menu. Check your work to make sure that each entry is correct. (The Menu Design Window allows you to edit menu entries at any time.) Then click the **OK** button to complete the menu definitions.

Returning to the **LoanInpt** form, you can examine the two new menus that you have defined. Click each menu in turn to view the drop-down menu lists. Figure 3.14 shows the **Principal Increment** list and Figure 3.15 shows the **Rate Increment** list. Notice that the middle entry is checked in each list. In both cases this check mark indicates the default increment value at the time the program begins its performance. To make a new selection, the user will simply pull down a menu and click the desired increment amount.

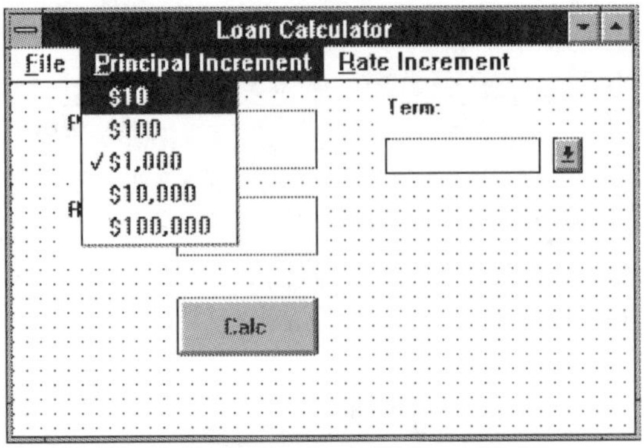

Figure 3.14 The **Principal Increment** menu list

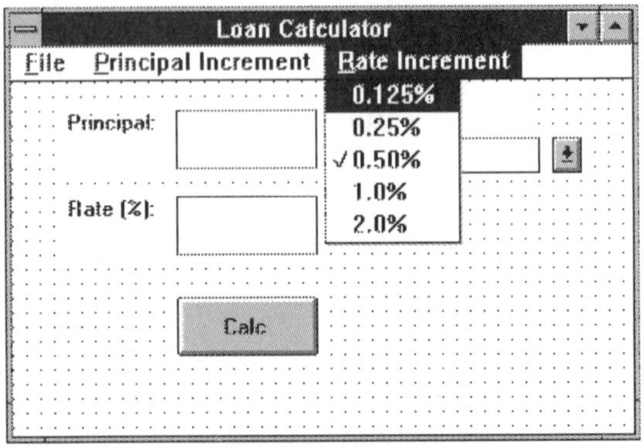

Figure 3.15 The **Rate Increment** menu list

SUMMARY: PROPERTIES IN A VISUAL BASIC APPLICATION

So far you've examined a handful of properties that apply to forms, controls, and menu entries, and you've seen how various settings can change the appearance and the functional elements of your application. Here is a summary of the form properties that you have learned about in this chapter:

- **Name** is a name that you use to identify a form in code. (The setting is a one-word text value.)

- **Caption** is a descriptive name displayed in the form's title bar. (The setting is a text value.)

- **BackColor** is the color or pattern displayed in the background area of a form. (The setting is an integer, but you can use the Color Palette to select a color or pattern.)

- **BorderStyle** determines whether the form can be sized by dragging the border during run time; it also specifies the graphic style of the border. (A fixed list of several settings is available.)

- **MaxButton** specifies whether or not there will be a maximize button at the upper-right corner of the form. (Settings are **True** or **False**.)

- **MinButton** specifies whether or not there will be a minimize button at the upper-right corner of the form. (Settings are **True** or **False**.)

- **ControlBox** determines whether there will be a control-menu box at the upper-left corner of the form. (Settings are **True** or **False**.)

These are the major control properties that you have worked with in applications up to this point:

- **Caption** is a text value displayed on a control; it applies to labels, command buttons, frames, check boxes, and option buttons.

- **Text** is the initial text value in a text box or a combo box.

- **Picture** selects the icon to be displayed in an image control or picture box.

- **TabIndex** specifies the order in which controls will be selected when the user presses the Tab key during run time. (The setting is an integer.)

- **Value** is the status of an option button or a check box. (Settings for an option button are **True** or **False**. Settings for a check box are **0Unchecked**, **1-Checked**, or **2-Grayed**.)

- **Name** is the name that you use to identify a control in code.

- **Index** is the index number of a control that is an element of a control array.

- **Rows** and **Cols** determine the size of the table in a grid control, and **FixedRows** and **FixedCols** specify the number of rows and columns that do not scroll.

Here are the menu properties that you have seen illustrated in this chapter and the previous chapter:

- **Caption** is the name of a menu or the name of a command in a pull-down menu list.

- **Name** is the name that you use to identify a menu element in code.
- **Index** is the index number of a command that is an element of a control array.
- **Checked** specifies whether or not a given command in a menu list is checked. (The setting is **True** or **False**.)

You'll learn about other properties and settings as you continue working with Visual Basic applications.

4

Building an Application,
Step 3: Writing Code

INTRODUCTION

In the third stage of application development you write code to handle the specific events you want your program to recognize. The forms and controls you have already selected—and the properties you have defined for them—give your application its visual and functional qualities. The code you now write will determine what the program can actually do.

If you are an experienced Basic programmer, you might be surprised at how little code you have to write in a Visual Basic application to achieve impressive results. In a traditional version of the Basic language you spend much of your programming effort on the detailed task of developing an interface for your programs—creating menus, developing input and output techniques, and generally finding ways to make your program work as simply as possible. In Visual Basic these design tasks are already complete by the time you reach the coding stage.

This chapter guides you through the process of planning and writing code for a Visual Basic application. You'll continue working on the *Loan Calculator* application you've been developing in the previous two chapters. For this chapter's hands-on exercise, you'll once again begin by opening the project from files supplied on the exercise disk. The first version of the exercise—up to the point you completed in Chapter 3—is stored as CH4EX1.MAK.

Your goals in this chapter are: first, to learn how to create procedures and to practice entering code; and second, to gain a broad understanding of Visual Basic program organization. After a brief hands-on programming exercise, you'll have the chance to examine the complete code for the *Loan Calculator* in both its versions. (The final versions of the program are stored on the exercise disk as LOANCALC.MAK and LOANCA2.MAK.) Before you begin, take a moment to review the concepts behind Visual Basic, and to compare this new language with what you know about Basic programming in other environments.

THE EVENT-DRIVEN PROGRAMMING MODEL

During run time a Visual Basic application waits for events to take place before performing code. A given procedure is performed when triggered by a specific event. This operating mode—known as the *event-driven programming model*—governs the action in a Visual Basic application.

Visual Basic defines groups of relevant events for each type of control. Most events are actions performed by the the person using the program—actions as simple as clicking a mouse button or pressing a key on the keyboard. Each event has a name, such as **Click**, **Load**, and **GotFocus**. The same name identifies the corresponding event procedure that Visual Basic looks for when the event takes place. The full name of an event procedure is:

```
ObjectName_EventName
```

where *ObjectName* identifies the form or control that is the object of the action, and *EventName* identifies the event that has occurred. For example, consider the command button named **Options** in the *Loan Calculator*. The action of clicking this control with the mouse initiates a **Click** event. When this event takes place, Visual Basic performs the event procedure named **Options_Click** in your code.

The event procedures for a form always use the object name **Form**, no matter what the actual name of the form is. For example, **Form_Load** is the name of the procedure that is called at the time a form is first loaded into memory at run time.

Not every event is followed by execution of code. When an event occurs, Visual Basic looks for a procedure you have written to define the program's reaction to the event. If the event procedure is found—that is, if you have supplied the target code—it is performed. If not, nothing happens. In short, an application loops repeatedly through the following process during run time:

1. Wait for the next event.

2. When an event occurs, look for the corresponding event procedure in the program's code.

3. If the event procedure exists, perform it; otherwise, do nothing.

4. Start again at Step 1.

Your job in this final stage of program development is to anticipate events and to plan your program's reactions to them. You organize your code around forms and controls you have already placed in your project. Before writing code, you select the objects that will be central to the action of the program, and you choose the events that you want the application to recognize for those objects. You then write event procedures to define the response to each anticipated event.

You will probably not write event procedures for every control in your application. Some screen objects have inherently simple roles, defined entirely by the built-in characteristics of the controls themselves. For example, consider some controls you have placed in the *Loan Calculator*. The labels in the main dialog box—with the captions **Principal**, **Rate**, and **Term**—describe the program's input requirements. No recognized events will take place around these label controls; therefore, you do not need to write code for them. Likewise, the frame controls on the second dialog box—labeled **Principal Increment** and **Text Increment**—serve only as containers for the groups of option buttons. Again, no event procedures are required for these controls in this particular program.

By design, the main action of the *Loan Calculator* application takes place when the user clicks a command button or an icon. For example, clicking the command button labeled **Table values** results in a second dialog box of options. Clicking the **Calc** button produces a payment table on the screen. Clicking one of the two icons sends the output to a selected destination—the printer or a text file on disk. These controls are therefore the objects around which you'll organize the code for the application.

VISUAL BASIC AND OTHER VERSIONS OF BASIC

If you are already an experienced Basic programmer, your first task is to orient yourself to Visual Basic's object-oriented event-driven programming model. After that, your previous programming experience—however brief or extensive—becomes an asset.

Traditional versions of the Basic programming language are *procedure oriented* rather than event oriented. In a procedure-oriented language, a program typically consists of a structured hierarchy of procedures. At the top of the structure is a main program section that controls the action by making *calls* to the program's procedures. In general, the action is sequential: The main program calls procedures one after another in a prescribed order, and the program performance ends after the last call. The sequence of procedure calls is determined by the logic and structure of the program itself.

By contrast, the order and sequence of a Visual Basic program depends on the events that occur at run time. Some event procedures may be called many times, each time the user performs an action and triggers the corresponding event. Some procedures may never be performed at all if the anticipated event never takes place.

Other versions of Basic do allow you to set up *event traps* to anticipate specific events during a program performance. In this sense you can create event-driven programs even in previous versions of the language, but you have to write the code to control all the mechanical details of the event. What is new in Visual Basic is the match between visual objects on the screen—objects that you select for your application without programming—and the predefined events relating to those objects.

Despite the differences between Visual Basic and other Basics, many of the keywords, tools, and built-in procedures in Visual Basic are the same as in other versions. For example, here is a selective list of Visual Basic programming structures and tools that you will recognize as identical, or nearly identical, to equivalent features in other Basics:

- *Procedures* and *functions*, the two structures designed for organizing individual sections of code.
- Numeric and string *data types*, and the operations and functions that apply to these data types.
- *Variables*, names that represent individual data values in a program.
- Data structures—*arrays* and *records*—representing multiple data values by a single name.
- *Assignment statements* for storing values in variables.
- Control structures, such as *loops* and *decisions*.
- Data file procedures, including *sequential* and *random-access* file input and output.
- *Error-trapping* techniques.

In many of the chapters of this book you'll find **Review Boxes** that will help you re-examine Basic programming topics such as these. The first, **Review Box 4.1**, covers the general syntax of procedures and functions. In the upcoming sections of this chapter, you'll begin exploring the different ways of using procedures and functions to organize your code in a Visual Basic application.

PROGRAM ORGANIZATION

Visual Basic distinguishes between two categories of code: *event procedures* and *general procedures*. The main distinction lies in the way procedures are called for execution:

- As you have seen, a call to an event procedure occurs automatically whenever the corresponding event occurs. Event procedures are always **Sub** procedures and appear only in forms.

- A call to a general procedure is performed explicitly via a procedure call, never triggered by an event. General procedures include both **Sub** procedures and **Function** procedures, and may appear in either forms or code modules. (**Review Box 4.1** describes the difference between **Sub** and **Function** procedures.)

You can write general procedures to help organize your program into small, manageable parts. Small procedures with carefully limited tasks to perform are always easier to work with than large ones. Another reason for writing general procedures is to avoid repetition of code. A general procedure can be called from any number of different locations in your program.

When you are ready to write code for any kind of procedure, Visual Basic takes care of creating the appropriate procedure *template*, consisting of the **Sub** and **End Sub** statements, or the **Function** and **End Function** statements. You have already seen how to find the template for an event procedure. Here is a quick review of the steps:

1. Click the **View Code** button in the Project window to view the Code window for a selected form.

2. Use the **Object** and **Proc** combo boxes at the top of the Code window to select the event procedure: First choose the name of the object from the **Object** list, and then the name of the event from the **Proc** list.

Review Box 4.1

Procedures and Functions

Code in Visual Basic is organized in sections known as **Sub** procedures and **Function** procedures. A procedure performs a disinct task and has its own unique name in an application. A *call* is a statement or expression that results in a performance of a procedure.

A **Sub** procedure—sometimes known simply as a *procedure*—is a block of code enclosed within **Sub** and **End Sub** statements:

```
Sub ProcedureName (ArgumentList)
  ' Block of statements.
End Sub
```

The optional *ArgumentList* is a list of variables that will receive argument values sent to the procedure at the time of a call. Variables in the list are separated by commas. The type of each variable can be identified by a type-declaration character (**%** for an integer, **&** for a long integer, **!** for a single-precision floating-point value, **#** for a double-precision floating-point value, **@** for a currency value, or **$** for a string), or by an **As** *Type* clause:

```
Argument1 As Type, Argument2 As Type
```

A call to a **Sub** procedure is a statement consisting of the name of the procedure followed by a list of the argument values sent to the procedure:

```
ProcedureName ArgumentValueList
```

As a result of the call statement, each argument value is assigned to its corresponding argument variable in the procedure definition, and then the block of statements in the procedure is performed.

When you complete these steps, the template for the event procedure you have selected appears inside the Code window, ready for you begin writing the code.

For example, suppose you want to write the **Calc_Click** procedure for the *Loan Calculator* application. When you choose the **Calc** object and the

Review Box 4.1 *(continued)*

Argument values in a call can be expressed as literal values, expressions, or variables. By default, argument values that appear as variables are sent *by reference*. This means that any change the procedure makes in the value of the argument is passed back to the variable in the original call. You can protect a variable from such a change by passing the argument *by value* instead. To do so, include the keyword **ByVal** in the argument list of the **Sub** procedure definition:

```
Sub ProcedureName (ByVal Argument1 As Type)
```

Alternatively, you can enclose an individual argument in parentheses in the call statement; this also prevents the procedure from changing the value of the variable:

```
ProcedureName (ArgumentVariable1)
```

A **Function** procedure—also known simply as a *function*—is a block of code enclosed within **Function** and **End Function** statements. Like a **Sub** procedure, a function has an optional list of argument variables. Unlike a **Sub** procedure, a function returns a value of a specified data type:

```
Function FunctionName (ArgumentList) As ReturnType
  ' Block of statements.
   FunctionName = ReturnValue
End Function
```

An assignment statement inside the function block specifies the function's return value by assigning an expression to the function name. A call to a function never stands alone as a statement by itself, but always appears as an expression that represents the function's return value.

Click event from the boxes at the top of the Code window, the event procedure template appears in the window as follows:

```
Sub Calc_Click ()

End Sub
```

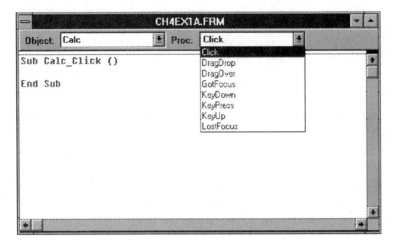

Figure 4.1 Finding the **Calc_Click** procedure template

The flashing edit cursor appears between these two lines, ready for you to type your first line of code. Figure 4.1 shows the Code window at this point in the process.

To create the template for a general procedure, you use the **New Procedure...** command from Visual Basic's **View** menu. This command is available when the current selection is a Code window. Here are the steps for creating a template for a new general procedure:

1. Pull down the **View** menu and select **New Procedure**. A dialog box appears on the screen, as shown in Figure 4.2.

2. Select either **Sub** or **Function** in the **Type** box.

3. Enter the name you want to give to the new procedure in the **Name** text box. Then click the **OK** button or press Enter. The new procedure template appears in the active Code window.

Whether the template in the Code window is for an event procedure or a general procedure, the next step is to begin writing code. The first lines you write should be a brief comment explaining the procedure's purpose.

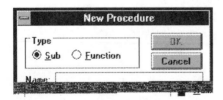

Figure 4.2 The **New Procedure** dialog box

As you know, comments in Visual Basic begin with the single-quote character; for example:

```
Sub Calc_Click ()

    ' Produce the output table when
    ' the user clicks the Calc button.
```

The more carefully and consistently you document your code in this way, the more easily you will be able to revise and debug your program later.

Hands-On Exercise: Entering Code

The **LoanInpt** form, which displays the main dialog box of the *Loan Calculator*, will eventually require a number of event procedures. You'll have the opportunity to examine all of these procedures later in this chapter, but for this first programming exercise, you'll create just three procedures yourself:

- An abbreviated and temporary version of **Calc_Click**, designed to display single-payment calculations in the **LoanTabl** form rather than entire payment tables.

- A short function named **Payment**, which the program uses to calculate all monthly payment figures.

- The **ExitButton_Click** procedure, which consists of one line of code allowing the user to stop the program performance.

Load the *Loan Calculator* project into memory from the exercise disk file CH4EX1.MAK. Then follow these steps to create the three procedures:

1. Select the **LoanInpt** form in the Project window and click the **View Code** button.

2. In the resulting Code window, use the **Object** and **Proc** boxes to display the template for the **Calc_Click** procedure.

3. Type the lines of this procedure in its initial form:

```
Sub Calc_Click ()

    ' Produce the output table when
    ' the user clicks the Calc button.

    Dim Princ, LRate, Term, TempPmt, PmtStr
    Dim i As Integer

    ' Read the input values.
```

```
Princ = InPrinc.Text
LRate = InRate.Text / 100
Term = Val(InTerm.Text)

' Calculate and display a payment amount.

TempPmt = Payment(Princ, LRate / 12, Term * 12)
PmtStr = Format$(TempPmt, "$#,#####.00")
LoanTabl.Show

For i = 0 To 5
  LoanTabl!LoanGrid.ColAlignment(i) = 1
  LoanTabl!LoanGrid.ColWidth(i) = 1260
Next i

LoanTabl!LoanGrid.Col = 0
LoanTabl!LoanGrid.Row = 0
LoanTabl!LoanGrid.Text = PmtStr

End Sub   ' Calc_Click
```

4. Use the **Object** and **Proc** boxes to display the template for the **ExitButton_Click** procedure.

5. The procedure consists of a comment and one line of code, the keyword **End**. Type the lines:

```
Sub ExitButton_Click ()

  ' Terminate the program performance.
  End
End Sub   ' ExitButton_Click
```

6. Use the **New Procedure** command in the **View** menu to create a template for the **Payment** function. Click the **Function** button in the dialog box, and enter **Payment** into the **Name** box. Then click **OK.**

7. In the code window, type the lines of the function, including the argument list and the **As Currency** clause on the **Function** line:

```
Function Payment (P, MoRate, Months) As Currency

  ' Calculate the monthly payment.

  Payment = (P * MoRate) / (1 - (1 + MoRate) ^ (-Months))

End Function   ' Payment
```

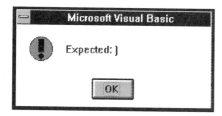

Figure 4.3 A message from the smart editor

As you enter the code of these first procedures, you may encounter a useful feature that is part of the Visual Basic code editor. If you attempt to enter a line that contains a syntax error, the "smart" editor immediately spots the problem and displays an error message on the screen. For example, imagine that you inadvertently enter the following line from the **Payment** function without its final closing parenthesis character:

```
Payment = (P * MoRate) / (1 - (1 + MoRate) ^ (-Months)
```

When you do so, the warning box shown in Figure 4.3 appears on the screen. This is the first of several Visual Basic features designed to help you correct errors in your programs.

You are ready to try running this abbreviated verison of the *Loan Calculator* application. Press the F5 function key to begin a performance. At this point, Visual Basic finds any structural errors that might exist in your code—errors that prevent the program from running. If such errors exist, you will see appropriate error messages on the screen. For example, imagine that you have omitted one of the arguments in the call to the **Payment** function (a call made from within the **Calc_Click** procedure):

```
TempPmt = Payment(LRate / 12, Term * 12)
```

The first argument, **Princ**, is missing from this function call. The function itself requires three arguments, not two:

```
Function Payment (P, MoRate, Months) As Currency
```

When you press F5 to run the program, Visual Basic immediately finds this inconsistency. It scrolls to the **Calc_Click** procedure in your code, highlights the mistaken function call, and displays the error message shown in Figure 4.4.

Before you can run the program, you must examine the highlighted line of code, determine exactly what is wrong with it, and correct the error. Additional errors might be highlighted in your subsequent attempts to run the program. But when you have corrected the final error, the program

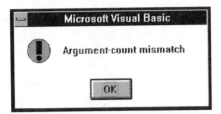

Figure 4.4 Error message after an attempt to run the program

performance begins. The main dialog box for the *Loan Calculator* appears on the screen, ready for your input.

To test the program, type the parameters of an imaginary loan into the program's text boxes. Enter a principal of **15000** and an interest rate of **10**. Select a term of **5 years** from the the list attached to the **Term** combo box. Then click the **Calc** button. As shown in Figure 4.5, the value **$318.71** appears in the first cell of the grid control in the **Loan Table** form. This is the monthly payment for the loan. Try additional calculations if you wish. When you are finished, click the **Exit** button. The performance stops, and you return to the Visual Basic design mode.

Examining the Code

Now take a brief look at the three procedures you have created. The **Calc_Click** procedure, called when the user clicks the **Calc** button, has the initial task of reading input from the text boxes and combo box. Then the procedure sends these three input values as arguments in a call to the **Payment** function to calculate the monthly payment amount. Finally, **Calc_Click** adjusts the grid properties in the **LoanTabl** form and displays the calculated payment in the first cell of the grid.

In Visual Basic 2.0 and 3.0, text boxes and combo boxes can accept and recognize input values belonging to string, numeric, or chronological data types. (By contrast, text boxes in Version 1.0 accept all data entries as

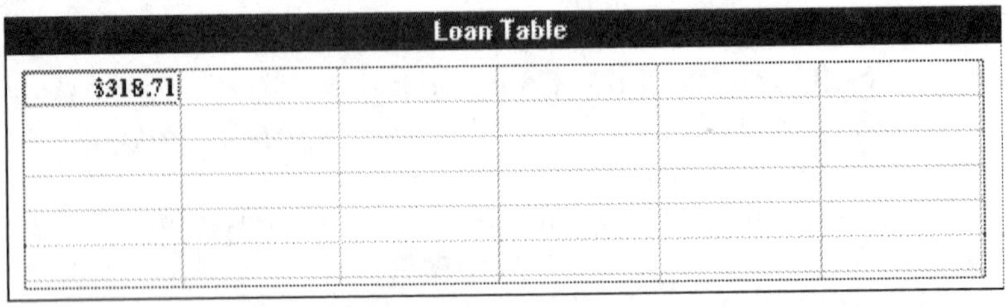

Figure 4.5 A single payment calculation in the **Loan Table** form

strings. Your program is then responsible for converting each entry into the appropriate data type if necessary.) Correspondingly, the default data type for variables in Visual Basic 2.0 and 3.0—unless you explicitly declare a variable differently—is a versatile new type known as the **Variant**. Traditional Basic variables always belong to unique and explicit data types; in contrast, a **Variant**-type variable can store a value belonging to any one of a variety of types, including a string, a numeric value, or a date or time value. (See **Review Box 4.2** for a description of variables and data types, including the new **Variant** type.)

Furthermore, Visual Basic handles data-type conversions automatically when you use **Variant**-type variables. In some programming contexts this new flexibility may simplify the way you handle data. On the other hand, you can still use standard data types if you prefer—for example, when you need to perform specific tests on input in the process of converting from one data type to another. This is a topic you'll continue to explore in several of the programs presented later in this book.

The five major variables in the **Calc_Click** procedure illustrate the use of the **Variant** type; they are declared as follows:

```
Dim Princ, LRate, Term, TempPmt, PmtStr
```

Because no data type is specified in this **Dim** statement, all of these variables belong to the default **Variant** type. Here are the three lines in the **Calc_Click** procedure that read the user's input and store the values in the appropriate **Variant**-type variables:

```
Princ = InPrinc.Text
LRate = InRate.Text / 100
Term = Val(InTerm.Text)
```

The input values are read through a reference to the current **Text** property setting for each of the three controls, **InPrinc**, **InRate**, and **InTerm**. During design time you assigned a blank string as the **Text** setting for these three controls. When the user enters a value into one of these controls, the new **Text** property setting represents the input value. Assuming the user enters valid numeric values into the three text boxes, Visual Basic automatically stores these values in numeric form in the three variables **Princ**, **LRate**, and **Term**.

A program uses the following general format to read the current setting of a property defined for any object in the application:

```
ObjectName.PropertyName
```

Given this format, you can see that **InPrinc.Text**, **InRate.Text**, and **InTerm.Text** represent the three input values that the user has entered

Review Box 4.2

Data Types, Operations, Variables, and Constants

Visual Basic supports five numeric data types named **Integer**, **Long**, **Single**, **Double**, and **Currency** along with a related group of numeric operations. Visual Basic also has two forms of the **String** type: variable length and fixed length. Finally, Visual Basic 2.0 and 3.0 have a versatile new **Variant** type that can represent chronological, numeric, or string data. A *variable* is a name that represents a data value belonging to a specific type. You can define the type of a variable by declaring the variable in a **Dim** statement or a **Global** statement, or by appending a type-declaration character as a suffix at the end of the variable name (%, &, !, #, and @ for the five numeric types, or $ for a string).

The *integer* types represent whole numbers within specific ranges of values. Integer representation is always perfectly precise, and also provides the fastest operations. Operations available for integers include ^ (exponentiation), * (multiplication), / (division), \ (integer division), **Mod** (modulo arithmetic), + (addition), and – (subtraction). The following table summarizes the characteristics of the two integer types:

Name	Variable Suffix	Storage	Low Value	High Value
Integer	%	2 bytes	-32768	32768
Long	&	4 bytes	-2147483648	2147483647

The *floating point* types represent numbers with decimal points within very large ranges but with limited precision. Operations are exponentiation, multiplication, division, addition, and subtraction. This table summarizes the two floating point types:

Name	Variable Suffix	Storage	Negative Values	Positive Values
Single	!	4 bytes	-3.4E+38 to -1.4 E-45	1.4 E-45 3.4E+38
Double	#	8 bytes	-1.7D+308 to -4.9D-324	4.9D-324 to 1.7D+308

Review Box 4.2 *(continued)*

The **Currency** type represents *fixed-decimal* values without loss of precision. Values belonging to this type may have up to 15 digits to the left of the decimal point and 4 digits after the decimal point:

Name	Variable Suffix	Storage	Low Value	High Value
Currency	**@**	8 bytes	-9.22E+14	9.22E+14

A *string* value is a sequence of characters, which may include letters of the alphabet, digits from "0" to "9", punctuation characters, and other special characters as defined in the ANSI code. Visual Basic defines one string operation, *concatenation*, represented by the + operator. Concatenation combines two strings to form a third string. In addition, Visual Basic has a large library of string procedures and functions. The **Len** function returns the length, in characters, of a string. A variable-length string can contain any number of characters up to an approximate length of 64K bytes. A fixed-length string has a predeclared length. You use a **Dim** statement to declare a fixed-length string:

```
Dim StringVarName As String * StringLength
```

where *StringLength* is an integer representing the length of the string.

A **Variant**-type variable can store a date/time value, a number, a string, or the **Null** value. This type matches the new versatility of text box controls in Visual Basic 2.0 and 3.0. (A text box can now accept and recognize an input value belonging to any data type.) Visual Basic supplies special functions such as **IsNumeric**, **IsDate**, and **IsNull** to determine the data type of the value stored in a **Variant** variable. For example, if you assign the value of a text box to a **Variant**-type variable, you can use these functions to find out whether the user has entered a value belonging to the expected data type.

An *assignment statement* stores a value in a variable. This statement has the general form:

```
VariableName = value
```

Review Box 4.2 *(continued)*

The value stored in a variable can—and typically does—change frequently during a program performance.

By contrast, a *constant* is a name that represents an unchanging value throughout the performance. You use the **Const** statement for declaring constants. This statement can appear in a code module, in form or module declaration sections, or in procedures. Visual Basic 2.0 and 3.0 supply the built-in constants **True** and **False** to represent logical values, equivalent to -1 and 0. If you have previously been in the habit of defining these two names in **Const** statements, you should no longer do so.

An undeclared variable in Visual Basic 2.0 or 3.0 belongs to the default **Variant** type. If you want Visual Basic to require declarations for all variables in a program, you can include the following statement in the declarations section of each form or module of your application:

```
Option Explicit
```

Under this option, Visual Basic displays the compile-time error message **Variable not defined** if it encounters any variable that has not been explicitly declared in a **Dim** statement or **Global** statement.

---

into the two text boxes and the combo box. Alternatively, Visual Basic 2.0 and 3.0 also allow you to refer implicitly to the defined *value* of a given control, without reference to the property name. Each type of control has one property that is designated as its value. For example, the **Text** property is defined as the value of a text box. You can therefore refer to the value in a text box without explicit naming the **Text** property. For example, you could read the value of the **InPrinc** text box as:

```
Princ = InPrinc
```

rather than:

```
Princ = InPrinc.Text
```

Omitting the **Text** property name in this case saves you a few keystrokes as you are entering your code. On the other hand, your code is arguably clearer and easier to read if you include the full reference to **InPrinc.Text**.

For this reason, the programs in this book use the full *ObjectName.PropertyName* reference format even when it is optional.

Notice the two operations that the **Calc_Click** procedure performs on the input data it reads: First the program divides the user's input for the interest rate by 100 to convert the percentage into a decimal value:

```
LRate = InRate.Text / 100
```

In addition, the program uses Visual Basic's built-in **Val** function to guarantee that the **Term** value will be numeric:

```
Term = Val(InTerm.Text)
```

If the user selects a term such as **5 years** from the combo box list, the **Val** function reads only the intial numeric portion of the selection—**5**—and discards the nonnumeric characters.

After reading the three input values and storing them in the variables **Princ**, **LRate**, and **Term**, the **Calc_Click** procedure sends these values to the **Payment** function to calculate the monthly payment:

```
TempPmt = Payment(Princ, LRate / 12, Term * 12)
```

Actually, the **LRate** value must first be divided by 12 to produce a monthly interest rate amount, and the **Term** value must be multiplied by 12 to give the loan term in months. Given these three arguments, the **Payment** function calculates the monthly loan payment, which is stored in the variable **TempPmt**. The built-in Visual Basic function named **Format$** then produces an output string in dollars-and-cents format, and stores the string in the variable **PmtStr**:

```
PmtStr = Format$(TempPmt, "$#,#####.00")
```

(Visual Basic 3.0 has a new built-in **PMT** function that you can use instead of the **Payment** function you have written. But you'll probably find **Payment** easier to use and more intuitive.)

Finally, the **Calc_Click** procedure displays the **LoanTabl** form on the screen and shows the result of the payment calculation in the first cell of the **LoanGrid** control. The first of these two tasks is performed by a call to one of Visual Basic's built-in *methods*. You'll recall that a method is a procedure that performs an operation on a particular object. (In Chapter 2 you used the **AddItem** method to build the drop-down list for the combo box in the *Loan Calculator*.) The format for calling a method is:

```
ObjectName.MethodName
```

Calc_Click uses a method that applys to forms: The **Show** method brings a hidden form to the screen. The following instruction shows the **LoanTabl** form:

```
LoanTabl.Show
```

Once the **LoanTabl** form is displayed, the program makes adjustments in five properties of the **LoanGrid** control:

- **ColAlignment** controls the alignment of data in a given column of the grid. Settings of **0**, **1**, or **2** produce left-justified, right-justified, or centered text.

- **ColWidth** changes the width (in *twips*) of a specified column.

- **Col** and **Row** identify the *current cell* in the grid.

- **Text** changes the value displayed in the current cell.

These five grid-control properties are available only at run time; in other words, you can work with them only in the code of your program, not in the design-mode environment. Because **ColAlignment** and **ColWidth** affect an indexed column of the grid, the program sets these properties within a **For** loop:

```
For i% = 0 to 5
  LoanTabl!LoanGrid.ColAlignment(i%) = 1
  LoanTabl!LoanGrid.ColWidth(i%) = 1260
Next i%
```

For the first six columns of the grid, indexed from 0 to 5, this loop changes the alignment to right-justification, and sets the width to 1260 twips. Notice the format for referring to the properties of a control that is located on a different form:

```
FormName!ControlName.PropertyName
```

In the special punctuation of this reference, the form name and the control name are separated by an exclamation point, and the control name and property name are separated by a period. The program uses this same format to select the upper-left corner cell of the grid and to display the calculated payment value in this cell:

```
LoanTabl!LoanGrid.Col = 0
LoanTabl!LoanGrid.Row = 0
LoanTabl!LoanGrid.Text = PmtStr
```

(Note that in Visual Basic 1.0, this reference uses a period rather than an exclamation point to separate the form name from the control name:

```
FormName.ControlName.PropertyName
```

This alternate notation is still legal in Visual Basic 2.0 and 3.0, but the new notation is preferable.)

In this first version of the *Loan Calculator*, each click of the **Calc** button displays a single value in the first cell of the **LoanGrid** control. Finally, clicking the **Exit** button ends the program performance. As you know, the exit is performed by a single Visual Basic command, **End**:

```
Sub ExitButton_Click ()
  End
End Sub
```

These three short procedures illustrate many features of Visual Basic programming. Here is a summary of what you have learned so far:

- The code you write in a Visual Basic program is divided into event procedures and general procedures. The format for naming an event procedure is *ObjectName_EventName*—for example, **Calc_Click**. An event procedure is called when the corresponding event occurs during run time. A general procedure (such as the **Payment** function) is performed as the result of an explicit call.

- The Visual Basic language has many *built-in* general procedures and functions. Examples you have seen illustrated so far are **Val** and **Format$**. Tools such as these are likely to be familiar to you from your work in other versions of Basic.

- Visual Basic also has a group of built-in procedures called methods. Each method performs an operation on a particular object. The format for calling a method is *ObjectName.MethodName*. For example, **LoanTabl.Show** calls the **Show** method for the **LoanTabl** form.

- A program uses the format *ObjectName.PropertyName* to access the current setting of any property. For example, **InPrinc.Text** represents the value entered into the **InPrice** text box.

- The notation *FormName!ControlName.PropertyName* refers to a control that is not on the active form. For example, **LoanTabl!LoanGrid.Text** is the value of the grid control on the **LoanTabl** form.

As you now turn to the complete code listings of the *Loan Calculator* application, you'll see more examples of each of these features. For now, don't worry about specific details, but concentrate instead on broad categories of programming tools. Event procedures, general procedures, methods, and properties—these are the elements of Visual Basic programming that you'll be studying and using in the chapters ahead.

Procedures in the Loan Calculator

You can now open the complete *Loan Calculator* application from the files supplied on the exercise disk. The name of the project file is LOAN-CALC.MAK. Run the application if you wish, and review the program's various operations. Enter an initial set of values into the **Principal**, **Rate**, and **Term** boxes, and click the **Calc** button to see the resulting payment table. Then click the **Table values...** button and change the increment values for the table. Click **Calc** again to view the result of your changes. Finally, try saving the table as a text file on disk, and sending the table to the printer. Click the **Exit** button when you are finished experimenting with the program.

This version of the application has procedures stored in both the **LoanInpt** and **LoanOpts** forms. Begin by focusing on the first of these forms, **LoanInpt**. Select the form and click the **View Code** button on the Project window. By scrolling through the code, you'll find that the form contains the following nine event procedures:

- **Form_Load** performs several initialization tasks at the beginning of the program's performance. (You've already seen part of this procedure; it contains the sequence of **AddItem** method calls that build the drop-down list of the combo box.)

- **Form_UnLoad** terminates the program performance if the user chooses the **Close** command from the control menu of the startup form.

- **Options_Click** is called when the user clicks the command button labeled **Table values**. It displays the application's second dialog box on the screen.

- **Calc_Click** is called when the user clicks the **Calc** command button. It creates and displays the payment table in the **LoanTabl** form.

- **SaveTabl_Click** is called when the user clicks the disk drive icon. It saves the payment table to disk in a text file named LOANTEMP.TXT.

- **PrntTabl_Click** is called when the user clicks the printer icon. It sends the payment table to the printer.

- **InPrinc_GotFocus** is called when the user selects the **InPrinc** text box. This procedure selects (and highlights) the entire text currently in the text box so the user can easily enter a new value.

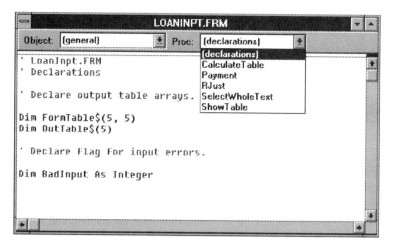

Figure 4.6 The list of general procedures in the **LoanInpt** form

- **InRate_GotFocus** is called when the user selects the **InRate** text box. Again, it highlights the entire text inside the text box.
- **ExitButton_Click** is called when the user clicks the button labeled **Exit**. As you have seen, it terminates the program performance.

In addition, the form contains a collection of five general procedures. You can see the names of these procedures by first selecting **(general)** entry in the **Object** list at the top of the Code window and then pulling down the **Proc** list. The list appears as shown in Figure 4.6. (You can jump directly to any of these procedures by selecting a name in the list.) There are two **Function** procedures: **Payment**, which performs the monthly-payment calculation; and **RJust**, which the program uses for aligning columns of figures in the output tables. The three **Sub** procedures are designed to simplify the program's overall organization: **CalculateTable** builds the entire table and stores it in convenient ways for the actual output procedures. **ShowTable** displays the table in the **LoanGrid** control of the **LoanTable** form. **SelectWholeText** is a general procedure for highlighting the current text in a text box.

You can examine all the program's procedures in Listings 4.1 to 4.8. In the sections ahead you'll survey a few of the most important programming techniques represented in this code.

Declaring and Initializing Variables

As in other advanced versions of Basic, the *scope* of variables is always an important issue. Scope refers to the level at which a given variable is recognized and available for use. There are three general levels of scope in Visual Basic:

- *Global* variables, declared by **Global** statements in a code module, are available everywhere in a program.

- Form-level or module-level variables are available only in the form or module that declares them. Each form or module has its own *declarations section* for declaring these variables.

- *Local* variables are defined inside a **Sub** or **Function** procedure, and are available only within the procedure that defines them.

The *Loan Calculator* application illustrates all three of these levels. Listing 4.1 shows the declarations stored in **LOANGLOB.BAS**, the application's code module, and in the declaration section of the **LoanInpt** form. You can view the **Global** module on the screen by selecting the **LOANGLOB.BAS** in the Project window and then clicking the **View Code** button. To view the declarations section of a form, select the word **(general)** in the **Object** list and the word **(declarations)** in the **Proc** list at the top of the Code window (Figure 4.6).

The program has two global variables named **CurPrincInc** and **CurRateInc**. They represent the current settings for the two increment values that determine the range of the payment table—the principal increment from one row to the next in the table, and the interest rate increment from one column to the next. Visual Basic has a special **Global** statement for use in the declaration section of a code module. Here is the statement that declares **CurPrincInc** and **CurRateInc**:

```
Global CurPrincInc As Currency, CurRateInc As Single
```

The **As** clause declares the data type of each variable. (Without the **As** clause, a variable takes on the default **Variant** type, as you have already seen.) These two variables are *initialized* in the **Form_Load** procedure (Listing 4.2):

```
CurPrincInc = 1000
CurRateInc = .005
```

Form_Load is always a good place to assign first values to a program's global variables. In the *Loan Calculator* these values remain fixed until the user clicks the **Table values** button and selects new settings on the **LoanOpts** form. Later you'll see how the values of the two variables are reset in the **LoanOpts** procedures. But you can already understand why these two variables are defined globally: Procedures in both the **LoanInpt** and the **LoanOpts** forms need access to them.

Displaying the Table

In this complete version of the *Loan Calculator,* the **Calc_Click** procedure (Listing 4.3) performs some input validation checks before attempting to create the output table. If any of the three input values is equal to 0, the procedure assumes that the user has made a mistake. (Note that the **Val** function returns a value of 0 if its string argument cannot be successfully converted to a number.) In this case, **Calc_Click** displays an error message on the screen, as shown in Figure 4.7.

If **Calc_Click** finds that the three input values are usable, the event procedure makes calls to two general procedures that do all the work of calculating and displaying the output table:

```
CalculateTable Princ, LRate, Term
ShowTable
```

The **CalculateTable** procedure (Listing 4.4) builds the entire table of monthly payment figures, and stores it in two different arrays, one for the convenience of the procedure that displays the table on the screen (**FormTable$**) and another for the procedures that save and print the table (**OutTable$**). For this work, the procedure makes extensive use of Visual Basic's built-in **Format$** function, and also the **Payment** function, which is one of the general procedures in the **LoanInpt** form.

Once the figures of the output table have been calculated and stored in memory, the **ShowTable** procedure (Listing 4.5) has the job of displaying the table in the **LoanGrid** control of the **LoanTabl** form. Before doing so, however, the procedure changes the **ColAlignment** and **ColWidth** settings of each column in the grid control. Then, within a pair of nested **For** loops, the procedure assigns a value to the **Text** property for each cell in the grid:

```
LoanTabl!LoanGrid.Text = FormTable$(i%, j%)
```

Figure 4.7 Error message for invalid input

Saving and Printing the Table

The **PrntTabl_Click** and **SaveTabl_Click** procedures (Figure 4.6) both begin by calling the **Calc_Click** procedure to make sure that the current payment table is based on the latest input data:

```
Calc_Click
```

This call illustrates an important point: Although an event procedure is normally called when the corresponding event takes place, you can also force a performance of an event procedure by writing a regular call statement.

The **PrntTabl_Calc** procedure then goes on to send the payment table to the printer. For this task, Visual Basic provides an object called **Printer**. Unlike other objects you've worked with up to now, the **Printer** object is not visible on the screen; however, it has properties and methods, which you access in familiar ways. For example, you can use the following format to change a **Printer** property:

```
Printer.PropertyName
```

The printer has some properties in common with other objects—such as **FontName**—and others that are uniquely its own.

Calls to **Printer** methods have the same format as other method calls:

```
Printer.MethodName
```

The **PrntTabl_Click** procedure has three examples of **Printer** method calls. The **Print** method, as you might expect, sends items and lines of information to the printer; the **NewPage** method moves the printing position to the top of the next page; and the **EndDoc** method completes a print job and releases it to the output device.

The **SaveTabl_Click** procedure uses standard Visual Basic tools for creating a sequential file on disk. The output is saved in a text file named LOANTEMP.TXT. The first step in the process is to open the file for output:

```
Open FileName$ for Output as #1
```

Then a sequence of **Print #** statements send the table to the open file, one line at a time; for example:

```
Print #1, OutTable$(i%)
```

And finally, the procedure closes the file when the entire table has been saved:

```
Close #1
```

Listing 4.6 also shows two additional event procedures from the **LoanInpt** form: **Options_Click** and **ExitButton_Click**. The first of these contains only one line of code, the statement that displays the **LoanOpts** form on the screen:

```
LoanOpts.Show
```

Changing the Increment Values

The **LoanOpts** form contains three event procedures, all of which are shown in Listing 4.7. When the user clicks one of the option buttons in the **Principal Increment** frame, the event procedure named **PInc_Click** is called. Likewise, clicking a button in the **Rate Increment** frame results in a call to **RInc_Click**. To understand these two procedures, recall that you defined these two groups of buttons as *control arrays*. For this reason, a single event procedure is sufficient for handling each group of buttons. When one of these two procedures is called, Visual Basic automatically passes the procedure an argument representing the **Index** number of the option button that the user has clicked. **PInc_Click** and **RInc_Click** use this number to determine the new values for the variables **CurPrincInc** and **CurRateInc**.

The third event procedure, **OkOpts_Click**, simply closes the **LoanOpts** form when the user clicks the **OK** button.

Controlling the Text Boxes

The remaining three procedures in the **LoanInpt** form (Listing 4.8) address a small detail in the behavior of the two text boxes. In short, these procedures highlight the entire contents of a text box as soon as the box is activated. This highlighting allows the user to enter a new value into a box without first erasing the old value. (Any new typing from the keyboard automatically replaces the highlighted text.)

The procedures are interesting for a number of reasons. First, they introduce a new event named **GotFocus**. This event occurs when a control receives the focus. (During run time, one control has the focus at a given time.) The **InPrinc_GotFocus** and **InRate_GotFocus** procedures are called when one of these text boxes is activated. Each procedure makes a call to a general procedure named **SelectWholeText**.

The **SelectWholeText** procedure illustrates an important feature: You can write a procedure that accepts a control as an argument:

```
SelectWholeText (InTextBox As Control)
```

This arrangement allows you to write general-purpose procedures for controls, performing the same set of operations on any object received as an argument. For example, **SelectWholeText** highlights the text contained in any text box. To do so, it uses two text box properties named **SelStart** and **SelLength**, which set the starting point and the length of the text highlight.

Code in the Second Version of Loan Calculator

Now that you have a sense of how the first version of the *Loan Calculator* works, you might want to take a look at the code in the second version. You can load the second version from files included on the exercise disk; the project name is LOANCA2.MAK. Run the program, and notice the differences in the way the two versions operate. The second version has only one command button, **Calc**. All the other options, including output destinations and table increments, are presented in the pull-down menu system.

The code for the second version is similar to the first, but organized differently. For one thing, all the code in the second version is contained in one form, named **LoanIn2**. In addition, the event procedures that save and print the form—and other procedures that change the table increments—are associated with menu objects rather than command buttons and icons. Finally, the **LoanTabl** form for the second version does not contain a grid control. Instead, the program displays a formatted table of numbers directly on the form itself. You can examine the steps for accomplishing this output operation in the **ShowTable** procedure.

As you look at the code for the second version, you might also want to review the structure of the menu system. To do so, open the **LoanTabl** form and then choose the **Menu Design** command from the **Window** menu. As you'll recall, this window shows you all the properties of each element in the menu.

You'll return to the second version of the *Loan Calculator* for debugging exercises in Chapter 5.

SUMMARY: THE ELEMENTS OF VISUAL BASIC PROGRAMMING

A Visual Basic program is centered around events—and the forms and controls that are the objects of events.

The code you write is organized into two general kinds of procedures: An *event procedure* is called whenever the corresponding event takes place during run time. A *general procedure*—which may be structured as a **Sub** or **Function** procedure—is performed by a call statement or a call expression. Interestingly, Visual Basic also allows you to call event procedures explicitly—that is, to force a performance of an event procedure even when the corresponding event has not taken place.

As in all versions of Basic, data in a Visual Basic program is represented by variable names. But a program can also access another variety of data—the properties of each form and control in the application, identified as *ObjectName.PropertyName*. A program can *read* the current setting of a property, or *change* the setting by placing the property name at the left side of an assignment statement:

```
ObjectName.PropertyName = Value
```

Visual Basic provides many built-in routines. A large library of general functions and procedures is available. In addition, Visual Basic provides *methods*, procedures that operate on specific categories of objects. Each object, including forms, controls, and special objects such as **Printer**, has its own library of associated methods.

Listing 4.1 Global declarations and form-level declarations from **LoanInpt**

```
' LoanGlob.BAS

Global CurPrincInc As Currency, CurRateInc As Single


' LoanInpt.FRM
' Declarations

' Declare output table arrays.

Dim FormTable$(5, 5)
Dim OutTable$(5)

' Declare flag for input errors.

Dim BadInput As Integer
```

Listing 4.2 The **Form_Load** and **Form_UnLoad** procedures from **LoanInpt**

```
Sub Form_Load ()

  ' Build the drop-down list for
  ' the Term combo box.

  InTerm.AddItem "4 years"
  InTerm.AddItem "5 years"
  InTerm.AddItem "10 years"
  InTerm.AddItem "15 years"
  InTerm.AddItem "20 years"
  InTerm.AddItem "30 years"

  ' Initialize the increment values.

  CurPrincInc = 1000
  CurRateInc = .005

End Sub   ' Form_Load


Sub Form_Unload (Cancel As Integer)
  End
End Sub
```

Listing 4.3 The **Calc_Click** procedure

```
Sub Calc_Click ()

  ' Produce the output table when
  ' the user clicks the Calc button.

  Dim Princ As Currency, LRate As Single, Term As Integer

  ' Read the input values and convert them to numbers.

  Princ = Val(InPrinc.Text)
  LRate = Val(InRate.Text) / 100
  Term = Val(InTerm.Text)

  ' Check for input errors or missing values,
  ' and display an error message if necessary.
```

```
    BadInput = (Princ = 0) Or (LRate = 0) Or (Term = 0)
    If BadInput Then
      Msg$ = "Input values are not valid."
      Title$ = "Loan Parameters"
      MsgBox Msg$, 48, Title$
    Else

    ' If input is OK, calculate and display the loan table.

      CalculateTable Princ, LRate, Term
      ShowTable
    End If

End Sub   ' Calc_Click
```

Listing 4.4 The **CalculateTable** procedure and the **Payment** function

```
Sub CalculateTable (P As Currency, R As Single, T As Integer)

  ' Build the payment table in the output arrays:
  '    -- FormTable$ is for displaying the table.
  '    -- OutTable$ is for printing and saving the table.

  Const W = 12
  Dim StartPrinc As Currency
  Dim StartRate As Single
  Static PRange(5) As Currency, RRange(5) As Single
  Dim LPmt As Currency

  ' Calculate the starting principal and rate for the
  ' table, given the current increment values.

  StartPrinc = P - 2 * CurPrincInc
  StartRate = R - 2 * CurRateInc

  ' Compute the first column and row of the table.

  OutTable$(0) = Space$(W)
  For i% = 1 To 5
    PRange(i%) = StartPrinc + CurPrincInc * (i% - 1)
    RRange(i%) = StartRate + CurRateInc * (i% - 1)
```

(continued)

```
    FormTable$(i%, 0) = Format$(PRange(i%), "$#,######")
    FormTable$(0, i%) = Format$(RRange(i%), "0.00%")

    OutTable$(0) = OutTable$(0) + RJust$(FormTable$(0, i%), W)
    OutTable$(i%) = RJust$(FormTable(i%, 0), W)
  Next i%

  ' Fill in the rest of the table.

  For i% = 1 To 5
    For j% = 1 To 5
      LPmt = Payment(PRange(i%), RRange(j%) / 12, T * 12)
      If i% = 3 And j% = 3 Then
        FormTable$(i%, j%) = Format$(LPmt, "\[$#,####.00\]")
      Else
        FormTable$(i%, j%) = Format$(LPmt, "$#,####.00")
      End If
      OutTable$(i%) = OutTable$(i%) + RJust$(FormTable$(i%, j%), W)
    Next j%
  Next i%

End Sub   ' CalculateTable


Function Payment (P@, MoRate!, Months%) As Currency

  ' Calculate the monthly payment.

  Payment = (P@ * MoRate!) / (1 - (1 + MoRate!) ^ (-Months%))

End Function   ' Payment
```

Listing 4.5 The **ShowTable** procedure and the **RJust$** function

```
Sub ShowTable ()

  ' Display the payment table in the LoanGrid
  ' grid control of the LoanTabl form.

  LoanTabl.Show
```

```
  For j% = 0 To 5
    LoanTabl!LoanGrid.Col = j%
    LoanTabl!LoanGrid.ColAlignment(j%) = 1
    LoanTabl!LoanGrid.ColWidth(j%) = 1260
    For i% = 0 To 5
      LoanTabl!LoanGrid.Row = i%
      LoanTabl!LoanGrid.Text = FormTable$(i%, j%)
    Next i%
  Next j%

End Sub   ' ShowTable


Function RJust$ (InString$, JustWidth%)

  ' Right-justify a string within a width.

  TempStr$ = Space$(JustWidth%)
  RSet TempStr$ = InString$
  RJust$ = TempStr$

End Function   ' RJust$
```

Listing 4.6 Click procedures for command buttons and image controls

```
Sub PrntTabl_Click ()

  ' Print the payment table.

  Calc_Click

  If Not BadInput Then
    Printer.Print OutTable$(0)
    Printer.Print
    For i% = 1 To 5
      Printer.Print OutTable$(i%)
    Next i%

    Printer.NewPage
```

(continued)

```
      Printer.EndDoc
   End If

End Sub  ' PrntTabl_Click


Sub SaveTabl_Click ()

   ' Save the table as a text file.

   Const FileName$ = "LoanTemp.Txt"

   Calc_Click
   If Not BadInput Then
     Open FileName$ For Output As #1
     Print #1, OutTable$(0)
     Print #1,
     For i% = 1 To 5
       Print #1, OutTable$(i%)
     Next i%
     Close #1
   End If

End Sub  ' SaveTabl_Click


Sub Options_Click ()

   ' Give the user the opportunity to select
   ' new increment values for the payment table.

   LoanOpts.Show

End Sub  ' Options_Click


Sub ExitButton_Click ()

   ' Terminate the program performance.
   End

End Sub  ' ExitButton_Click
```

Listing 4.7 Event procedures from the **LoanOpts** form

```
Sub PInc_Click (Index As Integer)

  ' Calculate the principal increment
  ' value, using the Index number of the
  ' currently selected option button.

  CurPrincInc = 10 ^ (Index + 1)

End Sub  ' PInc_Click


Sub RInc_Click (Index As Integer)

  ' Determine the rate increment value,
  ' using the Index number of the currently
  ' selected option button.

  Select Case Index
    Case 0
      CurRateInc = .00125
    Case 1
      CurRateInc = .0025
    Case 2
      CurRateInc = .005
    Case 3
      CurRateInc = .01
    Case 4
      CurRateInc = .02
  End Select

End Sub  ' RInc_Click


Sub OkOpts_Click ()

  ' When the user clicks the OK button,
  ' close the Table Values dialog box,
  ' and recalculate the payment table.

  LoanOpts.Hide

End Sub  ' OkOpts_Click
```

Listing 4.8 GotFocus event procedures and the **SelectWholeText** procedure

```
Sub InPrinc_GotFocus ()

  ' Highlight current entry when
  ' text box is selected.

  SelectWholeText InPrinc

End Sub   ' InPrinc_GotFocus


Sub InRate_GotFocus ()

  ' Highlight current entry
  ' when text box is selected.

  SelectWholeText InRate

End Sub   ' InRate_GotFocus


Sub SelectWholeText (InTextBox As Control)

  ' Highlight current entry when the
  ' user selects a text box.

  InTextBox.SelStart = 0
  InTextBox.SelLength = Len(InTextBox.Text)

End Sub   ' SelectWholeText
```

5

Debugging and Compiling an Application

INTRODUCTION

Mistakes are a fact of life in programming. Like all programming languages, Visual Basic demands a level of perfection that seldom emerges from the first version of code—or even the second or third versions—however skillful the programmer. For just this reason, the Visual Basic development environment includes a collection of tools and commands that will help you find the bugs in any application.

You've already seen two kinds of error correction that take place in the Visual Basic environment. At the first and most immediate level, the "smart" editor catches syntax errors as you enter lines of code. Given a line that contains an error, the editor displays an error message on the screen explaining what is wrong with the line. (Refer back to Figure 4.3 for an example.) In the code window, the edit cursor appears at the location of the error. This kind of error takes place during design time, and is usually easy to correct.

At the next stage of application development—when you first try running your new program—Visual Basic finds and describes any structural inconsistencies that prevent the performance from starting. For example, in Chapter 4 you saw the *compile-time* error that is displayed when the number of arguments in a procedure call does not match the number of arguments actually required by the procedure itself (Figure 4.4). Again, you will seldom need much time to fix this kind of error.

Bugs you discover during your program's performance are often much more troublesome, and can launch you into long and detailed investigations of your own code. Broadly speaking, there are two kinds of problems that show up during run time:

- A *run-time* error interrupts the program's performance because of some condition that Visual Basic cannot handle in any other way. A common example is an attempt to perform division by zero. In response to such an error, Visual Basic stops the program and displays an error message on the screen.

- A *logical error* does not interrupt the program, but creates unexpected and unwanted results. This kind of error can be the most difficult to correct. Your program completes its performance from beginning to end, but produces bad output, incorrect calculations, or an inappropriate sequence of operations.

Analysis of run-time errors and logical errors takes place primarily in Visual Basic's *break mode*. This is the third operating mode for application development, and is the mode in which debugging tools are available. You can always keep track of the mode you are in—design mode, run time, or break mode—by looking at the Visual Basic title bar. As you can see in Figure 5.1, a mode indicator appears in brackets after the program name.

In this chapter you'll learn to use Visual Basic's debugging tools to correct errors in your code. In particular, you'll focus on the commands offered in the **Debug** menu, shown in Figure 5.2. You'll also learn to use an important window that always appears on the desktop while you are running a program in the development environment—the Debug window.

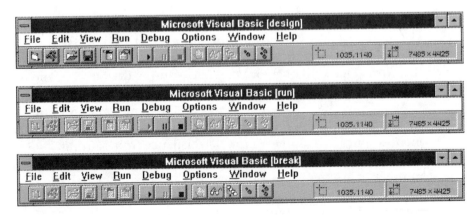

Figure 5.1 The three operating modes in the development environment

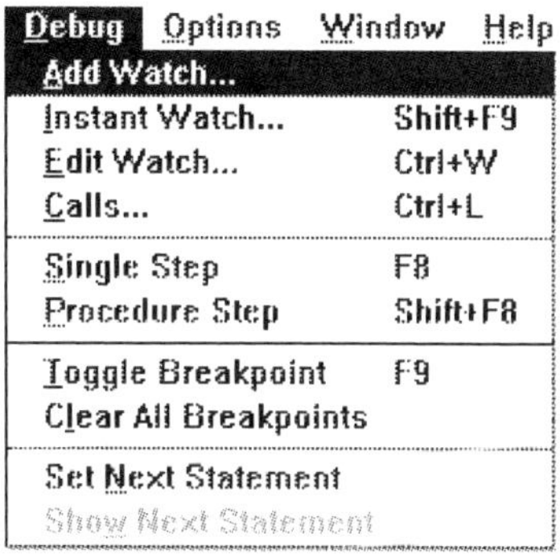

Figure 5.2 The **Debug** menu during break mode

This chapter guides you through a sequence of hands-on exercises designed to help you experiment with debugging features. The context for these exercises is a version of the *Loan Calculator* stored on the exercise disk as CH5EX1.MAK. Begin now by opening this project into the Visual Basic environment. Then select the **LoanInpt** form in the Project window and click the **View Code** button. In the declarations section of the code you will find the following message, presented as a sequence of comment lines:

```
'   ****************************************
'   ***        Debugging Exercise       ***
'   ***          (Chapter 5)            ***
'   ***     -----------------------     ***
'   ***     This program has errors.    ***
'   ****************************************
```

The deliberate errors introduced into this version of the program will give you opportunities to try out Visual Basic's debugging tools.

CORRECTING PERFORMANCE ERRORS

When you notice something going wrong with a program, your first task is to enter into the break mode so you can take advantage of debugging tools. There are a number of ways to do this. Perhaps the simplest—but sometimes least helpful—way is to pull down the **Run** menu and select the **Break** command, or click the Break icon in Visual Basic's Toolbar. Then you can click the **View Code** button in the Project window and see where you are in the performance. The problem with this entry into the break mode is that you can't easily control the point at which the break occurs. In fact, you are most likely to break during *idle time*, when Visual Basic is waiting for the next event to take place. In general, you need a more precise way to find the code that is causing the problem.

Visual Basic automatically provides an appropriate break when a run-time error interrupts the program performance. You can see how this happens by starting up the *Loan Calculator* now:

1. Close the Code window and then press F5 to start the program. (Keep in mind that this version—CH5EX1.MAK—has some built-in errors.)

2. Enter values for the three loan parameters: **15000** for the principal, **10** for the rate, and **5 years** for the term.

3. Click the **Calc** button.

You may be surprised by what happens next. Rather than producing the payment table at the bottom of the screen, Visual Basic stops your program and displays an error box with the one-word message **Overflow** (Figure 5.3). When you click the **OK** button on the error box, you'll see the Code

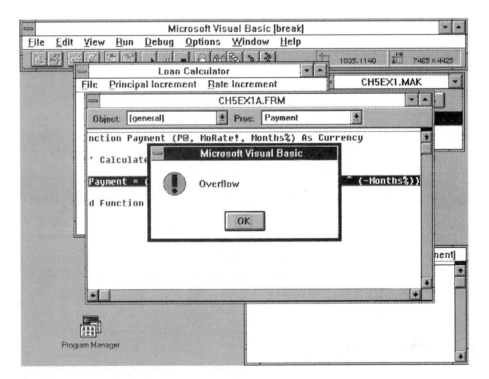

Figure 5.3 Interruption of the program due to an **Overflow** error

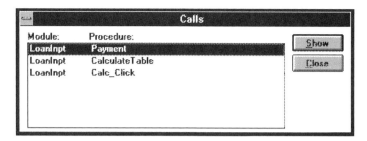

Figure 5.4 The **Calls** dialog box

window displaying part of your code, specifically, the **Payment** function. You'll also notice—by glancing up at the title bar—that you are now in the break mode. Clearly something has gone wrong.

An *overflow* error occurs when a variable is assigned a value outside the range of the variable's defined data type. Probably the most common cause of an overflow error is division by zero. As you examine the **Payment** function for errors, division by zero is the first possibility that comes to mind. But no matter how carefully you look, you can't see anything wrong with the function itself. It *looks* just like the code that worked perfectly well before. (It *is*.) You conclude that the problem must be elsewhere in your program, probably somewhere in the routine that *calls* the **Payment** function.

You can quickly find out the sequence of procedure calls that has led to the **Payment** function either by pulling down the **Debug** menu now and choosing the **Calls** command or simply by clicking the Calls tool, the third-to-last icon on the Toolbar. When you do so, Visual Basic displays the **Calls** dialog box, as shown in Figure 5.4. As you can see in the list of calls, the **Payment** function was called by the **CalculateTable** procedure. You speculate that this procedure has passed one or more inappropriate arguments to the function. (Click the **Close** button to close the **Calls** dialog box.)

So here is your problem: You need to see exactly what is happening to the data passed to the **Payment** function. Then you'll want to investigate the program's activities at some point *before* this overflow error occurs.

Visual Basic Debugging Features

The Debug window is the place to find out the current values of variables when your program performance is interrupted automatically, or when you switch manually to break mode. To control debugging activities once you are in the break mode—and to specify subsequent entry points into the break mode—you use the commands in the **Debug** menu.

The Debug Window and the Debug Object

At this point in your work, the Debug window is partially hidden behind the code window at the lower-right corner of your screen (Figure 5.3). To view the Debug window, click it with the mouse. It is empty at the moment, but its title bar gives you some important information: the name of the active form and the *current* procedure—that is, the procedure in control when the program was interrupted (Figure 5.5). By implication, this information tells you which groups of variables are now available for you to examine:

- Variables defined locally in the procedure that is named in the title bar of the Debug window.

- Variables defined in the declarations section of the active form.

- Global variables—that is, variables defined with **Global** statements in a code module. (These variables, if any are defined, are always available for viewing in the Debug window.)

The Debug window does not allow you to examine variables defined elsewhere—that is, local variables defined in other procedures of the active form or variables in other forms.

To view values in the Debug window, you type **Print** statements directly into the window in this format:

```
Print expression
```

When you do so, Visual Basic evaluates the *expression* and displays its value directly beneath the **Print** statement.

For now, you would like to know the values of the variables that were passed to the **Payment** function—on the theory that one of these values has probably caused the overflow error. The function's argument variables are **P@** (a currency-type variable representing the principal of the loan), **MoRate!** (a single-precision floating-point variable representing the

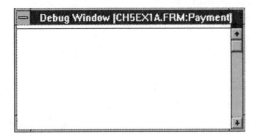

Figure 5.5 The Debug window

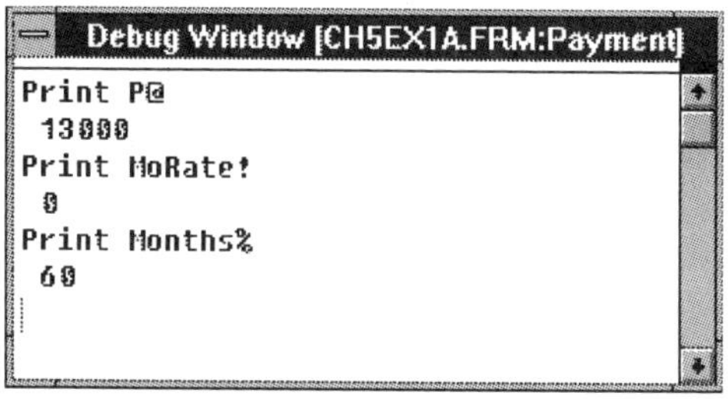

Figure 5.6 Viewing the values of variables in the Debug window

monthly interest rate), and **Months%** (an integer variable representing the number of months in the term of the loan). The function does not change the values of these variables, so you can view the original three values by entering the following three statements into the Debug window, one at a time:

```
Print P@
Print MoRate!
Print Months%
```

After each statement, the value of the variable appears in the window, as shown in Figure 5.6.

Two of these argument variables have the values you would have predicted: The value of **P@**, 13000, has been reduced by two one-thousand-dollar increments from the original **Principal** entry of 15000. (Keep in mind that the payment table displays two rows of monthly payment calculations for principal amounts that are *smaller* than the target amount and two for *larger* ones.) The value of **Months%**, 60, is also correct; it represents the number of months in a five-year loan term.

But the value displayed for **MoRate!**, 0, cannot be right. **MoRate!** should contain a reasonable interest rate amount, never zero. Obviously, the **CalculateTable** procedure has sent an unusable value to the **Payment** function for this argument. Furthermore, a quick review of the function's formula for monthly payment calculations shows why the overflow error occurred:

```
Payment = (P@ * MoRate!) / (1 - (1 + MoRate!) ^ (-Months%))
```

A **MoRate!** value of 0 produces a 0 in the denominator of this division operation—in short, division by zero.

Thanks to the Debug window, you've quickly identified the problem. The next step is to trace the error back to its source and correct it. Before you continue, however, you may be interested to learn another technique for displaying variable values in the Debug window.

In a long and detailed debugging process, it is sometimes convenient to write temporary **Print** statements directly in your code to display the values of certain key variables. The point is to monitor variables as they change over the course of the program performance. In Visual Basic you accomplish this by using an object named **Debug**. This is one of several objects that Visual Basic defines for special programming uses. (Another special object that you learned about in Chapter 4 is the **Printer** object.) There is only one method associated with **Debug**—the **Print** method. The **Debug.Print** statement sends a data value directly to the Debug window for display. A sequence of **Debug.Print** statements placed inside a procedure is therefore a convenient way to view the changing values of variables.

To experiment with this feature, add four **Debug.Print** statements now to the **Payment** function as follows:

```
Function Payment (P@, MoRate!, Months%) As Currency

   ' Calculate the monthly payment.

   Debug.Print "P@ = "; P@
   Debug.Print "MoRate! = "; MoRate!
   Debug.Print "Months% = "; Months%
   Debug.Print
   ' Payment = (P@ * MoRate!) / (1 - (1 + MoRate!) ^ (-Months%))

End Function   ' Payment
```

In addition, place a single-quote character at the beginning of the line containing the function's one assignment statement. This technique, sometimes known as *commenting out* a statement, is an easy way to deactivate a line of code temporarily while you are trying to find out what is going wrong in your program.

After you make these revisions, close the code window. If you wish, you can move the Debug window to a convenient place at the upper-right corner of the desktop so you'll be able to watch what happens when the program performance resumes. (You can also change the size and shape of the Debug window by dragging the borders of its frame with the mouse. For example, in this exercise you might want to reduce the width of the window by about half. If you do so, the window will be small enough to stay out of the way of other screen activity, yet large enough to display all the information that it receives.) Pull down the **Run** menu and select the **Continue** command—or simply press F5—to continue the program performance.

Keep your eye on the Debug window as the program proceeds with its attempt to calculate the loan payment table. No run-time error occurs this

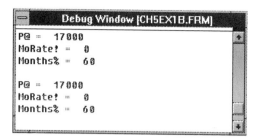

Figure 5.7 The output from **Debug.Print** statements

time, because you have commented out the statement that previously caused the premature break. Instead, three lines of information appear in the Debug window for each call that the program makes to the **Payment** function (Figure 5.7). The lines scroll by quickly, but you'll still be able to observe the fact that is most relevant to your current investigation: The value of the variable **MoRate!** is 0 for each call to the function, not just for the first call. Knowing this will help you locate the problem.

Now, exit from the program. Pull down the **File** menu in the *Loan Calculator* dialog box—*not* Visual Basic's **File** menu—and select the **Exit** command. Reopen the code window for the **LoanInpt** form, and locate the **Payment** function. Then delete three of the four of the **Debug.Print** statements; keep the one that displays the value of the **MoRate!** variable:

```
Debug.Print "MoRate! = "; MoRate!
```

(To delete a line in the code window, position the cursor at the line and press Ctrl+Y.) In the next exercise you'll use another technique for viewing the values of variables during run time.

Select the general procedure named **CalculateTable** in the code window. The calls to the **Payment** function occur within a pair of nested **For** loops, located near the end of the procedure:

```
For i% = 1 To 5
  For j% = 1 To 5
    LPmt = Payment(PRange(i%), RRange(h%) / 12, T * 12)
    FormTable$(i%, j%) = Format$(LPmt, "$#,####.00")
    OutTable$(i%) = OutTable$(i%) + RJust$(FormTable$(i%, j%), W)
  Next j%
Next i%
```

This passage will now become the focus of your investigation as you continue searching for the bug.

Take a close look at the loops. For convenience, the **CalculateTable** procedure arranges the calculated data for the payment table in a group of one-dimensional and two-dimensional arrays. (**Review Box 5.1** describes the variety of loop structures available in Visual Basic, and **Review Box 5.2** discusses arrays in Visual Basic.) Two of these arrays, named **PRange** and **RRange**, are defined locally for the **CalculateTable** procedure. The re-

---

Review Box 5.1

Loop Structures

Structures that control repetition in a program are known as *loops*. Visual Basic's two categories of repetition structures are **For** loops and **Do** loops. Both kinds of loops repeat the performance of a block of code for a controlled number of *iterations*. In some programming situations you can conveniently choose either kind of loop, but the general difference between them lies in the way they control the number of iterations:

- A **For** loop has a *counter*, or *control variable*, that keeps track of the number of iterations. The looping stops when the counter reaches an expressed stopping point.
- A **Do** loop is controlled by a conditional expression. The iterations continue until the value of the expression changes from true to false, or false to true.

In a **For** loop, the block of statements is marked off by a **For** statement and a **Next** statement:

```
For Counter = FirstValue To LastValue
        ' Block of statements.
Next Counter
```

This is the simplest form of the **For** loop: At the beginning of the loop performance, *FirstValue* is assigned to the *Counter* variable. If *Counter* is less than or equal to *LastValue*, Visual Basic performs the block of statements one time. At the end of the block, the value of *Counter* is increased by one, and again compared with *LastValue*. Iterations continue until *Counter* is greater than *LastValue*.

The optional **Step** clause allows you to specify an increment or decrement amount for the counter variable:

```
For Counter = FirstValue To LastValue Step ChangeValue
```

maining two, **FormTable$** and **OutTable$**, are created for the benefit of other procedures in the program. They are therefore defined in the declarations section of the **LoanInpt** form, making them available to all procedures in the program.

Review Box 5.1 *(continued)*

At the end of each iteration, *ChangeValue* is added to the current value of *Counter*. If *ChangeValue* is a positive number (and *FirstValue* is less than *LastValue*) the looping stops when *Counter* is greater than *LastValue*. If *ChangeValue* is a negative number (and *FirstValue* is greater than *LastValue*) the looping stops when *Counter* is less than *LastValue*. Without a **Step** clause, the default increment amount is 1.

The block of code in a **Do** loop is enclosed between the **Do** statement and a **Loop** statement. The loop usually contains either a **While** condition or an **Until** condition to control the repetition. Traditionally, a **While** clause appears at the top of the loop in the **Do** statement; or, the **Until** clause appears at the bottom of the loop in the **Loop** statement. But Visual Basic is flexible on this point: Either clause can be placed at the top or the bottom of the loop.

In a **Do While** loop, the repetition continues as long as the condition is true:

```
Do While Condition
  ' Block of statements.
Loop
```

In a **Do...Until** structure, looping continues as long as the condition is false:

```
Do
  ' Block of statements.
Loop Until Condition
```

The looping stops when the value of the *Condition* changes from false to true in an **Until** clause, or from true to false in a **While** clause.

A *nested* loop appears completely inside another loop structure. Nested loop structures can perform complex and powerful operations in very economical blocks of code.

You need to understand how these arrays are organized in order to proceed with this debugging session:

- The one-dimensional array **PRange** contains the range of principal amounts that appear in the first column of the output table. (These numbers, calculated earlier in the **CalculateTable** procedure, are stored in **PRange(1)** to **PRange(5)**.)

- Likewise, the one-dimensional array **RRange** contains the range of interest rates that appear in the top row of the output table (in **RRange(1)** to **RRange(5)**).

- The two-dimensional array **FormTable$** is designed to store formatted string versions of each individual value in the table. The first dimension represents the rows of the table, and the second dimension the columns. The **ShowTable** procedure uses this array to display the table in the **LoanTabl** form.

- The one-dimensional string array **OutTable$** is for storing each row of the table as a single string. The program builds this array for use in the procedure that prints the table (**PrintTableCommand_Click**) and also for use in the procedure that saves the table on disk as a text file (**SaveTableCommand_Click**).

The role of the **For** loops at the end of the **CalculateTable** procedure is to calculate the monthly payment amounts one at a time and to store them as formatted strings in the **FormTable$** and **OutTable$** arrays. The control variables of the loops—**i%** and **j%**—are meant to be used as indexes into the four arrays. By the time the performance reaches these loops, the one-dimensional arrays **PRange** and **RRange** are already supposed to contain the range of principal amounts and interest rates for the first column and first row of the payment table. Individual elements of these arrays—**PRange(i%)** and **RRange(j%)**—can therefore be sent as arguments to the **Payment** function.

Consider the numbers represented by **RRange(j%)**—the range of interest rates. Because you already know that these interest rates are not reaching the **Payment** procedure, you can speculate that one of the following two situations is the source of the problem:

- The range of interest rates has not been successfully stored in the **RRange** array, or

- The correct elements of **RRange** are not actually being sent to the **Payment** function.

To discover which of these hypotheses is true, you need to monitor three values in the **CalculateTable** procedure: the control variable **j%**, the array element **RRange(j%)**, and the expression **RRange(j%) / 12**—the calculation for the *monthly* interest rate. In the next steps of this exercise, you'll establish these three items as *watch expressions* whose values you can monitor in the Debug window during the course of a program performance. (If you have already spotted the error in the **CalculateTable** procedure, continue along through the following exercise anyway.)

Watch Expressions and Breakpoints

The Debug window actually has two *panes:* The *immediate pane*, where you've been examining values up to now; and the *watch pane*, which displays the values of watch expressions that you define. In the following steps, you'll create watch expressions for monitoring the three items that you want to examine in the **CalculateTable** procedure:

1. Pull down the **Debug** menu and choose the **Add Watch** command. In the resulting **Add Watch** dialog box (Figure 5.8), Visual Basic is prepared to accept a watch expression from **CalculateTable**, the procedure that is currently displayed in the Code window.

2. In the **Expression** box, enter the first of the three watch expressions, **j%**, and then click **OK**.

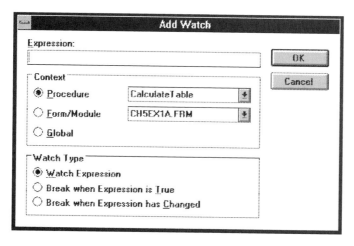

Figure 5.8 The **Add Watch** dialog box

Review Box 5.2

Arrays

An *array* is a data structure that represents a list, table, or multidimensional arrangement of data values. The name of an array is followed by one or more *indexes* enclosed in parentheses and separated by commas. For example, a one-dimensional array reference has one index—in the format *ArrayName(i)*—referring to the *i*th *element* in a list of values. A two-dimensional array has two indexes—in the format *ArrayName(i, j)*—referring to the element in the *i*th row and the *j*th column of a table; and so on. All elements of an array belong to the same data type; however, a **Variant**-type array has the flexibility of storing data values of different types.

In addition to arrays of data, Visual Basic also recognizes *control arrays*, which represent groups of visual controls in a frame—for example, an array of option buttons, text boxes, or menu items. The discussion that follows applies to data arrays (sometimes also called *variable arrays*), not to control arrays.

Visual Basic supports *fixed* arrays and *dynamic* arrays. The length of a fixed array is set for the entire duration of the program. In contrast, the length of a dynamic array can be adjusted at run time to meet changing requirements for data storage. In either event, you must declare an array before using it.

The keyword you use for a fixed array declaration depends upon the statement's location: **Global** to create a global array in a code module, **Dim** in the declaration section of a form or module, or **Static** in a procedure. In these declarations you give the length of each dimension in the array. Consider the following examples:

```
Global CodeNum(5) As Currency   ' A global array.
Dim FormTable$(5, 5)            ' A module-level array.
Static A(5, 6, 7) As Integer    ' A local array.
```

By default, the first *element* in each dimension of an array has an index of 0. For example, the first example above has six elements, from **CodeNum(0)** to **CodeNum(5)**. However, you can define a nondefault

Review Box 5.2 *(continued)*

indexing system by specifying the upper and lower bounds in the array's declaration statement. The syntax for defining the bounds uses the keyword **To**; for example:

```
Dim PM%(13 To 24)   ' A one-dimensional array with 12 elements.
```

You can declare the data type of an array either by appending a type-declaration character to the end of the array name, or by declaring the type in an **As** clause.

A dynamic array is declared in two steps. First, a **Dim** (or **Global**) statement establishes the scope of the array, using the following syntax:

```
Dim ArrayName()
```

Notice that the parentheses are empty in this statement; the length of the array is not yet defined. Next, a **ReDim** statement gives the length of the array and the number of dimensions:

```
ReDim ArrayName(Length)
```

ReDim is an executable statement, and therefore must appear inside a procedure. The length of a dynamic array can be changed at any time by another **ReDim** statement, but the number of dimensions remains fixed after the original declaration. By default, **ReDim** has the side effect of reinitializing all the elements of the array—numeric elements to zero, or string elements to empty strings. However, you can include the **Preserve** keyword in a **ReDim** statement to prevent this effect:

```
ReDim Preserve ArrayName(Length)
```

There is an important functional relationship between arrays and **For** loops in Basic programming. For example, you can use the counter variable of a **For** loop as the index into a one-dimensional array; this gives you an efficient way to process all the elements of the array in very economical code. Likewise, you can use the counter variables in a pair of nested **For** loops as the indexes into a two-dimensional array.

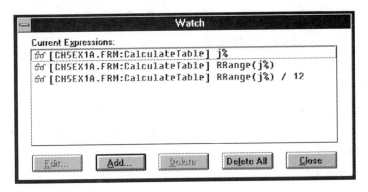

Figure 5.9 Examining watch expressions in the **Watch** dialog box

3. Repeat Steps 1 and 2 to create two additional watch expressions: **RRange(j%)** and **RRange(j%)/12**.

4. To confirm that you've correctly defined the three watch expressions, pull down the **Debug** menu and choose **Edit Watch**. The resulting **Watch** dialog box (Figure 5.9) shows the three watch expressions that you've created. Check them carefully. (If any expression is incorrect, highlight its line in the **Current Expressions** list and then click the **Edit** button. In response, Visual Basic opens the **Edit Watch** window, where you can modify the watch expression.) Click the **Close** button when you have made sure that all three expressions are correct.

Once you have narrowed your search down to a particular passage of code, you next need a way to stop the program when the performance reaches the target passage. *Breakpoints* are the answer. A breakpoint is a statement in your program that you specify in advance as a temporary stopping point in the performance. Upon reaching a breakpoint, Visual Basic switches into the break mode. The program is interrupted *before* the breakpoint statement is performed.

Establishing a breakpoint takes two simple steps:

1. Position the cursor on the target line of code.

2. Pull down the **Debug** menu and select the **Toggle Breakpoint** command. (Alternatively, use one of two available shortcuts to toggle a breakpoint: Press the F9 function key; or click the Breakpoint tool, the fifth-to-last icon on Visual Basic's Toolbar.)

Visual Basic highlights the breakpoint line in red. (When you finish working with a particular breakpoint, you use these same two steps to toggle the line of code back to its normal status.)

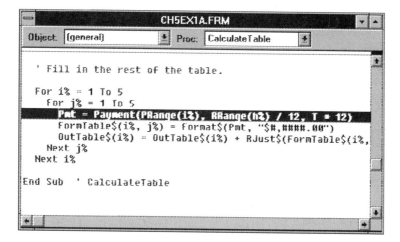

Figure 5.10 A breakpoint

In this stage of the debugging process, you want the program performance to stop just before the call to the **Payment** function. Move the cursor to the assignment statement that contains this call and press F9. When you do so, your code window appears as shown in Figure 5.10. Review the steps you have taken to prepare for your investigation:

- The statement that originally caused the error in the **Payment** function is commented out.

- The three watch expressions that you have defined for variables in the **CalculateTable** procedure—and the one **Debug.Print** statement remaining in the **Payment** function—will allow you to compare argument values before and after the function call.

- A breakpoint in the **CalculateTable** procedure will stop the performance just before the function call.

You are now ready to try running the program again. Press F5 to begin. When the dialog box appears on the screen, enter the same three input values as before (**15000** for the principal, **10** for the interest rate, and **5** for the term). Then click the **Calc** button. As expected, the performance stops at the breakpoint you have established. For convenience, you may now want to rearrange sizes and positions of the Code window and the Debug window, placing them one above the other across the width of the screen as in Figure 5.11. This way you can view both windows at once. The code window displays the target passage from the **CalculateTable** procedure, and the watch pane of the Debug window displays the initial values of **j%**, **RRate(j%)**, and **RRate(j%) / 12**. (Keep in mind that the watch pane, in the

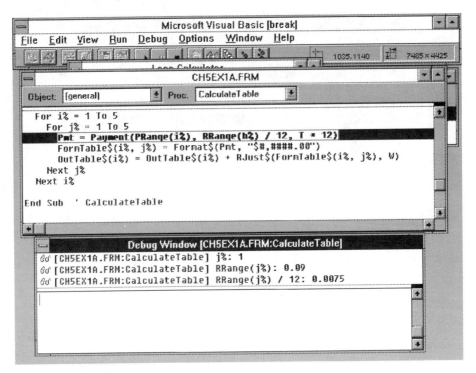

Figure 5.11 Rearranging the Code and Debug windows during break mode

upper portion of the Debug window, displays the values of the watch expressions you have defined. The immediate pane, in the lower portion, displays the result of **Debug.Print** statements.You can scroll each of these panes separately, and you can drag the division between them up or down to change the sizes of the panes.)

Single-Step Performance

While you are in break mode, Visual Basic gives you two ways to step through a passage of code one statement at a time. These techniques are represented both by the **Single Step** and **Procedure Step** commands in the **Debug** menu and by the last two tools in the Toolbar. Both of these commands perform the *next* statement in the path of execution. The difference between them is in the way they handle procedure calls:

- The **Single Step** command traces into a procedure and performs its executable statements one at a time. The keyboard shortcut for this command is the F8 function key.

- The **Procedure Step** command executes a procedure call as a single step, without tracing into the individual statements of the procedure. The keyboard shortcut is Shift-F8.

At this point, you can use these commands to step through the loops that build the payment table. As you do so, the Debug window will show you values from both the **CalculateTable** procedure and the **Payment** function.

Click the Procedure Step tool (the last icon in the Toolbar) now to perform the function call in a single step. Then examine the information displayed in the Debug window. The window, shown in Figure 5.12, displays a value of .0075 for the expression **RRange(j%) / 12**. This is the value that should have been sent to the **Payment** function as the interest rate argument. But, corresponding argument variable **MoRate!** still has a value of 0 when the function is called.

Click the Procedure Step tool repeatedly to step through several more iterations of the loop. For each iteration you see the same results: The **CalculateTable** procedure always calculates an appropriate interest rate value, but the value is never sent to the **Payment** function. From this you conclude definitively that the error is in the function call itself. Finally, a close examination of the function call reveals the problem:

```
LPmt = Payment(PRange(i%), RRange(h%) / 12, T * 12)
```

The **RRange** array in this statement is indexed incorrectly by an undefined variable, **h%**. The correct index variable is **j%**. Mistakes like this one commonly occur as the result of simple keystroke errors during coding. You can correct the mistake now while you are still in the break mode. Delete the **h%** index and type the correct one, **j%**:

```
LPmt = Payment(PRange(i%), RRange(j%) / 12, T * 12)
```

```
─           Debug Window [CH5EX1A.FRM:CalculateTable]
ᠪᠤᡝ [CH5EX1A.FRM:CalculateTable]  j%: 1
ᠪᠤᡝ [CH5EX1A.FRM:CalculateTable]  RRange(j%): 0.09
ᠪᠤᡝ [CH5EX1A.FRM:CalculateTable]  RRange(j%) / 12: 0.0075

MoRate! =  0
```

Figure 5.12 Comparing argument values before and after the call

```
──  Debug Window [CH5EX1A.FRM:CalculateTable]
&& [CH5EX1A.FRM:CalculateTable]  j%: 4
&& [CH5EX1A.FRM:CalculateTable]  RRange(j%): 0.105
&& [CH5EX1A.FRM:CalculateTable]  RRange(j%) / 12: 0.00875
MoRate! =   0
MoRate! =   0
MoRate! =   .00875
```

Figure 5.13 The correct argument sent to the **Payment** function

Then click the Procedure Step tool several more times to step through one more iteration of the loop. The Debug window now shows that the correct interest rate value has finally been sent to the **Payment** function (Figure 5.13).

In retrospect, the detailed debugging process you have just completed—just to correct a one-letter typographical error—may seem excessive. But errors as simple as this one *do* often occur, and programmers *do* spend many hours trying to find and correct them. The process is much more efficient with the tools you have used in this exercise: watch expressions, breakpoints, single-step performance, and the Debug window.

Now you have several small tasks to perform to return the program to its normal condition:

1. Position the cursor over the call to the **Payment** function and press F9 to toggle the statement out of the breakpoint mode.

2. Choose the **Edit Watch** command from the **Debug** menu and click the **Delete All** button in the resulting **Watch** dialog box. This deletes all the watch expressions you have been working with. Click the **Close** button to close the dialog box.

3. Go to the **Payment** function and delete the last remaining **Debug.Print** statement from its code. Then remove the single-quote character from the beginning of the assignment statement. The function is now operational again.

4. Close the Code window and then press F5 to continue the program performance. (This switches you from the break mode to the run mode.)

5. Click the **Calc** button on the dialog box and watch as the program displays a correctly calculated payment table.

Now you should continue testing all the program's operations. Pull down the **Rate Increment** menu and select a new value of **0.25%** for the

Loan Table					
	9.50%	9.75%	10.00%	10.25%	10.50%
$14,980	$314.61	$316.44	$318.28	$320.13	$321.98
$14,990	$314.82	$316.65	$318.49	$320.34	$322.19
$15,000	$315.03	$316.86	**$318.71**	$320.55	$322.41
$15,010	$315.24	$317.07	$318.92	$320.77	$322.62
$15,020	$315.45	$317.29	$319.13	$320.98	$322.84

Figure 5.14 A mistake in the **Principal Increment** menu

table's interest rate increments. Check the resulting table to make sure it is correct.

Next try an equivalent change with the **Payment Increment** menu: Select **$100** as the new increment for the rows of principal amounts. Check the output table (Figure 5.14). There seems to be something wrong here. The principal amounts in the table increase by $10 for each new row, not $100. Another bug.

Correcting a Logical Error

This time the error does not prevent the program from completing its performance, but the output is wrong. You know that the principal increment is calculated in a short event procedure named **PInc_Click**, so the error shouldn't be too difficult to correct. Follow these steps to get started:

1. Pull down the **Run** menu and select the **Break** command, or click the Break icon on the Toolbar.

2. Activate the **LoanInpt** form and click the **View Code** button in the Project window.

3. Go to the **PInc_Click** procedure in the code window, and find the statement that calculates the global **CurPrincInc** value:

```
CurPrincInc = 10 ^ Index
```

4. Place the cursor on the next executable statement after this assignment statement—a **For** statement—and press F9 to make this line a breakpoint. Visual Basic highlights the line in red.

5. Close the code window and press F5 to continue the program performance. In the dialog box, pull down the **Principal Increment** menu and select the **$1,000** option. The performance stops at the line in **PInc_Click** that you established as a breakpoint.

6. Activate the Debug window. (If necessary, choose **Debug** from the **Window** menu to open and activate the window.) Enter the following two lines in the immediate pane:

```
? Index
? CurPrincInc
```

(Note that the **?** command is a shorthand equivalent for **Print** in the Debug window.)

The Debug window now shows you the values of the **Index** argument—that is, the integer representing the most recent menu selection—and the calculated value of **CurPrincInc** (Figure 5.15). You can see the likely source of the problem right away. The **Index** values for the menu selections range from 0 to 4, but the formula for calculating **CurPrincInc** is based on powers of 10 from 1 to 5. A value of 1 needs to be added to **Index** to compute the correct exponent of 10 in the formula.

The next step illustrates another important feature of the Debug window. During break mode, you can perform individual commands that relate to your program by entering statements directly into the Debug window. Using this technique, you can test commands before you actually make changes in your code.

To see how this works, enter the following two commands into the window:

```
CurPrincInc = 10 ^ (Index + 1)
Calc_Click
```

The first of these statements performs the **CurPrincInc** calculation over again, this time using the corrected formula. The second actually makes a call to the **Calc_Click** procedure so that you can view the resulting payment table. Examining the output table, you can see that the new formula for **CurPrincInc** is correct—the principal increment amount is now $1,000.

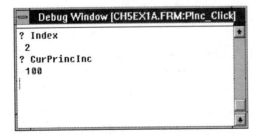

Figure 5.15 Examining the problem in the **PInc_Click** procedure

Complete this exercise by correcting the formula in the code of the **PInc_Click** command. (You can actually use the **Copy** and **Paste** commands from Visual Basic's **Edit** menu to copy the formula from the Debug window to the Code window.) Then clear the breakpoint from the procedure and close the code window. Press F5 to continue the program performance. Test the **Principal Increment** menu again to make sure it works properly now.

The program seems to be working correctly. But part of your job as a developer of Visual Basic applications is to test each program as thoroughly as possible. This means trying out as many different combinations of input data as you can—even combinations that may seem unlikely to you.

For example, in the *Loan Calculator* application you can still generate a run-time error with the following input:

1. Enter a value of **2** as the interest rate.

2. Pull down the **Rate Increment** menu and select **1.0%** as the increment.

In response, the program attempts to start the payment table with an interest rate of 0, and an overflow error occurs when the **Payment** function is called. (Choose the **End** command from the **Run** menu to return to the Design mode after this experiment.)

When you find a bug like this one, you have to rethink the design of your application and decide how you want the program to react to this particular combination of input parameters. Should the program reject the input and refuse to create a table? Should a special explanatory message be displayed on the screen? Or should the program make an automatic adjustment in the increment amount—not quite following the user's instructions, but avoiding a run-time error? Once you decide how you want your application to react, your next step is to write the appropriate code to implement your design. Then the testing process begins again. At some point you might want to try correcting this design problem as an additional exercise with the *Loan Calculator*.

COMPILING AN APPLICATION

After you design, write, test, and debug your application, the final step is to compile the program as an EXE file that can be run directly from the Windows environment. To accomplish this you use the **Make EXE File** command in the **File** menu.

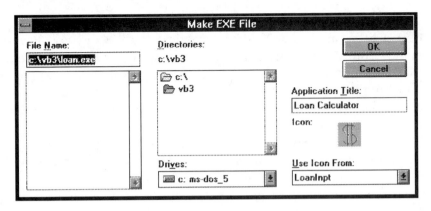

Figure 5.16 The **Make Exe File** dialog box

As an exercise with this command, open the project named LOAN.MAK from the exercise disk. Then pull down the **File** menu and select **Make EXE File**. The dialog box shown in Figure 5.16 appears on the screen. The box suggests default values for the file name, the directory path in which the EXE file will be saved, and application's name and icon. (This final version of the *Loan Calculator* application has a custom-made icon to represent the program in Windows. You'll learn how to work with icons in Chapters 9 and 12 .) If all of these details are satisfactory, click the **OK** button. The compilation process takes only a couple seconds.

Use the **Run** command from the Windows Program Manager's **File** menu to run an EXE file you have created in Visual Basic. In the dialog box that appears when you select this command (Figure 5.17) enter the program's path and file name. The program appears on the desktop, just like any other Windows application. (By the way, if you click the minimize button on the *Loan Calculator* application's dialog box, the program will be reduced to the custom icon that appears in Figure 5.16.)

Reading Parameters from the Command Line

An additional design feature that you can program into an application is the ability to read input parameters directly from the **Run** command line in Windows. For example, imagine being able to enter the principal, interest rate, and term of a loan into the **Run** input box at the time you start up the *Loan Calculator* from Windows. Figure 5.17 shows how this might appear. If the program is properly designed to read these values from the command line, the three numbers can appear as the initial input parameters in the dialog box when the program begins.

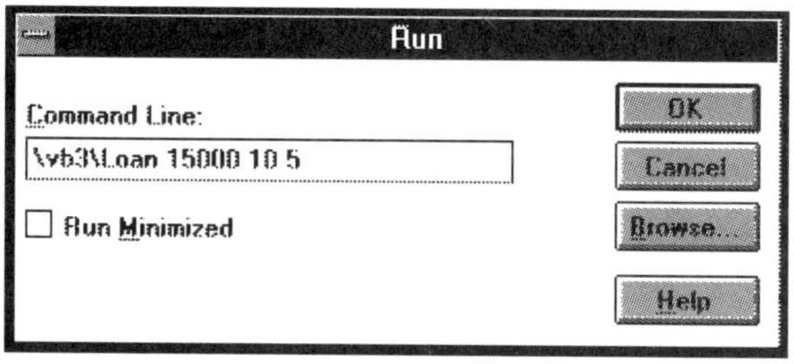

Figure 5.17 Entering input values from the **Run** command line in Windows

This feature does not happen automatically. You have to include code in your program to read the command line string and parse the string into individual data values. Visual Basic has a number of tools that help you in this process. First, the built-in **Command$** function returns the *command-line string*—that is, everything the user types into the **Command Line** box after the name of the program itself. In the example shown in Figure 5.17, **Command$** returns the string "15000 10 5". In the procedure you create to read the command line, you can use tools from Visual Basic's library of string functions—for example, the **Left$**, **Right$**, and **Mid$** functions, which return substring portions from a larger string.

The following procedure, named **ReadCommandLine**, is included in the **LoanIn** form of LOAN.MAK:

```
Sub ReadCommandLine ()

  ' Read the user-supplied command line.
  ' The line should be in the format:

  '        principal rate term

  ' where one or more spaces separate each
  ' numeric data item. This routine ignores
  ' any command line that does not conform
  ' to this format.

  Dim InLine As String, S1%, S2%

  InLine = LTrim$(RTrim$(Command$))

  ' Continue only if InLine is not blank.

  If Len(InLine) <> 0 Then
```

```
' Find locations of two space-character
' separators. Eliminate any extra spaces.

S1% = InStr(InLine, " ")
Do While Mid$(InLine, S1% + 1, 1) = " "
  S1% = S1% + 1
Loop

S2% = InStr(S1% + 1, InLine, " ")
Do While Mid$(InLine, S2% + 1, 1) = " "
  S2% = S2% + 1
Loop

' Continue only if separators are present.

If (S1% <> 0) And (S2% <> 0) Then

    ' Enter the loan parameters from the command line.
    ' Use Val and Str$ to convert any non-numeric
    ' input value into "0".

    InPrinc.Text = Str$(Val(Left$(InLine, S1% - 1)))
    InRate.Text = Str$(Val(Mid$(InLine, S1% + 1, S2% - S1%)))
    InTerm.Text = Str$(Val(Right$(InLine, Len(InLine) - S2%)))

  End If
End If

End Sub   ' ReadCommandLine
```

This procedure reads the principal, rate, and term from the command line, and copies these input values to the application's input controls, **InPrinc**, **InRate**, and **InTerm**. As you can see, **ReadCommandLine** uses a detailed sequence of nested loops and **If** decisions to accomplish its task. (You can read about Visual Basic's decision structures in **Review Box 5.3**. In this context, you may also want to examine the **RInc_Click** procedure in the **LoanInpt** form for an example of a **Select Case** structure.)

A call to **ReadCommandLine** appears in the program's **Form_Load** procedure. While you are developing a procedure like this one, you can use another Visual Basic feature to test the code designed to read the command line. The **Project** command in the **Options** menu contains a **Command Line Argument** option in which you can enter a command-line string. The **Command$** function then returns this string to your program as though the string had been entered from the Windows command line.

Review Box 5.3

Decision Structures

Visual Basic's two decision structures—**If** and **Select Case**—can both be used to select between two or more alternative blocks of code during run time. In general, the **If** structure makes its decision by evaluating logical conditions as true or false. In contrast, the **Select Case** structure chooses a block of code by comparing a single test value with lists of **Case** values; when a match is found, the corresponding block of code is performed.

The **If** structure has several formats, the simplest of which is:

```
If Condition Then
  ' Block of code.
End If
```

In this case, the block of code is performed only if *Condition* is evaluated as true. An **Else** clause provides an alternate block of code for the structure:

```
If Condition Then
  ' Block 1
Else
  ' Block 2
End If
```

Here the **If** statement chooses between the two blocks: If *Condition* is true, *Block 1* is performed; if *Condition* is false, *Block 2* is performed. The **If** statement can also include any number of **ElseIf** clauses, each of which introduces its own condition into the statement; for example:

```
If Condition1 Then
  ' Block 1
ElseIf Condition2 Then
  ' Block 2
ElseIf Condition3 Then
  ' Block 3
Else
  ' Block 4
End If
```

This structure selects only one block of code for performance. If a true condition is found, the corresponding block is performed and the

Review Box 5.3 *(continued)*

remainder of the structure is skipped. If there is no true condition, the **Else** block is performed.

The **Select Case** structure defines a test value—a numeric or string expression—that is used to select among a sequence of blocks:

```
Select Case TestValue
  Case ValueList1
    ' Block 1
  Case ValueList2
    ' Block 2
  Case ValueList3
    ' Block 3
  Case Else
    ' Block 4
End Select
```

This structure looks for a match between *TestValue* and an element in one of the *ValueLists.* When a match is found, the corresponding block is performed. Any number of **Case** blocks can be included in the structure. If no match is found, the **Case Else** block is performed. A *ValueList* can be a list of values, a range of values (expressed with the reserved word **To**), or a relational expression (using the reserved word **Is**).

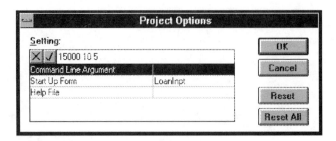

Figure 5.18 The **Project Options** dialog box

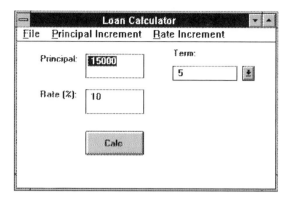

Figure 5.19 Input values from the command line

This final exercise with the *Loan Calculator* application (LOAN.MAK) gives you the opportunity to see how the **Project Options** feature works:

1. Pull down the **Options** menu and select the **Project** command. In the **Setting** box of resulting dialog box (Figure 5.18) enter the following line of data:

    ```
    15000  10  5
    ```

    Make sure each number is separated from the next by one or more spaces. Click **OK** or press the Enter key to complete your entry.

2. Press the F5 function key to run the *Loan Calculator* application. Figure 5.19 shows the opening dialog box. Notice that the program has copied your command-line input into the appropriate text boxes.

This is a simulation of what will occur when you enter command-line values in the Windows **Run** command.

SUMMARY: THE FINAL STEPS OF APPLICATION DEVELOPMENT

Even in a relatively simple application like the *Loan Calculator*, you may find yourself spending a long time testing and debugging—and sometimes redesigning—your program after you have finished writing the code. As you now turn to more ambitious programming projects, the tools and features you have used in this chapter will prove their value and flexibility over and over again:

- The break mode gives you the opportunity to stop your program, examine variables, test new approaches, and work through problematic passages of code one step at a time.
- The **Calls** command in the **Debug** menu shows you the sequence of calls that have led to the current break point in your program.
- The Debug window lets you move aside temporarily from your program's code to perform commands and to view the data that your program is working with.
- Watch expressions allow you to designate variables and expressions that you want to examine during run time.
- Breakpoints give you flexible control over your program's entry into the break mode.
- Single-step execution allows you to examine and analyze the effect of each separate line of code.

When all the testing and debugging is complete, the **Make EXE File** command efficiently transforms your program into an independent Windows application stored in an EXE file. This step meets the final goal of program development in Visual Basic—creating a working application that you can place alongside the other tools you use every day in the Windows environment.

P A R T   I I

Visual Basic 3 Applications

6

Input and Output Techniques: The Sales Week Application

INTRODUCTION

Input and *output* operations in Visual Basic take place interactively inside the windows you create for an application. In a typical dialog box, you might designate some controls for receiving the user's input from the keyboard and others for presenting the information your program generates. Sometimes the two operations may even seem to blend together when the same controls from which your program *reads* input data later become the tools for *displaying* output data. In this way, Visual Basic's controls take the place of specific input and output commands you may be familiar with in other versions of Basic.

For example, traditional Basics offer the INPUT statement for displaying an input prompt and reading a data item from the keyboard:

```
INPUT "Sales"; InSales
```

When this particular statement is executed, Basic displays a prompt on the screen—*Sales?*—and waits for the user's keyboard entry. The resulting input value is stored in the variable *InSales.* As you have seen, the approach to this input operation is very different in Visual Basic. You could plan for an equivalent event by placing a label and a text box on a form (Figure 6.1), and assigning settings to the relevant properties: **InSales** as the **Name** property of the text box, and **Sales** as the label's **Caption** property. During run time, your program reads the user's input as **InSales.Text**, a reference to the **Text** property of the text box.

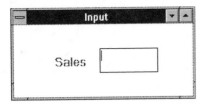

Figure 6.1 An input operation in Visual Basic

The advantages of the Visual Basic approach are immediately clear to the user. During run time, a text box is a versatile Windows-style input object: Entries can be edited, deleted, inserted, selected with the mouse, or even copied from one place to another. In an application containing several text boxes, the user can skip around between boxes, entering values in any order. In short, the event-driven programming model gives the user greater control over interactive input operations.

There are also advantages from your point of view as designer of the application. For one, a text box that serves as an input control in one operation can later be used for displaying output. The following assignment statement resets the **Text** property of the **InSales** text box:

```
InSales.Text = NewSalesVal
```

As a result of this statement, a new value appears inside the text box.

As a context for studying input and output techniques, this chapter presents a business database application named *Sales Week.* You can use this program for recording, reviewing, and analyzing sales figures. Examining the elements of this application—its controls, properties, and code—you'll see several interesting examples of input and output activities:

- Reading data from text boxes and performing specific input validation tests.

- Providing the user with different ways to issue instructions to the program—using the mouse, the keyboard, and menu selections.

- Reading data from, and writing data to, a sequential data file on disk.

- Displaying text, data, and graphics in a variety of Visual Basic controls—labels, text boxes, and picture boxes.

- Providing textual information in special Visual Basic windows called *message boxes.*

These events and operations will be the focus of your work in this chapter.

THE *SALES WEEK* APPLICATION

The *Sales Week* program is a tool for recording the daily and weekly sales activity of a retail business. The data you enter is saved as a database on disk, giving you a permanent chronological record of weekly sales. The program also builds bar graphs representing the sales for a given week or for a series of consecutive weeks.

The program is set up to work with a directory named \SALESWK on the C drive. All weekly sales files that the program creates are saved in this directory. One of the program's first actions is to search for the directory, and to create it if it does not yet exist.

Load the program from the exercise disk now. Its project name is SALESWK.MAK. When you open it, you'll see that the entire program is contained within a single form named **SaleGrph**, and stored on disk as SALEGRPH.FRM. Press the F5 function key to run the program. The program's dialog box immediately appears on the screen, as shown in Figure 6.2.

At the left side of the dialog box are two columns of cells for the current week's sales data. The days of the week, from Sunday to Saturday, appear in the first column, and seven zeros appear initially in the second column. Imagine that you are ready to begin using the program to record this week's daily sales figures. In the cell for Sunday, type a value of 512 (representing $512 or 512 units, the total sales for the day). Press the Tab key or the down arrow key to move the focus to the next cell down. In the picture box at

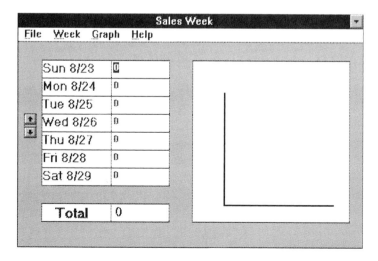

Figure 6.2 The initial dialog box from the *Sales Week* application

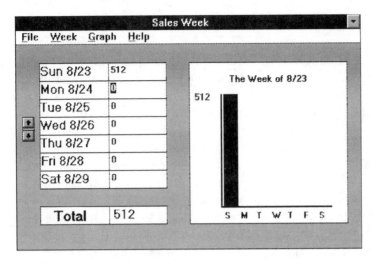

Figure 6.3 The first sales entry

the right side of the window, the program displays a single vertical bar representing the sales figure you have entered (Figure 6.3).

The graph becomes more significant as you enter more sales figures for the week. For example, try entering the following data into the cells for Monday through Saturday:

```
420
388
480
535
677
759
```

Each time you complete a new entry, the program adds a bar to the graph. The label at the top of the graph's vertical axis always shows the value of the largest sales figure for the week. The total of all the sales entries is tallied at the bottom of the sales column, at the lower-left corner of the window. Figure 6.4 shows what the dialog box looks like when you have completed the sales entries for the week. (Of course the dates you see will be different.)

You can make changes in the data at any time, and the program automatically redraws the bar graph in response. For example, suppose you discover an error in the data for Thursday: The correct sales figure is 700. When you enter this number into the appropriate cell, the new graph reflects your correction.

Now imagine that you have been using this program to record weekly sales data for some time, and now you want to review the figures for

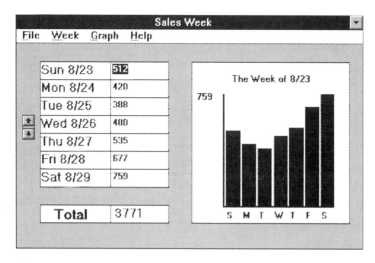

Figure 6.4 An entire week's sales data

previous weeks. To move backward in time by one week you can use either
the keyboard or the mouse:

- On the keyboard, press the PgUp key to view the data for the previous
  week; press PgDn for the next week.

- With the mouse, click the up arrow icon at the left side of the dialog
  box to view the previous week; click the down arrow for the next week.

Whenever you move to the display of another week's data, the program
saves the current week's sales figures in the database on disk. The saved
figures reappear when you scroll back to the current week.

To experiment fully with the features of the *Sales Week* application you'll
need at least ten weeks of sales data. The program is designed for quick
and easy data entry. Go back nine weeks from the current week, and enter
a set of imaginary sales data for each week up to the current week. Use the
data shown in Table 6.1.

When you have entered all the data, return to this week's sales figures.
The program has a convenient shortcut key for displaying this week's sales:
Simply press the F5 function key. Now you can view another kind of bar
graph, comparing this week's sales with the nine weeks in the immediate
past. The program calls this a *trend* graph. To display this graph, press the
F8 function key. The result is shown in Figure 6.5. Examining the new
graph, you see an increase in sales over the last few weeks; you may conclude
that your recent advertising campaign in local newspapers has been a
success. To toggle back to the one-week graph for the current week, press
the F7 function key.

Table 6.1 Nine weeks of sales data

	1	2	3	4	5	6	7	8	9
Sun.	237	219	195	119	139	151	225	288	388
Mon.	312	288	347	245	225	235	301	369	463
Tue.	288	315	265	259	201	215	255	342	425
Wed.	366	395	310	305	292	310	319	425	519
Thu.	432	399	405	391	355	376	400	490	588
Fri.	488	450	382	400	410	419	452	550	637
Sat.	450	488	401	391	388	410	429	515	619

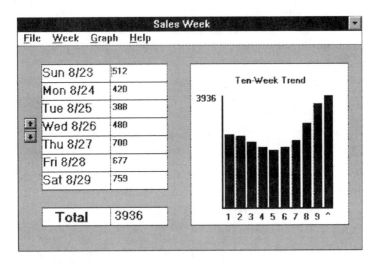

Figure 6.5 A ten-week graph of sales

Menus in the *Sales Week* Application

You'll notice that the main dialog box includes a menu line with four pull-down menus named **File**, **Week**, **Graph**, and **Help**. These menus offer a variety of commands designed to make the application more convenient and versatile.

The **File** menu (Figure 6.6) has a **Print** command, which prints the data and graph currently displayed in the dialog box; and an **Exit** command, which ends the program performance. Both of these commands, like several of the other commands in the application's menu system, have

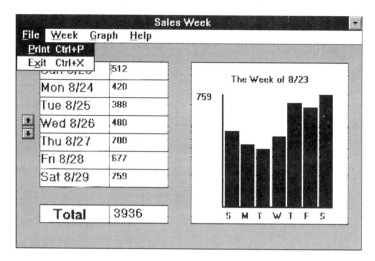

Figure 6.6 The **File** menu of the *Sales Week* application

shortcut keys. To print a screen of data, you can press Ctrl+P, and to exit from the program, press Ctrl+X.

The four commands in the **Week** menu (Figure 6.7) help you select a particular week's data. The commands named **This Week** and **Last Week** have shortcut keys of F5 and F6, respectively. The **Move Backward** and **Move Forward** commands are equivalent to pressing the PgUp or PgDn keys on the keyboard or clicking the up or down arrow icons in the dialog box.

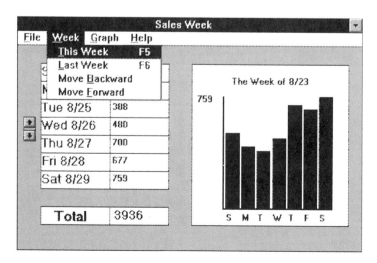

Figure 6.7 The **Week** menu of the *Sales Week* application

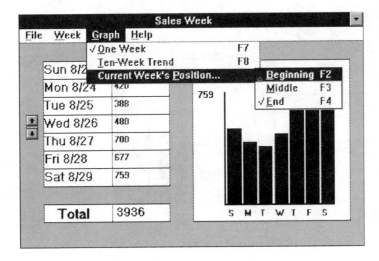

Figure 6.8 The **Graph** menu of the *Sales Week* application

The **Graph** menu (Figure 6.8) lets you select the kind of graph that you want to view in the application's picture box. As you have already seen, the **One Week** and the **Ten-Week Trend** commands have keyboard shortcuts of F7 and F8. A third command in the **Graph** menu—named **Current Week's Position**—results in a submenu with three selections, **Beginning**, **Middle**, and **End**. These selections control the position in the trend graph of the week that is currently displayed on the screen. The default is **End**, which means that the currently displayed week of data appears as the last

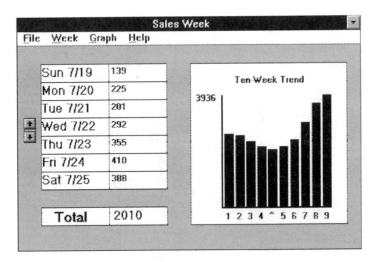

Figure 6.9 Using the **Middle** option

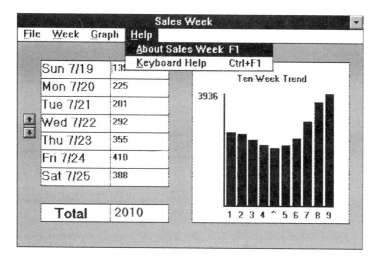

Figure 6.10 The **Help** menu of the *Sales Week* application

column of the graph. Figure 6.9 shows what happens when you move back five weeks in time, press F8 to switch to the trend graph, and then press F3 to select the **Middle** option: The displayed data appears in the middle of the graph. The currently displayed week is always represented by a caret character (^) along the graph's horizontal axis.

Finally, the **Help** menu (Figure 6.10) offers two help screens. The **About Sales Week** command displays a succinct description of the program (Figure 6.11) and the **Keyboard Help** command displays a list of the program's shortcut keys (Figure 6.12). You can view these help windows by pressing F1 or Ctrl+F1.

As you continue experimenting with the *Sales Week* application, try out all of the various menu commands and make sure you understand the function each one serves.

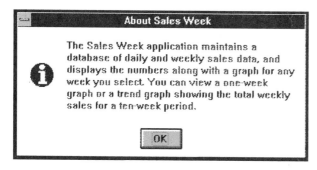

Figure 6.11 The **About Sales Week** help window

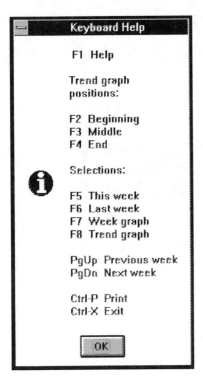

Figure 6.12 The **Keyboard Help** window

The Filing System for the Sales Database

The *Sales Week* application saves the sales database as a series of small text files rather than one large random-access file. Each individual file contains the sales data for one week. The program creates the file for a given week as soon as you enter the data and move on to another week.

File names are derived from the date of the first day of the week, Sunday. Each file has an extension name of SLS. For example, the file for the week of August 23, 1992 is named 08-23-92.SLS. The file contains the seven sales figures entered for the week:

```
512
420
388
480
700
677
759
```

As you have learned, the program is set up to store these files in the directory named C:\SALESWK. If you want to change this default directory location, you must revise the following **Const** declaration, located in the declaration section of the **SaleGrph** form:

```
Const PathName$ = "C:\SalesWk"
```

Because the database is stored in text files, you can use the TYPE command to view the contents of any file from the DOS prompt. You can also load any file into the Windows Notepad accessory.

THE STRUCTURE OF THE *SALES WEEK* PROGRAM

The central input controls in the *Sales Week* application are organized as an array of text boxes named **SalesDay**. Actually, the program uses the **SalesDay** boxes for both input and output. On the one hand, this is the column of text boxes in which you originally enter the sales data for a given week; then, when you later scroll to weeks for which you have previously saved data, the program uses these same text boxes to display the existing sales figures.

Other controls in the program's dialog box include an array of labels, a picture box, a vertical scroll bar, and, of course, the system of menu commands. Figure 6.13 shows what these controls look like in the design

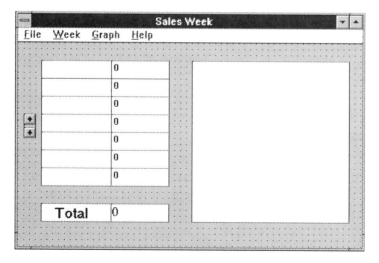

Figure 6.13 The controls of the *Sales Week* application

mode. Before you begin studying the program's code, take a brief look at these controls and their property settings.

Controls and Properties

The **SalesDay** text boxes have **Index** settings from **0** to **6**. As you can see in Figure 6.13, each box has an initial **Text** value of **0**. The column of controls just to the left of these text boxes is an array of labels named **WkDay**. During run time, the program displays a day of the week and a date in each one of these label controls. Like the **SalesDay** array, the **WkDay** labels have **Index** settings from **0** to **6**. Their initial **Caption** settings are blank and their **FontSize** settings are **12**, somewhat larger than the default size.

Just below these two control arrays is a pair of bordered labels. The label on the left displays the word **Total** as its fixed **Caption** setting. The label on the right is designed to display the total sales for a given week. Its **Name** setting is **Total**, and its initial **Caption** setting is **0**. The **Total** label has a **FontSize** setting of **12** in order to display the total more boldly than the other numbers that appear on the form.

The picture box in which the program displays bar graphs has a **Name** setting of **GraphBox**. As you'll see later, Visual Basic provides several important methods for displaying text and graphics inside a picture box.

The application also contains a vertical scroll bar, located at the left side of the dialog box. The bar's **Name** setting is **ScrollWeek**. This control has been sized down to a very small height setting; as a result, it looks like nothing more than a pair of arrow buttons. Normally, a vertical scroll bar has a *scroll box* that slides up and down the bar, but the **ScrollWeek** bar is too small to display the scroll box. You'll recall that the purpose of this scroll bar is to allow the user to scroll forward or backward one week at a time.

Several properties determine the behavior and value of a vertical scroll bar in Visual Basic:

- The **Value** property is the numeric equivalent of a selected position on the scroll bar.

- The **Min** property represents the scroll bar's smallest possible value— that is, the **Value** setting when the scroll box is positioned at the top of the bar.

- The **Max** property is the scroll bar's largest possible value—that is, the **Value** setting when the scroll box is positioned at the bottom of the bar.

- The **SmallChange** property is the increment by which the scroll bar's value changes when the user clicks one of the two arrows located at opposite ends of the bar. (Scroll bars also have a **LargeChange** property, representing the increment of change when the user clicks inside the bar.)

The **ScrollWeek** control in the *Sales Week* application has only three possible **Value** settings:

- **1** is the default setting.
- **0** is the **Min** setting. This value means that the user has just clicked the up arrow icon.
- **2** is the **Max** setting. This value means that the user has just clicked the down arrow icon.

The control's **SmallChange** setting is **1**. As you'll see shortly, changes in the value of this control are monitored by an event procedure named **ScrollWeek_Change**.

Finally, the application's menu system is designed to give the user a variety of mouse and keyboard techniques for selecting options and operations. As usual, the menu is created at design time in the Menu Design Window. In Figure 6.14 you can see definitions for the **File**, **Week**, and **Graph** menus.

Notice that the shortcut keys for individual menu commands are displayed in a column at the right side of the menu list box. As you are creating a menu, you use the **Shortcut** option in the Menu Design Window to select

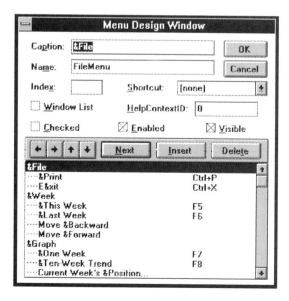

Figure 6.14 Menu definitions for the *Sales Week* application

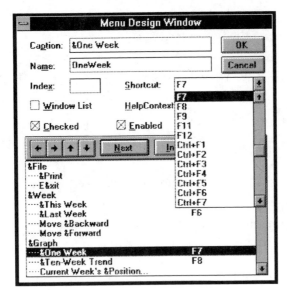

Figure 6.15 The drop-down list of the **Shortcut** option

an appropriate key for any menu command. This option has a drop-down list (Figure 6.15) that displays the available shortcut keys, including function keys and various keyboard combinations that use the Ctrl and Shift keys. To assign a shortcut key to a command, you simply select the key from this drop-down list.

Table 6.2 shows the **Name** settings and the shortcut keys assigned to the menu commands in the *Sales Week* application. A number of important events in this program are associated with menu commands and menu selections. To understand these events you should be familiar with the property settings defined for the menu.

Events

The user's keyboard and mouse activities are monitored and captured by a variety of event procedures in the *Sales Week* application. Broadly, the application recognizes two categories of user input: data entries into the daily sales boxes and commands to perform the program's defined operations and procedures.

As you have seen, many of the program's operations are defined as menu commands. Each command has an associated **Click** procedure in the program's code. This procedure is called when the user pulls down a menu

Table 6.2 Properties and shortcut keys in the *Sales Week* menu

Level	Caption	Name	Shortcut
menu	&File	FileMenu	—
----command	&Print	PrintSales	Ctrl+P
----command	E&xit	Quit	Ctrl+X
menu	&Week	WeekMenu	—
----command	&This Week	ThisWeek	F5
----command	&Last Week	LastWeek	F6
----command	Move &Backward	Backward	—
----command	Move &Forward	Forward	—
menu	&Graph	GraphMenu	—
----command	&One Week	OneWeek	F7
----command	&Ten-Week Trend	TenWeeks	F8
----command	&Current Week's Position...	Position	—
--------command	&Beginning	BeginPos	F2
--------command	&Middle	MidPos	F3
--------command	&End	EndPos	F4
menu	&Help	HelpMenu	—
----command	&About Sales Week	GeneralHelp	F1
----command	&Keyboard Help	KeyboardHelp	Ctrl+F1

and selects a command. From the user's point of view there are several different ways to perform menu commands:

- Click a menu with the mouse and then click a command in the drop-down menu list.

- Use the Alt key to pull down a menu and select a command or option by its *access key*. For example, to pull down the **Graph** menu and select the **Ten-Week Trend** option you can press Alt+G and then T.

- Press one of the defined shortcut keys to invoke a menu command. For example, pressing the F8 function key selects the **Ten-Week Trend** option.

All these user actions trigger the same **Click** event for a given menu command. No matter how the user selects a menu command—using the mouse or one of the keyboard techniques—the corresponding **Click** procedure is called and performed. From your point of view as an application developer, a menu is a powerful programming tool that allows you to monitor several varieties of user activity at once, with a minimum of code. This is particularly true when you include access keys and shortcut keys in a menu.

Aside from menu commands and their associated **Click** procedures, the *Sales Week* application recognizes several other events. First of all, the **Form_Load** event procedure is performed at the beginning of a program run and accomplishes several important initialization tasks. Once the dialog box appears on the screen, a **Change** event procedure is available for the vertical scroll bar, **ScrollWeek**. The **Change** event takes place in the application whenever the user clicks the up or down arrow icon on the scroll bar. In response, the program scrolls backward or forward to a new week in the sales database.

Finally, the program recognizes three events associated with the array of text boxes, **SalesDay**:

- The **LostFocus** event takes place when the user activates a new cell in the array of text boxes. The text box that *loses* the focus in this action is the object of the event. The program reads the value in the text box, and checks to see if the value has changed—that is, if the user has entered a new sales figure. If so, the program updates the graph to reflect the new figure.

- The **GotFocus** event is triggered by the same action, but in this case the object of the event is the text box that *receives* the focus. When this event takes place, the program highlights the entire value currently stored in the newly selected text box.

- The **KeyDown** event takes place when the user presses a key at the keyboard. The object of the event is the text box that currently has the focus. The purpose of the corresponding event procedure, **Sales-Day_KeyDown**, is to trap an up or down arrow keypress, or a PgUp or PgDn keypress. In response to one of these keys, the program selects a new text box or scrolls to a new week in the database.

You'll have the opportunity to examine all these event procedures now as you turn your attention to the application's code.

Procedures and Methods

The declaration section in the **SaleGrph** form defines several variables and arrays that are central to the program's operations. Because the application consists of a single form, these variables are, in effect, global to the program. You can examine the declarations, along with the **Form_Load** procedure, in Listing 6.1.

Form-Level Variable Declarations

Two of the most important form-level variables are **WeekRef&** and **FileName$**. **WeekRef&** is a long integer that always represents a date in the week that is currently displayed; **FileName$** is the name of the data file for the displayed week:

```
Dim WeekRef&, FileName$
```

WeekRef& is designed to store a *serial* date. A serial date is a positive or negative long integer that specifies a number of days forward or backward from an abitrarily defined starting point in time. The starting date in Visual Basic's serial date system is December 30, 1899, which has a serial value of 0. Prior dates have negative serial values, and subsequent dates have positive values. Extending this idea by a step, a complete serial value is a double-precision number in which the decimal portion represents the time of day.

Visual Basic has an extremely valuable library of date and time functions. For example, the **Now** function returns a **Variant**-type value representing the current date from the system calendar and the time from the system clock. Depending on the context in which **Now** is used, this **Variant** value can appear either as a date in a displayable format or a serial number representing a date. For example, the **Form_Load** procedure uses this function to initialize the value of **WeekRef&** to the serial value for today's date:

```
WeekRef& = Int(Now)
```

Because the time portion of the value returned by **Now** is not relevant to the *Sales Week* application, the program uses **Int** to drop the decimal part of the serial value.

In Chapters 8 and 9 you'll learn more about serial numbers and their use in representing date and time values. You'll also explore the advantages of using the **Variant** type along with Visual Basic's built-in **IsDate** function in applications that read date values as input from the user. In the case of the *Sales Week* program—which uses date values primarily for its own internal operations—the integer representation of serial dates is just as convenient as the **Variant** type.

Another variable declared in the form-level declarations section is **Back-Weeks**:

```
Dim BackWeeks As Integer
```

The program uses this integer to determine the position of the displayed week in a ten-week bar graph. The variable's initial value is established in the **Form_Load** procedure:

```
BackWeeks = 63
```

This initial value represents nine weeks—9 weeks times 7 days equals 63. It means that nine weeks will appear before the current week in the ten-week graph.

Finally, two important numeric arrays are declared in the form-level declarations section:

```
Dim WeekOnDisk(6) As Single, WeekOnScreen(6) As Single
```

As you can infer from their names, these arrays represent a week's sales data as currently stored on disk and as displayed on the screen. Comparisons between these two arrays give the program a simple way to determine when and if a week's data needs to be updated on disk.

Displaying a Week's Sales Data

The **Form_Load** procedure makes a call to a general procedure named **ShowWeek** (Listing 6.2) to display the current week's data in the dialog box. This procedure is called whenever the user selects a new week. The procedure displays the days of the selected week as the **Caption** settings of the array of labels named **WkDay**. The first part of this task is to determine the date of the first day of the week, Sunday:

```
WeekStart& = WeekRef& - (Weekday(WeekRef&) - 1)
```

Visual Basic's **Weekday** function receives a serial date as its argument and returns an integer from 1 to 7 representing the corresponding day of the week. **WeekStart&** is thus the serial date for Sunday of the currently selected week. Given this starting date, the following **For** loop sets the **Caption** properties for the array of labels in the dialog box:

```
For i% = 0 to 6
  WkDay(i%).Caption = Format$(WeekStart& + i%, "ddd m/d")
Next i%
```

Notice the use of Visual Basic's **Format$** function to produce a custom date-display format from the serial date values. The format "ddd m/d" is the representation you see in the dialog box.

The **ShowWeek** procedure uses **Format$** again to create the file name for the current week's data on disk:

```
FileName$ = PathName$ + "\" + Format$(WeekStart&, "mm-dd-yy") + ".SLS"
```

Given this file name, a call to the **ReadNewWeek** procedure reads the week's sales data from disk, if it exists.

Reading Sales Data from Disk and Writing Data to Disk

The **ReadNewWeek** procedure (Listing 6.3) uses an error trap to determine whether a data file exists yet for the currently selected week. The **Open** statement normally causes a run-time error if an attempt is made to open a nonexistent file for input. The error trap is triggered if this error occurs:

```
CannotRead = False
On Error Goto FileProblem
  Open FileName$ For Input As #1
On Error Goto 0
```

The file exists if the **CannotRead** variable still has a value of **False** after this passage.

The **ReadNewWeek** procedure next assigns **Text** property settings for the array of text boxes named **SalesDay**. The procedure displays a column of zeros in the **SalesDay** text boxes, if the file does not exist; or a column of sales data—read from the file on disk—if the file does exist:

```
If CannotRead Then
  SalesDay(i%).Text = 0
Else
  Input #1, SalesVal
  SalesDay(i%).Text = SalesVal
End If
```

Notice that the procedure reads each value from the open file into the **Variant**-type variable **SalesVal** and then assigns this value directly to the **Text** property. Thanks to the versatility of text boxes in Visual Basic 2.0 and 3.0, no data type conversion is necessary.

After displaying the sales data, **ReadNewWeek** sets the values of the arrays **WeekOnDisk** and **WeekOnScreen**. At this point, before the user has

had an opportunity to make changes in the data, the two arrays contain
the same values:

```
WeekOnDisk(i%) = SalesDay(i%).Text
WeekOnScreen(i%) = WeekOnDisk(i%)
```

When the user later selects a new week, the **SaveCurWeek** procedure
(Listing 6.4) uses these two arrays to determine whether the current week
needs to be updated on disk—that is, whether there are any new data values
to save:

```
For i% = 0 to 6
  If WeekOnScreen(i%) <> WeekOnDisk(i%) Then
SomethingtoSave% = True
Next i%
```

The **ReadNewWeek** and **SaveCurWeek** procedures use Visual Basic's
Open, **Input#**, **Print#**, and **Close#** statements to manage the sequential-
access data files on disk. You can read about these statements in **Review
Box 6.1**.

Drawing the Graphs

After reading a new week's sales data from disk, the **ReadNewWeek**
procedure makes a call to the **UpdateTotal** procedure (Listing 6.5) to
compute the week's total sales and to draw the appropriate bar graph.
UpdateTotal begins by assigning the total sales value to **Total.Caption**.
Then a call to the **DrawAxes** procedure (also in Listing 6.5) draws the
vertical and horizontal axes for the graph.

You'll recall that the picture box in the *Sales Week* application has a **Name**
setting of **GraphBox**. The **DrawAxes** procedure illustrates one property
and two methods that apply to picture boxes. The **Cls** method clears all
text and graphics currently displayed in the box. The **DrawWidth** property
determines the width of lines drawn in the box. (A setting of **2** gives slightly
thicker lines than the default). The **Line** method draws a line between two
points in the graph box:

```
GraphBox.Cls
GraphBox.DrawWidth = 2
GraphBox.Line (20, 20)-(20, 90), 0
GraphBox.Line (20, 90)-(90, 90), 0
```

Finally, **UpdateTotal** chooses between a call to the **DrawWeekGraph** or
the **DrawTrendGraph** procedure, depending upon the current **Checked**
setting of the **OneWeek** menu command:

```
If OneWeek.Checked Then
  DrawWeekGraph
Else
  DrawTrendGraph
End If
```

The kind of graph actually drawn therefore depends upon the user's current selection in the **Graph** menu.

The **DrawWeekGraph** procedure (Listing 6.6) and the **DrawTrend-Graph** procedure (Listing 6.7) both use **For** loops to draw the elements of the bar graphs. Within these loops, the **BF** argument of the **Line** method produces a filled box for each bar of the graph; for example:

```
GraphBox.Line (x%, 90)-Step(5, y%), , BF
```

To prepare for displaying a label at the proper position along the x-axis, each procedure resets the **CurrentX** and **CurrentY** properties of the picture box. A call to the **Print** method then displays the label:

```
GraphBox.CurrentX = x%
GraphBox.CurrentY = 92
GraphBox.Print WeekChar$(i%);
```

Reading Data from the Keyboard

The **SalesDay_LostFocus** event procedure (Listing 6.8) is called whenever the user selects a new text box in the dialog box. Several keyboard and mouse actions trigger this event in the application, including:

- Pressing the Tab key or Shift+Tab.
- Pressing the up or down arrow key.
- Clicking a new text box with the mouse.

The object of the **LostFocus** event in this case is the text box that *previously* had the focus. The program uses this event as an opportunity to read and validate the number in the previously selected text box and to update the total and the graph if the value represents a new or revised sales entry.

The **SalesDay_LostFocus** procedure uses the **Val** function to perform a simple validation check on the input value. **Val** supplies the numeric equivalent of the value stored in the box:

```
CurVal = Val(SalesDay(Index).Text)
```

(Keep in mind that the **Index** argument refers to the text box that has just lost the focus in the **SalesDay** array.) The **Val** function reads digital characters to the end of the entry, or up to the first nondigital character if

Review Box 6.1

Sequential Data Files

Read and write operations in an ASCII data file are performed *sequentially*—that is, one value at a time from the beginning to the end of the file. To open such a file for reading, use the **Open** statement as follows:

```
Open FileName For Input As #FileNum
```

FileName is the name of an existing file on disk, and *FileNum* is an integer that you use to identify the open file in subequent I/O statements. If *FileName* cannot be found on disk, an attempt to open the file for input results in a run-time error. However, you can prevent an interruption in the program performance by setting up an error trap:

```
On Error Goto ErrorTrapLabel
   Open FileName For Input As #FileNum
On Error Goto 0
```

ErrorTrapLabel is a line label that identifies the beginning of the error trap routine. Typically, the routine sets a flag variable indicating the **Open** failure.

The **Input#** statement reads individual data values from a data file that is open for reading:

```
Input #FileNum, VariableList
```

FileNum is the number assigned to the open file in the corresponding **Open** statement. *VariableList* consists of one or more variable names, with data types corresponding to the data expected from the file. **Input#** recognizes a comma or an end-of-line marker—**Chr$**(13) + **Chr$**(10)— as a delimiter between any two data values; in addition, a space character serves as a valid delimiter between two numeric values. The **Line Input#**

the entry contains characters that cannot be converted to numbers. For example, if the user happens to enter the value **123 items** into a text box, **Val** reads only the three digits and returns the numeric value **123**. If the user enters a string that *begins* with a nondigital character—for example, **q1234**—the **Val** function returns a value of 0.

Review Box 6.1 *(continued)*

statement reads an entire line of text from the file, regardless of commas or spaces contained in the line:

```
Line Input #FileNum, VariableName
```

The **EOF** function returns a value of true after an **Input#** or **Line Input#** statement reads the last data value from the file. Before this point, **EOF** gives a value of false:

```
EOF(FileNum)
```

You can use this function in a **DO** loop to read a file whose length is not known in advance.

To open a file for writing, use the **Open** statement in one of these forms:

```
Open FileName For Output As #FileNum
Open FileName For Append As #FileNum
```

The **Output** mode creates a new file and opens it for writing. The **Append** mode opens an existing file and prepares to append data values to the end of the file. The **Print#** and **Write#** statements both send individual data items to a file that is open in one of these two modes:

```
Print #FileNum, DataList
Write #FileNum, DataList
```

Print# sends the items as is, without delimiters. **Write#** encloses each string value in quotation marks and separates each data item from the next by a comma.

The **Close#** statement closes an open file:

```
Close #FileNum
```

The next statement in the **SalesDay_LostFocus** redisplays the validated input value in the text box:

```
SalesDay(Index).Text = CurVal
```

Together, these two assignment statements eliminate any nondigital characters from the user's input. In the case where the user enters **123 items**, the display will now be simply **123**. If the entry was **q1234**, this statement replaces the display with **0**.

Next the **LostFocus** procedure compares the text box entry with the value that was originally stored there. The previous value is recorded in the program's **WeekOnScreen** array. If the current value is not the same as the original value, the program copies the new value to **WeekOnScreen** and calls the **UpdateTotal** procedure to recompute the total and redraw the graph:

```
If CurVal <> WeekOnScreen(Index) Then
  WeekOnScreen(Index) = CurVal
  UpdateTotal
End If
```

When a new text box receives the focus, the **SalesDay_GotFocus** event procedure (also in Listing 6.8) highlights the entire text currently stored in the box. This operation, performed by changing the settings of the **SelStart** and **SelLength** properties, is designed to simplify subsequent data entry into the text box. Anything the user types replaces the current selection in the text box.

Reading Commands from the Keyboard

The third event procedure that applies to the **SalesDay** array is **Sales-Day_KeyDown**, shown in Listing 6.9. The **KeyDown** event—and its counterpart, the **KeyUp** event—monitor the keyboard for all keys the user presses; but these two events are especially useful for recognizing special keys such as editing and navigation keys. The *Sales Week* program uses **KeyDown** to give the user extra ways to make selections in the dialog box. In particular, the **SalesDay_KeyDown** procedure responds to four keys:

- The up arrow and down arrow keys, for moving the focus to the previous or the next text box in the **SalesDay** array.

- The PgUp and PgDn keys, for scrolling backward or forward to a new week of sales data.

Each of these keys has its own keyboard code number, as recorded in **Const** statements in the application's form-level declarations section:

```
Const PgDn = &H22
Const PgUp = &H21
Const Up = &H26
Const Down = &H28
```

The **KeyDown** event procedure passes an argument named **KeyCode**, which gives the keyboard code of the key that has been pressed. The **SalesDay_KeyDown** procedure uses a **Select Case** decision structure to respond to this key code:

```
Select Case KeyCode
```

For the up arrow and down arrow keys, the procedure uses the **SetFocus** method to move the focus to the previous or the next text box. If the current focus is on the first or the last text box, the procedure circles around to the opposite end of the column of boxes. For example, here is the response to the up arrow key:

```
Case Up
  If Index = 0 Then
    SalesDay(6).SetFocus
  Else
    SalesDay(Index - 1).SetFocus
  End If
```

For the PgUp and PgDn keys, the procedure changes the setting of the **ScrollWeek.Value** property, thus triggering a **Change** event for the vertical scroll bar:

```
Case PgUp
  ScrollWeek.Value = ScrollWeek.Min
```

The **ScrollWeek_Change** procedure (also shown in Listing 6.9) responds to a change in the setting of **ScrollWeek.Value**. (This change is usually caused when the user clicks the up or down arrow icon on the scroll bar, but as you've now seen, this can also be caused by a special call from the **SalesDay_KeyDown** procedure.) **ScrollWeek_Change**, in turn, calls either **Backward_Click** or **Forward_Click**, two of the event procedures designed for responding to menu selections.

Responding to Menu Commands

The rest of the routines in the code for the *Sales Week* application are event procedures for the menu commands. The procedures for the **File** menu appear in Listing 6.10. Listing 6.11 shows the **Week** menu procedures; Listings 6.12 and 6.13, the **Graph** menu; and Listing 6.14, the **Help** menu. Each of these procedures responds to the **Click** event that occurs when the user selects a menu command.

The **PrintSales_Click** procedure prints the *Sales Week* window, with the data and graph for the currently displayed week. Accomplishing this task is a simple matter of calling Visual Basic's **PrintForm** method, with the **SaleGrph** form as the object of the call:

```
SaleGrph.PrintForm
```

The **PrintSales_Click** procedure takes care of one additional detail. To avoid printing the vertical scroll graph inside the application window, the procedure temporarily toggles the setting of the **ScrollWeek.Visible** property to **False**. When the printing operation is complete, this property setting is switched back to **True**.

The **Quit_Click** procedure terminates the program performance when the user selects the **Exit** command from the **File** menu. Before doing so, however, the program calls the **SaveCurWeek** procedure to save to disk any new data in the currently displayed sales week.

The four event procedures for the **Week** menu are designed to display a newly selected week's data and graph on the screen. Each procedure makes an appropriate adjustment in the serial date stored in the **WeekRef&** variable, and then makes a call to **ShowWeek**.

The **OneWeek_Click** and **TenWeeks_Click** procedures adjust the **Checked** properties of the two menu commands, **OneWeek** and **Ten-Weeks**. Then each procedure makes a call to **UpdateTotal** to display the newly selected graph on the screen. You'll recall that **UpdateTotal** reads the settings of the two commands' **Checked** properties to decide which graph to create.

The **BeginPos_Click**, **EndPos_Click**, and **MidPos_Click** procedures also switch the **Checked** properties of the appropriate menu selections. Then each procedure assigns a new value to **BackWeeks**, the variable used to determine the current week's position in the ten-week graph. A call to **UpdateTotal** redraws the graph.

Finally, the two procedures that display help messages are named **Key-boardHelp_Click** and **GeneralHelp_Click**. Each one of these builds a help string and then calls Visual Basic's **MsgBox** procedure to display the message box on the screen. A call to **MsgBox** takes three arguments:

```
MsgBox MessageString, TypeCode, TitleString
```

The first argument is the string that will be displayed inside the message box. End-of-line markers (**Chr$**(13) + **Chr$**(10)) can be included explicitly in this string; otherwise, Visual Basic controls line wrapping in the message box. The second argument is a code number that selects from among the various message box icons available. (For example, an argument of 64 displays the *information* icon that you can see in Figures 6.11 and 6.12.) The third argument is the string that will appear in the title bar for the message box.

SUMMARY: INPUT AND OUTPUT IN VISUAL BASIC

The *Sales Week* application illustrates a number of techniques for accepting data and commands from the user:

- Reading the **Text** property of a text box.
- Monitoring **Click** events for commands in a menu system.
- Recognizing *shortcut* keys and *access* keys in a menu definition.
- Using the **KeyDown** (or **KeyUp**) event to read special keys from the keyboard.
- Monitoring the **Change** event for a scroll bar.

In addition, this application has many interesting examples of output techniques, including:

- Using text boxes for both output and input.
- Drawing graphs and displaying text in a picture box.
- Performing sequential-access file operations to save data to disk in a text file.
- Sending a form to the printer.

Input and output operations are central to every program, and programmers never stop experimenting with new techniques for simplifying and improving these procedures. You'll see many more examples of I/O operations in other applications presented in this book.

Listing 6.1 Declarations and the **Form_Load** procedure

```
' Declarations.

' The directory for weekly sales files.

Const PathName$ = "C:\SalesWk"

' Keyboard navigation keys.

Const PgDn = &H22
Const PgUp = &H21
Const Up = &H26
Const Down = &H28

' Serial number and file name for the current week.

Dim WeekRef&, FileName$

' Position of current week in trend graph.

Dim BackWeeks As Integer

' Arrays for current week's sales amounts.

Dim WeekOnDisk(6) As Single, WeekOnScreen(6) As Single


Sub Form_Load ()

  ' Initialize this week's serial number,
  ' and show the week's graph.

  SearchForPath
  WeekRef& = Int(Now)
  ShowWeek

  ' Initialize the position value
  ' for the trend graph.

  BackWeeks = 63

End Sub   ' Form_Load
```

Listing 6.2 The **ShowWeek** procedure

```
Sub ShowWeek ()

  ' Display the data for a new week.

  ' First save the data for the current week.

  SaveCurWeek

  ' Calculate the serial value for the first day
  ' of the week, and display the day captions.

  WeekStart& = WeekRef& - (Weekday(WeekRef&) - 1)
  For i% = 0 To 6
    WkDay(i%).Caption = Format$(WeekStart& + i%, "ddd m/d")
  Next i%

  ' Build the file name for the new week's data,
  ' and read the data from disk.

  FileName$ = PathName$ + "\" + Format$(WeekStart&, "mm-dd-yy") + ".SLS"
  ReadNewWeek

End Sub  ' ShowWeek
```

Listing 6.3 The **ReadNewWeek** procedure

```
Sub ReadNewWeek ()

  ' Read data from disk for the newly selected week.

  ' First check to see if the week's file exists yet.

  CannotRead = False
  On Error GoTo FileProblem
    Open FileName$ For Input As #1
  On Error GoTo 0

  ' If the file exists, read it and display individual
  ' data values in the SalesDay text boxes. Otherwise,
  ' display a value of zero in each box.

  For i% = 0 To 6
```

(continued)

```
      If CannotRead Then
        SalesDay(i%).Text = 0
      Else
        Input #1, SalesVal
        SalesDay(i%).Text = SalesVal
      End If
      WeekOnDisk(i%) = SalesDay(i%).Text
      WeekOnScreen(i%) = WeekOnDisk(i%)
    Next i%
    Close #1

    ' Update the total for the week.

    UpdateTotal
    Exit Sub

  ' Error trap to handle non-existent file.

  FileProblem:
    CannotRead = True
  Resume Next

  End Sub   ' ReadNewWeek
```

Listing 6.4 The **SaveCurWeek** procedure

```
Sub SaveCurWeek ()

  ' Save the revised data for the current week.

  ' First check to see if there is any new data to save.

  SomethingToSave% = False
  For i% = 0 To 6
    If WeekOnScreen(i%) <> WeekOnDisk(i%) Then SomethingToSave% = True
  Next i%

  ' If there is any new data, save the entire
  ' week's data as a sequential text file.

  If SomethingToSave% Then
    Open FileName$ For Output As #1
    For i% = 0 To 6
      Print #1, SalesDay(i%).Text
```

```
      WeekOnDisk(i%) = SalesDay(i%).Text
    Next i%
    Close #1
  End If

End Sub  ' SaveCurWeek
```

Listing 6.5 The **UpdateTotal** and **DrawAxes** procedures

```
Sub UpdateTotal ()

  ' Update the data total after new input.

  Total.Caption = 0
  For i% = 0 To 6
    Total.Caption = Total.Caption + WeekOnScreen(i%)
  Next i%

  ' Redraw the graph.

  DrawAxes
  If OneWeek.Checked Then
    DrawWeekGraph
  Else
    DrawTrendGraph
  End If

End Sub  ' UpdateTotal


Sub DrawAxes ()

  ' Draw the horizontal and vertical
  ' axes in the graph box.

  GraphBox.Cls
  GraphBox.DrawWidth = 2
  GraphBox.Line (20, 20)-(20, 90), 0
  GraphBox.Line (20, 90)-(90, 90), 0

End Sub  ' DrawAxes
```

Listing 6.6 The **DrawWeekGraph** procedure

```
Sub DrawWeekGraph ()

  ' Draw the graph for a single week's data.

  Const MaxHeight = 70
  Dim MaxDay, x%, y%, i%

  ' Find the largest single day's sales amount.

  MaxDay = WeekOnScreen(0)
  For i% = 1 To 6
    If WeekOnScreen(i%) > MaxDay Then MaxDay = WeekOnScreen(i%)
  Next i%

  ' Draw the seven bars of the graph.

  If MaxDay <> 0 Then
    For i% = 0 To 6
      x% = 22 + i% * 10
      y% = -(WeekOnScreen(i%) / MaxDay) * MaxHeight

      ' Display x-axis label.

      GraphBox.Line (x%, 90)-Step(8, y%), , BF
      GraphBox.CurrentX = x%
      GraphBox.CurrentY = 92
      GraphBox.Print Left$(WkDay(i%).Caption, 1);
    Next i%

    ' Display y-axis label and title.

    GraphBox.CurrentX = 1
    GraphBox.CurrentY = 18
    GraphBox.Print MaxDay;
    GraphBox.CurrentX = 25
    GraphBox.CurrentY = 7
    GraphBox.Print "The Week of"; Mid$(WkDay(0).Caption, 4);

  End If

End Sub   ' DrawWeekGraph
```

Listing 6.7 The **DrawTrendGraph** procedure

```
Sub DrawTrendGraph ()

  ' Draw the ten-week trend graph.

  Const MaxHeight = 70
  Dim CurWeekStart As Long, MaxTrendWeek
  Static TrendWeeks(9), WeekChar$(9)

  SaveCurWeek
  WeekStart& = WeekRef& - (Weekday(WeekRef&) - 1)
  MaxTrendWeek = 0
  For i% = 0 To 9

    ' Build the file name for each week's data.

    CurWeekStart = WeekStart& - (BackWeeks - (i% * 7))
    TrendFileName$ = PathName$ + "\" + Format$(CurWeekStart, "mm-dd-yy")
    TrendFileName$ = TrendFileName$ + ".SLS"

    ' Determine the x-axis label for the week.

    If CurWeekStart = WeekStart& Then
      WeekChar$(i%) = "^"
    ElseIf CurWeekStart < WeekStart& Then
      WeekChar$(i%) = Format$(i% + 1, "#")
    Else
      WeekChar$(i%) = Format$(i%, "#")
    End If

    ' Check to see if file exists.

    FileFound% = True
    On Error GoTo NoTrendFileName
      Open TrendFileName$ For Input As #1
    On Error GoTo 0

    ' Read the file and compute the total sales for the week.

    TrendWeeks(i%) = 0
    If FileFound% Then
      For j% = 1 To 7
        Input #1, dayVal
        TrendWeeks(i%) = TrendWeeks(i%) + dayVal
      Next j%
      Close #1
      If TrendWeeks(i%) > MaxTrendWeek Then MaxTrendWeek = TrendWeeks(i%)
    End If
  Next i%

  ' Draw the bar for each week.
```

(continued)

```
  If MaxTrendWeek <> 0 Then
    For i% = 0 To 9
      x% = 22 + i% * 7
      y% = -(TrendWeeks(i%) / MaxTrendWeek) * MaxHeight
      GraphBox.Line (x%, 90)-Step(5, y%), , BF
      GraphBox.CurrentX = x%
      GraphBox.CurrentY = 92
      GraphBox.Print WeekChar$(i%);
    Next i%

    ' Display the y-axis label and the title.

    GraphBox.CurrentX = 1
    GraphBox.CurrentY = 18
    GraphBox.Print MaxTrendWeek;
    GraphBox.CurrentX = 28
    GraphBox.CurrentY = 7
    GraphBox.Print "Ten-Week Trend";
  End If
  Exit Sub

' The error trap for a non-existent file.

NoTrendFileName:
  FileFound% = False
Resume Next

End Sub   ' DrawTrendGraph
```

Listing 6.8 The **SalesDay_LostFocus** and **SalesDay_GotFocus** procedures

```
Sub SalesDay_LostFocus (Index As Integer)

  ' Read a new daily sales figure from a text box.

  Dim CurVal

  ' Read and validate the input value.

  CurVal = Val(SalesDay(Index).Text)

  ' Eliminate any invalid characters from the display.

  SalesDay(Index).Text = CurVal

  ' Update the graph only if this is a new input value.
```

```
   If CurVal <> WeekOnScreen(Index) Then
     WeekOnScreen(Index) = CurVal
     UpdateTotal
   End If

End Sub


Sub SalesDay_GotFocus (Index As Integer)

  ' Extend the highlight over the entire text
  ' entry when the user selects an input box.

  SalesDay(Index).SelStart = 0
  SalesDay(Index).SelLength = Len(SalesDay(Index).Text)

End Sub  ' SalesDay_GotFocus
```

Listing 6.9 The **SalesDay_KeyDown** and **ScrollWeek_Change** procedures

```
Sub SalesDay_KeyDown (Index As Integer, KeyCode As Integer, Shift As
Integer)

  ' Respond to navigation keys for selecting the daily
  ' values in a week's data, and for scrolling through weeks.

  Select Case KeyCode

    ' Scroll back to the previous week.

    Case PgUp
      ScrollWeek.Value = ScrollWeek.Min

    ' Scroll forward to the next week.

    Case PgDn
      ScrollWeek.Value = ScrollWeek.Max

    ' Select the previous day's text box.

    Case Up
      If Index = 0 Then
        SalesDay(6).SetFocus
      Else
        SalesDay(Index - 1).SetFocus
      End If
```

(continued)

```
      ' Select the next day's text box.

    Case Down
      If Index = 6 Then
        SalesDay(0).SetFocus
      Else
        SalesDay(Index + 1).SetFocus
      End If
  End Select

End Sub  ' SalesDay_KeyDown



Sub ScrollWeek_Change ()

  ' Scroll backward or forward to a new week.

  ' ScrollWeek.Min (0) is the setting for an
  ' up-arrow click, and ScrollWeek.Max (2) is
  ' the setting for a down-arrow click. The
  ' neutral ScrollWeek.Value setting is 1.

  If ScrollWeek.Value = ScrollWeek.Min Then
    Backward_Click
  ElseIf ScrollWeek.Value = ScrollWeek.Max Then
    Forward_Click
  End If

  ' Reset the ScrollWeek value.

  If ScrollWeek.Value <> 1 Then
    ScrollWeek.Value = 1
    SalesDay(0).SetFocus
  End If

End Sub  ' ScrollWeek_Change
```

Listing 6.10 The **PrintSales_Click** and **Quit_Click** procedures

```
Sub PrintSales_Click ()

  ' Print the current week's data and graph.
  ' (Temporarily make the ScrollWeek control invisible.)

  ScrollWeek.Visible = False
  SaleGrph.PrintForm
```

```
   ScrollWeek.Visible = True

End Sub  ' PrintSales_Click


Sub Quit_Click ()

   ' Exit from the program, but save the
   ' current week's data first.

   SaveCurWeek
   End

End Sub  ' Quit_Click
```

Listing 6.11 Event procedures for the **Week** menu commands

```
Sub ThisWeek_Click ()

   ' Display the current week's data and graph.

   WeekRef& = Int(Now)
   ShowWeek

End Sub  ' ThisWeek_Click


Sub LastWeek_Click ()

   ' Display last week's data and graph.

   WeekRef& = Int(Now) - 7
   ShowWeek

End Sub  ' LastWeek_Click


Sub Backward_Click ()

   ' Scroll back to the previous week.
```

(continued)

```
   WeekRef& = WeekRef& - 7
   ShowWeek

End Sub  ' Backward_Click


Sub Forward_Click ()

  ' Move forward by one week.

   WeekRef& = WeekRef& + 7
   ShowWeek

End Sub  ' Forward_Click
```

Listing 6.12 The event procedures for the **Graph** menu

```
Sub OneWeek_Click ()

  ' Display the graph for one week's data.

   OneWeek.Checked = True
   TenWeeks.Checked = False
   UpdateTotal

End Sub  ' OneWeek_Click



Sub TenWeeks_Click ()

  ' Switch to the ten-week trend graph.

   TenWeeks.Checked = True
   OneWeek.Checked = False
   UpdateTotal

End Sub  ' TenWeeks_Click
```

Listing 6.13 The event procedures for the **Position** options

```
Sub BeginPos_Click ()

  ' Establish new setting for Position submenu.

  BeginPos.Checked = True
  MidPos.Checked = False
  EndPos.Checked = False

  ' Assign correct number of days to the
  ' global variable BackWeeks.

  BackWeeks = 0

  ' Redisplay graph to show new position.

  If TenWeeks.Checked Then UpdateTotal

End Sub  ' BeginPos_Click


Sub EndPos_Click ()

  ' Establish new setting for Position submenu.

  EndPos.Checked = True
  MidPos.Checked = False
  BeginPos.Checked = False

  ' Assign correct number of days to the
  ' global variable BackWeeks.

  BackWeeks = 63

  ' Redisplay graph to show new position.

  If TenWeeks.Checked Then UpdateTotal

End Sub  ' EndPos_Click
```

(continued)

```
Sub MidPos_Click ()

  ' Establish new setting for Position submenu.

  MidPos.Checked = True
  BeginPos.Checked = False
  EndPos.Checked = False

  ' Assign correct number of days to the
  ' global variable BackWeeks.

  BackWeeks = 28

  ' Redisplay graph to show new position.

  If TenWeeks.Checked Then UpdateTotal

End Sub   ' MidPos_Click
```

Listing 6.14 The event procedures for the **Help** menu

```
Sub GeneralHelp_Click ()

  ' Display a message box with general help.

  Help$ = "The Sales Week application maintains a database of daily "
  Help$ = Help$ + "and weekly sales data, and displays the numbers "
  Help$ = Help$ + "along with a graph for any week you select. You "
  Help$ = Help$ + "can view a one-week graph or a trend graph showing "
  Help$ = Help$ + "the total weekly sales for a ten-week period."

  MsgBox Help$, 64, "About Sales Week"

End Sub   ' GeneralHelp_Click



Sub KeyboardHelp_Click ()

  ' Display a message box with keyboard help.

  Dim HelpMsg$

  CrLf$ = Chr$(13) + Chr$(10)
  HelpMsg$ = "  F1  Help" + CrLf$ + CrLf$
```

```
   HelpMsg$ = HelpMsg$ + "  Trend graph" + CrLf$
   HelpMsg$ = HelpMsg$ + "  positions:" + CrLf$ + CrLf$
   HelpMsg$ = HelpMsg$ + "  F2  Beginning" + CrLf$
   HelpMsg$ = HelpMsg$ + "  F3  Middle" + CrLf$
   HelpMsg$ = HelpMsg$ + "  F4  End" + CrLf$ + CrLf$

   HelpMsg$ = HelpMsg$ + "  Selections:" + CrLf$ + CrLf$
   HelpMsg$ = HelpMsg$ + "  F5  This week" + CrLf$
   HelpMsg$ = HelpMsg$ + "  F6  Last week" + CrLf$
   HelpMsg$ = HelpMsg$ + "  F7  Week graph" + CrLf$
   HelpMsg$ = HelpMsg$ + "  F8  Trend graph" + CrLf$ + CrLf$

   HelpMsg$ = HelpMsg$ + "  PgUp  Previous week" + CrLf$
   HelpMsg$ = HelpMsg$ + "  PgDn  Next week" + CrLf$ + CrLf$

   HelpMsg$ = HelpMsg$ + "  Ctrl-P  Print" + CrLf$
   HelpMsg$ = HelpMsg$ + "  Ctrl-X  Exit"

   MsgBox HelpMsg$, 64, "Keyboard Help"

End Sub  '  KeyboardHelp_Click
```

Listing 6.15 The **SearchForPath** procedure

```
Sub SearchForPath ()

  ' Search for the directory in which weekly sales files
  ' are to be stored. Create the directory (on drive C)
  ' if it does not exist yet.

  ' Note: PathName$ is declared at the declarations-level
  ' of the SaleGrph form.

  Dim CDir$

  ' Record the current directory.
  CDir$ = CurDir$("C")

  ' Set up an error-handling mode.
  On Error Resume Next

  ' Attempt to change to the target directory.
  ChDir PathName$

  ' If the directory doesn't exist, create it.
```

(continued)

```
    MkDir PathName$

    ' Restore the original directory
    ChDir CDir$

End Sub   ' SearchForPath
```

7

Data Structures and Control Arrays: The Address File Application

INTRODUCTION

A *data array* is an efficient way to organize multiple data items under one variable name. Likewise, a *control array* simplifies your work with certain groups of Visual Basic controls on a form. Although data arrays and control arrays are not identical in usage, the two structures are parallel in concept. In both cases, you refer to an individual array element by its indexed position in the array. The index appears as an integer in parentheses after the array name:

```
DataArray(Index)
ControlArray(Index)
```

A **For** loop is useful for focusing successively on the individual elements of a data array or a control array. The loop's control variable serves as the index into the array.

You have seen examples of data arrays and control arrays—and the **For** loops that process them—in earlier chapters. For example, the *Sales Week* application uses an array of text boxes to display sales information on the screen and a pair of data arrays to store the same values in memory. Significantly, each of the arrays in the *Sales Week* program has a fixed length of seven elements, representing the seven days of the week. Fixed length, or *static*, arrays are ideal in any context where the dimensions of the data are known in advance.

In contrast, data arrays and control arrays both can be used *dynamically* in Visual Basic—as structures that increase or decrease in length during run time. For data arrays, this means that you can design a structure to store any group of data items, even if you do not know how many items there will ultimately be. You create a dynamic array by declaring its name, but not its length, in an initial **Dim** statement. A pair of empty parentheses after the array name indicates that the size of the array will be defined later:

```
Dim DataArray()
```

Then, inside a procedure that uses the array, you use the **ReDim** statement to define the necessary length for the array:

```
ReDim DataArray(NewLength)
```

ReDim is an executable statement that allocates space during run time for an array of the indicated length. A dynamic array can be resized any number of times during a program performance. By default, **ReDim** also *reinitializes* the values of an array, setting numeric array elements to 0 and string elements to empty strings. Alternatively, you can use the **ReDim Preserve** statement to save the data in an array from one resizing to the next.

A comparable dynamic quality in control arrays allows you to create and display entirely new controls *at run time* in response to specific events that occur during program execution. As you know, you normally create a control array at design time by giving the same **Name** setting to a group of controls. When you do so, Visual Basic automatically assigns a sequential **Index** setting to each control you add to the array.

To create a control array whose length will change during run time, you can begin by placing a single control on a form at design time. You then assign a numeric setting to the control's **Index** property, thus defining the control explicitly as an element of an array. Given this initial control, your program uses a special Visual Basic statement named **Load** to create new elements of the control array at run time. The **Load** statement takes as its argument the name and index number of a control element that will be created:

```
Load ControlArray(NewIndex)
```

As a result of the **Load** statement, a new control element, numbered **NewIndex**, is added to the array.

Try the following brief experiment to see how controls can be created at run time:

1. In the design mode, place a single option button on an empty form.

2. Assign the button a **Name** setting of **OptionButton**, an **Index** setting of **0**, **Width** and **Height** settings of **1215** and **375**, **Left** and **Top** settings of **960** and **120**, and a **Caption** setting of **0**.

3. Enter the following lines of code into the form's **Form_Load** procedure:

```
Sub Form_Load ()
  For i% = 1 To 10
    Load OptionButton(i%)
    OptionButton(i%).Visible = True
    OptionButton(i%).Height = 375
    OptionButton(i%).Width = 1215
    OptionButton(i%).Left = 960
    OptionButton(i%).Top = 120 + i% * 375
    OptionButton(i%).Caption = i%
  Next i%
End Sub
```

4. Press F5 to run the program. The resulting form displays an array of eleven option buttons, as shown in Figure 7.1.

Only the first of these eleven option buttons was created at design time. The remaining ten were placed on the screen by the **Load** statement, performed repeatedly by a **For** loop in the **Form_Load** procedure. After creating each control, the **Form_Load** procedure also establishes the new control's properties.

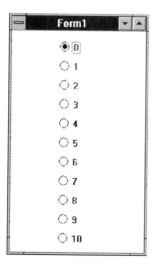

Figure 7.1 Controls created at run time

Now pull down the **Run** menu and choose the **End** command. Back in the design mode, you'll see that the form contains only the one control that you originally placed on it. The **Load** statement affects only the run-time contents of the form. (You can now close this experimental program without saving it.)

As you'll see shortly, you can use **Load** to expand the options provided in an application.

THE *ADDRESS FILE* APPLICATION

This chapter's *Address File* application illustrates control arrays and data arrays that change size during program execution. The application is a menu-driven database program, designed to manage a personal or business address file stored on disk. You can use this program to:

- Add new addresses to your file.
- Retrieve and view the address and phone number for any person you have already entered into the file.
- Revise or update existing addresses.
- Print envelopes.

To search for specific records, the program uses an alphabetized index list—similar in many ways to the index at the end of a book—to keep track of the location of each address in the database. Because the database and its index can increase in size whenever you run the application, this list is stored in memory as a dynamic data array. Each time you add a new record to the database, the program resizes the index array to accommodate the new database length.

The *Address File* application also contains an important example of a control array. The program displays an array of option buttons named **Title** from which you can choose an appropriate title for the person in an address record. Initially, the array offers a list of five titles: *Mr., Ms., Mrs., Miss,* and *Dr.*; but the program allows you to add more titles to this list to meet the requirements of your own address database. For example, you might add option buttons for new titles such as *The Honorable* for writing to representatives in Congress, *Professor* or *Dean* for academic correspondence, and *The Reverend* or *Rabbi* for religious leaders. Each time you add an entry to this list, the *Address File* program increases the length of the **Title** array.

In addition to its data arrays and control array, the program also illustrates another type of data structure: the user-defined type, also known as the *record* type. A record is a variable that represents multiple data *fields*—values that may belong to different data types. **Review Box 7.1** describes Visual Basic's user-defined record type. A record structure is a particularly effective way to organize information in a database management program like the *Address File* application. (Chapter 8 gives a more detailed look at the file techniques associated with database management.)

Data arrays, control arrays, and data records—these structures are the focus of your work in this chapter. Begin now by loading the *Address File* application from the exercise disk. The name of the project file is AD-DRESS.MAK. Use the **Open Project** command in Visual Basic's **File** menu to open the application, then press F5 or click the Run tool on Visual Basic's Toolbar to begin a performance.

Running the Program

The *Address File* application offers simple keyboard techniques for saving, retrieving, and printing addresses. When you first run the program, an input form appears on the screen with eight empty text boxes labeled *First Name, Last Name, Company Name, Address, City, State, Zip Code*, and *Phone Number*. To the left of these text boxes is a vertical group of option buttons labeled *Mr., Ms., Mrs., Miss*, and *Dr.* You create an address record by entering information into the text boxes and clicking one of the option buttons with the mouse.

A complete sample entry appears in Figure 7.2. When you complete an address entry like this one and you are ready to store the record, a single keystroke instructs the program to write the address to the database file: *Press the F2 function key to save the current address entry.* The program saves the address, creates a new entry in the index, and leaves the address displayed in the input form.

You can leave some of the text boxes blank and still save a record to the database. All the fields of the address record are optional except for *First Name* and *Last Name,* the two fields that the program uses for identifying a record in the index to the database. Normally, you'll fill most of the text boxes with information, but in some cases you might omit a field such as *Company Name* or *Phone Number.* You can also leave all the option buttons unselected.

After saving an address, you may want to clear the input form so you can enter a new address or view an address already stored in the database. Again, the action takes a single keystroke: *Press F3 to clear the current address entry from the input form.* The focus returns to the *First Name* text box, where you can begin a new entry.

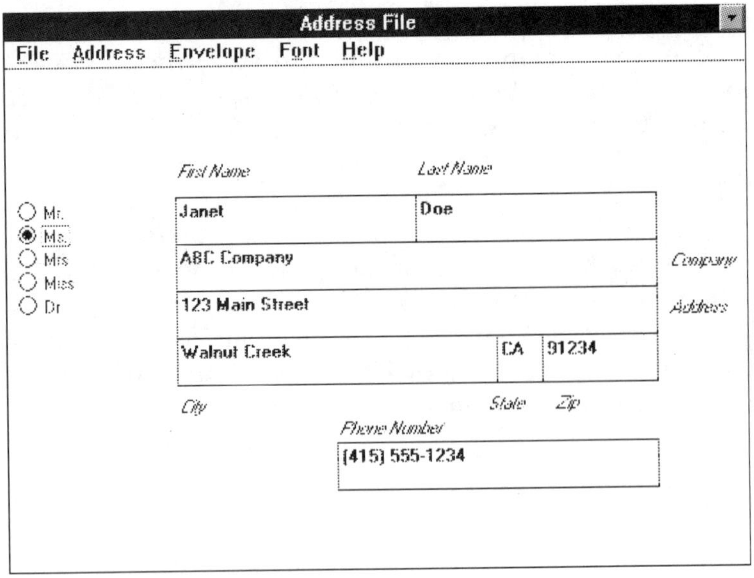

Figure 7.2 An address entry

Searching for and viewing an existing address is a two-step process. First you enter the full name—*First Name* and *Last Name*—of the person whose address you want to retrieve. Then you press the key that requests a record search: *Press **F4** to retrieve an address.* In response, the program looks up the name in the index. The index in turn supplies the location of the address in the database. Given this location, the program reads the address and displays the complete record in the form. On the other hand, if the program cannot find the name entry in the index, a message box appears on the screen (Figure 7.3). When this happens, you should check the spelling of the name you have entered. If the spelling is correct, you can assume that there is not yet an address recorded for this person. (Alphabetic case is not significant in a record search; you can enter a name in any combination of uppercase or lowercase letters.)

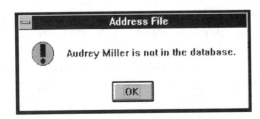

Figure 7.3 An unsuccessful record search

Figure 7.4 Updating an existing address record

Once you have retrieved an address record from the database, you can make revisions in the address and phone number and then save the revised address back to the database. Again, you simply press the F2 function key to save the address. In this case, the program recognizes that you are revising an existing record and asks you to confirm the *save* operation. Figure 7.4 shows the message box that appears on the screen. Click the **Yes** button to update the address record or click **No** to cancel the operation.

Before you print an envelope for a given address, you may want to create a record of your return address. To do so, you clear the input form (F3) and enter your name and address. Then you instruct the program to record the entry as the return address: *Press **Ctrl+R** to save the current address entry as the return address.* The program stores the return address in a separate file on disk. Once you have saved a return address, the program includes it on all envelopes that you print. You can view the recorded return address at any time: *Press **F8** to view the return address.* In response, the program displays a message box like the one in Figure 7.5. To change the return address, simply enter a new address in the input form and press Ctrl+R again. If you want to omit the return address from a printed envelope, save a blank address entry as the return address: Press F3 to clear the input form and then Ctrl+R to save the return address.

Figure 7.5 Viewing the return address

```
Mr. Jack Smith
XYZ Corp.
888 Maple Drive
St. Louis, MO


                        Ms. Janet Doe
                        ABC Company
                        123 Main Street
                        Walnut Creek, CA 91234
```

Figure 7.6 A printed envelope

The *Address File* application offers three groups of options for printing envelopes: font, orientation, and envelope size. By default, the program is set up to do *landscape*-oriented printing in a fixed-space font on a business-size envelope. (Under these default options, the program generates printer code commands that work on an HP LaserJet or compatible.) To print an envelope, you begin by retrieving an existing address or entering a new address; then feed the envelope into the printer and instruct the program to begin printing: *Press Ctrl+E to print an envelope.* Figure 7.6 shows an example of the result.

The program's **Envelope** and **Font** menus provide other options for printing envelopes. In addition, the menu system supplies alternate ways of performing the program's other operations.

The Menu System

The **File** menu (Figure 7.7) and the **Address** menu (Figure 7.8) contain the commands for the program features you've seen up to now. The **File** menu has commands for saving an address to the database, clearing an address from the input form, and printing an envelope. The menu's final command is **Exit**, which terminates the program. (You also can press Ctrl+X from the keyboard to end the program performance.) The **Address** menu includes commands for retrieving an address from the database, for saving and viewing the return address, and for adding a new title to the list of option buttons displayed at the left side of the form.

The **Envelope** menu (Figure 7.9) offers three envelope-size settings, described as **Business**, **Home**, and **Personal**. There are also two orientation settings. For feeding envelopes sideways into a laser printer, use the default

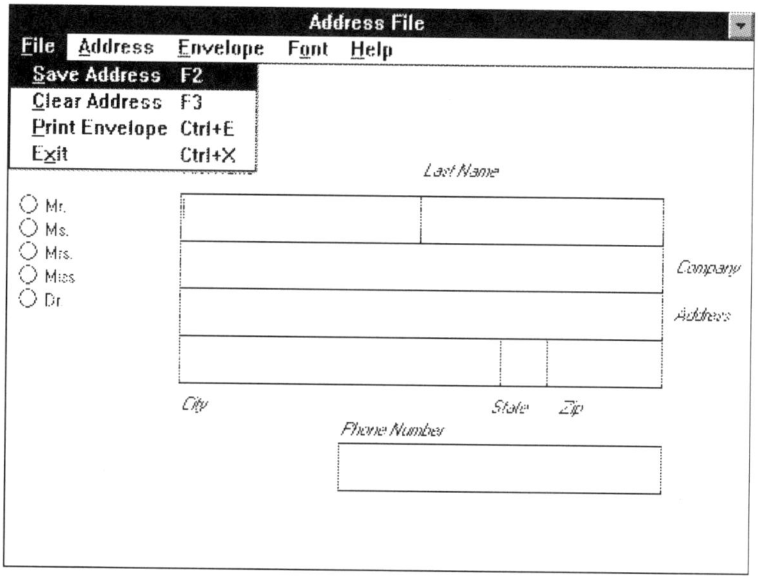

Figure 7.7 The **File** menu

Landscape Orientation setting; for tractor-fed envelopes on other kinds of printers, use the **Portrait Orientation**. (The program's code, which you'll examine later in this chapter, illustrates two completely different printing

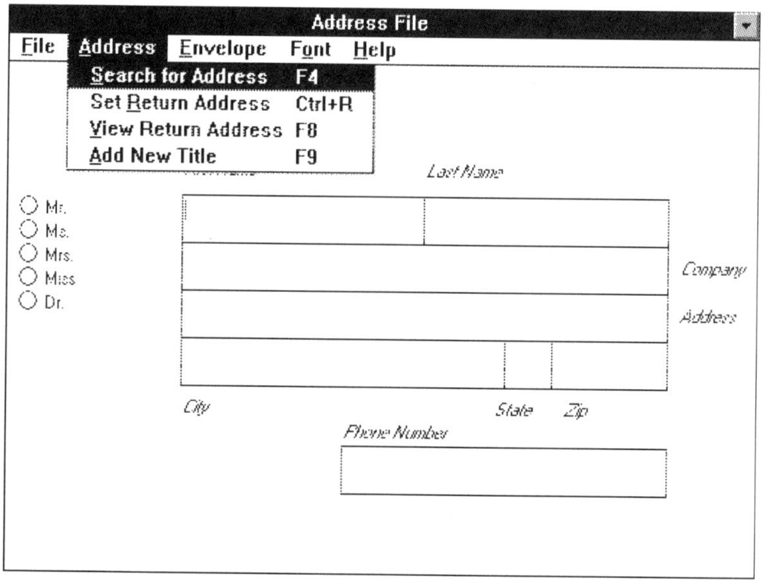

Figure 7.8 The **Address** menu

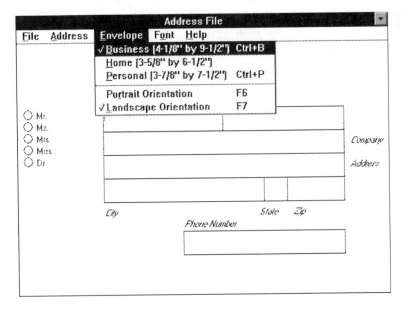

Figure 7.9 The **Envelope** menu

techniques corresponding to these two options. You may want to revise parts of the code to take advantage of the features of your own printer.) The **Font** menu contains two options (Figure 7.10), **Fixed-Space Font** and

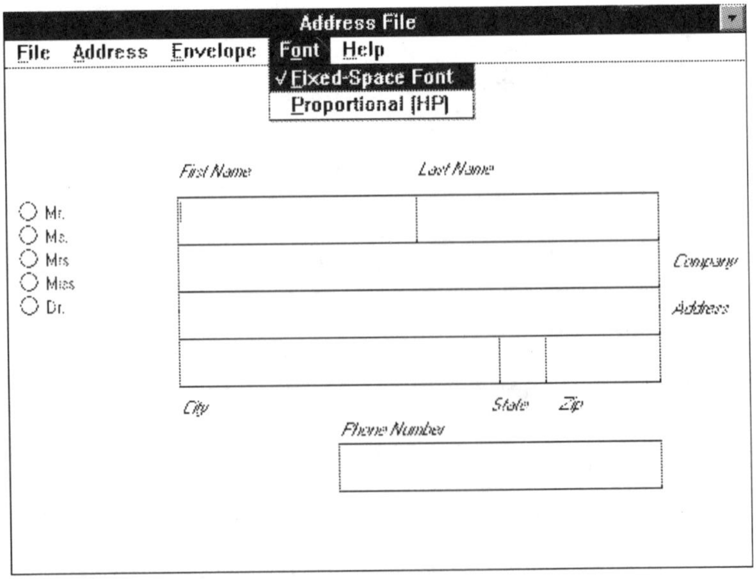

Figure 7.10 The **Font** menu

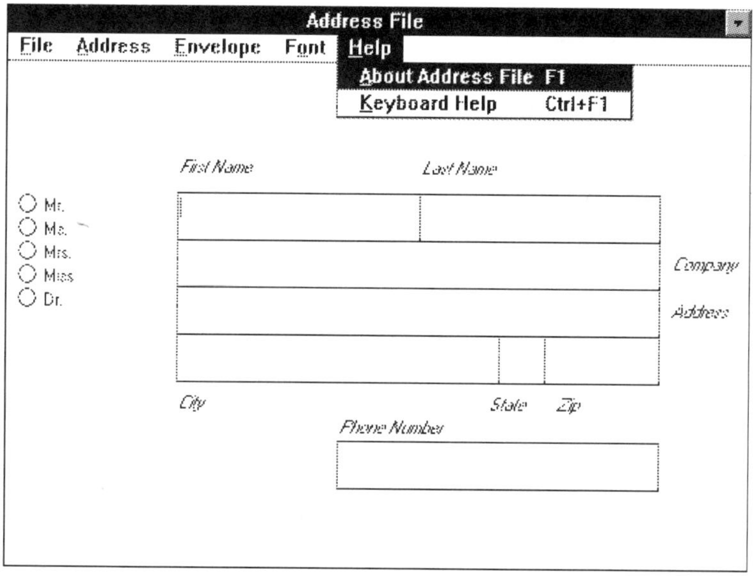

Figure 7.11 The **Help** menu

Proportional. The second of these two options is dimmed if you choose the **Portrait Orientation** option in the **Envelope** menu.

Finally, the **Help** menu (Figure 7.11) has two commands. The first, **About Address File**, gives a brief description of the program. The second, **Keyboard Help**, displays a message box (Figure 7.12) with a list of the special keys you use for the program's operations.

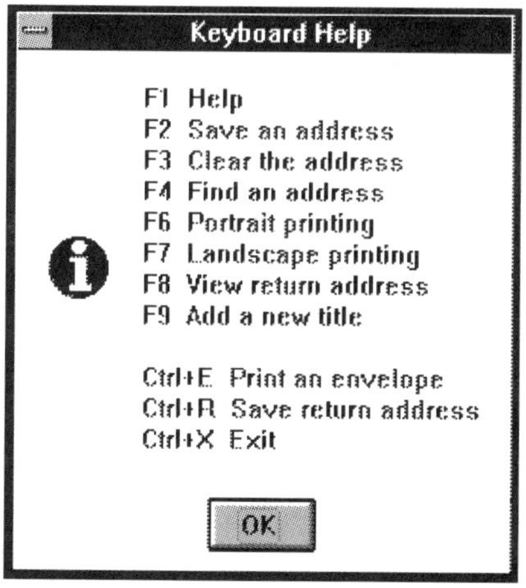

Figure 7.12 The **Keyboard Help** message box

Figure 7.13 The Add a Title dialog box

Adding a Title

The program provides a special dialog box for adding a new title to the list of option buttons. *To add a new title, press the **F9** function key.* The dialog box shown in Figure 7.13 appears on the screen. Enter a new title in the text box at the bottom of the dialog box and then click the **OK** button. In response, the program adds the new title to the bottom of the list of option buttons. For example, in Figure 7.14 an option button has been added for the title *Mr. and Mrs.* Once you add a new title, you can select it as the option for any new or existing address record.

The program allows you to add as many as ten new titles to the list. In addition, you can add the special option *(none)* to the list if your address database includes records from which you want to remove the title. To add the *(none)* option, press F9 and enter any part of the label "(none)" into the text box—for example, enter **none**, or **no**, or simply **n**. When you later select this option for a given record, the program prints the record without a title.

The complete list of titles becomes a permanent part of your customized address database: The titles that you add to the list reappear in the *Address File* form each time you restart the program.

The Filing System for the Address Database

The *Address File* application creates and works with four files, all stored in the root directory of drive C. The main database, named ADDRESS.DAT, is opened as a *random-access* file. This means that the program can read any individual record directly from the file—or rewrite any record to the file—if the correct record number is available. For example, to read the

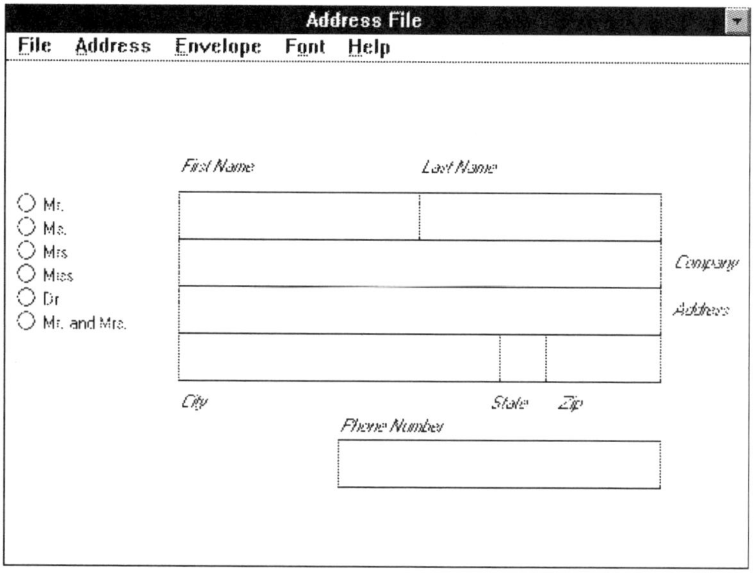

Figure 7.14 Adding a new title option

tenth record in the file, the program does *not* first have to read through the first nine records; rather, the program can go directly to the tenth record position and read the address information.

The purpose of the index array is to supply the program with the record number for any address stored in the database. The index file, ADDRESS.NDX, contains a list of the names from the database, along with the corresponding record numbers. Each time you store a new address record in the database, the program also appends another index line to the end of ADDRESS.NDX. Here is how the index might appear after you have stored a dozen addresses in your database file:

```
"MATSEN ELIZA",1
"HARRIS JOHN",2
"CLARK MARY",3
"WU NANCY",4
"ANDERSON SHEILA", 5
"DOE JANET",6
"BARTON RUDY",7
"JOHNSON DIANE",8
"SANDBERG TOM",9
"PETERSON SALLY",10
"VAN DYKE MARTHA",11
"SANCHEZ JACK",12
```

Each line consists of a string and an integer. The string gives the last name and first name entries from a record in the database, and the integer represents the record number. Notice that the index is not stored on disk in alphabetical order. The program alphabetizes the index in memory at the beginning of a run, and then realphabetizes the list each time a new name is added. Given this alphabetized list, the program uses an efficient search technique for finding a particular name whenever you press the F2 key. If the name is found in the index list, the program then reads the entire address directly from the specified record location in the database.

The file named ADDRESS.RTN stores your return address. Here is an example:

```
Mr. Jack Smith
XYZ Corp.
888 Maple Drive
St. Louis, MO 63123
```

This file contains three or four lines of text, depending on whether your return address includes a company name. The program rewrites the file whenever you record a new return address. When you print an envelope, the program reads the text of the return address directly from this file and prints it in the upper-left corner of the envelope.

Finally, the program creates a file named ADDRESS.TTL to save any new titles you add to the list of option buttons. This text file contains a line for each title you include in the list; for example:

```
Mr. and Mrs.
Madame
The Honorable
Professor
Dean
The Reverend
Rabbi
```

The program looks for this file each time you start the application. If the file exists, the program adds each title in the file to the list of option buttons in the **Title** array.

THE ELEMENTS OF THE *ADDRESS FILE* PROGRAM

The *Address File* project consists of a single form, plus a code module containing global declarations. The form is stored on disk as INADDR.FRM and the code module is ADDRGLOB.BAS. The form contains a small variety of controls: eight text boxes, eight descriptive labels, and an array of option buttons.

The events in the program are primarily **Click** events for the menu commands. The program recognizes keyboard commands—such as F2, F4, or Ctrl+E—thanks to the shortcut keys defined for the menu system. Before examining the code, take a brief look at the application's controls and menu definition.

Controls, Properties, and Menus

The application's eight text boxes have predictable **Name** settings: **FirstName**, **LastName**, **Company**, **Address**, **City**, **State**, **Zip**, and **Phone**. Their **Text** settings all start out as empty strings. In addition, each text box has a **MaxLength** property setting that matches the defined length of the corresponding field in the address database; this setting prevents the user from typing name and address entries that are longer than the database itself can store.

The group of option buttons located at the left of the text boxes is defined as a control array named **Title**. The initial five controls in the array have **Index** numbers from **0** to **4**.

The program's menu definition includes five menu lists. The **Envelope** menu illustrates the use of a *separator bar*—a line that separates two groups of commands in the menu. Refer back to Figure 7.9 to see what this line looks like in the menu display. It separates the three commands related to envelope size, **Business**, **Home**, and **Personal**, from the two printer orientation commands, **Portrait** and **Landscape**.

Figure 7.15 shows how the separator bar is created in the Menu Design Window. A **Caption** entry consisting of a single hyphen character instructs Visual Basic to insert the separator bar in the menu. Like all other menu entries, the separator bar has its own **Name** setting.

Events

Three categories of events occur in the *Address File* application:

- As usual, the **Form_Load** event is the first to take place. The program's **Form_Load** procedure performs a series of initializations and other start-up tasks.

- A **GotFocus** event occurs each time the user selects one of the text boxes. As you have seen in other applications, each **GotFocus** procedure in the program arranges to highlight the contents of the text box that has received the focus.

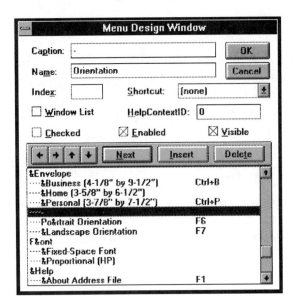

Figure 7.15 The separator bar for the *Envelope* menu

- Finally, a **Click** event occurs whenever you select a command or an option from one of the program's menus. Keep in mind that the same **Click** event is triggered by any keyboard or mouse technique that you use to invoke a particular menu command. For example, any one of these operations results in a call to the event procedure named **PrintEnv_Click:** Pressing the shortcut key Ctrl+E, typing the sequence of access keys Alt+F+P, or clicking the **Print Envelope** command with the mouse.

Procedures and Methods

The complete code for the *Address File* application is shown in Listings 7.1 to 7.20. As you examine the code, you'll concentrate on three main programming topics:

1. Creating and managing dynamic data arrays.

2. Using a control array to customize the application's options.

3. Sending data and commands to the printer.

The program contains about three dozen event procedures and general procedures. The following section guides you through a first brief look at the code.

An Overview of the Code

The program's central data structures are a record variable and an array of records. As explained in **Review Box 7.1**, record types can be defined only in a code module. Accordingly, this program's **AddrGlob** module (Listing 7.1) defines two record types. The first, **AddrRecType**, outlines the structure of a database record:

```
Type AddrRecType
  TitleField As Integer
  FirstField As String * 20
  LastField As String * 20
  CoField As String * 50
  AddrField As String * 50
  City Field as String * 30
  StateField As String * 2
  ZipField As String * 10
  PhoneField As String * 30
End Type
```

The second, **IndexType**, represents an element of the index array:

```
Type IndexType
  FullName As String * 41
  RecNum As Integer
End Type
```

In the form-level declaration section (also Listing 7.1), two variables are created from these record types. The record variable named **AddrRec** is defined to store the current address record throughout the program performance:

```
Dim AddrRec As AddrRecType
```

And the dynamic array of records named **AddrIndex** represents the database index:

```
Dim AddrIndex() As IndexType
```

Notice that the length of the index array is not specified at this point.

The **Form_Load** procedure (Listing 7.2) opens the address database file and computes the number of records currently in the database. This number is stored in the global variable **AddrCount**. Assuming **AddrCount** is greater than 0, the program calls a general procedure named **ReadIndex** (Listing 7.3) to read the index file into memory.

Review Box 7.1

Record Structures

A *user-defined type* is a compound structure representing multiple data *fields*. Programmers sometimes refer to a this data type as a *record structure*. Two steps are necessary for defining a record variable. The first is to write a **Type** definition that outlines the field structure of the record type. The second component is a **Dim** statement that declares a variable belonging to the defined record type.

In Visual Basic, **Type** statements appear only in code modules. The statement supplies a name for the user-defined type, followed by a list of field definitions:

```
Type RecordTypeName
   FieldName1 As type
   FieldName2 As type
   FieldName3 As type

   ' ...
End Type
```

Each field definition consists of a field name followed by an **As** clause giving the field's data type. The *type* specification can be any of Visual Basic's **Variant**, numeric, or string data types, or even a previously defined record type. Visual Basic permits both fixed-length and variable-length strings as field types, but you should use only fixed-length strings in a record destined for random-access data file programming. Visual Basic 2.0 and 3.0 also allow static arrays as fields.

The **Dim** statement for a record variable may appear in the declaration section of a form or module or in a procedure, depending on the scope you want to establish for the variable. To declare a variable representing a single record, the **Dim** syntax is:

```
Dim VariableName As RecordTypeName
```

Subsequent action depends on the user's activities and commands. For example, the user might begin by entering a new record in the input form and pressing F2 for a *save* operation. In response, the **SaveAddr_Click** procedure (Listing 7.4) saves the new record to the database file, first

---

Review Box 7.1 *(continued)*

You can also define an array of records, in which each array element represents a separate record. In this case, the **Dim** syntax is:

```
Dim ArrayName(length) As RecordTypeName
```

for a static one-dimensional array, or:

```
Dim ArrayName() As RecordTypeName
```

for a dynamic array of records.

Visual Basic recognizes a special format for references to individual fields in a record variable. In this format, the record variable name is followed by a period and then the field name:

```
VariableName.FieldName
```

The format for a record element in an array of records is only slightly more complicated:

```
ArrayName(Index).FieldName
```

In both cases, this field reference can be used in any statement that normally takes a simple variable name. For example, the following assignment statement stores a value in a field:

```
AddrRec.CityField = "Dakar"
```

It is easy to confuse field references with Visual Basic property references. For this reason, you should try to name records and fields in a way that clearly identifies their structural roles:

```
City.Text = AddrRec.CityField
```

---

checking to make sure that the target name does not already exist in the database. After storing a new address record, the program also adds the current name to the index list. The **SortAddrIndex** procedure (Listing 7.6) realphabetizes the list.

When the user enters a name and presses F4 to retrieve the corresponding address record, the **SearchAddr_Click** procedure (Listing 7.5) reads the record from the database. This procedure in turn uses a function named **SearchIndex%** (Listing 7.6) to search efficiently through the index list for the target name.

Three procedures are in charge of saving and displaying the user's return address. The **SetRtnAddr_Click** procedure (Listing 7.8) writes the address to a text file on disk. The **ViewRtnAddr_Click** procedure (Listing 7.9) displays the address in a message box when the user presses F8. **ReadReturnAddr** (Listing 7.10) reads the address from disk and stores it in a special string array in memory, where it is available whenever the user wants to print an envelope.

A variety of simple **Click** procedures respond to the user's other menu choices. For example, **ClearAddr_Click** (Listing 7.12) blanks out all the text boxes in the input form when the user presses F3. **GeneralHelp_Click** and **KeyHelp_Click** (Listing 7.14) supply help messages if the user selects a command from the **Help** menu. The **Landscape_Click** and **Portrait_Click** procedures (Listing 7.15) make the appropriate selections in the menu system when the user selects one of the two orientation options from the **Envelope** menu. Likewise, **FixedFont_Click** and **PropFont_Click** (Listing 7.16) are in charge of adjusting the settings for fixed- or proportional-font printing.

The program's most detailed procedures are the ones that print envelopes. The **PrintEnv_Click** procedure (Listing 7.17) chooses between two different approaches for printing, depending upon currently selected menu options. **PrintLandscapeEnv** (Listing 7.19) is the default printing procedure. It bypasses Visual Basic's **Printer** object, instead using the **Print#** statement to send text directly to the printer. This allows the program to send a greater variety of printer codes to a laser printer, including the code for landscape printing. In contrast, the **PrintPortraitEnv** procedure (Listing 7.20) takes the much simpler approach of printing data via the **Printer** object.

Finally, the three procedures that deal with additions to the **Title** array are shown in Listing 7.18. **AddTitle_Click** is called when the user presses F9 or chooses the **Add New Title** command from the **Address** menu. This procedure uses Visual Basic's **InputBox$** function to display a dialog box on the screen, eliciting the text for the user's new title entry. When the entry is complete, the procedure calls the **LoadNewTitle** routine (also listed in Listing 7.18) to add the new option button to the *Address File* form and then opens ADDRESS.TTL to append the new entry to the file.

The program calls the **ReadTitleFile** procedure (Listing 7.18) at the beginning of each performance to read ADDRESS.TTL—if the file exists— and add the custom titles to the form.

Using a Dynamic Data Array

The **AddrIndex** array allows the program to locate address records or to determine whether a given name has been stored in the database. The **ReadIndex** procedure (Listing 7.3) is responsible for resizing this array whenever new records are added to the database. Two event procedures make calls to **ReadIndex**. First, the **Form_Load** procedure determines the initial size of the database; the number of records is stored in the global variable **AddrCount**. If **AddrCount** is greater than 0, the program calls **ReadIndex**:

```
If AddrCount > 0 Then ReadIndex
```

Each time the user adds a new record to the database, the **SaveAddr_Click** procedure increases the value of **AddrCount** by one:

```
AddrCount = AddrCount + 1
```

The **SaveAddr_Click** procedure then appends a new entry to the end of the index file and calls **ReadIndex** to rebuild the index array:

```
Open IndexFile For Append As #1
  Write #1, BuildIndexName(), PutPos
Close #1
ReadIndex
```

In short, the **AddrCount** variable always has a new value at the time **ReadIndex** is called. Accordingly, **ReadIndex** begins by defining a new size for the **AddrIndex** array:

```
ReDim AddrIndex(AddrCount) As IndexType
```

The array now contains an element for each record in the database. To rebuild the index, the **ReadIndex** procedure reads the index file from disk and then makes a call to the **SortAddrIndex** procedure to alphabetize the new index:

```
Open IndexFile For Input As #1
  For i% = 1 to AddrCount
    Input #1, AddrIndex(i%).FullName, AddrIndex(i%).RecNum
```

```
    Next i%
Close #1

SortAddrIndex
```

To summarize, here are the steps that the program uses to maintain the database index in the **AddrIndex** array:

1. Use a **Dim** statement to declare the dynamic array—without specifying a length—in the form-level declaration section.

2. After calculating the number of records in the database, define the initial length of the array in a **ReDim** statement. Read the index file into the array, and alphabetize the list.

3. Perform the **ReDim** statement again each time the user adds a new address record. After redimensioning, reread the index file into the array and sort the array once again.

Using a Control Array to Customize the Title Options

As you've seen, the *Address File* application allows additions to the list of titles at the left side of the main dialog box. The three routines that manage this feature are all shown in Listing 7.18. When the user first presses F9 (or selects the **Add New Title** command), the **AddTitle_Click** procedure elicits the caption for a new option button and calls the **LoadNewTitle** procedure to add the new control to the form:

```
NewTitle$ = InputBox$("Enter a new title:", "Add a Title")
   If RTrim$(NewTitle$) <> "" Then


      '  ...


      LoadNewTitle NewTitleIndex%, NewTitle$
```

The **LoadNewTitle** routine receives the index as **i%** and the title text as **TitleCaption$**. Accordingly, it uses the **LOAD** command to add a new element to the **Title** array and then sets the caption and other properties of the new option button:

```
Sub LoadNewTitle (i%, TitleCaption$)

   Load Title(i%)
   Title(i%).Visible = True
   Title(i%).Enabled = True
```

```
Title(i%).Height = 255
Title(i%).Width = 1575
Title(i%).Left = 120
Title(i%).Top = 1320 + i% * 240
Title(i%).Caption = TitleCaption$
```

Back in the **AddTitle_Click** procedure, the program increments the value of the **NewTitleIndex%** variable and stores the text of this new option button in the ADDRESS.TTL file:

```
NewTitleIndex% = NewTitleIndex + 1

Open TitleFile For Append As #1
  Print #1, NewTitle$
Close #1
```

These custom additions to the **Title** array are defined only during run time. (You can confirm that this is true by examining the *Address File* form again in the design mode; you'll see that only the original five option buttons appear on the form.) But to maintain the integrity of the database, the application must redisplay these added titles whenever the user restarts the application. After all, the user can select any option button from the list as the title field for an address record that is stored in the database.

For this reason, the program makes a call to the **ReadTitleFile** procedure at the beginning of each program run. This routine checks to see if the ADDRESS.TTL file exists. If it finds the file, the routine reads each line of text and loads a new option button onto the *Address File* form for each custom title:

```
Do While Not EOF(1)
  Line Input #1, NewTitle$
  LoadNewTitle NewTitleIndex%, NewTitle$
  NewTitleIndex% = NewTitleIndex% + 1
Loop
```

Finally, the procedure checks to see if the **NewTitleIndex%** counter has gone past the maximum number allowed for the list of title options. If so, the program disables the **Add New Title** command in the **Address** menu:

```
If NewTitleIndex% > MaxTitles Then AddTitle.Enabled = False
```

This prevents any further additions to the **Title** array.

Printing Techniques

The **Printer** object is a versatile tool for sending information to the printer. Visual Basic defines a useful assortment of properties and methods for this object—properties that control printer settings, or supply information about the current settings; and methods that perform printing operations. You have seen examples of some of these properties and methods already. Here is a summary of several of the most important tools among them:

- Among the properties related to fonts are **FontName**, which you can use to identify or change the current font; **FontSize**, **FontItalic**, and **FontBold**, which change the printing characteristics in the current font; **FontCount**, which supplies the number of fonts available on the system printer; and **Fonts**, an indexed property that supplies the names of the available fonts.

- Properties that identify and set the current printing area and position include **ScaleWidth**, **ScaleHeight**, **CurrentX**, and **CurrentY**.

- Among the printing methods are **Print**, for printing text; **Circle** and **Line**, for printing graphics; and **NewPage**, for feeding forward to the top of the next piece of paper.

Despite the power and versatility of all these tools, you may occasionally need a way to send printer-specific commands directly to the printer device, without passing through the **Printer** object. Your printer might have capabilities that are not covered by the existing properties and methods of the **Printer** object. For example, Visual Basic does not supply a property that switches between landscape and portrait orientation for a laser printer. You need a different technique for sending commands to the printer for these characteristics.

One solution to this problem lies with traditional I/O statements that Visual Basic inherits from previous versions of the language. Specifically, the following form of the **Open** command opens an output channel for sending text directly to the printer:

```
Open "Prn" For Output As #1
```

Once this channel is open, you can use **Print #1** statements to send text output to the printer. The output can include lines of printable characters, along with control sequences and other special characters that your printer interprets as commands and option selections.

The *Address File* application illustrates both of these very different approaches to printing. The **PrintLandscapeEnv** procedure (Listing 7.19) uses **Print#** statements to send specific printing commands to a laser printer. In contrast, the **PrintPortraitEnv** procedure (Listing 7.20) takes advantage of the tools associated with the **Printer** object. Take a brief look at both of these procedures now.

Using the Print# Statement   The **PrintLandscapeEnv** procedure defines four string constants to represent specific command codes for the HP LaserJet printer:

```
Const FixedCode = "(s0P"       ' Fixed-space font.
Const PropCode = "(s1P"        ' Proportional font.
Const LandCode = "&l1O"        ' Landscape printing.
Const PortraitCode = "&l0O"    ' Portrait printing.
```

Given these codes, the routine begins its output to the printer with two command sequences:

```
Print #1, Chr$(Esc) + CurFont$
Print #1, Chr$(Esc) + LandCode
```

These commands represent a font setting and the landscape-orientation switch for the HP LaserJet printer. Each begins with the escape character, **Chr$(Esc)**, which signals the beginning of a control command. (The constant **Esc** represents 27; **Chr$(27)** is the escape character.) The **Cur-Font$** string contains one of two settings, either **FixedCode** or **PropCode**, depending on the current setting in the **Font** menu.

After sending the two control commands, the **PrintLandscapeEnv** procedure writes the text for the return address and the destination address, again using the **Print#** statement. For example, here is the output for the return address:

```
For i% = 0 to 3
  Print #1, Indent$; ReturnAddrLines$(i%)
Next i%
```

A form-feed character completes the printing operation after the text for the two addresses has been sent:

```
Print #1, Chr$(FormFeed)
```

(The procedure defines **FormFeed** as an integer constant with a value of 12. **Chr$(12)** is the form-feed character.) Finally, when both addresses have been printed, the output channel is closed again:

```
Close #1
```

This approach requires detailed understanding of your printer's capabilities and command codes. For this reason, you should use the **Open** and

Print# commands for printer output only when the **Printer** object does not contain a simpler answer to your printing requirements.

Using the Printer Object   The **PrintPortraitEnv** procedure uses the **Printer.Print** method to send the two addresses to the printer. For example, here is the sequence for the return address:

```
For i% = 0 To 3
  Printer.Print Indent$; ReturnAddressLines$(i%)
Next i%
```

When both addresses have been printed, calls to the **NewPage** and **EndDoc** methods complete the output operation:

```
Printer.NewPage
Printer.EndDoc
```

EndDoc sends a signal that the completed document can be released to the printer.

SUMMARY: DATA STRUCTURES AND CONTROL ARRAYS

Visual Basic's data arrays and control arrays give you flexible ways to manage data and controls in an application.

You can define data arrays as *static* or *dynamic* structures. The length of a static array remains fixed throughout program execution; in contrast, a program establishes the dimensions of a dynamic array at run time. Both kinds of arrays have important uses. In general, you should use static arrays whenever you can be certain of the amount of data that an application will generate; the *Loan Calculator* and *Sales Week* applications both contain examples.

On the other hand, a dynamic array is the better choice when the dimensions of the data are not known until run time, or when the length of data can change one or more times during run time. For example, the *Address File* application builds an index that increases in length each time the user adds a new record to the address database. Defining this index as a static array could cause two different problems:

- For a small address database, the array might actually be larger than necessary, and therefore waste memory space.

- As the address database grows over time, the array might at some point turn out to be too small, placing an upper limit on the number of records the program can handle.

The *Address File* program rereads the index list from disk after redimensioning the array.

Like data arrays, Visual Basic's control arrays have a built-in flexibility that proves very useful in applications that must respond dynamically to run-time events. You can use control arrays—along with the **Load** and **UnLoad** statements—to add or remove controls during run time.

Finally, this chapter's application example illustrates another Visual Basic data structure known as a *user-defined structure*, or simply a *record*. A record structure, representing multiple fields belonging to different data types, is an important structure in database management applications. You can learn more about records and databases by reviewing the *Real Estate* application. This program, originally introduced in Chapter 1, is described in much greater detail in Chapter 8.

Listing 7.1 Code module and form-level declarations

```
' The Address Program (ADDRESS.MAK)

' ADDRGLOB.BAS Global Declarations

' The address record type.

Type AddrRecType
  TitleField As Integer
  FirstField As String * 20
  LastField As String * 20
  CoField As String * 50
  AddrField As String * 50
  CityField As String * 30
  StateField As String * 2
  ZipField As String * 10
  PhoneField As String * 30
End Type


' The index record type.

Type IndexType
  FullName As String * 41
  RecNum As Integer
End Type
```

(continued)

```
' The Address Program (ADDRESS.MAK)

' INADDR.FRM
' Declarations.

' The names of the four files
' this program creates and reads.

Const AddrFile = "C:\ADDRESS.DAT"
Const IndexFile = "C:\ADDRESS.NDX"
Const ReturnAddr = "C:\ADDRESS.RTN"
Const TitleFile = "C:\ADDRESS.TTL"

' The maximum number of titles in the
' list of options buttons.

Const MaxTitles = 14

Dim AddrRec As AddrRecType        ' An address record.
Dim AddrIndex() As IndexType      ' The index array.
Dim AddrCount As Integer          ' Current number of records.

Dim TitleStr$                     ' "Mr. ", "Mrs. ", etc.
Dim NewTitleIndex%                ' Index for new title.
Dim ReturnAddrLines$(3)           ' Return address lines.

Dim CrLf$                         ' Carriage-return, line-feed.

' End of form-level declarations for INADDR.FRM.
```

Listing 7.2 The **Form_Load** procedure

```
Sub Form_Load ()

   ' Initialize variables and menu options, and
   ' check the length of the address database.

   ' Carriage-return, line feed.
   CrLf$ = Chr$(13) + Chr$(10)
```

```
  ' Open the database file and find
  ' out how many records it contains.

  Open AddrFile For Random As #1 Len = Len(AddrRec)
     AddrCount = LOF(1) / Len(AddrRec)
  Close #1

  ' If the database is not empty, read the index.

  If AddrCount > 0 Then ReadIndex

  ' Initialize the title list.

  NewTitleIndex% = 5
  ReadTitleFile

End Sub  ' Form_Load
```

Listing 7.3 The **ReadIndex** procedure

```
Sub ReadIndex ()

  ' Read the index file for the address database.

  ' First redimension the AddrIndex array for
  ' storing the index at its current length.

  ReDim AddrIndex(AddrCount) As IndexType

  Open IndexFile For Input As #1
    For i% = 1 To AddrCount
      Input #1, AddrIndex(i%).FullName, AddrIndex(i%).RecNum
    Next i%
  Close #1

  ' Arrange the index in alphabetical order.
  SortAddrIndex

End Sub  ' ReadIndex
```

Listing 7.4 The **SaveAddr_Click** procedure

```
Sub SaveAddr_Click ()

  ' Save the current address in the database.

  Const Yes = 6, No = 7
  Dim LocPos As Integer, PutPos As Integer
  Dim DoSave As Integer, NewRecord As Integer

  ' Don't save a blank record.

  If Trm$(FirstName) = "" Or Trm$(LastName) = "" Then
    MsgBox "Can't save a record without a name.", 48, "Address File"
    Exit Sub
  End If

  ' Don't allow quotation marks in name.

  Q$ = Chr$(34)
  If Instr(FirstName, Q$) <> 0 Or InStr(LastName, Q$) <> 0 Then
    MsgBox "Can't save a name with quotation marks.", 48, "Address File"
    Exit Sub
  End If

  ' Check index to see if this name already exists.

  LocPos = SearchIndex%()

  ' If so, give the user the options of writing over the
  ' existing record or abandoning the save operation.

  If LocPos > 0 Then
    Msg$ = "This name is already in the database."
    Msg$ = Msg$ + " Do you want to change the address record? "

    If MsgBox(Msg$, 4, "Address File") = Yes Then
      DoSave = True
      NewRecord = False
      PutPos = LocPos
    Else
      DoSave = False
    End If

  Else   ' This is a new record.

    DoSave = True

    ' Increment the record count.

    AddrCount = AddrCount + 1
```

```
      PutPos = AddrCount
      NewRecord = True
    End If

    ' Save the record.

    If DoSave Then
      AddrRec.TitleField = 0
      For i% = 0 To NewTitleIndex% - 1
        If Title(i%).Value Then AddrRec.TitleField = i% + 1
      Next i%

      AddrRec.FirstField = FirstName.Text
      AddrRec.LastField = LastName.Text
      AddrRec.Cofield = Company.Text
      AddrRec.AddrField = Address.Text
      AddrRec.CityField = City.Text
      AddrRec.StateField = State.Text
      AddrRec.ZipField = Zip.Text
      AddrRec.PhoneField = Phone.Text

      Open AddrFile For Random As #1 Len = Len(AddrRec)
        Put #1, PutPos, AddrRec
      Close #1

      ' If this is a new record, add a new entry to the index.

      If DoSave And NewRecord Then
        Open IndexFile For Append As #1
          Write #1, BuildIndexName(), PutPos
        Close #1
        ReadIndex
      End If

    End If

End Sub   ' SaveAddr_Click
```

Listing 7.5 The **SearchAddr_Click** procedure

```
Sub SearchAddr_Click ()

  ' Search for the current address in the database.

  Dim TargetPos%
```

(continued)

```
' Find the name in the index, and read the record's
' position. (A return value of zero indicates that
' the record is not in the database.)

TargetPos% = SearchIndex%()

If TargetPos% <> 0 Then

  ' Read the record.

  Open AddrFile For Random As #1 Len = Len(AddrRec)
    Get #1, TargetPos%, AddrRec
  Close #1

  ' Display the fields of the record in
  ' the appropriate text boxes.

  FirstName.Text = AddrRec.FirstField
  LastName.Text = AddrRec.LastField
  Company.Text = AddrRec.Cofield
  Address.Text = AddrRec.AddrField
  City.Text = AddrRec.CityField
  State.Text = AddrRec.StateField
  Zip.Text = AddrRec.ZipField
  Phone.Text = AddrRec.PhoneField

  ' Display the title field as a selected option button.

  If AddrRec.TitleField <> 0 Then
    If AddrRec.TitleField < NewTitleIndex% Then
      Title(AddrRec.TitleField - 1).Value = True
    End If
  End If

' If the record does not exist, inform the user.

Else
  Msg$ = FirstName.Text + " " + LastName.Text
  Msg$ = Msg$ + " is not in the database."
  MsgBox Msg$, 48, "Address File"
End If

End Sub  ' SearchAddr_Click
```

Listing 7.6 The **SortAddrIndex** and **SearchIndex%** routines

```
Sub SortAddrIndex ()

  ' Alphabetize the index.

  Dim TempAddrRec As IndexType

  For i% = 1 To AddrCount - 1
    For j% = i% + 1 To AddrCount
      If AddrIndex(i%).FullName > AddrIndex(j%).FullName Then
        TempAddrRec = AddrIndex(i%)
        AddrIndex(i%) = AddrIndex(j%)
        AddrIndex(j%) = TempAddrRec
      End If
    Next j%
  Next i%

End Sub   ' SortAddrIndex


Function SearchIndex% ()

  ' Search through the index for the name that
  ' the user has entered into the FirstName and
  ' LastName text boxes.

  Dim AddrFound%, StartPos%, EndPos%, CenterPos%, SearchName$

  AddrFound% = 0
  StartPos% = 1
  EndPos% = AddrCount

  ' Build the target name in the format used in the index.

  SearchName$ = BuildIndexName$()

  ' Perform a binary search.

  Do While ((AddrFound% = 0) And (StartPos% <= EndPos%))
    CenterPos% = (StartPos% + EndPos%) \ 2

    Select Case SearchName$
```

(continued)

```
      Case RTrim$(AddrIndex(CenterPos%).FullName)
        AddrFound% = AddrIndex(CenterPos%).RecNum
      Case Is > AddrIndex(CenterPos%).FullName
        StartPos% = CenterPos% + 1
      Case Else
        EndPos% = CenterPos% - 1
    End Select
  Loop

  ' Return the record number if the name was found,
  ' or a value of zero if the name was not found.

  SearchIndex% = AddrFound%

End Function   ' SearchIndex%
```

Listing 7.7 The **BuildIndexName$** and **Trm$** functions

```
Function BuildIndexName$ ()

  ' Prepare the current name in the
  ' correct format for the index.

  Dim TempName$

  TempName$ = Trm$(LastName) + " " + Trm$(FirstName)
  BuildIndexName$ = UCase$(TempName$)

End Function   ' BuildIndexName$


Function Trm$ (TextBox As Control)

  ' Trim spaces from the beginning
  ' and the end of a string.

  Trm$ = LTrim$(RTrim$(TextBox.Text))

End Function   ' Trm$
```

Listing 7.8 The **SetRtnAddr_Click** procedure

```
Sub SetRtnAddr_Click ()

  ' Save the current address as the return address.
  ' (Note: A blank address can be saved if the user does
  ' not want to print a return address on an envelope.)

  Dim Co$, Place$

  Open ReturnAddr For Output As #1

    Print #1, TitleStr$;
    Print #1, Trm$(FirstName); " ";
    Print #1, Trm$(LastName)

    Co$ = Trm$(Company)
    If Co$ <> "" Then Print #1, Co$

    Print #1, Trm$(Address)
    Place$ = Trm$(City)
    If Place$ <> "" Then Print #1, Place$; ", ";
    Print #1, Trm$(State); " ";
    Print #1, Trm$(Zip)

  Close #1

End Sub   ' SetRtnAddr_Click
```

Listing 7.9 The **ViewRtnAddr_Click** procedure

```
Sub ViewRtnAddr_Click ()

  ' Display a message box with the return address.

  If ReadReturnAddr() Then
    Msg$ = ""
    For i% = 0 To 3
      Msg$ = Msg$ + ReturnAddrLines$(i%) + CrLf$
    Next i%
```

(continued)

```
   Else
     Msg$ = "No return address found on disk."
   End If

   MsgBox Msg$, 64, "Return Address"

End Sub  ' ViewRtnAddr_Click
```

Listing 7.10 The **ReadReturnAddr** function

```
Function ReadReturnAddr () As Integer

   ' Read the return address from its
   ' text file on disk.

   Dim OkReturn As Integer, LineNum As Integer

   ' First check to see if the file exists.

   OkReturn = True
   On Error GoTo NoReturnAddress
     Open ReturnAddr For Input As #2
   On Error GoTo 0

   If OkReturn Then

     ' Blank out any previous return address.

     For i% = 0 To 3
       ReturnAddrLines$(i%) = ""
     Next i%

     LineNum = 0
     Do While Not EOF(2)
       Line Input #2, ReturnAddrLines$(LineNum)
       LineNum = LineNum + 1
     Loop
     Close #2
   End If

   ' Return a boolean value indicating
   ' whether or not the file exists.
```

```
   ReadReturnAddr = OkReturn

   Exit Function

' Error routine for missing file.

NoReturnAddress:
   OkReturn = False
Resume Next

End Function   ' ReadReturnAddr
```

Listing 7.11 The **HighlightText** and **GotFocus** event procedures

```
Sub HighlightText (TextBox As Control)

  ' Highlight the contents of a text box.

  TextBox.SelStart = 0
  TextBox.SelLength = Len(TextBox.Text)

End Sub   ' HighlightText


Sub Address_GotFocus ()

  ' Highlight the contents of the text box.

  HighlightText Address

End Sub   ' Address_GotFocus


Sub City_GotFocus ()

  ' Highlight the contents of the text box.

  HighlightText City

End Sub   ' City_GotFocus
```

(continued)

```
Sub Company_GotFocus ()

  ' Highlight the contents of the text box.

  HighlightText Company

End Sub  ' Company_GotFocus


Sub FirstName_GotFocus ()

  ' Highlight the contents of the text box.

  HighlightText FirstName

End Sub  ' FirstName_GotFocus


Sub LastName_GotFocus ()

  ' Highlight the contents of the text box.

  HighlightText LastName

End Sub  ' LastName_GotFocus


Sub Phone_GotFocus ()

  ' Highlight the contents of the text box.

  HighlightText Phone

End Sub  ' Phone_GotFocus


Sub State_GotFocus ()

  ' Highlight the contents of the text box.

  HighlightText State

End Sub  ' State_GotFocus
```

```
Sub Zip_GotFocus ()

  ' Highlight the contents of the text box.

  HighlightText Zip

End Sub  ' Zip_GotFocus
```

Listing 7.12 The **ClearAddr_Click** and **Quit_Click** procedures

```
Sub ClearAddr_Click ()

  ' Clear the current address.

  TitleStr = ""
  FirstName.Text = ""
  LastName.Text = ""
  Company.Text = ""
  Address.Text = ""
  City.Text = ""
  State.Text = ""
  Zip.Text = ""
  Phone.Text = ""

  ' Deselect all the option buttons.

  For i% = 0 To NewTitleIndex% - 1
    Title(i%).Value = False
  Next i%

  FirstName.SetFocus

End Sub  ' ClearAddr.Click


Sub Quit_Click ()

  ' Terminate the program.

  End

End Sub  ' Quit_Click
```

Listing 7.13 Click event procedures for envelope size options

```
Sub BusinessEnv_Click ()

  ' Display a check next to the Business
  ' option in the Envelope menu.

  BusinessEnv.Checked = True
  HomeEnv.Checked = False
  PersonalEnv.Checked = False

End Sub   ' BusinessEnv_Click


Sub HomeEnv_Click ()

  ' Display a check next to the Home
  ' option in the Envelope menu.

  BusinessEnv.Checked = False
  HomeEnv.Checked = True
  PersonalEnv.Checked = False

End Sub   ' HomeEnv_Click


Sub PersonalEnv_Click ()

  ' Display a check next to the Personal
  ' option in the Envelope menu.

  BusinessEnv.Checked = False
  HomeEnv.Checked = False
  PersonalEnv.Checked = True

End Sub   ' PersonalEnv_Click
```

Listing 7.14 Click event procedures for **Help** menu options

```
Sub GeneralHelp_Click ()

    ' Display a message box describing the program.

    Dim Msg$

    Msg$ = "The Address File application manages "
    Msg$ = Msg$ + "an address database. You can "
    Msg$ = Msg$ + "press F2 to save an address, "
    Msg$ = Msg$ + "or F4 to find the address for "
    Msg$ = Msg$ + "a given name. The program also "
    Msg$ = Msg$ + "prints envelopes in a variety "
    Msg$ = Msg$ + "of sizes."

    MsgBox Msg$, 64, "About Address File"

End Sub   ' GeneralHelp_Click


Sub KeyHelp_Click ()

  ' Display a list of special keys
  ' that the program uses.

  Msg$ = "F1  Help" + CrLf$
  Msg$ = Msg$ + "F2  Save an address" + CrLf$
  Msg$ = Msg$ + "F3  Clear the address" + CrLf$
  Msg$ = Msg$ + "F4  Find an address" + CrLf$
  Msg$ = Msg$ + "F6  Portrait printing" + CrLf$
  Msg$ = Msg$ + "F7  Landscape printing" + CrLf$
  Msg$ = Msg$ + "F8  View return address" + CrLf$
  Msg$ = Msg$ + "F9  Add a new title" + CrLf$ + CrLf$


  Msg$ = Msg$ + "Ctrl+E  Print an envelope" + CrLf$
  Msg$ = Msg$ + "Ctrl+R  Save return address" + CrLf$
  Msg$ = Msg$ + "Ctrl+X  Exit"

  MsgBox Msg$, 64, "Keyboard Help"

End Sub   ' KeyHelp_Click
```

Listing 7.15 The **Landscape_Click** and **Portrait_Click** procedures

```
Sub Landscape_Click ()

  ' Switch to the landscape printing mode.

  ' Make the switch only if the Landscape
  ' option is not currently checked.

  If Not Landscape.Checked Then

    Landscape.Checked = True
    Portrait.Checked = False

    ' Enable the Home and Personal envelope options.

    HomeEnv.Enabled = True
    PersonalEnv.Enabled = True

    ' Enable the Proportional font option.

    PropFont.Enabled = True

  End If

End Sub   ' Landscape_Click


Sub Portrait_Click ()

  ' Switch to the Portrait printing mode.

  ' Make the switch only if the Portrait
  ' option is not currently checked.

  If Not Portrait.Checked Then

    Portrait.Checked = True
    Landscape.Checked = False
```

```
     ' Disable the Home and Personal envelope options.

     BusinessEnv_Click
     HomeEnv.Enabled = False
     PersonalEnv.Enabled = False

     ' Disable the Proportional font option.

     PropFont.Enabled = False
     FixedFont_Click

   End If

End Sub   ' Portrait_Click
```

Listing 7.16 The **FixedFont_Click** and **PropFont_Click** procedures

```
Sub FixedFont_Click ()

  ' Change to the fixed-font option.

  PropFont.Checked = False
  FixedFont.Checked = True

End Sub   ' FixedFont_Click



Sub PropFont_Click ()

  ' Change to the proportional-font option.

  PropFont.Checked = True
  FixedFont.Checked = False

End Sub   ' PropFont_Click
```

Listing 7.17 The **PrintEnv_Click** procedure

```
Sub PrintEnv_Click ()

  ' Read the title selection.

  TitleStr$ = ""
  For i% = 0 To NewTitleIndex% - 1
    If Title(i%).Value Then
      If Title(i%).Caption <> "(none)" Then
        TitleStr$ = RTrim$(Title(i%).Caption) + " "
      End If
    End If
  Next i%

  ' Choose between two printing modes.

  If Portrait.Checked Then
    PrintPortraitEnv
  Else
    PrintLandscapeEnv
  End If

End Sub  ' PrintEnv_Click
```

Listing 7.18 **AddTitle_Click**, **LoadNewTitle**, and **ReadTitleFile**

```
Sub AddTitle_Click ()

  ' Give the user the opportunity to add a new title
  ' to the list (Mr., Ms., Miss, etc.)

  NewTitle$ = InputBox$("Enter a new title:", "Add a Title")

  If RTrim$(NewTitle$) <> "" Then

    ' Test for an entry of "(none)"

    If InStr("(none)", NewTitle$) > 0 Then NewTitle$ = "(none)"

    ' Load a new option button for the title.
```

```
   LoadNewTitle NewTitleIndex%, NewTitle$
   NewTitleIndex% = NewTitleIndex% + 1

   ' Save the title to ADDRESS.TTL

   Open TitleFile For Append As #1
     Print #1, NewTitle$
   Close #1

   ' Limit the number of new titles.

   If NewTitleIndex% > MaxTitles Then AddTitle.Enabled = False
 End If

End Sub   ' AddTitle_Click


Sub LoadNewTitle (i%, TitleCaption$)

  ' Add a title to the list of option buttons.

   Load Title(i%)
   Title(i%).Visible = True
   Title(i%).Enabled = True
   Title(i%).Height = 255
   Title(i%).Width = 1575
   Title(i%).Left = 120
   Title(i%).Top = 1320 + i% * 240
   Title(i%).Caption = TitleCaption$

End Sub   ' LoadNewTitle


Sub ReadTitleFile ()

  ' Read ADDRESS.TTL and add the titles
  ' to the list of option buttons.

  Dim TitleFileExists As Integer

  ' First check to see if the file exists.

  TitleFileExists = True
```

(continued)

```
    On Local Error GoTo NoTitleFile
      Open TitleFile For Input As #1
    On Error GoTo 0

    If TitleFileExists Then

      Do While Not EOF(1)
        Line Input #1, NewTitle$
        LoadNewTitle NewTitleIndex%, NewTitle$
        NewTitleIndex% = NewTitleIndex% + 1
      Loop
      Close #1

      If NewTitleIndex% > MaxTitles Then AddTitle.Enabled = False

    End If

    Exit Sub

  ' Error routine for missing file.

  NoTitleFile:
    TitleFileExists = False
  Resume Next

  End Sub  ' ReadTitleFile
```

Listing 7.19 The **PrintLandscapeEnv** procedure

```
Sub PrintLandscapeEnv ()

  ' Print the envelope in the landscape mode.
  ' (This routine uses HP LaserJet printer commands.)

  Const FormFeed = 12  ' Chr$(12) is a form-feed.
  Const No = 7         ' The code "No" in a message box.
  Const Esc = 27       ' Escape code.

  ' HP printer commands:

  Const FixedCode = "(s0P"      ' Fixed-space font.
  Const PropCode = "(s1P"       ' Proportional font.
```

```
Const LandCode = "&l1O"        ' Landscape printing.
Const PortraitCode = "&l0O"    ' Portrait printing.

Dim OkReturnAddr As Integer, i%
Dim Indent1$, Indent2$, CurFont$
Dim FirstLine As Integer, SkipLines As Integer

' Read the setting for the envelope size, and
' adjust the indent strings accordingly.

If BusinessEnv.Checked Then
  Indent1$ = Space$(20)
ElseIf HomeEnv.Checked Then
  Indent1$ = Space$(45)
Else
  Indent1$ = Space$(35)
End If

Indent2$ = Space$(70)

' Read the selection in the font menu and
' set the correct HP LaserJet code.

If FixedFont.Checked Then
  CurFont$ = FixedCode
Else
  ' Proportional font.
  CurFont$ = PropCode
  Indent1$ = Indent1$ + Indent1$
  Indent2$ = Indent2$ + Indent2$
End If

FirstLine = 10
SkipLines = 6

' Set an error trap, in case the printer is
' not ready. Then attempt to print the envelope.

On Local Error GoTo NotReady
  Open "Prn" For Output As #1

  ' Send the font code and the code
  ' for landscape printing.
```

(continued)

```
   Print #1, Chr$(Esc) + CurFont$
   Print #1, Chr$(Esc) + LandCode

   For i% = 1 To FirstLine
     Print #1,
   Next i%

   ' Print the return address if one exists.

   OkReturnAddr = ReadReturnAddr()
   For i% = 0 To 3
     Print #1, Indent1$; ReturnAddrLines$(i%)
   Next i%

   For i% = 1 To SkipLines
     Print #1,
   Next i%

   Print #1, Indent2$;
   Print #1, TitleStr$;
   Print #1, Trm$(FirstName); " "; Trm$(LastName)

   Co$ = Trm$(Company)
   If Co$ <> "" Then Print #1, Indent2$; Co$

   Print #1, Indent2$; Trm$(Address)
   Print #1, Indent2$; Trm$(City); ", ";
   Print #1, Trm$(State); " "; Trm$(Zip)
   Print #1, Chr$(FormFeed)

   ' Restore portrait printing and fixed space.

   Print #1, Chr$(Esc) + PortraitCode
   Print #1, Chr$(Esc) + FixedCode

   Close #1
 On Error GoTo 0

 Exit Sub

' Allow the user to abort the printing operation or try again.

NotReady:
 Ans = MsgBox("Printer not ready. Try again?", 4, "Printer Error")
```

```
   If Ans = No Then
     Close #1
     Exit Sub
   End If

 Resume

 End Sub  ' PrintLandscapeEnv
```

Listing 7.20 The **PrintPortraitEnv** procedure

```
Sub PrintPortraitEnv ()

  ' Print the envelope in the portrait mode.

  Dim OkReturnAddr As Integer, i%

  Indent1$ = Space$(5)
  Indent2$ = Space$(50)

  ' Print the return address.

  OkReturnAddr = ReadReturnAddr()
  For i% = 0 To 3
    Printer.Print Indent1$; ReturnAddrLines$(i%)
  Next i%

  For i% = 1 To 6
    Printer.Print
  Next i%

  ' Print the destination address.

  Printer.Print Indent2$; TitleStr$;
  Printer.Print Trm$(FirstName); " ";
  Printer.Print Trm$(LastName)

  Co$ = Trm$(Company)
  If Co$ <> "" Then Printer.Print Indent2$; Co$

  Printer.Print Indent2$; Trm$(Address)
```

(continued)

```
   Printer.Print Indent2$; Trm$(City); ", ";
   Printer.Print Trm$(State); " ";
   Printer.Print Trm$(Zip)

   Printer.NewPage
   Printer.EndDoc

End Sub  ' PrintPortraitEnv
```

8

Random-Access Files:
The Real Estate *Application*

INTRODUCTION

The *random-access file* structure is the key to creating efficient database management applications in Visual Basic. Thanks to a fixed-length record structure, a random-access file gives you direct access to individual data records in a database. Your programs can perform three essential input and output operations with such a file:

- Read a record directly from a target location in the database, without having to read any other records before or after.
- Write revised data over a target record position, without danger of destroying any other information in the database.
- Append a new record to the end of the database file.

(In Visual Basic 3.0 you can also write applications that employ databases from other software environments, such as Microsoft Access or dBASE. This new alternative approach is described in the appendix.)

The *Address File* application, presented in Chapter 7, is an example of a database application that creates and maintains a random-access file. Chapter 7 discusses the major data structures you are likely to use in this kind of application: a record variable to represent individual records in the database (see **Review Box 7.1**), and an array to store the index that the program builds for the database. The alphabetized index contains two items of information about each record in the database:

1. A unique key field for each record.

2. Each record's numeric location in the database.

With this index, the process of retrieving a target record is simple and direct: The program searches through the index for the key field and makes note of the record number that the index supplies. Given this record number, the program opens the database file and goes directly to the target record to perform an input or output operation.

Along with these two essential data structures, you use three Basic commands for working with a random-access file:

- An **Open** statement opens the file in the **Random** mode and establishes the fixed record length.

- The **Get** statement reads a record from a target record position in the file.

- The **Put** statement writes a record to the file, either appending a record to the end of the file or overwriting an existing record.

Review Box 8.1 summarizes the use of these statements.

In this chapter you'll return to another example of a database management program, the *Real Estate* application, first introduced in Chapter 1. The project is stored on the exercise disk under the name REALEST.MAK. Open the application now so that you can review its operations and examine its code during the course of this chapter. You'll use this application to explore specific random-access file-handling techniques for a variety of tasks: reading records from the file, revising existing records, appending new records, and maintaining the database index.

THE *REAL ESTATE* APPLICATION

As you'll recall, the *Real Estate* program creates and maintains a residential real estate database. The program is useful when you are in the market for a new home to buy. Each record in the database contains information about a particular home that is on the market. Figure 8.1 shows a sample record. The fields include the address of the home, the asking price, the date you viewed the home, and additional details about the property for sale. There is also a **Comments** field in which you can record your own impressions and reactions to the home.

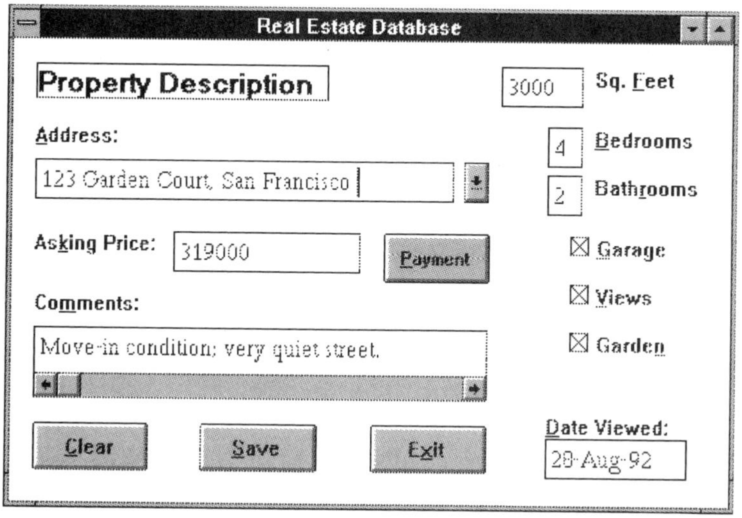

Figure 8.1 The *Real Estate* application

This application performs the basic operations of a typical database management program. To create a new home record, you enter information about the home and click the **Save** button. You can easily retrieve an existing record by clicking the target address from the **Address** combo box list. When you do so, the program displays all the information about the home you have selected. You can also revise an existing record: Simply retrieve the record, make changes in any of the data fields other than the address, and click the **Save** button. The program saves your revisions as the new version of the record.

Although this chapter focuses on the main database component of the *Real Estate*, the program also has a useful mortgage calculator, which you activate by clicking the **Payment** button. The mortgage calculator is similar to the *Loan Calculator* application that you worked on in Chapters 2 through 5.

One of the important features of this application is its ability to check for appropriate input as you enter the fields of a home record into the main input form. Input validation applies to numeric fields and to the program's one date field, labeled **Date Viewed**. Take a moment to experiment with this feature now.

Entering the Fields of a Home Record

The main input form has four numeric fields: **Asking Price**, **Sq. Feet**, **Bedrooms**, and **Bathrooms**. When you enter a number into one of these

Review Box 8.1

Random-Access Data Files

A random-access file is organized into individual units of data called *records*. Each record in a random-access file contains a structured group of data items known as *fields*. All the records in a given file have the same fixed length. Thanks to this characteristic, Visual Basic can provide direct access to any record in the file. A record is identified by its *record number*, an integer ranging from 1 up to the number of records currently stored in the file.

Visual Basic's *user-defined structure*, also known as a record structure, is the ideal data structure to use for the definition and creation of a random-access file. A **Type** statement defines a record structure, and a subsequent **Dim** statement creates a corresponding record variable. (Refer back to **Review Box 7.1** for details.) Along with a defined record structure, the major tools you are likely to use in a random-access file program are the **Open** and **Close** statements, the **LOF** function, and the **Get** and **Put** statements.

The following form of the **Open** statement opens a file in the random-access mode:

```
Open FileName for Random As #FileNum Len = Len(RecordVariable)
```

In this syntax, *FileName* is the name of the file on disk, *FileNum* is an integer that identifies the open file in subsequent I/O statements, and *RecordVariable* is the name of a variable defined to represent records as they are read from the file or written to the file. This form of the **Len** clause defines the file's fixed record length to be equal to the length of the record variable. Visual Basic's **Len** function supplies the length, in bytes, of *RecordVariable*.

Once open, a random-access file is available for both reading and writing. At the outset, a program typically needs to find out the number

text boxes and then move to another control on the form, the program checks your input. If you have entered a valid number, your input remains as it is. If, however, you inadvertently enter a nonnumeric value, the program changes the entry to 0. Finally, if you enter a string of digits

Review Box 8.1 *(continued)*

of records currently stored in the file. The following formula uses Visual Basic's **LOF** ("length of file") function to compute the record count:

```
RecordCount% = LOF(FileNum) / Len(RecordVariable)
```

The **LOF** function takes an integer argument—the file number of the open file—and returns the length, in bytes, of the file. Dividing this value by the length of the record structure gives the number of records in the file.

The **Get** statement reads a single record from a specified position in the open file:

```
Get #FileNum, RecordNumber, RecordVariable
```

The value of *RecordNumber* ranges from 1 up to the current *RecordCount*. As a result of this statement, the entire record stored at the *RecordNumber* position in the file is assigned to the fields of *RecordVariable*.

You can use a **For** loop to read a random-access file sequentially:

```
For i% = 1 To RecordCount
  Get #FileNum, i%, RecordVariable
  ' Process the record.
Next i%
```

The **Put** statement writes a single record to a specified position in the open file:

```
Put #FileNum, RecordNumber, RecordVariable
```

If *RecordNumber* is equal to *RecordCount* + 1, this **Put** statement appends a new record to the end of the open file. On the other hand, if *RecordNumber* is in the range from 1 to *RecordCount*, **Put** writes the current contents of *RecordVariable* over an existing record. In this case, the value of the record previously stored at *RecordNumber* is lost.

followed by a string of nonnumeric characters, the program drops the invalid characters from the entry. For example, an entry of **1234 sq ft** becomes simply **1234**. You have seen this kind of numeric input validation before in the *Sales Week* application.

Figure 8.2 Error message for invalid date input

The *Real Estate* program also checks dates. The default date entry in the **Date Viewed** field is always the current date. If you are entering a record into the database for a home you have looked at today, you don't have to change the date entry for the record. Otherwise, if you wish to enter a date other than today's date, the program is flexible in the date input formats it recognizes. For example, any of the following input formats results in a date display of **28-Aug-92**, assuming the current year is 1992:

```
8/28/92
8/28
8-28
8 Aug
Aug 8, 92
```

Date formats that do not include a year, such as 8/28 and 8-28, are assumed to be in the current year. When you enter a date and then move the focus to a new control on the input form, the *Real Estate* automatically converts your entry into the program's standard date display format, represented generally as **d-mmm-yy**.

On the other hand, if you enter a text value that the program cannot convert into a date, an error message appears on the screen, as shown in Figure 8.2. When you click the **OK** button on this message box, the program automatically resets the default date in the **Date Viewed** box. The program accomplishes its date validation and formatting with the help of built-in date functions that Visual Basic supplies. You'll examine these functions later when you turn to the program's code.

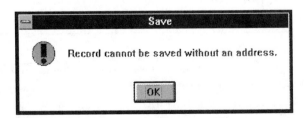

Figure 8.3 Error message for a missing address field

The program also produces an error message if you try to save a home record before entering an address field (Figure 8.3). Because the address is the key for retrieving a record, the program has to insist on a non-blank entry in the **Address** box before appending a new record to the database.

The Database File

The *Real Estate* program creates a single file on disk for the home database. The file's name is HOMES.DB, and it is stored in the root directory of drive C. Because HOMES.DB is structured as a random-access file, each home record takes up the same number of bytes. To maintain this fixed record length, Visual Basic stores each numeric field in a specific fixed-length binary format. For this reason, a random-access file is not like a text file; you cannot expect load the file into a text editor and read the information contained in the file. Text fields in the database may be recognizable, but numeric fields will appear on the screen as unreadable sequences of characters. In short, a random-access file is designed to be read by a database program, not by a person.

Unlike the *Address File* application, this program does not maintain a separate disk file for storing the index to the database. Instead, the *Real Estate* application rebuilds the index from scratch at the beginning of each program run. This alternate program design is based on the assumption that the homes database will normally be relatively small, containing, say, dozens of records rather than hundreds. Here are the initial steps that the program takes to build the index:

1. Open the database file and determine the number of records currently stored in the file.

2. Read through the entire database sequentially, from beginning to end, and build the index array with two items of information for each record: the address, which serves as the key field for retrieving records, and the numeric record number.

3. After reading these two data items from each record in the database, alphabetize the index array by the key field.

You'll see the code that performs these steps shortly.

THE ELEMENTS OF THE *REAL ESTATE* APPLICATION

The *Real Estate* project consists of four forms and a module (Figure 8.4). The main input form, named HOMEINPT.FRM on disk, is the focus of

Figure 8.4 The *REALEST.MAK* project

your attention in this chapter; the other three forms are related to the mortgage calculator.

Controls and Properties

The **HomeInpt** form contains a varied assortment of controls: six text boxes, a combo box, three check boxes, and four command buttons, along with various labels that identify the controls. In order to follow the structure of the program's code, you'll need to be familiar with the **Name** settings of these controls:

- The text boxes represent the major features of a home on the market, along with the date of your visit and your comments: **AskPrice**, **SqFeet**, **Bedrooms**, **Bathrooms**, **DateViewed**, and **Comments**.

- The combo box, named **Address**, represents the data field that is the key for retrieving records from the database.

- The three check boxes, **Garage**, **Views**, and **Garden**, complete the information about the home. Each of these has, in effect, a *yes* or *no* setting that the user establishes at run time by checking or unchecking a box. (Note that the **Value** property of a Visual Basic check box actually has three possible settings: **0-Unchecked**, **1-Checked**, and **2-Grayed**. This application makes use of only the first two settings.)

- Finally, the command buttons represent the program's database and computational operations: **PmtButton**, **ClearButton**, **SaveButton**, and **ExitButton**.

One of the text boxes has a special property setting you should notice. The **Comments** box has an attached horizontal scroll bar, giving the user an easy way to scroll through a comment that is too long to be displayed on the screen in its entirety. The **ScrollBars** property controls the presence of this feature. In the case of the **Comments** text box, the **ScrollBars** setting is **1-Horizontal**. (To display and activate the horizontal scroll bar on this control, the property named **MultiLine** requires a setting of **True**.)

The **Address** combo box also has an important characteristic that makes the user interface more convenient. Combo boxes have a property named **Sorted**, which determines whether or not the items in a drop-down list will appear in sorted order. The default setting for this property is **False**. The **Address** control's **Sorted** property has a nondefault setting of **True**. Under this setting, Visual Basic automatically alphabetizes the addresses in the drop-down list, even as the program adds new records to the database.

Events

The events recognized in the *Real Estate* application include:

- A **GotFocus** event for each of the text boxes. The corresponding event procedure arranges to highlight the entire current contents of the text box. This is an operation you have seen in other applications, including *Sales Week* and *Address File*.

- A **LostFocus** event for the text boxes that represent date and numeric fields. The **LostFocus** event procedures perform the application's input validations.

- **Click** events for the command buttons.

- A **Click** event for the **Address** combo box. When the user selects an address from the drop-down list of addresses, the **Address_Click** event retrieves the corresponding home record and displays it in the input form.

Procedures and Methods

The event procedures and general procedures from the **HomeInpt** form appear in Listings 8.1 to 8.9. (Listings 8.10 to 8.13 show the code from the **MortInpt** form, and Listing 8.14 lists the one procedure from the **LoanOpts** form.) As you examine the **HomeInpt** procedures, your main focus will be on the database operations they perform: saving, retrieving, and revising records. In addition, you'll learn how the program handles date input for the **Date Viewed** text box.

Opening the Database and Building the Index

The application's code module (HOMEGLOB.BAS, shown in Listing 8.1) contains definitions for two record types: **HomeRecordType** identifies the ten fields of a record stored in the database itself:

```
Type HomeRecordType
  Address As String * 50
```

```
      AskPrice As Long
      SqFeet As Integer
      Bedrooms As Integer
      Bathrooms As Integer
      Garage As Integer
      Views As Integer
      Garden As Integer
      DateViewed As Double
      Comments As String * 125
   End Type
```

IndexRecordType defines the two fields of the index structure: the key address field and the record number:

```
Type IndexRecordType
   AddressRef As String * 50
   RecNo As Integer
End Type
```

The form-level declaration section in the **HomeInpt** form (also Listing 8.1) creates a variable and an array belonging to these two record types. First, **HomeRecord** is the variable that will represent individual records read from or written to the database:

```
Dim HomeRecord As HomeRecordType
```

The **AddressList** array serves as the index into the database:

```
Dim AddressList(MaxRecords) As IndexRecordType
```

Unlike the *Address File* application, *Real Estate* uses a static array rather than a dynamic array to represent the index. The fixed length of the **AddressList** array is specified in the following constant definition:

```
Const MaxRecords = 200
```

It is important to understand the significance of this defintion. Because the index for the database has a fixed length, the program must place an upper limit on the number of records that can be entered into the database itself. In a practical sense this limitation is not likely to matter to users of the *Real Estate* application; there is, after all, an upper limit to the number of places a house-hunter will view before making a decision. If, however, you find that you want to expand the home database beyond the length currently allowed by the program, you can take either of two approaches to revise the code:

- Increase the value of the **MaxRecords** constant.
- Restructure the database index, **AddressList**, as a dynamic array.

The second of these two revisions is a particularly interesting programming exercise, which you might want to try after you have finished studying the current version of the program.

The form-level declaration section also defines a string constant that represents the file name of the database:

```
Const HomeDataBase = "C:\HOMES.DB"
```

The **Form_Load** procedure for the **HomeInpt** form (Listing 8.2) issues an **Open** statement to open this database as a random-access file:

```
Open HomeDataBase For Random As #1 Len = Len(HomeRecord)
```

Notice that this statement uses the length of the **HomeRecord** variable to define the record length inside the file. The program then divides the length of the open file by the length of a single record to calculate the current number of records in the file.

```
RecCount = LOF(1) / Len(HomeRecord)
```

The **RecCount** variable is declared at the form level and is therefore available to all the procedures in the **HomeInpt** form.

After determining the size of the database, the **Form_Load** procedure reads sequentially through the entire file and builds the index. A **For** loop reads each record from the first to the last:

```
For i% = 1 To RecCount
  Get #1, i%, HomeRecord
```

Immediately after reading a record, the program adds the record's address to the drop-down list attached to the **Address** combo box. The **AddItem** method accomplishes this task:

```
Address.AddItem HomeRecord.Address
```

Finally, the procedure assigns the address string to the **AddressRef** field of the current **AddressList** record and the record number to the **RecNo** field:

```
AddressList(i%).AddressRef = UCase$(HomeRecord.Address)
AddressList(i%).RecNo = i%
```

The final step for building the index is to sort the list of addresses. A call to a general procedure named **SortAddressList** (Listing 8.4) does the job:

```
SortAddressList
```

This procedure uses a pair of nested **For** loops to compare each address in the index list with each address after it. Whenever two addresses are out of order, they are swapped. At the end of the looping, the addresses in the list are sorted in alphanumeric order. Now the index is ready to be used for retrieving records from the database.

The next events in the program depend upon the user's input activities and command choices.

Database Management Techniques

If the user enters the ten fields of a new home record and then clicks the **Save** button, the **SaveButton_Click** procedure (Listing 8.3) writes the record to the database. This procedure needs a way to distinguish between a new record that the user wants to append to the database and a revised record that the user wants to write over an existing record. To find out which of these is the case, the program searches through the index for the current **Address** field. If the address already exists the program assumes this is a revision; if not, this is a new record.

A call to the **SearchHomeRec%** function (Listing 8.4) searches for the current address entry in the index:

```
CurRec% = SearchHomeRec%(HomeRecord.Address)
```

The **SearchHomeRec%** function performs an efficient operation known as the *binary search*. This process continually divides the sorted address list into smaller and smaller pairs of sections, always focusing the search on the section in which the target address will ultimately be found if it exists. This approach minimizes the number of actual comparisons that take place during the search. If the routine finds the address in the index list, **SearchHomeRec%** returns the corresponding record number—that is, the position of the record in the database. If the address is not found, **SearchHomeRec%** returns a value of 0.

The **SaveButton_Click** procedure stores this return value in the **CurRec%** variable. If **CurRec%** is 0, the current text box entries represent a new home record. Accordingly, **SaveButton_Click** must perform several steps to add the record to the database:

1. Increase **RecCount** by 1:

    ```
    RecCount = RecCount + 1
    ```

2. Copy the address and the record number to the index and then sort the index once again:

    ```
    AddressList(RecCount).AddressRef = UCase$(HomeRecord.Address)
    AddressList(RecCount).RecNo = RecCount
    SortAddressList
    ```

3. Copy all the fields of the new record to the **HomeRecord** variable. Some of these fields are copied by the appropriate **LostFocus** procedures as soon as the user completes a numeric data entry. For example, the **AskPrice_LostFocus** procedure copies the asking price into the **HomeRecord.AskPrice** field:

```
HomeRecord.AskPrice = Val(AskPrice.Text)
```

The remaining fields are copied by the **SaveButton_Click** procedure, for example:

```
HomeRecord.Comments = Comments.Text
HomeRecord.Garage = Garage.Value
HomeRecord.Views = Views.Value
HomeRecord.Garden = Garden.Value
```

4. Write the complete home record to the end of the database:

```
CurRec% = RecCount
'  ...
Open HomeDataBase For Random As #1 Len =
Len(HomeRecord)
   Put #1, CurRec%, HomeRecord
Close #1
```

If the record already exists, **CurRec%** is the record's position in the database. In this case, the same **Open**, **Put**, and **Close** statements write the new version of the record to its correct place in the database.

SaveButton_Click anticipates one additional contingency. If the number of records in the database reaches the defined maximum—**MaxRecords**—the procedure cannot allow the user to save any new records:

```
ElseIf CurRec% = 0 And RecCount = MaxRecords Then
```

The program displays an alert box on the screen and performs a premature exit from the **SaveButton_Click** procedure:

```
MsgBox Msg$, 48, "Real Estate"
Exit Sub
```

Figure 8.5 shows the message that appears on the desktop in this situation.

Of course, if you decide to revise the program—restructuring the database index as a dynamic array—you can eliminate this passage from the **SaveButton_Click** procedure. Here is an outline of the steps required for this revised version:

1. A **ReDim Preserve** statement increases the size of the **AddressList** array after each new record is added to the database.

Figure 8.5 Error message displayed when database is "full"

2. The procedure adds an index entry for the newly appended record.

3. Finally, a call to the **SortAddressList** procedure rearranges the index, using the address field as the key to the sort.

The action of selecting an address from the drop-down **Address** list triggers a call to the **Address_Click** event procedure (Listing 8.5). This procedure's job is to read the selected record from the database and then to display its fields in the **HomeInpt** form. The first step is to look up the record number from the index, a task performed by a call to the **SearchHomeRec%** function:

```
GetRec% = SearchHomeRec%((Address.Text))
```

This call illustrates an important detail regarding procedures and arguments. By default, an argument variable is passed to a procedure or a function *by reference* in Visual Basic. This means that the procedure receives the argument's *address* in memory, and can potentially change the value of the variable. However, Visual Basic does not allow the value of a control property—for example, the **Text** property of a text box or combo box—to be sent by reference as an argument. Instead, a control property must be sent *by value*. This means that Visual Basic makes a copy of the argument and sends the copy to the procedure or function, thus protecting the original argument from changes.

There are two ways to send an argument by value in Visual Basic. One is simply to enclose the argument in parentheses in the procedure call. This is the technique used in the call to the **SearchHomeRec%** function:

```
SearchHomeRec((Address.Text))
```

Notice the double parentheses. The outer parentheses are required in the syntax of any function call. The inner parentheses indicate that the argument **Address.Text** is to be sent by value.

The other technique is to use the keyword **ByVal** in the argument list of the procedure or function itself. For example, here is how you could rewrite the first line of the **SearchHomeRec%** function:

```
Function SearchHomeRec% (ByVal InAddress$)
```

Because this function makes no attempt to change the value of **InAddress$**, the **ByVal** keyword is a reasonable alternative in this case. But note that some procedures and functions are designed to use argument variables—specifically, arguments that are passed by reference—to send information back to the calling procedure. In this case, you should use parentheses in the procedure call—rather than **ByVal** in the procedure definition—if you want to protect a particular argument variable from changes.

After the call to the **SearchHomeRec%** function, the **Address_Click** procedure uses the record number—stored in the variable **GetRec%**—to read the selected record directly from its position in the database:

```
Open HomeDataBase For Random As #1 Len = Len(HomeRecord)
Get #1, GetRec%, HomeRecord
Close #1
```

This **Get** statement reads the record stored at position **GetRec%** and stores the entire record in the fields of the **HomeRecord** variable. The procedure subsequently copies each field to its corresponding control in the **HomeInpt** form:

```
AskPrice.Text = HomeRecord.AskPrice
SqFeet.Text = HomeRecord.SqFeet
Bedrooms.Text = HomeRecord.Bedrooms
Bathrooms.Text = HomeRecord.Bathrooms
Garage.Value = HomeRecord.Garage
Garden.Value = HomeRecord.Garden
Views.Value = HomeRecord.Views
DateViewed.Text = Format$(HomeRecord.DateViewed,
DateFormat)
Comments.Text = HomeRecord.Comments
```

As you know, the Text property of a Visual Basic 2.0 or 3.0 text box control can be assigned a value of any type—numeric, string, date, or **Variant**. Except for the statement that displays a formatted date, no data type conversion is required in this passage, even though the fields of the **HomeRecord** variable belong to a variety of data types.

Note the use of Visual Basic's **Format$** function to convert the **DateViewed** field into a displayable date format:

```
DateViewed.Text = Format$(HomeRecord.DateViewed, DateFormat)
```

HomeRecord.DateViewed is a serial date, stored in the database as a double-precision real value. As illustrated in the *Sales Week* application, the **Format$** function supports a great variety of formats for converting serial dates into date display strings. In the *Real Estate* applications, the following constant establishes the display format for any date that appears in the **Date Viewed** text box:

```
Const DateFormat = "d-mmm-yy"
```

In fact, the program takes care of converting any date entry into this standard date format.

Accepting Dates As Input from the Keyboard

The **DateViewed.LostFocus** procedure (Listing 8.7) validates any date that the user enters into the **Date Viewed** text box. If the entry is a valid date, the procedure copies the date to the **HomeRecord.DateViewed** field and redisplays the value in the standard date format. If the entry is not valid, the procedure displays an error message (Figure 8.2) and instead stores today's date in the text box.

To test the date entry, the procedure assigns the **DateViewed.Text** value to a **Variant**-type variable named **NewDate**, and then uses the **IsDate** function to determine whether the entry is a valid date:

```
NewDate = DateViewed.Text
If IsDate(NewDate) Then
```

If **IsDate** returns a value of **True**, the procedure stores the serial equivalent of the date in the **HomeRecord.DateViewed** field:

```
SerialEquiv = DateValue(NewDate)
HomeRecord.DateViewed = SerialEquiv
```

On the other hand, if the user's date entry cannot be recognized, the program displays an error message and reinitializes the date display:

```
Else

  MsgBox "Illegal Date", 48, "Input Error"
  InitDate

End If
```

The **InitDate** procedure (also Listing 8.7) simply assigns today's date to the **DateViewed** field:

```
HomeRecord.DateViewed = Now
```

Then the following statement standardizes the display format:

```
DateViewed.Text = Format$(HomeRecord.DateViewed, DateFormat)
```

In short, the *Real Estate* application uses the following Visual Basic functions to handle date entries appropriately:

- The **DateValue** function returns the serial date value from a date string.

- The **Format$** function produces a formatted date string from a serial date. (**Format** returns a date as a **Variant**-type value.)

- The **Now** function supplies the serial date value for the current system date and time.

You'll learn more about serial values, the **Variant** data type, and Visual Basic's date and time functions in Chapter 9.

SUMMARY: DATABASE MANAGEMENT IN VISUAL BASIC

In any database programming environment the first step in creating a successful database is to define an appropriate record structure. The user-defined record structure is the tool to use for this definition in Visual Basic. A **Type** statement located in a code module outlines the fields of a record structure, and a subsequent **Dim** statement creates a record variable.

References to this record variable appear in several different file statements. First, the statement that opens the database uses the variable to establish the fixed record length of a random-access file:

```
Open FileName For Random As #1 Len = Len(RecordVariable)
```

Once the file is open, the record variable also has a role in the calculation of the number of records currently in the database. The record count is equal to the length of the open file divided by the length of the record variable.

```
RecordCount = LOF(1) / Len(RecordVariable)
```

Finally, the **Get** and **Put** statements that perform input and output operations on the database use the record variable to represent individual record values. As a result of a **Get** statement, a record is read from the database and stored in the record variable:

```
Get #1, RecordNumber, RecordVariable
```

And a **Put** statement writes a new record to the file:

```
Put #1, RecordNumber, RecordVariable
```

In advance of the **Put** statement, the program assigns a complete set of field values to the record variable.

A database management program typically builds an index structure to provide efficient access to records in the database. The index has at least two values for each record: a field value that serves as the key for a record search and the corresponding record number. The program keeps the index sorted by the key field. Given this sorted index, an algorithm known as the *binary search* performs an efficient search for a given record in the index. After a successful search, the index provides the numeric position in the database where the target record will be found.

Listing 8.1 Declarations from **HOMEGLOB.BAS** and the **HomeInpt** form

```
' The Real Estate Application
' HOMEGLOB.BAS Global Declarations

' The record type definition for a home description:

Type HomeRecordType
   Address As String * 50
   AskPrice As Long
   SqFeet As Integer
   Bedrooms As Integer
   Bathrooms As Integer
   Garage As Integer
   Views As Integer
   Garden As Integer
   DateViewed As Double
   Comments As String * 125
End Type
```

```
' The record type definition for the address index:

Type IndexRecordType
  AddressRef As String * 50
  RecNo As Integer
End Type

' The mortgage payment table.

Global PaymentTable(5, 5)
Global DisplayTable$(5, 5)

' The current increment settings for the payment table.

Global CurPrincInc, CurRateInc



' The Real Estate Application
' HOMEINPT.FRM Declarations

' The program's standard date display format.

Const DateFormat = "d-mmm-yy"

' The database file name.

Const HomeDataBase = "C:\HOMES.DB"

' The maximum number of home records.

Const MaxRecords = 200

' The HomeRecord and AddressList structures.
' (The TYPE statements for these structures are in the
' global declarations module, HomeGlob.)

Dim HomeRecord As HomeRecordType
Dim AddressList(MaxRecords) As IndexRecordType
Dim RecCount As Integer
```

Listing 8.2 The **Form_Load** procedure (**HomeInpt**)

```
Sub Form_Load ()

  ' When the form is first loaded, initialize
  ' the date field and its display.

  InitDate

  ' Then open the home database file and read
  ' the records sequentially.

  Open HomeDataBase For Random As #1 Len = Len(HomeRecord)
  RecCount = LOF(1) / Len(HomeRecord)

  ' Store the address field and the record number
  ' in the AddressList index.

  For i% = 1 To RecCount
    Get #1, i%, HomeRecord
    Address.AddItem HomeRecord.Address
    AddressList(i%).AddressRef = UCase$(HomeRecord.Address)
    AddressList(i%).RecNo = i%
  Next i%
  Close #1
  ClearHomeRecord

  ' Alphabetize the index.

  SortAddressList

End Sub  ' Form_Load
```

Listing 8.3 The **SaveButton_Click** procedure

```
Sub SaveButton_Click ()

  ' Save a new address in the database.

  Dim Msg$, CurRec%, HomeAddr$

  HomeAddr$ = LTrim$(RTrim$(Address.Text))
```

```
If HomeAddr$ = "" Then

  ' Do not try to save without an address field.

  Msg$ = "Record cannot be saved without an address."
  MsgBox Msg$, 48, "Save"
  Address.SetFocus

Else

  HomeRecord.Address = HomeAddr$

  ' Find out if this record exists already.

  CurRec% = SearchHomeRec%(HomeRecord.Address)

  ' If not, create a new record.

  If CurRec% = 0 And RecCount < MaxRecords Then

    ' First add the address to the index.

    RecCount = RecCount + 1
    AddressList(RecCount).AddressRef = UCase$(HomeRecord.Address)
    AddressList(RecCount).RecNo = RecCount
    SortAddressList

    ' Add the address to the combo box list.

    Address.AddItem HomeRecord.Address
    CurRec% = RecCount

  ElseIf CurRec% = 0 And RecCount = MaxRecords Then

    ' Display a message if the database is full,
    ' and go no further with the save operation.

    Msg$ = "The database has reached its maximum length. "
    Msg$ = Msg$ + "You cannot add this new record."
    MsgBox Msg$, 48, "Real Estate"
    Exit Sub

  End If
```

(continued)

```
        ' Read the fields that have not already been read.

      HomeRecord.Comments = Comments.Text
      HomeRecord.Garage = Garage.Value
      HomeRecord.Views = Views.Value
      HomeRecord.Garden = Garden.Value

      ' Write the record to the database. If this is a new
      ' record, CurRec% is the new length of the database.
      ' For revising a record, CurRec% is the numeric
      ' position of the existing record.

      Open HomeDataBase For Random As #1 Len = Len(HomeRecord)
        Put #1, CurRec%, HomeRecord
      Close #1
    End If

End Sub   ' SaveButton_Click
```

Listing 8.4 The **SortAddressList** and **SearchHomeRec%** routines

```
Sub SortAddressList ()

  ' Alphabetize the database index.

  Dim TempAddressRec As IndexRecordType

  For i% = 1 To RecCount - 1
    For j% = i% + 1 To RecCount
      If AddressList(i%).AddressRef > AddressList(j%).AddressRef
      Then
        TempAddressRec = AddressList(i%)
        AddressList(i%) = AddressList(j%)
        AddressList(j%) = TempAddressRec
      End If
    Next j%
  Next i%

End Sub   ' SortAddressList
```

```
Function SearchHomeRec% (InAddress$)

  ' Search for an address in the database index.

  AddrFound% = 0
  startPos% = 1
  endPos% = RecCount

  Do While ((AddrFound% = 0) And (startPos% <= endPos%))
    centerPos% = (startPos% + endPos%) \ 2
    Select Case UCase$(InAddress$)
      Case AddressList(centerPos%).AddressRef
        AddrFound% = AddressList(centerPos%).RecNo
      Case Is > AddressList(centerPos%).AddressRef
        startPos% = centerPos% + 1
      Case Else
        endPos% = centerPos% - 1
    End Select
  Loop

  ' Return the record number if the address was found;
  ' otherwise return a value of zero.

  SearchHomeRec% = AddrFound%

End Function  ' SearchHomeRec%
```

Listing 8.5 The **Address_Click** procedure

```
Sub Address_Click ()

  ' Retrieve an address record when the user selects
  ' an address from the Address combo box.

  GetRec% = SearchHomeRec%((Address.Text))
  If GetRec% <> 0 Then
    Open HomeDataBase For Random As #1 Len = Len(HomeRecord)
    Get #1, GetRec%, HomeRecord
    Close #1

    ' Copy the fields of the address record to the
    ' appropriate controls on the input form.
```

(continued)

```
      AskPrice.Text = HomeRecord.AskPrice
      SqFeet.Text = HomeRecord.SqFeet
      Bedrooms.Text = HomeRecord.Bedrooms
      Bathrooms.Text = HomeRecord.Bathrooms
      Garage.Value = HomeRecord.Garage
      Garden.Value = HomeRecord.Garden
      Views.Value = HomeRecord.Views
      DateViewed.Text = Format$(HomeRecord.DateViewed, DateFormat)
      Comments.Text = HomeRecord.Comments
   End If

End Sub   ' Address_Click
```

Listing 8.6 Click procedures and the **ClearHomeRecord** procedure

```
Sub ClearButton_Click ()

   ' Clear all the string and numeric text boxes,
   ' and reinitialize the date field.

   Address.Text = ""
   AskPrice.Text = ""
   Comments.Text = ""
   SqFeet.Text = ""
   Bedrooms.Text = ""
   Bathrooms.Text = ""
   InitDate
   Garage.Value = False
   Views.Value = False
   Garden.Value = False
   Address.SetFocus

   ClearHomeRecord

End Sub   ' ClearButton_Click


Sub ClearHomeRecord ()

   ' Clear the fields of the HomeRecord variable.
```

```
   HomeRecord.Address = ""
   HomeRecord.AskPrice = 0
   HomeRecord.SqFeet = 0
   HomeRecord.Bedrooms = 0
   HomeRecord.Bathrooms = 0
   HomeRecord.Garage = False
   HomeRecord.Views = False
   HomeRecord.Garden = False
   HomeRecord.Comments = ""

End Sub   ' ClearHomeRecord



Sub PmtButton_Click ()

   ' Display the dialog box for the Mortgage Calculator.

   MortInpt.Show

   ' Copy the asking price to the selling price box
   ' and clear the other text boxes on the
   ' MortInpt form.

   MortInpt!InPrice.Text = AskPrice.Text
   MortInpt!InDown = ""
   MortInpt!InTerm = ""
   MortInpt!InRate = ""

   ' Temporarily hide the main dialog box.

   HomeInpt.Hide

End Sub   ' PmtButton_Click



Sub ExitButton_Click ()

   ' Stop the program performance.

   End

End Sub   ' ExitButton_Click
```

Listing 8.7 DateViewed_LostFocus and InitDate

```
Sub DateViewed_LostFocus ()

  ' Validate the user's date entry
  ' and redisplay it in the program's
  ' standard format. Assign the serial
  ' equivalent to the HomeRecord.DateViewed
  ' field.

  Dim NewDate As Variant
  Dim SerialEquiv As Double

  NewDate = DateViewed.Text
  If IsDate(NewDate) Then

    SerialEquiv = DateValue(NewDate)
    DateViewed.Text = Format(SerialEquiv, DateFormat)
    HomeRecord.DateViewed = SerialEquiv

  Else

    ' If the user has entered an invalid date,
    ' display an error message and redisplay
    ' today's date.

    MsgBox "Illegal Date", 48, "Input Error"
    InitDate

  End If

End Sub   ' DateViewed_LostFocus


Sub InitDate ()

  ' Initialize the date field to today's date.

  HomeRecord.DateViewed = Now

  ' Display this date in the program's standard date format.

  DateViewed.Text = Format$(HomeRecord.DateViewed, DateFormat)

End Sub   ' InitDate
```

Listing 8.8 GotFocus procedures and the **HighlightEntry** procedure

```
Sub AskPrice_GotFocus ()

  ' Highlight the contents of the text box.

  HighlightEntry AskPrice

End Sub


Sub Bathrooms_GotFocus ()

  ' Highlight the contents of the text box.

  HighlightEntry Bathrooms

End Sub   ' Bathrooms_GotFocus


Sub Bedrooms_GotFocus ()

  ' Highlight the contents of the text box.

  HighlightEntry Bedrooms

End Sub   ' Bedrooms_GotFocus


Sub Comments_GotFocus ()

  ' Highlight the contents of the text box.

  HighlightEntry Comments

End Sub   ' Comments_GotFocus


Sub DateViewed_GotFocus ()

  ' Highlight the contents of the text box.

  HighlightEntry DateViewed

End Sub   ' DateViewed_GotFocus
```

(continued)

```
Sub SqFeet_GotFocus ()

  ' Highlight the contents of the text box.

  HighlightEntry SqFeet

End Sub  ' SqFeet_GotFocus


' HighlightEntry procedure (HOMEGLOB.BAS)

Sub HighlightEntry (TextBox As Control)

  ' Highlight the contents of the text box
  ' that has just received the focus.

  TextBox.SelStart = 0
  TextBox.SelLength = Len(TextBox.Text)

End Sub  ' HighlightEntry
```

Listing 8.9 The **LostFocus** event procedures

```
Sub AskPrice_LostFocus ()

  ' Validate the asking price entry when
  ' the user moves the focus to another control.

   HomeRecord.AskPrice = Val(AskPrice.Text)
   AskPrice.Text = HomeRecord.AskPrice

End Sub  ' AskPrice_LostFocus


Sub Bathrooms_LostFocus ()

  ' Validate the entry for the number of bathrooms.

  HomeRecord.Bathrooms = Val(Bathrooms.Text)
  Bathrooms.Text = HomeRecord.Bathrooms

End Sub  ' Bathrooms_LostFocus
```

```
Sub Bedrooms_LostFocus ()

  ' Validate the entry for the number of bedrooms.

  HomeRecord.Bedrooms = Val(Bedrooms.Text)
  Bedrooms.Text = HomeRecord.Bedrooms

End Sub   ' Bedrooms_LostFocus


Sub SqFeet_LostFocus ()

  ' Validate the entry for the square footage.

  HomeRecord.SqFeet = Val(SqFeet.Text)
  SqFeet.Text = HomeRecord.SqFeet

End Sub   ' SqFeet_LostFocus
```

Listing 8.10 Form-level declarations and the **Form_Load** procedure (**MortInpt**)

```
' MORTINPT.FRM Declarations

Dim BadInput As Integer


Sub Form_Load ()

  'Arrange windows and initialize variables.

  LoanTabl.Hide
  LoanOpts.Hide

  CurPrincInc = 1000
  CurRateInc = .005

  ' Build the combo box list for
  ' the term of the loan.

  InTerm.AddItem "4 years"
  InTerm.AddItem "5 years"
```

(continued)

```
   InTerm.AddItem "10 years"
   InTerm.AddItem "15 years"
   InTerm.AddItem "20 years"
   InTerm.AddItem "30 years"

End Sub  ' Form_Load
```

Listing 8.11 The **Calc_Click** and the **Payment** routines (**MortInpt**)

```
Sub Calc_Click ()

' When the user clicks the Calc button...
' Begin by reading the values
' that have been entered into the two input boxes
' and the combo box.

  d = Val(InDown.Text) / 100
  p = Val(InPrice.Text) * (1 - d)
  i = Val(InRate.Text) / 100
  t = Val(InTerm.Text)

' Determine whether the values are usable.

  BadInput = (p = 0) Or (i = 0) Or (t = 0)

' If not, display an error message.

  If BadInput Then
    msg$ = "Input values are not valid."
    title$ = "Loan Parameters"
    MsgBox msg$, 48, title$

' Otherwise, calculate the loan payment table,
' and display it in a window.

  Else
    CalculateTable p, CurPrincInc, i, CurRateInc, t
    ShowTable
  End If

End Sub  ' Calc_Click
```

```
Function Payment (Princ, MoRate, Months)

  ' Calculate a monthly mortgage payment.

  Payment = (Princ * MoRate) / (1 - (1 + MoRate) ^ (-Months))

End Function  ' Payment
```

Listing 8.12 The **CalculateTable** and **ShowTable** procedures (**MortInpt**)

```
Sub CalculateTable (Princ, DeltaP, YrRate, DeltaR, Years)

  ' Calculate the mortgage table.

  Dim StartPrinc, StartRate, Mult As Integer, i%, p%, r%

  ' Compute the starting parameters for the table.

  StartPrinc = Princ - 2 * DeltaP
  StartRate = YrRate - 2 * DeltaR

  ' Build the first row and the first column of the table.

  For i% = 1 To 5
    Mult = i% - 1
    PaymentTable(i%, 0) = StartPrinc + DeltaP * Mult
    DisplayTable$(i%, 0) = Format$(PaymentTable(i%, 0), "$#,######")
    PaymentTable(0, i%) = StartRate + DeltaR * Mult
    DisplayTable$(0, i%) = Format$(PaymentTable(0, i%), "0.000%")
  Next i%

  ' Fill in the remaining rows and columns of data.

  For p% = 1 To 5
    TempP = PaymentTable(p%, 0)
    For r% = 1 To 5
      TempR = PaymentTable(0, r%) / 12
      PaymentTable(p%, r%) = Payment(TempP, TempR, Years * 12)
      DisplayTable$(p%, r%) = Format$(PaymentTable(p%, r%), "$#,####.00")
    Next r%
  Next p%

End Sub  ' CalculateTable
```

(continued)

```
Sub ShowTable ()

  ' Display the mortgage table.

  LoanTabl.Show
  LoanTabl.FontName = "Tms Rmn"
  LoanTabl.FontSize = 10
  LoanTabl.FontBold = False
  LoanTabl.Cls

  TempStr$ = Space$(15)
  For i% = 0 To 5
    For j% = 0 To 5
      LoanTabl.Print Tab(15 * j%);
      RSet TempStr$ = RTrim$(DisplayTable$(i%, j%))
      If j% = 3 And i% = 3 Then

        ' Display the target calculation in bold.

        LoanTabl.FontBold = True
        SpLen% = 11 - Len(LTrim$(TempStr$))
        LoanTabl.Print Space$(SpLen%); LTrim$(TempStr$);
        LoanTabl.FontBold = False
      Else
        LoanTabl.Print TempStr$;
      End If
    Next j%
    LoanTabl.Print
    If i% = 0 Then LoanTabl.Print
  Next i%

  MortInpt.SetFocus

End Sub   ' ShowTable
```

Listing 8.13 Options_Click, ExitButton_Click, and GotFocus procedures

```
Sub Options_Click ()

  ' Display the Table Values window.

  LoanOpts.Show

End Sub   ' Options_Click
```

```
Sub ExitButton_Click ()

  ' Go back to the main dialog box.

  MortInpt.Hide
  LoanTabl.Hide
  HomeInpt.Show

End Sub  ' ExitButton_Click


Sub InDown_GotFocus ()

  ' Highlight the contents
  ' of the text box.

  HighlightEntry InDown

End Sub  ' InDown_GotFocus


Sub InPrice_GotFocus ()

  ' Highlight the contents
  ' of the text box.

  HighlightEntry InPrice

End Sub  ' InPrice_GotFocus


Sub InRate_GotFocus ()

  ' Highlight the contents
  ' of the text box.

  HighlightEntry InRate

End Sub  ' InRate_GotFocus
```

Listing 8.14 OkOpts_Click procedure (**LoanOpts**)

```
Sub OkOpts_Click ()

  Dim i%

  ' Read the new settings for the principal increment
  ' and the rate increment.

  For i% = 0 To 4
    If PInc(i%).Value Then

      ' Calculate the principal increment.

      CurPrincInc = 10 ^ (i% + 1)
    End If

    If RInc(i%).Value Then

      ' Select the rate increment.

      Select Case i%
        Case 0
          curRateInc = .00125
        Case 1
          curRateInc = .0025
        Case 2
          curRateInc = .005
        Case 3
          curRateInc = .01
        Case 4
          curRateInc = .02
      End Select
    End If

  Next i%

  ' Close the Table Values window.

  LoanOpts.Hide

End Sub  ' OkOpts_Click
```

9

Chronological Data and MDI: The Workday *Application*

INTRODUCTION

This chapter presents an application named *Workday,* designed to help you record billable hours or maintain daily time sheet files. As you explore the *Workday* project, you'll focus on two general programming topics:

1. Techniques for working with chronological data, a subject you've examined briefly in other chapters.
2. Visual Basic's new facility for creating *multiple-document interface* applications, also known as MDI.

Chronological data—consisting of both date and time values—are important in a large variety of business applications. For example, a customer billing program might keep track of several dates for a given customer's account: a closing date, a billing date, a due date, and the actual payment date. The program may need to perform specific operations with these dates, such as finding the number of days between the due date and the payment date. Similarly, a time sheet program calculates the amount of time that elapses between two time values—the time when an employee begins working on a particular job, and the time when the work ends. These operations and others like them are sometimes called *date arithmetic* and *time arithmetic.*

To perform efficient arithmetic operations on chronological values, a program needs a system for translating dates and times into representative numeric values. For this purpose, dates are often represented as integers. In general, a given date-integer value is equal to the number of days elapsed since a fixed reference point in the past. Given two date integers, you can easily find the number of days between the two corresponding dates by subtracting one number from the other. A time value, on the other hand, can be conveniently represented as a fractional value, expressing the portion of a 24-hour day that has gone by at a given point in time. For example, 6:00 A.M. is represented by the decimal fraction .25—because one-fourth of a day is over at six in the morning.

As you've seen, Visual Basic uses a practical format known as the *serial number* to represent date and time values together. Specifically, a serial number is a double-precision value that Visual Basic interprets as a particular date and time. The integer portion of a serial number—that is, the sequence of digits located before the decimal point—represents a date. The fractional portion—located after the decimal point—represents the time of day. The fixed reference date in the past that Visual Basic uses to calculate serial dates is December 30, 1899. This "starting date" has a serial value of 0. Subsequent dates have positive serial values, and prior dates have negative values.

The exercise disk has a simple application named the *Date Converter* that you can use to explore Visual Basic's serial date system. The project is stored on disk as DATES.MAK. Load it now into the Visual Basic environment and press F5 to run it. The form that appears on the screen has five boxes (Figure 9.1). In the two boxes at the left side of the form you can enter date strings in any recognizable format. (Enter a date and then press the Tab key to move the edit cursor to the next or previous text box.) In response, the program displays the corresponding serial date in the adjacent box to the right. When you then enter a second date string, the program calculates the difference between the two dates in days, and displays this value in the single text box at the right side of the form.

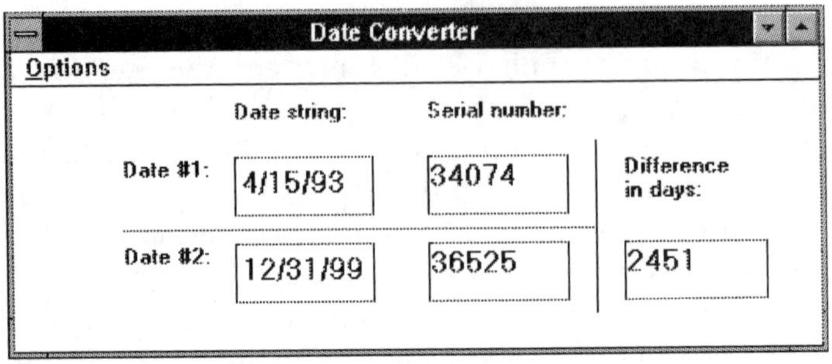

Figure 9.1 The *Date Converter* exercise

For example, in Figure 9.1 the dates 4/15/93 and 12/31/99 have been entered into the two text boxes. As you can see, the corresponding serial dates are **34074** and **36525**, respectively. In other words, the date April 14, 1993 is 34,074 days forward from December 30, 1899, the starting point of Visual Basic's serial date system. Likewise, December 31, 1999 is 36,525 days forward from the starting date.

The number of days between these two dates, shown as **2451**, is equal to the difference between their serial date equivalents. In general, you compute the number of days between any two dates by subtracting one serial date from the other:

```
DiffInDays = Date2 - Date1
```

Combined with a fractional value representing the time of day, a serial number is a complete date-and-time value. Consider the following example:

```
34074.75
```

You already know from Figure 9.1 that 34074 represents the date 4/15/93. The decimal value .75 represents 6:00 P.M., the time when three-quarters of the day is over. Consequently, Visual Basic interprets this serial number as April 15, 1993 at 6:00 P.M.

To use serial numbers effectively, you sometimes need techniques for converting string date formats—such as "April 15, 1993" or "4/15/93"—into serial dates, and conversely, for creating serial numbers from recognizable date strings. You may also need tools for converting between time strings—such as "7:55 A.M." or "21:15:38"—and their equivalent serial time values. As you might expect, Visual Basic has a useful library of functions that relate to this subject. Here are five of the most important among them:

- The **DateValue** function takes a date string (or **Variant**) as its argument, and provides the equivalent serial date value as a **Variant**.

- The **TimeValue** function takes a time string (or **Variant**) as its argument, and returns the equivalent serial time value as a **Variant**.

- The **Format$** function—useful for creating string displays in many different contexts—can produce date and time strings from serial numbers. (The **Format** function performs the same operations, but returns a **Variant**-type value.)

- The **Now** function returns a **Variant** representing the current date and time.

- The **IsDate** function determines whether the value of a **Variant**-type variable is a recognizable date.

As you saw in Chapter 8, the **Variant**-type variable is often the most convenient tool for working with date-type values that the user enters from the keyboard. If you take a look at the code in the *Date Converter* application (Listing 9.1), you'll see several uses of **Variant** variables for storing date values. In particular, the **DateString_LostFocus** event procedure defines a **Variant** variable named **InDate** to represent the user's date input:

```
Dim InDate As Variant
```

The procedure begins by assigning the user's input value (entered into the **DateStr** text box) to this variable, and then testing the value with the **IsDate** function:

```
InDate = DateStr(Index).Text
If IsDate(InDate) Then
```

If **InDate** contains a valid date entry, the program uses the **DateValue** function to find the date's serial equivalent, which is then displayed as the caption of the **SerialNum** label control:

```
SerialEquiv = DateValue(InDate)
SerialNum(Index).Caption = SerialEquiv
```

SerialEquiv is a long-integer variable, defined for storing the serial equivalent of a date.

Another event procedure named **TodayDate_Click** uses a **Variant** variable named **Today** to represent the current date. The **Int** and **Now** functions produce today's date:

```
Dim Today As Variant
Today = Int(Now)
```

To display the date, the program simply assigns this value to the **DateStr** text box. No conversion is necessary in this case, because the **Variant**-type variable stores the date in a displayable format. Then the program uses **DateValue** to find the equivalent serial number:

```
DateStr(Index).Text = Today
SerialEquiv = DateValue(Today)
SerialNum(Index).Caption = SerialEquiv
```

Finally, the procedure named **CalcDiff** finds the difference in days between two dates by subtracting one serial number from the other:

```
d1 = SerialNum(0).Caption
d2 = SerialNum(1).Caption

Diff.Caption = Abs(d1 - d2)
```

The use of the **Abs** function guarantees that the result will be a positive number of days, regardless of which date is earlier, **d1** or **d2**.

You'll see additional examples of these and other date and time techniques in the *Workday* application.

THE *WORKDAY* APPLICATION

Workday is a time sheet program, designed for tracking the amount of time spent on particular jobs or projects during the course of a given business day. The application is suitable for a variety of business people, including:

- Employees who are required to account in detail for time spent on the job.

- Managers who want to analyze the time requirements for a variety of tasks.

- Professionals who need to produce records of time that is billable to particular clients.

The *Workday* project is stored on the the exercise disk under the name WORKDAY.MAK. When you load it into the Visual Basic environment, you'll see that the project consists of four forms and a code module (Figure 9.2).

This project's startup form is named **TSMDI**, indicating that the application is an example of a *multiple-document interface*. The capacity for multiple-document interface applications, or MDI, is an important new feature in Visual Basic 2.0 and 3.0. In an MDI application the user can open and work with more than one document file at a time. Familiar Windows applications such as word processors and spreadsheet programs typically are designed as multiple-document interfaces.

An MDI application contains one MDI form along with one or more *child* forms. During run time, a child form appears as a window inside the

Figure 9.2 The WORKDAY.MAK project

background of the MDI form. At design time, Visual Basic provides simple techniques for creating MDI and child forms:

- To add an MDI form to an application, you choose the **New MDI Form** command from the **File** menu. (This command is dimmed for an application that already has an MDI form; no application may have more than one MDI form.)

- To create a child form, you select the form that is to become the child and set the form's **MDIChild** property to **True**.

As you'll learn in this chapter, your application can display multiple *instances* of a child form within the MDI form during run time.

In the *Workday* application, the form named **TimeSheet** (TMSHEET.FRM on disk) is the child form. As you can see in the project window, Visual Basic uses special icons to identify the MDI and child forms. Other forms in the *Workday* application are named **TSPrint** (TSPRINT.FRM) and **TSOpen** (TSOPEN.FRM). The code module is stored as TIMEPROC.BAS.

Press the F5 function key to run the program. When you do so, the program's MDI form—titled *Daily Work Records*—appears on the Windows desktop (Figure 9.3). The form contains several interesting visual elements, including:

- A menu bar with individual pull-down menus named **File**, **Pages**, **Time**, and **Windows**.

- A toolbar with seven icons representing some of the program's major operations.

- A display of the current date and time, just to the right of the toolbar. This display is updated every minute from the system clock.

- Two time sheet windows, which initially display today's and yesterday's time sheets. These windows are instances of the child form named **TimeSheet**.

The two windows are always available during run time so that you can view, edit, and compare the time sheets for any two dates of your choice. (No additional windows can be opened beyond the two, but you can open any date's time sheet into either window, as you'll see later.) In general, the operations represented by the program's menu commands and toolbar icons all apply to the time sheet displayed in the *active* window. To activate either of the two windows, pull down the **Windows** menu and choose the name of the window you want to view, or simply click the title bar of the inactive window.

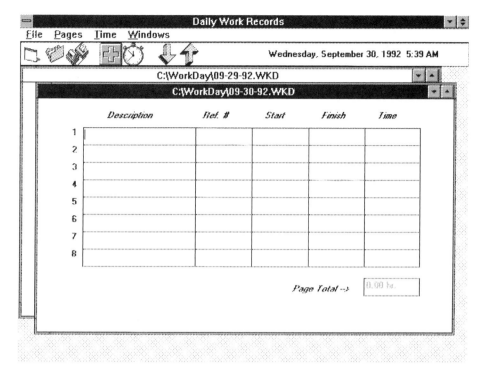

Figure 9.3 The *Workday* application

Inside each of the time sheet windows are columns of cells for recording and viewing the details of a workday. You'll see that both windows are organized in the same way. The time sheet grid has five columns:

- The *Description* column is for the name or description of a given job, project, or client.

- The *Ref #* column is for an optional reference number.

- The *Start* and *Finish* columns are for recording the starting time and finishing time for work on a particular job.

- Finally, the *Time* column ultimately displays the total amount of time spent on a job. The *Workday* program fills in this column after you supply values for *Start* and *Finish*.

Finally, there is a *Page Total* box at the lower-right corner of each window. The program uses this box to display the total hours of the jobs displayed on the current page of a time sheet window. A time sheet for a given date consists of as many as ten pages, each containing up to eight lines of job descriptions.

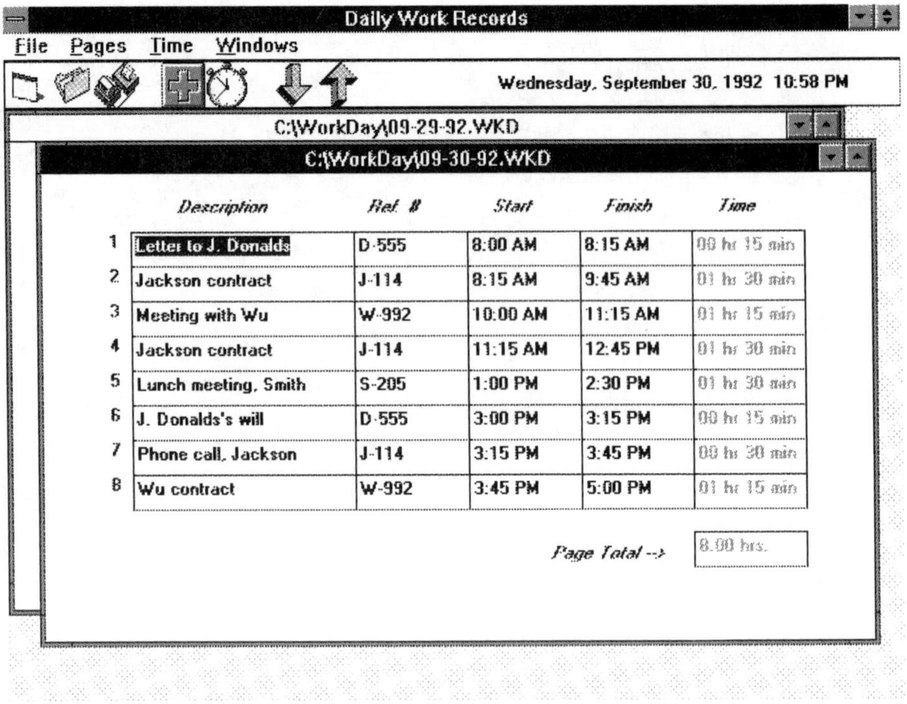

Figure 9.4 A completed daily work record, page 1

Each window's title bar shows the file name for the current time sheet. Although the program begins by displaying the time sheets for today's and yesterday's date, you can open and work with any two time sheet files at a time.

Figures 9.4 and 9.5 show an example of a two-page time sheet for a day's work. To scroll down to the next page in the active time sheet window, you can perform any one of the following three actions:

- Choose the **Next Page** command from the program's **Pages** menu.

- Press the F8 function key from the keyboard.

- Click the down arrow icon, the second-to-last item in the application's toolbar.

Conversely, to scroll up to the previous page, choose the **Previous Page** command, press F7, or click the up arrow icon.

Notice the variety of formats in which the program displays time values. Times in the *Start* and *Finish* columns appear in AM/PM format, for example:

```
8:15 AM
```

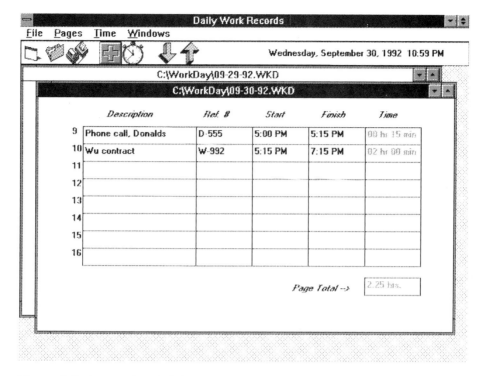

Figure 9.5 A completed daily work record, page 2

In contrast, the elapsed time amounts in the *Time* column are expressed in hours and minutes, such as:

```
01 hr 30 min
```

Finally, the *Total* box shows the total working time for the entire day, expressed as a decimal value:

```
8.00 hrs
```

You'll see how these displays are produced when you examine the program's code later in this chapter.

The *Workday* application has a number of features that make it particularly convenient for creating and using daily work records:

- The program's **Windows** menu gives you a choice between two arrangements for the two time sheet windows: **Cascade** (the default) or **Tile**. The tile arrangement is shown in Figure 9.6. You can use standard Windows keyboard techniques to copy entries from one window to the other: Select an entry in one window and press Ctrl+C to copy the entry to the Clipboard; then activate the other window,

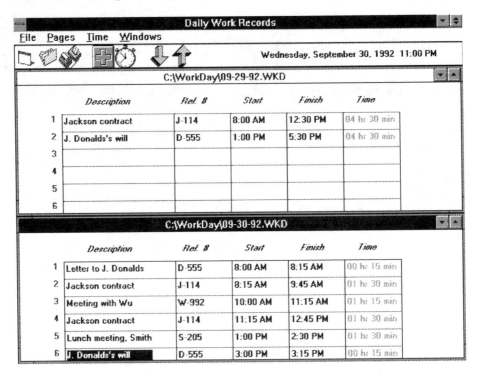

Figure 9.6 The tile arrangement for the two time sheet windows

select a text box, and press Ctrl+V to paste a copy of the entry in the new location.

- In the active window, the program allows you to enter times into the *Start* and *Finish* columns in two ways: If you type a time entry directly from the keyboard, the program checks your entry—making sure it represents a valid time value—and then converts it to a standard time display format. Alternatively, you can enter the *current* time into any *Start* or *Finish* box by selecting the box and pressing Ctrl-T from the keyboard.

- The times displayed in the *Time* column and the *Page Total* box are updated automatically each time you complete a job line or change a *Start* or *Finish* time. Furthermore, you can view the total hours for all the pages in the active time sheet window by choosing the **Show Total** command from the **Pages** menu. (Alternatively, press the F6 function key from the keyboard; or click the Total icon, the fourth tool in the application's toolbar.) When you do so, the program displays a message box like the one shown in Figure 9.7. As you can see, the sample time sheet contains records for a total of 10.25 hours.

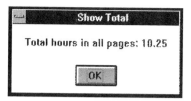

Figure 9.7 The total hours from both pages of a day's work record

- Options available in the program's **File** menu allow you to create a new time sheet or open any existing time sheet file in the active window. Each day's time sheet is stored in its own file on disk.

- The program allows you to print a variety of reports from a time sheet. For a simple printout of the time sheet in the active window, you can choose the **Print This Time Sheet** command from the **File** menu (or press Ctrl-P; or click the Print icon, the third tool in the toolbar). In response, the program prints all the nonblank lines of the open time sheet file, as shown in Figure 9.8. Alternatively, you can produce reports from any day's time sheet file. These printed reports are sorted by reference numbers, and include subtotals and a total. The example shown in Figure 9.9 is created from the two-page time sheets in Figures 9.4 and 9.5. You can send reports like this one directly to your printer, or save them to disk as text files for subsequent processing or editing.

- The program can also print summary reports for an entire week's work records. Weekly reports are sorted by reference numbers and also include subtotals and a total.

```
Time Sheet File: C:\WorkDay\09-30-92.WKD

Letter to J. Donalds      D-555      08:00 AM   08:15 AM    00 hr 15 min
Jackson contract          J-114      08:15 AM   09:45 AM    01 hr 30 min
Meeting with Wu           W-992      10:00 AM   11:15 AM    01 hr 15 min
Jackson contract          J-114      11:15 AM   12:45 PM    01 hr 30 min
Lunch meeting, Smith      S-205      01:00 PM   02:30 PM    01 hr 30 min
J. Donalds's will         D-555      03:00 PM   03:15 PM    00 hr 15 min
Phone call, Jackson       J-114      03:15 PM   03:45 PM    00 hr 30 min
Wu contract               W-992      03:45 PM   05:00 PM    01 hr 15 min
Phone call, Donalds       D-555      05:00 PM   05:15 PM    00 hr 15 min
Wu contract               W-992      05:15 PM   07:15 PM    02 hr 00 min

                                     Total --> 10.25 hrs.
```

Figure 9.8 A printout from the current time sheet

```
                    Time Sheet for 09-30-92
                    =========================

Job Description             Ref.      Start      Finish      Total Time
----------------            ----      -----      ------      ----------
J. Donalds's will           D-555     03:00 PM   03:15 PM    00 hr 15 min
Letter to J. Donalds        D-555     08:00 AM   08:15 AM    00 hr 15 min
Phone call, Donalds         D-555     05:00 PM   05:15 PM    00 hr 15 min

                            Total for D-555      --> 0.75 hr

Jackson contract            J-114     08:15 AM   09:45 AM    01 hr 30 min
Jackson contract            J-114     11:15 AM   12:45 PM    01 hr 30 min
Phone call, Jackson         J-114     03:15 PM   03:45 PM    00 hr 30 min

                            Total for J-114      --> 3.50 hrs

Lunch meeting, Smith        S-205     01:00 PM   02:30 PM    01 hr 30 min

                            Total for S-205      --> 1.50 hrs

Meeting with Wu             W-992     10:00 AM   11:15 AM    01 hr 15 min
Wu contract                 W-992     03:45 PM   05:00 PM    01 hr 15 min
Wu contract                 W-992     05:15 PM   07:15 PM    02 hr 00 min

                            Total for W-992      --> 4.50 hrs

                            *** Total Work Time ---> 10.25 hrs
```

Figure 9.9 A sorted time sheet report

You'll continue investigating the program's features in the sections ahead.

Entering Data into the Work Record Form

In all but the last column of the time sheet grid you can enter and edit information in any way you wish. To select a text box, click it with the mouse or use the keyboard:

- Press the Tab key to move from one box to the next inside the first four columns.

- Press the up or down arrow key to move to the previous or next box in the current column.

To enter the current time into a box in the *Start* or *Finish* column, you select the box and choose the **Enter the Current Time** command from the

Time menu, or press Ctrl+T from the keyboard, or click the stopwatch icon in the toolbar. To see how this works, try the following exercise:

1. In the *Description* column of line 1 in the active window, enter the following imaginary project name:

   ```
   Billing application
   ```

2. In the *Ref #* column, enter:

   ```
   B-112
   ```

3. Now move the mouse pointer to the *Start* column box in line 1, and click the stopwatch icon in the toolbar. The program enters the current time into the box (Figure 9.10).

These three steps simulate the actions you might take as you begin working on a particular project on the morning of a new workday. You enter your description of the project, then at the point in time when you are ready to begin your work you select the *Start* box and click the stopwatch icon. Then you go to work.

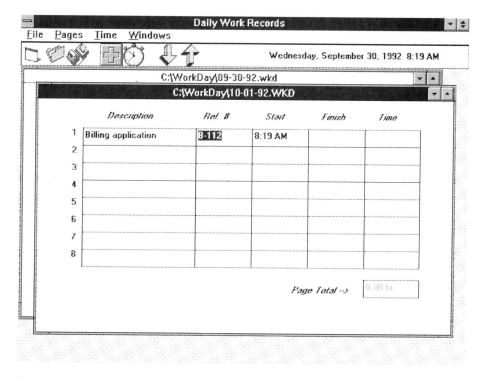

Figure 9.10 Entering a job description and a starting time

If you need to run other applications during your work, the compiled *Workday* application can be reduced to an icon on the Windows desktop—temporarily out of your way, but available at any time. To return to the application, you double-click the icon. Alternatively, you can exit from the *Workday* application altogether. When you later restart the program, it automatically reopens today's time sheet from its file on disk. Any entries you have already made for today's work reappear in the active window.

When you finish your work on this first project—or when you need to move on to another job—you return to the *Workday* application and select the *Finish* box in line 1; then click the stopwatch icon or press Ctrl+T. The program enters the current time into the box and instantly calculates the amount of time that has gone by since you began your work on the project. This elapsed time appears in the *Time* column. In addition, the program displays your current total work time in the *Page Total* box (Figure 9.11).

Sometimes you may prefer to enter time values manually into the time sheet grid instead of using the **Enter the Current Time** command. For example, you might forget to enter the finishing time for a particular job at the appropriate moment. When you finally get back to the *Workday*

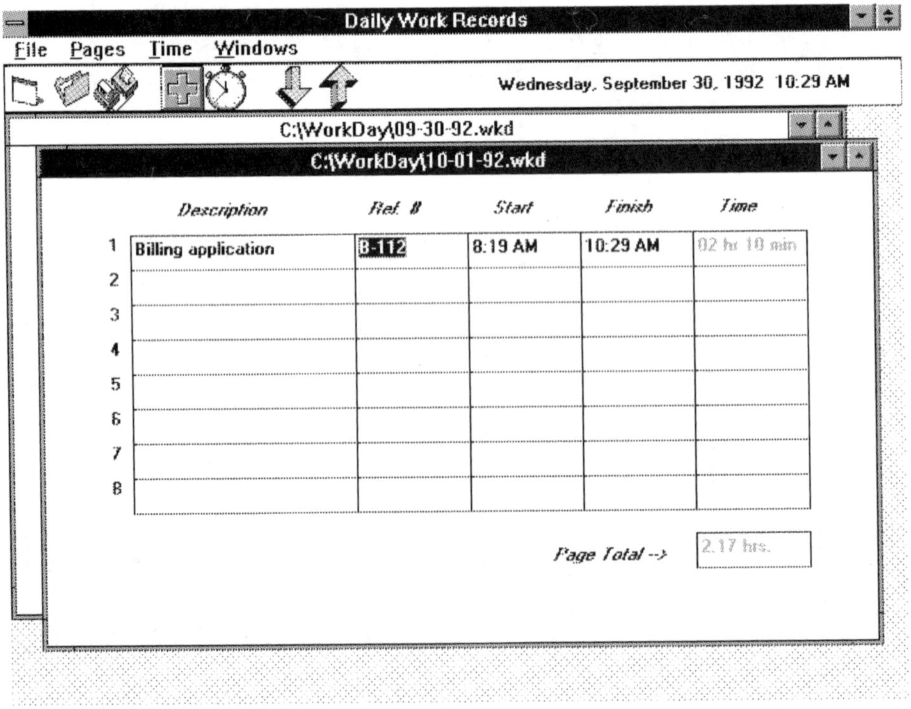

Figure 9.11 Completing a job line

application, several hours might have gone by since you actually completed the job. In this case, you can simply type the time directly into the appropriate *Finish* box. The program allows some flexibility in the format of time entries. For example, if you type "10 a" into a time text box, the program recognizes the entry and converts it to "10:00 AM." If, however, you make an entry that cannot be recognized as a time value, the program erases your entry and leaves the text box blank.

The program fills in the *Time* column for a given line whenever you supply valid entries for both the *Start* and *Finish* columns. Significantly, if you enter a *Finish* value that is earlier in time than the *Start* value for a given job, the program assumes that your work went past midnight and into the next day. For example, if you enter 10:00 PM as the *Start* time and 1:30 AM as the *Finish* time, the program calculates the elapsed time as 3 hours and 30 minutes.

Except for requiring valid time entries, the program leaves you free to fill in the time sheet form in any way you want. You can make entries in any order, and you can even reserve blank lines for later entries.

The File Menu Options

The application's **File** menu contains commands that allow you to open a day's work record from disk, and print reports from any day's work record. Here is the list of commands that appear in the menu:

Create a New Time Sheet...	F2
Open Today's Time Sheet	F3
Open an Existing Time Sheet...	F4
Print This Time Sheet	Ctrl+P
Print a Time Sheet Report...	F5
Exit	Ctrl+X

Notice that there is no **Save** command. This is because the program automatically takes care of creating files and saving your work at the appropriate moments. The program saves all files in a directory named WORKDAY on drive C. (If this directory does not initially exist, the application creates it at the beginning of the first program run.) The file name for a particular day's time sheet consists of the day's date followed by an extension name of WKD (for "workday"). For example, here is the path and file name for September 30, 1992:

```
C:\WORKDAY\09-30-92.WKD
```

Figure 9.12 Creating a new time sheet file

The **Create a New Time Sheet** command allows you to create a file for a time sheet that does not yet exist on disk. For example, you might want to use this command to record your work hours for a day in the past when you neglected to record entries in your time sheet. To create a new time sheet file, follow these steps:

1. Select the window in which you want to work on the new time sheet file. (The program will automatically save the window's current contents to disk before clearing the time sheet grid for the new file.)

2. Perform one of the following three actions: Choose the **Create New Time Sheet** command from the **File** menu; press the F2 function key; or click the New File icon, the first tool in the application's toolbar. The dialog box shown in Figure 9.12 appears on the screen.

3. In the text box at the bottom of the dialog box enter the date for which you want to create the new time sheet file. (You can enter the date in any recognizable format, such as 04-15-92 or April 15, 1992.)

Assuming the file for this date does not already exist on disk, the program creates the file and displays a blank time sheet grid in the active window, where you can begin recording your work hours for the day. The name of the new time sheet file is displayed in the title bar of the active window.

If you happen to enter a date in the *New Time Sheet* box for which a file exists, a message box appears on the screen with the following prompt:

```
This file already exists. Do you want to delete the previous version?
```

The prompt is followed by two buttons labeled **Yes** and **No**. Click **Yes** to abandon the previous version of the time sheet and start with a blank grid. Click **No** to open the previous version and view its contents on the screen.

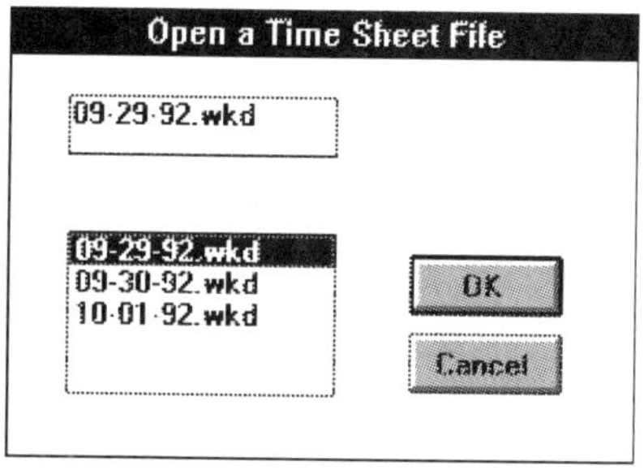

Figure 9.13 Opening an existing time sheet file

If the active window displays a time sheet for a date other than today, you can quickly open today's file by choosing the **Open Today's Time Sheet** command or simply by pressing F3.

You can open *any* file into the active window by choosing the **Open an Existing Time Sheet** command from the **File** menu—or by pressing F4 or clicking the Open File icon, the second tool in the program's toolbar. In response, the program displays the dialog box shown in Figure 9.13. To open a file, you select a name from the scrollable file list box and click **OK**. Before opening the newly selected file, the program saves any changes you may have made in the file that is currently open in the active window.

As you've seen, the **File** menu offers two printing options. The first, **Print This Time Sheet**, sends the data to the printer from all the pages of the time sheet file that is open in the active window (Figure 9.8). This command is useful if you simply want a quick printout of your current time sheet. The keyboard shortcut for this command is Ctrl+P. The Print icon in the toolbar also represents this operation.

The second printing option, **Print a Time Sheet Report**, gives you the opportunity to select a file from disk and create a printed report from data in the file. When you select this option, a new dialog box appears on the screen, as shown in Figure 9.14.

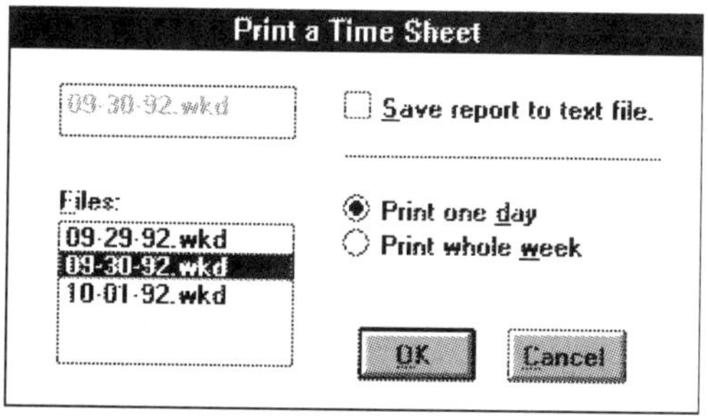

Figure 9.14 The **Print a Time Sheet** dialog box

The **Print a Time Sheet** box contains a scrollable list of all the WKD files that are stored in the C:\WORKDAY directory. When you click a file in the list, the file name also appears on the text box above the file list. To print a report, you select a file and then click the **OK** button, or you can simply double-click a file name in the file list. In the resulting report, the job data is sorted by reference numbers and contains a time subtotal for all the jobs of a given reference number. (Look back at Figure 9.9 to review the format of the printed report.)

The **Print a Time Sheet** dialog box contains two additional options:

- The **Save report to text file** option allows you to send the report to a text file on disk instead of printing it. To select this option, click the check box with the mouse or press Alt+S. An X appears inside the box. Use this option when you want to incorporate your report into a larger word processed document, or when you want to edit the report in some way before you print it. The application saves the report file in the WORKDAY directory with a TXT extension.

- A pair of option buttons give you a choice between printing a one-day report (**Print one day**) or a one-week summary report (**Print whole week**). By default, the application creates the output report from the single day's file that you select in the file list. However, if you select the **Print whole week** option, the program combines data from all the existing files of an entire week, Sunday through Saturday. To specify a week, you can select the file for any day that is in the week. The resulting report is in the same format as the one-day report (Figure 9.9), but contains data from as many as seven days. If you save this one-week summary report to disk instead of printing it, the application saves the file in the WORKDAY directory with an extension of WK.

The **Print whole week** option proves useful if you are keeping track of hours that are billable to a client. You can use the resulting report to produce detailed billing statements on a weekly basis.

The program can successfully generate time sheet reports even from a file that has missing data values. For example, if you omit the reference number from one or more lines in a time sheet file, the program creates a subgroup identified as *(no ref #)* and sorts the entries in this group by their job descriptions. Furthermore, if the starting or finishing time entry is missing from a given line in a time sheet, the program prints the line without including its time in the totals. You can see examples of both of these contingencies in the time sheet shown in Figure 9.15 and the resulting report in Figure 9.16.

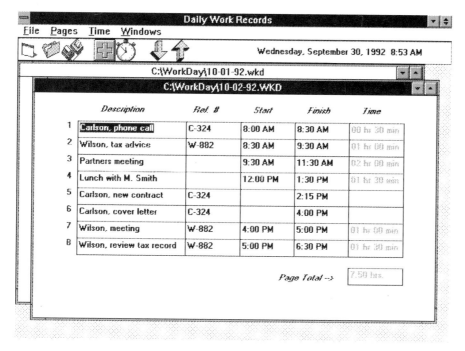

Figure 9.15 A time sheet with missing data entries

```
                         Time Sheet for 10-02-92
                         ========================


Job Description              Ref.        Start       Finish      Total Time
---------------              ----        -----       ------      ----------
Lunch with M. Smith          (no ref #)  12:00 PM    01:30 PM    01 hr 30 min
Partners meeting             (no ref #)  09:30 AM    11:30 AM    02 hr 00 min

                             Total for (no ref #) --> 3.50 hrs


Carlson, cover letter        C-324                   04:00 PM
Carlson, new contract        C-324                   02:15 PM
Carlson, phone call          C-324       08:00 AM    08:30 AM    00 hr 30 min

                             Total for C-324       --> 0.50 hr


Wilson, meeting              W-882       04:00 PM    05:00 PM    01 hr 00 min
Wilson, review tax record    W-882       05:00 PM    06:30 PM    01 hr 30 min
Wilson, tax advice           W-882       08:30 AM    09:30 AM    01 hr 00 min

                             Total for W-882       --> 3.50 hrs

                             *** Total Work Time ---> 7.50 hrs
```

Figure 9.16 The report resulting from the incomplete time sheet

THE ELEMENTS OF THE *WORKDAY* APPLICATION

Now that you've run the program, you can see the general purpose of each of the forms and modules contained in the *Workday* project:

- The **TSMDI** form is the main window for the application itself. Although it has no menu definition of its own, it displays the menu defined on the **TimeSheet** form. This is a general characteristic of MDI forms in Visual Basic 2.0 and 3.0: During run time, an MDI form displays the menu defined on the active child form. The **TSMDI** form contains a picture box, which in turn displays the row of icons that make up the application's toolbar. The picture box control is the only item that you can place directly on an MDI form, but the picture box itself can be a container for any number of other controls. For example, the picture box at the top of the **TSMDI** form contains seven image controls, one timer control, and one label for displaying the current date.

- The **TimeSheet** form displays the eight-line grid for entering a day's data. This form contains text boxes and labels. At run time, the program displays two instances of the **TimeSheet** form as the children of the **TSMDI** form. The code stored in this form responds to the events that take place around the time sheet grid and the menu commands.

- The **TSPrint** form is the dialog box that appears when you select the **Print a Time Sheet Report** command from the **File** menu. This form contains a text box, a check box, a pair of option buttons, two command buttons, and the *file list box* control from which you select a file to print. The code stored with this form is devoted to printing (or saving) data in the report formats.

- The **TSOpen** form appears when you select the **Open an Existing Time Sheet** command, also from the **File** menu. This form has a framed label, two command buttons, and a file list box.

- The code module TIMEPROC.BAS contains a record-type definition named **WorkRecordType**. This is the data structure definition that the program uses for file input and file output operations. (The daily work records are saved as random-access files.) The module also defines string constants that provide the path name and the extension name for saving files to disk, along with some essential global variables, which you'll be examining later in this chapter. Finally, TIMEPROC.BAS contains the general procedures and functions that the program uses to perform its major operations: time sheet display, file management, and report printing. (Recall that the procedures and functions stored in a module are available to all forms in the application.)

The upcoming sections of this chapter describe the program's organization and code, with a focus on the date and time operations the program performs, and on the structure of the application's multiple-document interface.

Controls, Properties, and Menus

The picture box in the **TSMDI** form is named **ToolsAndDate**. It contains seven image controls, which in turn display the icons that the user can click to perform some of the program's most important operations:

- The **NewFileIcon** control is for creating a new time sheet file.

- The **OpenFileIcon** control is for opening an existing time sheet file on disk.

- The **PrintSheetIcon** control is for printing the lines of an open time sheet.

- The **TotalIcon** control is for displaying the total number of hours recorded in a time sheet.

- The **CurTimeIcon** control is for entering the current time into a *Start* or *Finish* box.

- The **NextPageIcon** and **PrevPageIcon** controls are for scrolling through the pages of the active time sheet window.

The icon displayed in an image control is defined by the control's **Picture** property. To assign an icon to an image control at design time, you follow these steps:

1. Select the control and then scroll to the **Picture** property in the Properties window.

2. Click the **...** button displayed at the right side of the Settings box. As a result, Visual Basic displays the **Load Picture** dialog box, shown in Figure 9.17.

3. In the **Directories** box, select any of the icon subdirectories within the **Visual Basic** directory. These subdirectories contain the library of ICO files that are supplied with Visual Basic.

4. Select an ICO file in the **File Name** list and click **OK**. The selected icon appears inside the current image control.

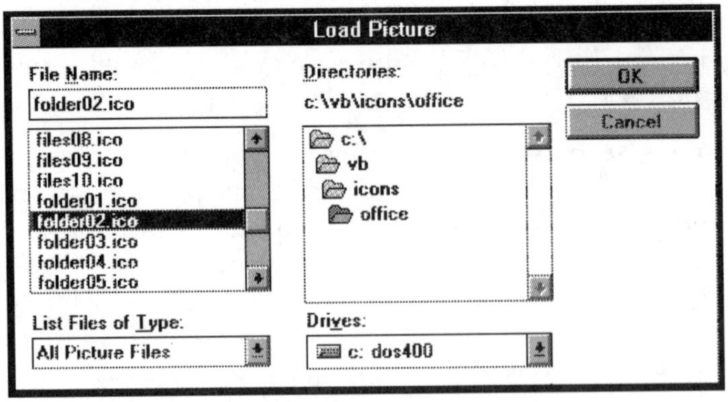

Figure 9.17 The **Load Picture** dialog box

Use the same steps to define the **Icon** property of an MDI form or a child form. This property determines the icon that will represent a minimized form during run time. For example, Figure 9.18 shows what happens when you minimize the two child forms inside the MDI form. As you can see, each form is represented by a clock icon. To restore a form to its original

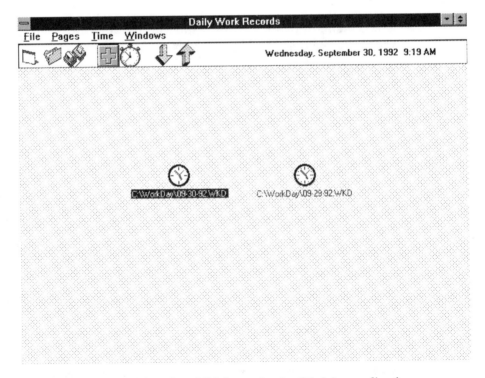

Figure 9.18 Minimizing the child forms in the *Workday* application

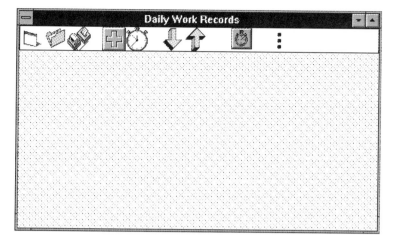

Figure 9.19 The **TSMDI** form during design time

size, double-click the icon that represents the form or select the form's name from the **Windows** menu.

The picture box in the **TSMDI** form contains two additional controls: a timer control named **DayTimer** and a label named **DateAndTime**. The label displays the current date and time, and the timer control is responsible for updating this display every minute. As you can see in Figure 9.19, the timer control is represented by a gray clock icon, located between the row of image control icons and the **DateAndTime** label. The icon for a timer control is always hidden during run time.

Visual Basic defines only a small number of properties—and a single event—for timer controls. Most important among the properties are **Name**, **Enabled**, and **Interval**. The **Interval** property setting is an integer representing the number of milliseconds in the interval defined for the timer. In this application, the **Interval** setting is 60000, for sixty seconds. The one event defined for this control is **Timer**. As long as the **Enabled** property remains **True**, the **Timer** event is called at the end of each time period defined by the **Interval** setting. Accordingly, the **DayTimer_Timer** event procedure is called every minute in the *Workday* application. This procedure's job is to update the current date and time displayed as the **Caption** property of the **DayAndTime** label.

The data area in the **TimeSheet** form consists of forty text boxes arranged in rows and columns, and an additional text box for the total time. Here are the properties of these controls:

- Each column is defined as a control array, with **Index** settings from **0** to **7**.

- The **Name** settings of the five control arrays are **Description**, **Ref**, **Start**, **Finish**, and **TotalTime**—similar to the label captions displayed at the top of the columns themselves.

- The eight text boxes in the **TotalTime** column have **Enabled** settings of **False**; this is because the program alone controls the contents of this particular column. The user never has access to these text boxes via the keyboard or the mouse.

- The text box at the lower-right corner of the form has a **Name** setting of **DayTotal** and an **Enabled** setting of **False**.

The **TSPrint** form (Figure 9.20) has a greater variety of controls than those in the **TimeSheet** form. The primary purpose of **TSPrint** is to prompt the user to select a file name for creating a report. In this context, the most important control in the form is the file list box, which displays the available file names.

Appropriately enough, the file list box has a **Name** setting of **FileList**. The program sets and reads other properties of this control at run time, starting in the **Form_Load** procedure of the **TSPrint** form. Three essential properties define the behavior and use of the file list box:

- The **Path** property specifies the path from which files will be accessed. (This property is available only at run time, not at design time.)

- The **Pattern** property gives the pattern of file names that will appear in the list.

- The **FileName** property (also available only at run time) provides the name of a file that the user has selected by clicking in the file list.

Here is how the program sets the **Path** and **Pattern** properties:

```
FileList.Path = PathName$
FileList.Pattern = "*." + ExtName$
```

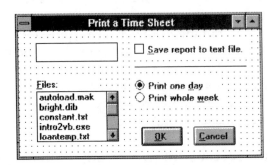

Figure 9.20 The controls on the **TSPrint** form

PathName\$ and **ExtName\$** are string constants, defined in the application's code module:

```
Global Const PathName$ = "C:\WorkDay"
Global Const ExtName$ = "WKD"
```

As a result of these definitions, the **FileList** box displays the names of all WKD files in the C:\WORKDAY directory.

When the user clicks a file name, Visual Basic assigns the name of the file to the **FileName** property of the file list box. The *Workday* program therefore gets the user's file selection from **FileList.FileName** and displays the file name in the text box located just above the file list box. The name of the text box is **DisplayFile**:

```
DisplayFile.Text = FileList.FileName
```

You will learn more about the characteristics of file list boxes—and the companion controls known as *drive list boxes* and *directory list boxes*—in Chapter 10. The application presented in Chapter 10 uses all three of these controls.

The remaining controls on the **TSPrint** form include:

- A check box control named **SaveReport**. This control's initial **Value** setting is **0-Unchecked**. If the user checks this control, the program sends the report output to disk rather than to the printer.

- A pair of option buttons organized as a control array. The buttons are named **WeekOrDay** and have **Index** settings of 0 and 1. The first of the two controls, **WeekOrDay(0)**, has an initial **Value** setting of **True**; the second is **False**. If the user accepts these default settings, the program creates a one-day report. Reversing the settings results in a one-week report.

- Two command buttons, named **OKButton** and **CancelButton**. The **CancelButton** control has an setting of **True** for a property named **Cancel**. When the **Cancel** setting is **True** for a given command button, the user can activate the button's **Click** event by pressing the Escape key on the keyboard.

Finally, notice the horizontal line that appears between the check box control and the pair of option buttons on the **TSPrint** form (Figure 9.20). This is an example of the line control, one of the new tools available in Visual Basic 2.0 and 3.0.

The menu definitions defined on the **TimeSheet** form are fairly straightforward. The six commands in the **File** menu have names of **NewSheet**, **OpenToday**, **OpenPrevious**, **PrintRec**, **PrintPrevRec**, and **ExitCommand**.

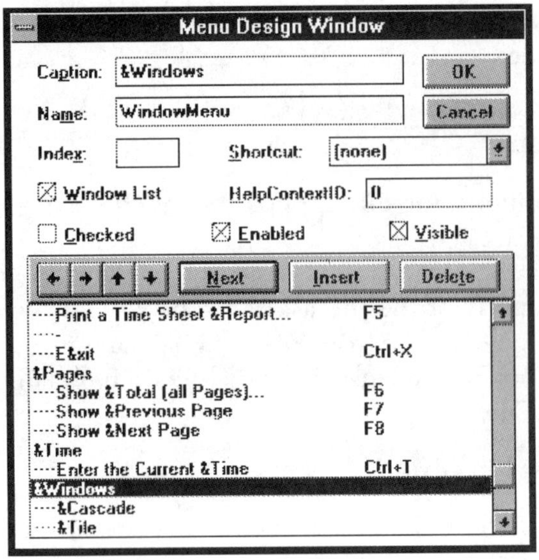

Figure 9.21 The menu design for the *Workday* application

The **Pages** commands are named **ShowTotal**, **PreviousPage**, and **Next-Page**. The **Time** menu command is named **CurTime**.

Finally, the **Windows** menu contains only two defined commands, named **CascadeArrangement** and **TileArrangement**. Conveniently, Visual Basic can automatically list the names of child forms in the **Windows** menu of an MDI application. To make this happen, you simply check the **Window List** box in the **Menu Design Window**, as shown in Figure 9.21.

Events

The **TSMDI** and **TimeSheet** forms respond to their own sets of **Click** events for toolbar clicks and menu selections. Keep in mind that the menu definition belongs to the child **TimeSheet** form, even though the pull-down menus themselves are displayed at the top of the MDI form during run time. For this reason, the **Click** procedures that respond to menu selections are stored in the **TimeSheet** form, whereas the **Click** procedures that respond to toolbar selections are stored in the **TSMDI** form.

But corresponding **Click** procedures in the MDI and child forms must perform identical operations. For example, the program must be prepared to print the active time sheet either when the user chooses the **Print This Time Sheet** command from the **File** menu, or when the user clicks the Print icon on the toolbar. In other words, the **PrintRec_Click** procedure in the

TimeSheet form and the **PrintSheetIcon_Click** procedure in the **TSMDI** form must both carry out the same task: print the current time sheet.

To accommodate these requirements, the *Workday* program is organized in a way that is typical of MDI applications containing both menus and toolbars:

- The child form (**TimeSheet** in this case) contains a set of short **Click** event procedures for responding to menu selections.

- The MDI form contains a set of short **Click** event procedures for responding to toolbar selections.

- A code module (**TIMEPROC.BAS** in the *Workday* program) contains the general procedures that actually carry out the tasks. These procedures are called by the **Click** event procedures in both the MDI and the child forms.

For the most part, the general procedures in the **TIMEPROC.BAS** module perform tasks that apply to the *active* child window. For this reason, each **Click** procedure needs a way of indicating to a general procedure which child window is active at the time of a given call. In the **TSMDI** form, the **Click** event procedures use the **ActiveForm** keyword to indicate the name of the active form. By contrast, the **Click** procedures in the **TimeSheet** form use a new Visual Basic keyword to represent the active child window; this important keyword is **Me**. You'll see how these keywords are used when you examine the program's code.

In addition to menu clicks and toolbar clicks, several other types of events take place on the **TSMDI** and **TimeSheet** forms:

- In the **TSMDI** form, a **Timer** event for the **DayTimer** control.

- In the **TimeSheet** form, **GotFocus** and **KeyDown** events for each of the text boxes; and **LostFocus** events for the **Start** and **Finish** text boxes.

The **GotFocus** event procedures arrange to highlight the current contents of a newly selected text box so that the user can easily replace or revise an entry; to do so, they make calls to a general procedure named **HighlightText** in the **TIMEPROC.BAS** module. The **KeyDown** event procedures respond to the up and down arrow keys. If the user presses up arrow or down arrow, these procedures move the focus to the text box just above or just below the current box.

The **Start_LostFocus** and **Finish_LostFocus** event procedures validate a new time entry when the user moves the focus away from a *Start* or *Finish* text box. In addition, these procedures update the hour values displayed in the *Time* column. Here is the sequence of steps performed by these two procedures:

1. Attempt to convert the user's entry to a serial time value.

2. If the conversion is successful, redisplay the time in a standard string format. (Otherwise, replace the entry with a blank string.)

3. If both time entries (*Start* and *Finish*) are available in the current line, display the difference between the two time values in the *Time* column.

4. Update the subtotal—that is, the number of hours on the current page of the time sheet.

The **TSPrint** form is displayed on the screen when the user chooses the **Print a Time Sheet Report** command from the **File** menu. In the **PrintPrevRec_Click** procedure, the **Show** method displays the previously hidden **TSPrint** form on the screen and temporarily transfers the program's focus to the controls contained in this secondary form:

```
TSPrint.Show 1
```

The main events in the **TSPrint** form are:

- The initial **Form_Load** event, which establishes the path and the pattern characteristics of the form's file list box.

- The **Click** event for the **FileList** control, which copies the user's file selection—represented by **FileList.FileName**—to the **DisplayFile** text box.

- The **Click** event for the **OKButton**, which makes a call to the appropriate report printing procedure.

Interestingly enough, the user can abbreviate this process by *double-clicking* a file name in the **FileList** box. The **FileList_DblClick** procedure simply makes a call to the **OKButton_Click** procedure to produce a report. But in Visual Basic's *event ordering* protocol, a **DblClick** event always first triggers an automatic **Click** event. For this reason, the following three event procedures are called in response to a double click:

```
FileList_Click
FileList_DblClick
OKButton_Click
```

The first of these procedures copies the selected file name to the **Display-File** text box, and the second and third procedures make the sequence of calls that result in the printing operation.

Procedures and Methods

The code for the *Workday* application appears in Listings 9.2 to 9.27. More specifically, here is where you will find the code for each of the program's forms and modules:

- The event procedures from the **TSMDI** form are shown in Listings 9.2 and 9.3.

- The event procedures from the **TimeSheet** form are in Listings 9.4 through 9.8.

- The global declarations from the **TIMEPROC.BAS** module are shown in Listing 9.9, and the module's general procedures are in Listings 9.10 through 9.19.

- The code from the **TSPrint** form is in Listing 9.20 to 9.26.

- The code from the **TSOpen** form is in Listing 9.27.

Because **TSMDI** is the startup form for the *Workday* application, the first event procedure to be executed at the beginning of a program run is **MDIForm_Load**, shown in Listing 9.2. (The name of this event procedure distinguishes it from the **Form_Load** procedures in ordinary forms.) As you examine this procedure—along with an important global variable declaration that appears in Listing 9.9—you'll begin to see some of the special programming techniques that are needed to manage an MDI application.

Programming Techniques for the Multiple-Document Interface

You can create an *instance* of a form dynamically at run time. You do so by declaring an *object variable* to represent the new instance of the form. The instance is an identical copy of the original form—with all its properties, controls, and code. In particular, if the original form is an MDI child, the new instance also appears as a child form. In the **Dim** or **Global** statement that you write to declare an instance of a form, you use a **New** clause to identify the name of the original form from which the instance will be created:

```
Dim NewInstance As New OriginalForm
```

or

```
Global NewInstance As New OriginalForm
```

Both of these statements declare *NewInstance* as a copy of *OriginalForm*. After this declaration, your program can use *NewInstance* as the name of a new form object.

The *Workday* program uses this technique to create an instance of the **TimeSheet** form. The object variable that represents this instance is declared globally in the module declaration section of **TIMEPROC.BAS**, shown in Listing 9.9:

```
Global TimeSheet2 As New TimeSheet
```

As a result, **TimeSheet** and **TimeSheet2** are the names of the two child forms available for displaying dated time sheets within the MDI form. From the user's point of view, these forms appear as two identical windows in which time sheet files can be displayed and edited. At run time, there is no visible or functional distinction between the original child form and the new instance of the form.

The **MDIForm_Load** procedure has the task of loading both forms and displaying a time sheet in each. As you'll recall, the two windows initially display the time sheet files for yesterday's and today's dates. **MDI-Form_Load** therfore begins by assigning the serial equivalent of today's date to the long-integer variable **Today**:

```
Today = Int(Now)
```

Before actually displaying the two child forms, the procedure assigns values to their **Caption** settings. The caption displayed in the title bar of each form is the actual file name of the time sheet that is open in the form:

```
TimeSheet.Caption = FileName$(Today - 1)
TimeSheet2.Caption = FileName$(Today)
```

The **FileName$** function (Listing 9.14) returns the full path and file name of the time sheet for a given date. Once both forms have captions in their title bars, the **MDIForm_Load** procedure is ready to display them as children of the MDI form. The **Show** method accomplishes this task:

```
TimeSheet.Show
TimeSheet2.Show
```

Finally, the program makes two calls to a general procedure named **OpenOnePage** (Listing 9.15) to display the first page of each time sheet file—if the files exist already on disk—inside the appropriate form:

```
OpenOnePage TimeSheet, 1, 8
OpenOnePage TimeSheet2, 1, 8
```

Notice that **OpenOnePage** takes three arguments: a **Form**-type variable representing the form on which the procedure will operate; and two integers, representing the first and last lines of the time sheet page. (For example, **1, 8** represents the first eight-line page; **9, 16** the second page; **17, 24** the third; and so on.) The procedure receives the arguments in variables named **CurSheet**, **FromLine%**, and **ToLine%**:

```
Sub OpenOnePage (CurSheet As Form, FromLine%, ToLine%)
```

This is the first of several examples you'll see of form objects as arguments.

Once the two time sheet windows are displayed, the user is free to select either form and perform any appropriate operations—by choosing menu commands or by clicking icons in the application's toolbar. This is where the **Click** event procedures in the **TSMDI** and the **TimeSheet** forms need ways of identifying the active child form. As you learned earlier, the **TSMDI** procedures use the **ActiveForm** keyword for this purpose, and the **TimeSheet** procedures use **Me**.

For example, consider the **Click** event that takes place when the user requests the total of the current time sheet. The subsequent procedure call depends upon whether the user clicks the Total icon in the toolbar or chooses the **ShowTotal** command from the **Pages** menu:

- In response to a click of the Total icon, the **TotalIcon_Click** procedure in the **TSMDI** form (Listing 9.3) is called.

- In response to the choice of the **Show Total** menu command, the **ShowTotal_Click** procedure in the **TimeSheet** form (Listing 9.5) is called.

Each **Click** procedure in turn makes a call to the **AllPagesTotal** to compute and display the total time recorded in the current time sheet.

The **AllPagesTotal** procedure (Listing 9.10) takes one **Form**-type argument, which identifies the window whose pages are to be totaled:

```
Sub AllPagesTotal (SheetToTotal As Form)
```

The **TSMDI** procedure uses **ActiveForm** to identify the active window in the procedure call:

```
AllPagesTotal ActiveForm
```

In contrast, the **TimeSheet** procedure uses **Me** for the same purpose:

```
AllPagesTotal Me
```

Thanks to these two simple techniques, the **TSMDI** and **TimeSheet** procedures both can make calls to the same general procedure to accomplish a given operation on the active form. You'll see examples of this approach throughout the *Workday* program.

The longest and most detailed routines in the program are the general procedures that perform file input and output operations. These include the **SavePage** procedure (Listing 9.17), responsible for saving a day's time sheet to disk; the **PrintADay** and **PrintAWeek** procedures (Listings 9.23 and 9.24), which read data from disk in preparation for printing a report; and **PrintWorkRecordList** (Listing 9.25), which actually creates an output report, sending it either to the printer or to a text file on disk. The following discussion will give you a general sense of how these operations take place. Then you'll examine specific illustrations of date and time operations in the *Workday* program.

Overview of File Procedures

A structured type named **WorkRecordType** is defined in the **TIME-PROC.BAS** module as follows:

```
Type WorkRecordType
  DescriptField As String * 25
  IDField As String * 10
  StartField As Double
  FinishedField As Double
End Type
```

This record type contains four fields, to represent a data entry from each of the four columns in a time sheet:

- **DescriptField** and **IDField** are string fields representing the description and reference number of a job.

- **StartField** and **FinishedField** are numeric fields representing the starting and finishing time for the job. The double-precision data type of these two fields accommodates Visual Basic's serial time format.

The program declares a single global record variable belonging to this structured type:

```
Global WorkRecord As WorkRecordType
```

When the program saves a page of entries to a time-sheet file, this record variable is used in the process of opening a file and writing data to the file. Specifically, the **SavePage** procedure has the job of saving the eight lines of the current page displayed in the active time sheet window.

SavePage receives a **Form**-type argument that identifies the active window:

```
Sub SavePage (SheetToSave As Form)
```

The procedure begins by reading the caption properties of the form's **LineNum** controls to determine which sequence of worksheet lines is currently displayed on the form:

```
FirstLine =  SheetToSave!LineNum(0).Caption
LastLine = SheetToSave!LineNum(7).Caption
```

Notice the format for referencing a control on the active form:

```
FormName!ControlName.PropertyName
```

An exclamation point separates the form name from the control name, and a period separates the control name from its property. This is the preferred format in Visual Basic 2.0 and 3.0, although you can also use an alternative format that is compatible with the previous version of Visual Basic:

```
FormName.ControlName.PropertyName
```

Next, the **SavePage** procedure assigns the file name for today's date to the string variable **CurFile$**. It reads this file name from the **Caption** property of the active form:

```
CurFile$ = SheetToSave.Caption
```

Then the procedure opens the file and initiates a **For** loop to write a page of records to the file:

```
Open CurFile$ For Random As #1 Len = Len(WorkRecord)
  For i% = FirstLine to LastLine
    Ndx = (i% - 1) Mod 8
```

The four fields are initially read as strings directly from the corresponding text boxes in the active form:

```
WorkRecord.DescriptField = SheetToSave!Description(Ndx).Text
WorkRecord.IDField = SheetToSave!Ref(Ndx).Text

S$ = RTrim$(SheetToSave!Start(Ndx).Text)
F$ = RTrim$(SheetToSave!Finish(Ndx).Text)
```

Then the **StartField** and **FinishedField** entries are converted to numeric values. If a nonblank time entry exists, the program uses Visual Basic's

TimeValue function to convert it to a serial time; but if the entry is blank, the program stores a value of -1 (represented by the constant **NoTime**) as the time field:

```
If Len(S$) > 0 Then
  WorkRecord.StartField = TimeValue(S$)
Else
  WorkRecord.StartField = NoTime
End If
```

Finally, when all four fields have been stored in the **WorkRecord** variable, a **Put** statement writes the record to the file:

```
Put #1, i%, WorkRecord
```

The **TSPrint** form (Listing 9.20) declares two **WorkRecordType** structures—a dynamic array of records named **WorkRecordList**, along with a single record variable named **WorkRecord**:

```
Dim WorkRecordList() As WorkRecordType
Dim WorkRecord As WorkRecordType
```

These structures are both used in the process of preparing data for output in reports. When the user requests a printed report, the **OKButton_Click** procedure (Listing 9.21) makes a call either to the **PrintADay** procedure or the **PrintAWeek** procedure, depending upon which of the **WeekOrDay** option buttons has been selected:

```
If WeekOrDay(0).Value Then PrintADay Else PrintAWeek
```

The **PrintADay** procedure (Listing 9.23) opens a day's work file, and calculates the number of records in the file, **RecCount**. Given this count, the procedure redimensions the **WorkRecordList** array accordingly and then reads the day's work data into the array:

```
ReDim WorkRecordList(RecCount) As WorkRecordType
For i% = 1 To RecCount
  Get #1, i%, WorkRecordList(i%)
```

If the **IDField** string is blank for a given record, the procedure replaces it with the string "(no ref #)":

```
If RTrim$(WorkRecordList(ListNum).IDField) = "" Then
  WorkRecordList(ListNum).IDField = "(no ref #)"
```

After reading the entire time sheet file, the program calls a procedure named **SortWorkRecordList** (Listing 9.26) to sort the array by the reference numbers—that is, the **IDField**. Then a call to **PrintWorkRecordList** (Listing 9.25) prints the report or saves it as a text file on disk.

The **PrintAWeek** procedure (Listing 9.24) is slightly more complicated. It begins by determining the date of the first day of the week corresponding to the user's selected file. Then the procedure opens each of the week's seven files in turn and calculates **WeekRecCount**, the total number of records in all seven files. This value defines the dynamic size of the **WorkRecordList** array:

```
ReDim WorkRecordList(WeekRecCount)As WorkRecordType
```

Next the procedure uses a pair of nested **For** loops to reopen each of the seven files in turn and read the records into the **WorkRecordList** array. Finally, a call to **SortWorkRecordList** sorts the array and a call to **PrintWorkRecordList** generates the one-week summary report.

The **PrintWorkRecordList** procedure begins by reading the current **Value** setting of the check box control named **SaveReport**. A setting of true means the user has requested text file output; a setting of false means the user wants a printed report. Accordingly, the procedure assigns either a file name or the device name "Prn" to the string variable **Dest**:

```
If SaveReport.Value Then
  Dest = OutFile
Else
   Dest = "Prn"
End If
```

(**OutFile**, the name used for a text file, is passed as an argument to the procedure.) Whichever destination has been selected, the following **Open** statement prepares for the output:

```
Open Dest For Output As #1
```

Finally, a sequence of **Print #1** statements write the report to the selected destination. As you can see, the use of the **Dest** variable in the **Open** statement simplifies the choice between printing or saving the report.

As the report is generated, the procedure tallies a running total of the hours recorded for a given reference number. Each time the reference number changes, a subtotal line is included in the report:

```
If ThisRef <> NexRef Then
  Print #1,
  Print #1, Tab(37); "Total for "; ThisRef; " -- > ";
  Print #1, Format$(RefTot * 24, "##0.00"); " hr";
```

Date and Time Operations

The *Weekday* application often converts date and time strings to serial numbers, or serial numbers back to time strings. Time values are read from disk as double-precision numeric values, but then are changed to a variety of display formats for the purpose of generating reports. When the program needs to perform an arithmetic operation on one or more chronological values, serial numbers are the most convenient way to store the data. However, a serial number would seem meaningless on a printed report, and therefore needs to be converted to a readable string format.

For example, the first such conversion takes place in the routine that displays the date and time at the top of the **TSMDI** form. The **Day-Timer_Timer** procedure (Listing 9.2) initially produces the display and then updates it every minute:

```
Cur$ = Format$(Now, "dddd, mmmm dd, yyyy  h:mm AM/PM")
DayAndTimeDisplay.Caption = Cur$
```

In this statement, the **Now** function supplies a **Variant** representation of the current date from the system calendar and time from the system clock. From the corresponding serial number, the **Format$** function supplies a customized date-and-time display string, which the program assigns to the **Caption** property of the **DayAndTime** label. Notice the syntax of the **Format$** function for creating date-and-time displays:

```
Format$(SerialNumber, "date-and-time format string")
```

You can also use **Format$** to produce either the date string or the time string alone from any serial number. In this case, the format string determines the content of the function's return value. For example, here is how the **EnterCurTime** procedure (Listing 9.13) displays an entry in the *Start* or *Finish* column of a time sheet grid:

```
CurControl.Text = Format$(Now, "h:mm AM/PM")
```

Even though the **Now** function provides the current date *and* the current time, this call to the **Format$** function produces a time display alone, thanks to a time-specific format string:

```
"h:mm AM/PM"
```

Another interesting example of the **Format$** function appears in the routine that builds the file names for saving time sheets to disk. The **FileName$** function (Listing 9.14) receives a serial date, **TargetDate**, as its argument, and returns a string that includes the path name, file name, and extension name for saving the day's data to disk. In this case, the **Format$** function returns the date-string equivalent of its serial number argument:

```
TempName$ = PathName$ + "\"
TempName$ = TempName$ + Format$(TargetDate, "mm-dd-yy")
FileName$ = TempName$ + "." + ExtName$
```

These lines produce a complete file name, such as:

```
C:\WORKDAY\04-17-92.WKD
```

The reverse operation—producing a serial number from a time string or a date string—is performed by Visual Basic's **TimeValue** and **DateValue** functions. Each of these functions takes one string (or **Variant**) argument—a time or a date—and provides the equivalent serial number:

```
SerialTime = TimeValue(TimeString)
SerialDate = DateValue(DateString)
```

(Actually, these functions return **Variant**-type values, which in turn can be assigned to numeric variables.) Both functions are very flexible in the variety of string arguments that they will accept and recognize. For example, the **TimeValue** function recognizes any of these time string formats:

```
6:35:15 PM
18:35:15
18:35
```

Likewise, **DateValue** recognizes any of these date strings:

```
September 15, 1992
Sept 15, 92
15 September 92
9/15/92
9-15-92
```

When each component of the date—*mm, dd,* and *yy*—is represented by an integer, **DateValue** recognizes the international date format you have selected for use in the Windows environment. For example, if you choose a European date format, **DateValue** recognizes 15-4-91 rather than 4-15-91.

As you might guess, **TimeValue** gets more use than **DateValue** in the *Workday* application. For example, the **SavePage** procedure uses **TimeValue** to store serial time values in the two time fields of the **Work-Record** structure, **StartField** and **FinishedField**:

```
WorkRecord.StartField = TimeValue(S$)
WorkRecord.FinishedField = TimeValue(F$)
```

TimeValue generates a run-time error if the functions receive an unrecognizable time-string argument. To avoid an interruption in your program's performance, you should write an error trap whenever there is a possibility that this function will receive an invalid argument. For example, the **Start_LostFocus** and **Finish_LostFocus** event procedures read the values the user has entered into the **Start** and **Finish** text boxes. If the user enters a valid time string, the **TimeValue** function successfully converts the entry. But if the user's input is not in a recognizable time string format, an error occurs when the program tries to convert the string to a serial time:

```
F = TimeValue(Finish(Index).Text)
```

For this reason, the **LostFocus** routines include error traps to handle unpredictable problems in the user's input; for example:

```
OKTime = True
On Local Error GoTo BadFinishTime
  F = TimeValue(Finish(Index).Text)
On Local Error GoTo 0
```

In this case, the error trap simply sets the variable named **OKTime** to false:

```
BadFinishTime:
  OKTime = False
Resume Next
```

This causes the routine to reject the user's input and replace it with a blank string in the text box.

Once the user has successfully entered valid *Start* and *Finish* time strings for a given line in the time sheet, the *Workday* application needs to compute the amount of time that has elapsed between the two time values, and display the difference in hours and minutes. After using **TimeValue** to convert each time string to a serial time, the program can simply subtract one time value from the other. This operation takes place in a function named **DoLineTotal**, displayed in Listing 9.13:

```
TempTotal = T2 - T1
```

The only complication is making the adjustment for a job entry that has gone past midnight. In this case, **T1**, the starting time, is greater than **T2**, the finishing time, and **TempTotal** is therefore a negative number. Adding 1 to this value gives the correct elapsed time:

```
If T2 < T1 Then TempTotal = TempTotal + 1

DoLineTotal = TempTotal
```

DoLineTotal therefore returns a double-precision number that represents the difference between two time values rather than an absolute time value. The program uses a string constant named **T$** to represent the format for converting these numbers to strings:

```
Global Const T$ = "hh \hr mm \m\i\n"
```

For example, here is how the **Finish_LostFocus** procedure displays the total time for a job line:

```
LineTot = DoLineTotal(S, F)
TotalTime(Index).Text = Format$(LineTot, T$)
```

As you have seen, this **Format$** function produces displays such as:

```
01 hr 30 min
```

The **UpdateDayTotal** procedure (Listing 9.19) tallies the total of all the times displayed on the current page of the active time sheet and displays the total in the **DayTotal** text box. In this case, the program displays the total time amount as a decimal value representing a number of hours; for example:

```
8.00 hrs
```

To produce this display, the program multiplies the total, **Tot**, by the number of hours in a day:

```
DispTot$ = Format$(Tot * 24, "###0.00")
```

Finally, the *Workday* application contains an interesting illustration of date arithmetic in the procedure that generates a one-week summary report, **PrintAWeek** (Listing 9.24). This procedure's first job is to determine the date of the first day of the week, given a date that the user has selected from the file list box. The user's selected date might be on any day of a given week, from Sunday to Saturday. **PrintAWeek** reads all the files for the corresponding week, beginning with the file for Sunday.

To find the date for the beginning of the week, **PrintAWeek** sends the user's selected date string to the **FirstDayOfWeek** function (Listing 9.22). This function begins by converting the date string to a serial date:

```
CurDate = DateValue(DayInWeek)
```

Then the routine uses Visual Basic's **Weekday** function in a formula that finds the date of the first day of the corresponding week:

```
FirstDayOfWeek = CurDate - (Weekday(CurDate) - 1)
```

Weekday returns an integer from 1 to 7, representing a day of the week from Sunday to Saturday. Subtracting 1 from the **Weekday** value gives an integer in the range from 0 to 6. Reducing **CurDate** by this amount results in the serial date for Sunday.

The **PrintAWeek** procedure, in turn, assigns the serial date for Sunday to the variable **FirstDay**, and then uses a **For** loop to go through an entire week of dates:

```
For i& = FirstDay To FirstDay + 6
```

Notice that the counter variable for the loop is a long integer variable, **i&**, to accommodate the range of serial dates.

SUMMARY: CHRONOLOGICAL VALUES AND MDI

In other languages—including previous versions of Basic—programmers have to write their own procedures for performing chronological operations like date and time arithmetic. But Visual Basic has built-in support for serial dates and serial time values, along with a library of functions for converting between strings and serial numbers. In addition, Visual Basic's **Variant** data type can represent both a displayable date value and the value's serial equivalent. Functions such as **DateValue**, **TimeValue**—and the converse operations performed by **Format$**—are simple to use, but extremely valuable in any application where date and time values are significant.

An MDI application consists of an MDI form along with one or more child forms. During run time a program can create multiple instances of a child form, producing two or more open document windows within the main application window. A **Dim** or **Global** statement with a **New** clause declares an object variable to represent the new instance of a form. To identify the active form at any given moment during run time, Visual Basic supplies two essential keywords: **ActiveForm**, for use in procedures that are not inside the child form; and **Me** for use in procedures that do belong to the child form.

Listing 9.1 Code from the *Date Converter* application

```
' The Date Converter Application
' DATES.MAK

' An experiment with date strings,
' serial numbers, and date arithmetic.


Sub CalcDiff ()

  ' Find the difference in days between the two dates.

  Dim d1 As Variant
  Dim d2 As Variant

  d1 = SerialNum(0).Caption
  d2 = SerialNum(1).Caption

  If d1 <> Empty And d2 <> Empty Then
    Diff.Caption = Abs(d1 - d2)
  End If

End Sub  ' CalcDiff


Sub ClearCommand_Click ()

  ' Clear all the text boxes.

  DateStr(0).SetFocus
  For i% = 0 To 1
    DateStr(i%).Text = ""
    SerialNum(i%).Caption = ""
  Next i%

  Diff.Caption = ""

End Sub  ' ClearCommand_Click
```

(continued)

```
Sub DateStr_GotFocus (Index As Integer)

  ' Highlight the existing text in the text box.

  DateStr(Index).SelStart = 0
  DateStr(Index).SelLength = Len(DateStr(Index).Text)

End Sub  ' DateStr_GotFocus


Sub DateStr_LostFocus (Index As Integer)

  ' Validate the user's date entry, and display
  ' the equivalent serial number in the adjacent text box.
  ' Then calculate the difference between the two dates
  ' if both are available.

  Dim SerialEquiv As Long
  Dim InDate As Variant

  InDate = DateStr(Index).Text
  If IsDate(InDate) Then
    SerialEquiv = DateValue(InDate)
    SerialNum(Index).Caption = SerialEquiv
    CalcDiff
  Else
    DateStr(Index).Text = ""
    SerialNum(Index).Caption = ""
    Diff.Caption = ""
  End If

End Sub  ' DateStr()_LostFocus


Sub ExitCommand_Click ()

  End

End Sub  ' ExitCommand_Click


Sub TodayDate_Click (Index As Integer)
```

```
   ' Enter today's date in the specified date box,
   ' and the equivalent serial number in the adjacent box.

   Dim SerialEquiv As Long
   Dim Today As Variant

   Today = Int(Now)
   DateStr(Index).Text = Today
   SerialEquiv = DateValue(Today)
   SerialNum(Index).Caption = SerialEquiv
   CalcDiff

End Sub  ' TodayDate_Click
```

Listing 9.2 MDIForm_Load and **DayTimer_Timer** from the **TSMDI** form

```
' The Workday application.

' Startup form: TSMDI.FRM


Sub MDIForm_Load ()

  Dim Today As Long

  ' Make sure the directory exists for storing
  ' time sheet files. If not, create it.

  SearchForPath

  Today = Int(Now)

  ' Open both time sheet windows
  ' and display the first pages of
  ' yesterday's and today's time
  ' sheet files.

  TimeSheet.Caption = FileName$(Today - 1)
  TimeSheet2.Caption = FileName$(Today)
```

(continued)

```
   TimeSheet.Show
   TimeSheet2.Show

   OpenOnePage TimeSheet, 1, 8
   OpenOnePage TimeSheet2, 1, 8

   ' Initialize the time.

   DayTimer_Timer

End Sub   ' MDIForm_Load


Sub DayTimer_Timer ()

   ' Display the date and time in the label control
   ' located at the top of the TSMDI form.

   Dim Cur$

   Cur$ = Format$(Now, "dddd, mmmm d, yyyy   h:mm AM/PM")
   DateAndTimeDisplay.Caption = Cur$

End Sub   ' DayTimer_Timer
```

Listing 9.3 Click procedures from **TSMDI**

```
Sub CurTimeIcon_Click ()

   ' Enter the current time in
   ' the active start or finish box.

   EnterCurTime ActiveForm, SCREEN.ActiveControl

End Sub   ' CurTimeIcon_Click


Sub NewFileIcon_Click ()
   ' Prepare the active sheet window
   ' for a new date's time sheet file.
```

```
   SavePage ActiveForm
   OpenNewSheet ActiveForm

End Sub  ' NewFileIcon_Click


Sub NextPageIcon_Click ()

   ' Scroll down to the next page
   ' of the current time sheet.

   ChangePage ActiveForm, True

End Sub  ' NextPageIcon_Click


Sub OpenFileIcon_Click ()

   ' Open an existing time sheet file
   ' and display its first page in
   ' the active time sheet window.

   SavePage ActiveForm
   OpenAFile ActiveForm

End Sub  ' OpenFileIcon_Click


Sub PrevPageIcon_Click ()

   ' Scroll up to the previous page of
   ' the time sheet file displayed in
   ' the active window.

   ChangePage ActiveForm, False

End Sub  ' PrevPageIcon_Click


Sub PrintSheetIcon_Click ()

   ' Print all the nonblank lines of
   ' the current time sheet file.
```

(continued)

```
   PrintCurSheet ActiveForm

End Sub  ' PrintSheetIcon_Click


Sub TotalIcon_Click ()

   ' Display the total of all the pages
   ' in the current time sheet file.

   AllPagesTotal ActiveForm

End Sub  ' TotalIcon_Click
```

Listing 9.4 Declarations and **Form_Load** from the **TimeSheet** form

```
' The Workday Application.

' TMSHEET.FRM
' Declarations.

Dim CurIndex As Integer ' The current line.
Dim CrLf$                ' Carriage return / line feed.

' Codes for the up and down arrow keys

Const Up = &H26
Const Down = &H28

' End of TMSHEET Declarations.


Sub Form_Load ()

   ' Initializations.

   CurIndex = 0

   ' Disable the Current Time command in the
   ' Time menu and the Current Time icon in
   ' the MDI toolbar.
```

```
  CurTime.Enabled = False
  TSMDI!CurTimeIcon.Enabled = False

  ' Set the dimensions of the sheet.

  Height = 5250
  Width = 9000

End Sub   ' Form_Load (TimeSheet)
```

Listing 9.5 Click procedures for menu commands from the **TimeSheet** form

```
Sub CascadeArrangement_Click ()

  ' Switch to a cascade arrangement
  ' of the two child windows.

  CascadeArrangement.Checked = True
  TileArrangement.Checked = False
  TSMDI.Arrange 0

  ' Set the dimensions of the windows.

  TimeSheet.Height = 5250
  TimeSheet.Width = 9000

  TimeSheet2.Height = 5250
  TimeSheet2.Width = 9000

End Sub   ' CascadeArrangement_Click


Sub CurTime_Click ()

  ' Enter the current time
  ' into a start or finish box.

  EnterCurTime Me, SCREEN.ActiveControl

End Sub   ' CurTime_Click
```

(continued)

```
Sub ExitCommand_Click ()

    ' Save the current page of each sheet,
    ' unload the sheets, and end the
    ' program performance.

    SavePage TimeSheet
    SavePage TimeSheet2

    End

End Sub   ' ExitCommand_Click


Sub NewSheet_Click ()

    ' Prepare a window for a new
    ' date's time sheet.

    SavePage Me
    OpenNewSheet Me

End Sub   ' NewSheet_Click


Sub NextPage_Click ()

    ' Scroll down to the next page
    ' in the active time sheet window.

    ChangePage Me, True   ' "True" means scroll down.

End Sub   ' NextPage_Click


Sub OpenPrevious_Click ()

    ' Open a time sheet file and display
    ' its first page in the active window.

    SavePage Me
    OpenAFile Me

End Sub   ' OpenPrevious_Click
```

```
Sub OpenToday_Click ()

  ' Open today's time sheet file and
  ' display its first page in the
  ' active window.

  SavePage Me
  Caption = FileName$(Int(Now))
  OpenOnePage Me, 1, 8

End Sub  ' OpenToday_Click


Sub PreviousPage_Click ()

  ' Scroll up to the previous page
  ' in the Active time sheet window.

  ChangePage Me, False  ' "False" means scroll up.

End Sub  ' PreviousPage_Click


Sub PrintPrevRec_Click ()

  ' Prepare to print a time sheet or a week of
  ' time sheets from files stored on disk.

  ' First save the current page.

  SavePage Me

  ' Then show the TSPrint form to elicit
  ' the user's choice of a file name.

  TSPrint.Show 1

End Sub  ' PrintPrevRec_Click


Sub PrintRec_Click ()

  ' Print the time sheet file shown
  ' in the active window.
```

(continued)

```
    PrintCurSheet Me

End Sub   ' PrintRec_Click


Sub ShowTotal_Click ()

   ' Show the total of all pages
   ' of the current time sheet file.

   AllPagesTotal Me

End Sub   ' ShowTotal_Click


Sub TileArrangement_Click ()

   ' Switch to a tile arrangement of
   ' the two time sheet windows.

   TileArrangement.Checked = True
   CascadeArrangement.Checked = False
   TSMDI.Arrange 1

End Sub   ' TileArrangement_Click
```

Listing 9.6 GotFocus procedures from the **TimeSheet** form

```
Sub Description_GotFocus (Index As Integer)

   ' Highlight the contents of a Description text box.

   HighlightText Description(Index)
   CurIndex = Index

End Sub   ' Description_GotFocus
```

```
Sub Finish_GotFocus (Index As Integer)

  ' Highlight the contents of a Finish text box.

  HighlightText Finish(Index)
  CurIndex = Index

  ' Enable the Current Time option in the Time menu
  ' and the Current Time icon in the MDI toolbar.

  CurTime.Enabled = True
  TSMDI!CurTimeIcon.Enabled = True

End Sub   ' Finish_GotFocus


Sub Ref_GotFocus (Index As Integer)

  ' Highlight the contents of a Ref text box.

  HighlightText Ref(Index)
  CurIndex = Index

End Sub   ' Ref_GotFocus


Sub Start_GotFocus (Index As Integer)

  ' Highlight the contents of a Start text box.

  HighlightText Start(Index)
  CurIndex = Index

  ' Enable the Current Time command in the
  ' Time menu and the Current Time icon in the
  ' MDI toolbar.

  CurTime.Enabled = True
  TSMDI!CurTimeIcon.Enabled = True

End Sub   ' Start_GotFocus
```

Listing 9.7 LostFocus procedures from the **TimeSheet** form

```
Sub Finish_LostFocus (Index As Integer)

  ' Validate a time entry.

  Dim OKTime As Integer
  Dim S As Double, F As Double

  ' Attempt to convert the text value
  ' to a time value.

  OKTime = True
  On Local Error GoTo BadFinishTime
    F = TimeValue(Finish(Index).Text)
  On Local Error GoTo 0

  If OKTime Then

    ' If the entry is valid, redisplay
    ' it in a standard time format.

    Finish(Index).Text = Format$(F, "h:mm AM/PM")

    ' If the Start entry is also available,
    ' fill in the total hours value for this line.

    If RTrim$(Start(Index).Text) <> "" Then
      S = TimeValue(Start(Index).Text)
      LineTot = DoLineTotal(S, F)
      TotalTime(Index).Text = Format$(LineTot, T$)
    End If
  Else

    ' Otherwise, replace the current time and
    ' total with blank strings.

    Finish(Index).Text = ""
    TotalTime(Index).Text = ""
  End If

  ' Recalculate the subtotal on the current page,
  ' and disable the Current Time option in the Time menu.
```

```
  UpdateDayTotal Me
  CurTime.Enabled = False
  TSMDI!CurTimeIcon.Enabled = False

  Exit Sub

BadFinishTime:
  OKTime = False
Resume Next

End Sub   ' Finish_LostFocus


Sub Start_LostFocus (Index As Integer)

  ' Validate a time entry.

  Dim OKTime As Integer
  Dim S As Double, F As Double

  OKTime = True

  ' Attempt to convert the time entry to
  ' a numeric time value.

  On Local Error GoTo BadStartTime
    S = TimeValue(Start(Index).Text)
  On Local Error GoTo 0

  ' If the entry is valid, redisplay it in
  ' a standard time format.

  If OKTime Then
    Start(Index).Text = Format$(S, "h:mm AM/PM")
    If RTrim$(Finish(Index).Text) <> "" Then
      F = TimeValue(Finish(Index).Text)
      LineTot = DoLineTotal(S, F)
      TotalTime(Index).Text = Format$(LineTot, T$)
    End If

  ' Otherwise, replace the entry with a blank.

  Else
```

(continued)

```
    Start(Index).Text = ""
    TotalTime(Index).Text = ""
  End If

  ' Update the total hours for the page.

  UpdateDayTotal Me

  ' Disable the Current Time command and icon.

  CurTime.Enabled = False
  TSMDI!CurTimeIcon.Enabled = False

  Exit Sub

BadStartTime:
  OKTime = False
Resume Next

End Sub   ' Start_LostFocus
```

Listing 9.8 KeyDown procedures from the **TimeSheet** form

```
Sub Description_KeyDown (Index As Integer, KeyCode As Integer, Shift As
Integer)

  ' Respond to up- or down-arrow key.

  Select Case KeyCode
  Case Up
    If CurIndex = 0 Then
      Description(7).SetFocus
    Else
      Description(CurIndex - 1).SetFocus
    End If
  Case Down
    If CurIndex = 7 Then
      Description(0).SetFocus
    Else
      Description(CurIndex + 1).SetFocus
    End If
  End Select

End Sub   ' Description_KeyDown
```

```
Sub Finish_KeyDown (Index As Integer, KeyCode As Integer, Shift As Integer)

  ' Respond to up- or down-arrow key.

  Select Case KeyCode
  Case Up
    If CurIndex = 0 Then
      Finish(7).SetFocus
    Else
      Finish(CurIndex - 1).SetFocus
    End If
  Case Down
    If CurIndex = 7 Then
      Finish(0).SetFocus
    Else
      Finish(CurIndex + 1).SetFocus
    End If
  End Select

End Sub  ' Finish_KeyDown


Sub Ref_KeyDown (Index As Integer, KeyCode As Integer, Shift As Integer)

  ' Respond to up- or down-arrow key.

  Select Case KeyCode
  Case Up
    If CurIndex = 0 Then
      Ref(7).SetFocus
    Else
      Ref(CurIndex - 1).SetFocus
    End If
  Case Down
    If CurIndex = 7 Then
      Ref(0).SetFocus
    Else
      Ref(CurIndex + 1).SetFocus
    End If
  End Select

End Sub  ' Ref_KeyDown


Sub Start_KeyDown (Index As Integer, KeyCode As Integer, Shift As Integer)

  ' Respond to up- or down-arrow key.

  Select Case KeyCode
  Case Up
    If CurIndex = 0 Then
      Start(7).SetFocus
```

(continued)

```
      Else
        Start(CurIndex - 1).SetFocus
      End If
  Case Down
    If CurIndex = 7 Then
      Start(0).SetFocus
    Else
        Start(CurIndex + 1).SetFocus
    End If
  End Select

End Sub   ' Start_KeyDown
```

Listing 9.9 Global declarations from the **TIMEPROC.BAS** module

```
' The Workday application.

' TIMEPROC.BAS
' Global declarations.

' The record structure for one line on a time sheet.

Type WorkRecordType
  DescriptField As String * 25
  IDField As String * 10
  StartField As Double
  FinishedField As Double
End Type

Global WorkRecord As WorkRecordType   ' A file record.

' The path name for storing time sheet files.

Global Const PathName$ = "C:\WorkDay"

' The extension name for time sheet files.

Global Const ExtName$ = "WKD"

' The maximum number of lines in a time sheet.

Global Const MaxLines = 80
```

```
' Flag for a blank time value.

Global Const NoTime = -1#

' Format for line totals.

Global Const T$ = "hh \hr mm \m\i\n"

' A second instance of the TimeSheet form.

Global TimeSheet2 As New TimeSheet

' End of global declarations.
```

Listing 9.10 AllPagesTotal and CurTot routines (TIMEPROC.BAS)

```
Sub AllPagesTotal (SheetToTotal As Form)

  ' When the user chooses the Total command
  ' from the Pages menu, display a message box
  ' showing the total hours in the current file.

  Dim TotStr$

  ' Prepare the message string. The CurTot function
  ' calculates the total hours for the file.

  TotStr$ = "Total hours in all pages: "
  TotStr$ = TotStr$ + Format$(CurTot(SheetToTotal), "###0.00")

  MsgBox TotStr$, 0, "Show Total"

End Sub   ' AllPagesTotal


Function CurTot (SheetToTot As Form) As Double

  ' Find the total number of hours in all
  ' of the pages of the current time sheet.
```

(continued)

```
    Dim S As Double, F As Double
    Dim TempTot As Double

    ' First save the current page.

    SavePage SheetToTot
    TempTot = 0

    ' Open the current file and read each record.

    Open SheetToTot.Caption For Random As #1 Len = Len(WorkRecord)
    Do While Not EOF(1)
      Get #1, , WorkRecord
      S = WorkRecord.StartField
      F = WorkRecord.FinishedField

      ' Add to the total only if both time fields
      ' contain nonblank values.

      If Not (S < 0 Or F < 0) Then TempTot = TempTot + DoLineTotal(S, F)
    Loop
    Close #1

    ' Multiply the time value by 24
    ' to compute the number of hours.

    CurTot = TempTot * 24

End Function   ' CurTot
```

Listing 9.11 The **ChangePage** procedure (**TIMEPROC.BAS**)

```
Sub ChangePage (CurSheet As Form, Forward As Integer)

   ' Display a new page of lines on the
   ' current time sheet. Go forward or backward
   ' depending on the boolean value passed
   ' as the Forward argument.

   SavePage CurSheet
   FirstLine% = Val(CurSheet!LineNum(0).Caption)
```

```
   If Forward Then

      ' Allow no more than MaxLines in the file.

      If FirstLine% + 15 <= MaxLines Then
        OpenOnePage CurSheet, FirstLine% + 8, FirstLine% + 15
      End If

   Else

      ' Don't try to go backward from the first page.

      If FirstLine% > 8 Then
        OpenOnePage CurSheet, FirstLine% - 8, FirstLine% - 1
      End If

   End If

End Sub    ' ChangePage
```

Listing 9.12 The **ClearLineTimes** and **ClearPage** procedures (**TIMEPROC.BAS**)

```
Sub ClearLineTimes (Sheet As Form, WLineNum As Integer)

   ' Clear the time values from
   ' one line in the time sheet.

   Sheet!Start(WLineNum).Text = ""
   Sheet!Finish(WLineNum).Text = ""
   Sheet!TotalTime(WLineNum).Text = ""

End Sub    ' ClearLineTimes


Sub ClearPage (SheetToClear As Form)

   ' Clear all lines of the time sheet page.

   Dim i%

   For i% = 7 To 0 Step -1
```

(continued)

```
      SheetToClear!Ref(i%).Text = ""
      ClearLineTimes SheetToClear, (i%)
      SheetToClear!Description(i%).Text = ""
   Next i%

   SheetToClear!DayTotal.Text = ""

   If CurIndex <> 0 Then
      CurIndex = 0
      SheetToClear!Description(CurIndex).SetFocus
   End If

End Sub   ' ClearPage
```

Listing 9.13 DoLineTotal, EnterCurTime, and HighlightText (TIMEPROC.BAS)

```
Function DoLineTotal (T1 As Double, T2 As Double) As Double

   ' Calculate the difference between two time
   ' values and return a serial time value.

   Dim TempTotal As Double

   TempTotal = T2 - T1

   ' If the Finish value is earlier than the start,
   ' assume that the work continued past midnight.

   If T2 < T1 Then TempTotal = TempTotal + 1

   DoLineTotal = TempTotal

End Function   ' DoLineTotal


Sub EnterCurTime (CurSheet As Form, CurControl As Control)

   ' Enter the current time into a
   ' Start or Finished text box.

   CurControl.Text = Format$(Now, "h:mm AM/PM")
```

```
  ' Move the focus to trigger the LostFocus event.

  i% = CurControl.Index
  CurSheet!Ref(i%).SetFocus

End Sub   ' EnterCurTime



Sub HighlightText (BoxToHighlight As Control)

  Dim T$

  T$ = BoxToHighlight.Text
  BoxToHighlight.SelStart = 0
  BoxToHighlight.SelLength = Len(RTrim$(T$))

End Sub   ' HighlightText
```

Listing 9.14 The **FileName$** and **OpenNewSheet** routines (**TIMEPROC.BAS**)

```
Function FileName$ (TargetDate As Long)

  ' Create a file name from a serial date.
  ' Note: PathName$ and ExtName$ are global constants.

  Dim TempName$

  TempName$ = PathName$ + "\"
  TempName$ = TempName$ + Format$(TargetDate, "mm-dd-yy")
  FileName$ = TempName$ + "." + ExtName$

End Function   ' FileName$



Sub OpenNewSheet (CurForm As Form)

  ' Create a new time sheet file when the user
  ' chooses the New command from the File menu.

  ' Settings and return values for the
  ' INPUTBOX function.
```

(continued)

```
Const YesNo = 4
Const Yes = 6
Const No = 7

Dim NoAnswer As Integer, OKDate As Integer
Dim NewDate As Long
Dim NewFile$
Dim Answer As Variant

' Input prompts.

Prompt1$ = "Enter the date for which you want to"
Prompt1$ = Prompt1$ + " create a new time sheet file."

Prompt2$ = "This file already exists. Do you want to"
Prompt2$ = Prompt2$ + " delete the previous version?"

NoAnswer = False

' Display an input box and repeat the prompt until
' the user clicks Cancel or enters a valid date.

NoAnswer = False
OKDate = False
Do
  Answer = InputBox$(Prompt1$, "New Time Sheet")
  If Answer = "" Then
    NoAnswer = True
  Else
    If IsDate(Answer) Then
      NewDate = DateValue(Answer)
      OKDate = True
    End If
  End If
Loop Until OKDate Or NoAnswer

' If the user has entered a valid date,
' create the new time sheet file.

If OKDate Then
  NewFile$ = FileName$(NewDate)

  Open NewFile$ For Random As #1 Len = Len(WorkRecord)
```

```
      NumRecs% = LOF(1) / Len(WorkRecord)
    Close #1

    ' If this file already exists on disk, find out
    ' whether the user wants to replace it with a blank file.

    If NumRecs% > 0 Then
      ans% = MsgBox(Prompt2$, YesNo, "New Time Sheet")
      If ans% = Yes Then Kill NewFile$
    End If

    CurForm.Caption = NewFile$
    OpenOnePage CurForm, 1, 8

  End If

End Sub   ' OpenNewSheet
```

Listing 9.15 The **OpenAFile** and **OpenOnePage** procedures (**TIMEPROC.BAS**)

```
Sub OpenAFile (CurForm As Form)

  Dim NewFileName As String
  Dim SelectedFile As String

  ' Open an existing time sheet file.

  ' Show the TSOpen form to elicit the user's
  ' file name selection.

  TSOpen.Show 1

  ' Display the first page of the
  ' newly opened file.

  SelectedFile = TSOpen!TSFileToOpen.Caption
  If RTrim$(SelectedFile$) <> "" Then
    NewFileName = PathName$ + "\" + SelectedFile
    CurForm.Caption = NewFileName
  End If

  OpenOnePage CurForm, 1, 8

End Sub   ' OpenAFile
```

(continued)

```
Sub OpenOnePage (CurSheet As Form, FromLine%, ToLine%)

  ' Open a time sheet file and display a page of entries.

  Dim S As Double, F As Double

  Const TimeFormat$ = "h:mm AM/PM"

  ClearPage CurSheet

  ' Read the file name from the caption property
  ' of the TimeSheet form. Then compute the number of
  ' records in the file.

  Open CurSheet.Caption For Random As #1 Len = Len(WorkRecord)
  RecCount = LOF(1) / Len(WorkRecord)

  ' Read and display a page of records.

  For i% = FromLine% To ToLine%

    ' Calculate the index number for the text arrays
    ' and display the line number.

    LineNdx% = (i% - 1) Mod 8
    CurSheet!LineNum(LineNdx%).Caption = Format$(i%, "## ")

    ' If this line contains a record, display it.

    If i% <= RecCount Then
      Get #1, i%, WorkRecord
      CurSheet!Description(LineNdx%).Text = WorkRecord.DescriptField
      CurSheet!Ref(LineNdx%).Text = WorkRecord.IDField

      S = WorkRecord.StartField
      F = WorkRecord.FinishedField

      ' Display time entries or blanks.

      If S >= 0 Then
        CurSheet!Start(LineNdx%).Text = Format$(S, TimeFormat$)
      Else
        CurSheet!Start(LineNdx%).Text = ""
      End If

      If F >= 0 Then
        CurSheet!Finish(LineNdx%).Text = Format$(F, TimeFormat$)
      Else
        CurSheet!Finish(LineNdx%).Text = ""
      End If

      ' If both time entries are available,
      ' calculate the total for the line.
```

```
      If Not (S < 0 Or F < 0) Then
        CurSheet!TotalTime(LineNdx%).Text = Format$(DoLineTotal(S, F), T$)
      End If

    End If
  Next i%

  Close #1

  ' Display the subtotal for the page.

  UpdateDayTotal CurSheet

End Sub   ' OpenOnePage
```

Listing 9.16 The **PrintCurSheet** and **BlankLine** routines (**TIMEPROC.BAS**)

```
Sub PrintCurSheet (SheetToPrint As Form)

  ' Print all the lines of the current time sheet.

  Dim S As Double, F As Double, Tot As Double

  SavePage SheetToPrint

  ' Set up an error trap to avoid a run-time
  ' error if the printer is not ready.

  On Local Error GoTo PrinterProblem

  ' Open the time sheet file as #2
  ' and the printer device as #3.

  Open SheetToPrint.Caption For Random As #2 Len = Len(WorkRecord)
  Open "Prn" For Output As #3
  NumRecs% = LOF(2) / Len(WorkRecord)

  Print #3, "Time Sheet File: "; SheetToPrint.Caption
  Print #3,

  ' Print each line of the file.

  For i% = 1 To NumRecs%
    Get #2, i%, WorkRecord

    ' Do not print blank lines.

    If Not BlankLine(WorkRecord) Then
      D$ = WorkRecord.DescriptField
      R$ = WorkRecord.IDField
```

(continued)

```
      S = WorkRecord.StartField
      F = WorkRecord.FinishedField

    ' Print each field, or the appropriate
    ' number of spaces for a blank field.

    If RTrim$(D$) <> "" Then
      Print #3, D$; "   ";
    Else
      Print #3, Space$(27);
    End If

    If RTrim$(R$) <> "" Then
      Print #3, R$; "   ";
    Else
      Print #3, Space$(12);
    End If

    If S < 0 Then
      Print #3, Space$(11);
    Else
      Print #3, Format$(S, "hh:mm AM/PM"); "    ";
    End If

    If F < 0 Then
      Print #3, Space$(11);
    Else
      Print #3, Format$(F, "hh:mm AM/PM"); "    ";
    End If

    ' If both time entries are available,
    ' print the total number of hours for the line.

    If Not (S < 0 Or F < 0) Then
      Tot = DoLineTotal(S, F)
      Print #3, Format$(Tot, T$)
    Else
      Print #3,
    End If
  End If

Next i%

Close #2

' Print the total hours for the file.

Print #3,
Print #3, Space$(46); "Total --> ";
TempTot = CurTot(SheetToPrint)
```

```
   Print #3, Format$(TempTot, "###0.00"); " hrs."
   Print #3, Chr$(12) ' form-feed.

AbortPrint:
  Close

Exit Sub

PrinterProblem:
  MsgBox "Check printer and try again.", 0, "Printer Problem"
Resume AbortPrint

End Sub   ' PrintCurSheet


Function BlankLine (LineRec As WorkRecordType) As Integer

  ' Check to see if the current
  ' time sheet line is blank.

  Dim D%, R%, S%, F%

  D% = (RTrim$(LineRec.DescriptField) = "")
  R% = (RTrim$(LineRec.IDField) = "") Or LineRec.IDField = "(no ref #)"
  S% = (LineRec.StartField < 0)
  F% = (LineRec.FinishedField < 0)

  BlankLine = D% And R% And S% And F%

End Function   ' BlankLine
```

Listing 9.17 The **SavePage** procedure (**TIMEPROC.BAS**)

```
Sub SavePage (SheetToSave As Form)

  ' Save the displayed page of entries
  ' to the current time-sheet file.

  Dim CurFile$, S$, F$
  Dim FirstLine As Integer, LastLine As Integer
  Dim Ndx As Integer

  ' Read the range of record numbers
  ' from the LineNum labels.
```

(continued)

```
    FirstLine = SheetToSave!LineNum(0).Caption
    LastLine = SheetToSave!LineNum(7).Caption

    ' Read the file name from the TimeSheet caption.

    CurFile$ = SheetToSave.Caption
    SheetToSave!Description(0).SetFocus

    ' Open the random-access file
    ' and save each line as a record.

    Open CurFile$ For Random As #1 Len = Len(WorkRecord)
      For i% = FirstLine To LastLine
        Ndx = (i% - 1) Mod 8
        WorkRecord.DescriptField = SheetToSave!Description(Ndx).Text
        WorkRecord.IDField = SheetToSave!Ref(Ndx).Text

        S$ = RTrim$(SheetToSave!Start(Ndx).Text)
        F$ = RTrim$(SheetToSave!Finish(Ndx).Text)

        ' Save each time entry as a double-precision
        ' numeric time value. For a blank time entry,
        ' save the value of the constant NoTime (-1).

        If Len(S$) > 0 Then
          WorkRecord.StartField = TimeValue(S$)
        Else
          WorkRecord.StartField = NoTime
        End If

        If Len(F$) > 0 Then
          WorkRecord.FinishedField = TimeValue(F$)
        Else
          WorkRecord.FinishedField = NoTime
        End If

        Put #1, i%, WorkRecord
      Next i%
    Close #1

End Sub ' SavePage
```

Listing 9.18 The **SearchForPath** procedure (**TIMEPROC.BAS**)

```
Sub SearchForPath ()

  ' Search for the directory in which work sheet files
  ' are to be stored. Create the directory (on drive C)
  ' if it does not exist yet.

  ' Note: PathName$ is a global constant.

  Dim CDir$

  ' Record the current directory.
  CDir$ = CurDir$("C")

  ' Set up an error-handling mode.
  On Local Error Resume Next

  ' Attempt to change to the target directory.
  ChDir PathName$

  ' If the directory doesn't exist, create it.
  MkDir PathName$

  ' Restore the original directory.
  ChDir CDir$

End Sub  ' SearchForPath
```

Listing 9.19 The **UpdateTotal** procedure (**TIMEPROC.BAS**)

```
Sub UpdateDayTotal (SheetToUpdate As Form)
' Calculate the total hours for the
  ' current page of the time sheet file.

  Dim Tot As Double, i%, DispTot$
  Dim S As Double, F As Double, T1$, T2$

  Tot = 0
```

(continued)

```
' Step through each line of the time sheet.

For i% = 0 To 7

  T1$ = RTrim$(SheetToUpdate!Start(i%).Text)
  T2$ = RTrim$(SheetToUpdate!Finish(i%).Text)

  If Len(T1$) > 0 And Len(T2$) > 0 Then
    S = TimeValue(T1$)
    F = TimeValue(T2$)
    Tot = Tot + DoLineTotal(S, F)
  End If

Next i%

' Display the Total value.

DispTot$ = Format$(Tot * 24, "###0.00")
If (Tot * 24) > 1 Then
  DispTot$ = DispTot$ + " hrs."
Else
  DispTot$ = DispTot$ + " hr."
End If

SheetToUpdate!DayTotal.Text = DispTot$

End Sub   ' UpdateDayTotal
```

Listing 9.20 Declarations and **Form_Load** procedure from the **TSPrint** form

```
' The Workday application.

' TSPRINT.FRM
' Declarations

' Dynamic array of work records.

Dim WorkRecordList() As WorkRecordType

' A single work record.
```

```
Dim WorkRecord As WorkRecordType

' End of TSPRINT Declarations


Sub Form_Load ()

  ' Initialize the path and pattern.

  FileList.Path = PathName$
  FileList.Pattern = "*." + ExtName$
  FileList.Refresh

End Sub  ' Form_Load (TSPrint)
```

Listing 9.21 Click procedures from the **TSPrint** form

```
Sub CancelButton_Click ()

  ' Return to the time sheet without printing.

  Unload TSPrint

End Sub  ' CancelButton_Click (TSPRINT.FRM)


Sub FileList_Click ()

  ' When the user clicks a file name in
  ' the file list, copy the file name to
  ' the DisplayFile text box.

  DisplayFile.Text = FileList.FileName

  ' Then enable the OK button.

  OKButton.Enabled = True

End Sub  ' FileList_Click
```

(continued)

```
Sub FileList_DblClick ()

  ' If the user double-clicks a file name
  ' in the file list, force a call to the
  ' OKButton_Click event procedure.

  OKButton_Click

End Sub  ' FileList_DblClick


Sub OKButton_Click ()

  ' When the user clicks the OKButton, call one
  ' of the two print procedures and then hide the
  ' TSPrint form.

  ' The choice between PrintADay and PrintAWeek
  ' depends on which of the two WeekOrDay option
  ' buttons is currently active.

  If LTrim$(DisplayFile.Text) <> "" Then
    If WeekOrDay(0).Value Then PrintADay Else PrintAWeek
  End If

  Unload TSPrint

End Sub  ' OKButton_Click (TSPRINT.FRM)
```

Listing 9.22 The **FirstDayOfWeek** function (**TSPrint** form)

```
Function FirstDayOfWeek (DayInWeek As String)

  ' Given a date string, find the serial date of
  ' the first day--Sunday--of the same week.

  Dim CurDate As Double

  ' Find the serial date of the argument.

  CurDate = DateValue(DayInWeek)
```

```
  ' Subtract enough days to reach Sunday.

  FirstDayOfWeek = CurDate - (Weekday(CurDate) - 1)

End Function  ' FirstDayOfWeek (TSPRINT.FRM)
```

Listing 9.23 The **PrintADay** procedure (**TSPrint**)

```
Sub PrintADay ()

  ' Print a single day of work records.

  Dim WorkFileName As String, RecCount As Integer
  Dim Heading As String, DateStr As String, OutFileName As String

  ' Create the complete file name for the time sheet.

  WorkFileName = PathName$ + "\" + DisplayFile.Text

  ' Open the file and count its records.

  Open WorkFileName For Random As #1 Len = Len(WorkRecord)
    RecCount = LOF(1) / Len(WorkRecord)

    ' Redimension the array of records accordingly.

    ReDim WorkRecordList(RecCount) As WorkRecordType

    ' Read the entire file into the array.

    For i% = 1 To RecCount
      Get #1, i%, WorkRecordList(i%)

      ' If a reference entry is blank, store the
      ' string "(no ref #)" as the IDField value.

      If RTrim$(WorkRecordList(i%).IDField) = "" Then
        WorkRecordList(i%).IDField = "(no ref #)"
      End If
    Next i%
  Close #1
```

(continued)

```
    ' Sort the array by the reference numbers (IDField)
    ' and descriptions (DescriptField).

    SortWorkRecordList RecCount

    ' Print the one-day time sheet.

    DateStr = Left$(DisplayFile.Text, 8)
    Heading = "Time Sheet for " + DateStr
    OutFileName = PathName$ + "\" + DateStr + ".TXT"
    PrintWorkRecordList Heading, RecCount, OutFileName

End Sub  ' PrintADay
```

Listing 9.24 The **PrintAWeek** procedure (**TSPrint** form)

```
Sub PrintAWeek ()

  ' Print a week's summary of work records.

  Dim WorkFileName As String, RecCount As Integer
  Dim WeekRecCount As Integer, Heading As String
  Dim FirstDay As Long, FirstDayStr As String, i&, j%
  Dim FirstFileName As String

  ' Find the serial number and the date string
  ' representing the first day of the target week.

  FirstDay = FirstDayOfWeek(Left$(DisplayFile.Text, 8))
  FirstDayStr = Format$(FirstDay, "mm-dd-yy")

  ' Count the records in all the time sheet
  ' files for the week (Sunday through Saturday).

  WeekRecCount = 0
  For i& = FirstDay To FirstDay + 6
    WorkFileName = PathName$ + "\" + Format$(i&, "mm-dd-yy") + "." + ExtName$
    Open WorkFileName For Random As #1 Len = Len(WorkRecord)
      WeekRecCount = WeekRecCount + LOF(1) / Len(WorkRecord)
    Close #1
  Next i&

  ' Redimension the work record array accordingly.

  ReDim WorkRecordList(WeekRecCount) As WorkRecordType
```

```
' Read work records into the array, from as
' many as seven time sheet files.

ListNum = 1
For i& = FirstDay To FirstDay + 6
  WorkFileName = PathName + "\" + Format$(i&, "mm-dd-yy") + "." + ExtName$
  Open WorkFileName For Random As #1 Len = Len(WorkRecord)
    RecCount = LOF(1) / Len(WorkRecord)
    For j% = 1 To RecCount
      Get #1, j%, WorkRecordList(ListNum)

      ' If a reference entry is blank, store the string
      ' "(no ref #)" as the IDField value.

      If RTrim$(WorkRecordList(ListNum).IDField) = "" Then
        WorkRecordList(ListNum).IDField = "(no ref #)"
      End If

      ListNum = ListNum + 1
    Next j%
  Close #1
Next i&

' Sort the array by the reference numbers (IDField)
' and the descriptions (DescriptField).

SortWorkRecordList WeekRecCount

' Print the one-week time sheet summary.

Heading = "Summary Time Sheet for the Week of " + FirstDayStr
FirstFileName = PathName$ + "\" + FirstDayStr + ".WK"
PrintWorkRecordList Heading, WeekRecCount, FirstFileName

End Sub   ' PrintAWeek (TSPRINT.FRM)
```

Listing 9.25 The **PrintWorkRecordList** procedure (**TSPrint** form)

```
Sub PrintWorkRecordList (Title As String, NumRecs As Integer, OutFile As
String)

  ' Print a daily or weekly report from a selected time sheet file.

  Dim T1 As Double, T2 As Double, RefTot As Double
  Dim ThisRef As String, NextRef As String
  Dim TabForCenter As Integer, Dest As String
  Dim GrandTot As Double
```

(continued)

```
' Read the SaveReport value to determine
' whether the output should be printed or
' saved as a text file on disk.

If SaveReport.Value Then
  Dest = OutFile
Else
  Dest = "Prn"
End If

' In either event, set up an error trap and
' use the Open statement to open the output file.

On Local Error GoTo DeviceNotReady
Open Dest For Output As #1

' Print the title and the column headings.

TabForCenter = (75 - Len(Title)) \ 2
Print #1, Tab(TabForCenter); Title
Print #1, Tab(TabForCenter); String$(Len(Title), "=")
Print #1,
Print #1, "Job Description"; Tab(26); "  Ref.          ";
Print #1, "Start      Finish";
Print #1, "     Total Time"
Print #1, "---------------"; Tab(26); "  ----         ";
Print #1, "-----      ------";
Print #1, "     ----------"
Print #1,

RefTot = 0
GrandTot = 0

' Print the entire array of records.

For i% = 1 To NumRecs

  ' Keep track of changes in the sorted
  ' column of reference numbers.

  If Not BlankLine(WorkRecordList(i%)) Then
    ThisRef = WorkRecordList(i%).IDField
    If i% <> NumRecs Then
      NextRef = WorkRecordList(i% + 1).IDField
    Else
      NextRef = ""
    End If

    ' Print a detail line.

    Print #1, WorkRecordList(i%).DescriptField; "  ";
    Print #1, ThisRef; "  ";
```

```
    T1 = WorkRecordList(i%).StartField
    T2 = WorkRecordList(i%).FinishedField

  ' If a time value is recorded as -1 (NoTime), the
  ' user has left this entry blank. Accordingly,
  ' print a space in the time column.

  If T1 >= 0 Then
    Print #1, Format$(T1, "hh:mm AM/PM"); "    ";
  Else
    Print #1, Space$(11);
  End If

  If T2 >= 0 Then
    Print #1, Format$(T2, "hh:mm AM/PM"); "    ";
  Else
    Print #1, Space$(11);
  End If

  ' Compute and print a total if
  ' both time values are available.

  If Not (T1 < 0 Or T2 < 0) Then
    Print #1, Format$(DoLineTotal(T1, T2), "hh \hr mm \m\i\n")

    ' Accumulate the total time for the
    ' current reference number.

    RefTot = RefTot + DoLineTotal(T1, T2)
  Else
    Print #1,
  End If

  ' If the reference number changes, print
  ' a total line for the previous reference number.

  If ThisRef <> NextRef Then
    Print #1,
    Print #1, Tab(37); "Total for "; ThisRef; " --> ";
    Print #1, Format$(RefTot * 24, "##0.00"); " hr";
    If RefTot * 24 > 1# Then Print #1, "s" Else Print #1,
    Print #1,
    GrandTot = GrandTot + RefTot
    RefTot = 0
  End If
  End If

Next i%

' Print a total line for the entire report.

Print #1,
```

(continued)

```
   Print #1, Tab(37); "*** Total Work Time ---> ";
   Print #1, Format$(GrandTot * 24, "##0.00"); " hr";
   If GrandTot * 24 > 1# Then Print #1, "s" Else Print #1,
   If Dest = "Prn" Then Print #1, Chr$(12) ' form-feed.
AbortPrint:
   Close #1

Exit Sub

DeviceNotReady:
   MsgBox "Check printer or disk and try again.", 0, "Device Problem"
Resume AbortPrint

End Sub   ' PrintWorkRecordList (TSPRINT.FRM)
```

Listing 9.26 The **SortWorkRecordList** procedure (**TSPrint** form)

```
Sub SortWorkRecordList (NumRecs As Integer)

   ' Sort the work record array, using the reference
   ' numbers (IDField) as the primary key, and the
   ' job description field as the secondary key.

   Dim i%, j%
   Dim TempWorkRec As WorkRecordType

   For i% = 1 To NumRecs - 1
     For j% = i% + 1 To NumRecs

       ' Concatenate the primary and secondary key values.

       field1$ = WorkRecordList(i%).IDField + WorkRecordList(i%).DescriptField
       field2$ = WorkRecordList(j%).IDField + WorkRecordList(j%).DescriptField

       ' Compare the values, and swap the record positions if necessary.

       If field1$ > field2$ Then
         TempWorkRec = WorkRecordList(i%)
         WorkRecordList(i%) = WorkRecordList(j%)
         WorkRecordList(j%) = TempWorkRec
       End If

     Next j%
   Next i%

 End Sub   ' SortWorkRecordList (TSPRINT.FRM)
```

Listing 9.27 Procedures from the **TSOpen** form

```
' The Workday Application.

' TSOPEN.FRM


Sub Form_Load ()

  ' Initialize the path and pattern
  ' of the file list box.

  TSFileList.Path = PathName$
  TSFileList.Pattern = "*." + ExtName$

  TSFileToOpen.Caption = ""
  OKButton.Enabled = False

  TSFileList.Refresh

End Sub  ' Form_Load (TSOPEN.FRM)


Sub CancelButton_Click ()

  ' Return to the time sheet without opening a file.

  TSFileToOpen.Caption = ""
  TSOpen.Hide

End Sub  ' CancelButton_Click (TSOPEN.FRM)


Sub OKButton_Click ()

  Dim TempName$

  ' Return to the time sheet form.

  TSOpen.Hide

End Sub  ' OKButton_Click  (TSOPEN.FRM)
```

(continued)

```
Sub TSFileList_Click ()

   ' When the user clicks a file name in the
   ' file list, copy the file name to the
   ' TSFileToOpen text box.

   TSFileToOpen.Caption = TSFileList.FileName

   ' Now enable the OK button.

   OKButton.Enabled = True

End Sub   ' TSFileList_Click (TSOPEN.FRM)


Sub TSFileList_DblClick ()

   ' If the user double-clicks a file name in
   ' the file list box, force a call to the
   ' OKButton_Click event procedure.

   OKButton_Click

End Sub   ' TSFileList_DblClick (TSOPEN.FRM)
```

10

File-System Controls and Graphics: The Pie Chart *Application*

INTRODUCTION

This chapter, like the preceding, examines two important programming topics in the context of a single project: The *Pie Chart* application produces graphs from data files that you have created in other applications. To simplify the process of opening those files, the program introduces a powerful trio of controls: the drive list box, the directory list box, and the file list box. You'll learn to use these three controls at the same time that you begin exploring the variety of graphics procedures available in Visual Basic.

Windows programs typically have an **Open** command to provide access to application-specific data files stored on disk. In the dialog box for this command you can expect to accomplish three steps in the process of locating and opening a file:

1. Change the disk drive if necessary—for example, to A, B, or C.
2. Find the directory where the file is stored.
3. Select the file itself and open it.

In general, each time you choose an application's **Open** command you can select the correct drive and directory for finding a particular file.

To match this capability in your own Visual Basic applications, you use three specially designed *file-system controls*, known as the *drive list box*, the *directory list box*, and the *file list box*. Examples of all three controls appear in Figure 10.1. Under the direction of a program's code, these three

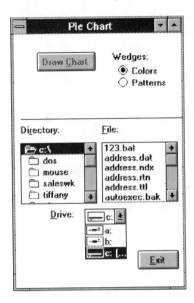

Figure 10.1 Examples of a drive list box, a directory list box, and a file list box

controls work together in a coordinated way to give the user access to any application-specific file on disk. The drive list box has a drop-down list displaying the drives on the current system. When the user clicks the name of a drive in this list, the directory list box in turn displays the hierarchy of directories available on the drive. Likewise, when the user selects and opens a directory, the file list box displays the names of files stored in the directory.

The coordination between the three controls is not quite automatic, but nonetheless requires very little programming on your part. To integrate the drive, directory, and file boxes, your program monitors the **Change** and **Click** events—and the resulting changes in property settings—that take place when the user makes selections in the boxes.

In particular, your program takes charge of exchanging specific items of information between the three controls:

- The drive list box has a **Drive** property that represents the name of the currently selected drive. When the user makes a new selection in the drive list box, the resulting **Change** event is an opportunity for your program to read the new **Drive** setting and pass it on to the directory list box.

- The directory list box has a property named **Path** that represents the current directory path. Your program assigns the **Drive** setting from the drive list box to the directory's **Path** property; this causes the directory box to display the directory hierarchy of the newly selected drive. When the user subsequently opens a directory, a **Change** procedure in your program reads the new setting of the directory control's **Path** property, and passes the value to the file list box.

- The file list box has its own **Path** property. In this case, the setting specifies the directory path from which the file list itself will be read. Your program assigns the new **Path** setting from the directory list box to the **Path** property of the file list box; as a result, file names from the selected directory are displayed. The file list box also has a **Pattern** property to which your program can assign a specific wild-card string, thus restricting the displayed file list to a particular set of file names.

- Finally, when the user clicks a file name in the file list box, a **Click** event procedure in your program reads the new setting of the control's **FileName** property. This property supplies the name of the file that the user has selected.

Your code is *not* responsible for building the lists displayed in these three boxes. **AddItem**—the method used for building the list in a combo box—does not exist for the drive, directory, or file controls. Rather, these controls automatically read file-system information directly from the operating system. All your program has to do is orchestrate the changes in the three lists and read the user's file selections.

Clearly these three controls are among Visual Basic's most powerful tools. When you first add a set of them to a new form, their default **Name** values are **Drive1**, **Dir1**, and **File1**. In this chapter you'll learn to use the following properties and events:

- **Drive1.Drive**, the current drive name, and **Dir1.Path**, the current directory path.

- **File1.Path** and **File1.Pattern**, the properties that determine the contents of the file list.

- **File1.FileName**, the name of the currently selected file in the file list.

- **Drive1_Change**, **Dir1_Change**, **File1_Click**, and **File1_DblClick**, the event procedures that are called when the user makes new selections in the three file-system controls.

As an exercise with these controls, properties, and events, this chapter presents the *Pie Chart* project. The application reads data files created by two other programs in this book—*Sales Week* (from Chapter 6) and *Workday* (from Chapter 9)—and creates pie charts from the numeric information stored in the files.

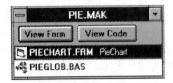

Figure 10.2 The PIE.MAK project

Open the *Pie Chart* application now into the Visual Basic environment. The project is stored on the exercise disk as PIE.MAK, and consists of a form and a code module (Figure 10.2). Press F5 to run the program. You'll see that the three file-system controls from Figure 10.1 are actually part of this program's dialog box.

THE *PIE CHART* APPLICATION

A pie chart shows how individual numeric data items relate to the sum of all the items in a data set. Each number is represented by a wedge in a circular pie. The angle of a wedge—and therefore the width of the slice—is determined by the ratio of one numeric data item to the sum of all the data. In short, a pie chart gives you a useful picture of the parts that create a whole. The *Pie Chart* application draws pie charts for two familiar kinds of data files you have worked with in earlier chapters:

- The time sheet files created by the *Workday* program. You'll recall that these files have extension names of WKD. For a WKD file, the *Pie Chart* application draws a pie depicting the number of work hours recorded for a given day. Each wedge in the pie represents the number of hours recorded for one particular project, identified by the project's reference number.

- The weekly sales files created by the *Sales Week* program. These files have SLS extensions. For an SLS file, *Pie Chart* draws a pie depicting the total dollar sales for a given week. Each wedge in the pie thus represents one day's sales, from Sunday to Saturday.

The *Workday* program creates random-access files, organized by individual job records. In contrast, the *Sales Week* program creates sequential-access data files consisting of a simple list of daily sales figures. The *Pie Chart* program therefore needs different procedures for reading each kind of file. On the other hand, a single procedure in the program draws the pie chart itself, regardless of the source of the data. For this reason you will find the application relatively easy to expand if you decide that you want

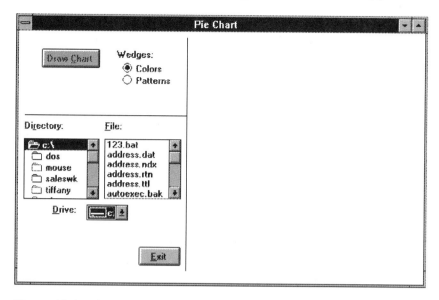

Figure 10.3 The initial dialog box from the *Pie Chart* application

to add other file types to the list of files that the program can recognize, read, and chart.

When you first run the application, the dialog box shown in Figure 10.3 appears on the desktop. The right side of the dialog box—where the application eventually draws a pie chart—is empty at first. The left side displays a variety of objects, including the familiar trio of file-system controls. The application is very simple to use: To open a data file you make appropriate changes in the current drive and directory if necessary, and then you select a WKD or SLS file name from the file list box. When you have made your selection, you click the **Draw Chart** button. (This button remains dimmed until you select a file that the program can work with.) The application draws a pie chart from the file you have selected. During a given run of the program you can examine charts for any number of different data files.

As a first exercise with the *Pie Chart* application, try the following sequence of steps:

1. Pull down the drive list, and note that the list contains the names of all the drives on your system. Drive C is currently selected. Assuming you have saved SLS and WKD files in directories on drive C, you do not need to change the drive.

2. In the directory list box, scroll down to the **WorkDay** directory, where the data files from the *Workday* application are stored.

3.   Double-click the directory name. The closed folder icon displayed at the left of the directory name changes to an open folder icon, symbolizing the opening of the directory. At the same time, the file list box changes to a list of all the WKD files in the directory.

4.   Click any one of the WKD files you have created with the *Workday* program. When you do so, the **Draw Chart** button is enabled and the name of your selected file appears just beneath the button in the dialog box (Figure 10.4).

5.   Click the **Draw Chart** button. The application opens the selected file, reads and reorganizes its data, and draws the chart. (All this happens after an almost unnoticable pause.) If you are working with a color graphics monitor, you can view the chart in color. On a mono-chrome monitor, click the **Patterns** option at the top of the dialog box and the wedges will be filled in with geometric patterns instead of colors. Figure 10.4 shows an example of the patterned pie chart.

At the far right side of the dialog box, the program displays a *legend* for the pie chart. For a WKD file, the legend identifies the reference number corresponding to each wedge in the chart. The application allows a maximum of seven wedges for depicting the data in any given file. If a WKD file happens to have more than seven different reference numbers, the pie depicts the total hours for the seven most significant projects—that is, the

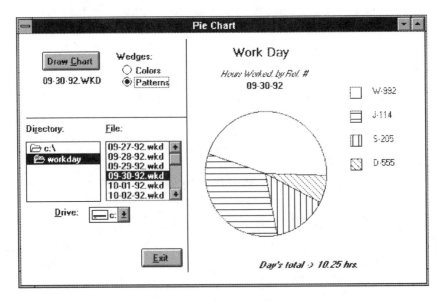

Figure 10.4 A pie chart created from a WKD file

```
                          Time Sheet for 09-30-92
                          =========================

Job Description           Ref.       Start       Finish      Total Time
---------------           ----       -----       ------      ----------
J. Donalds's will         D-555      03:00 PM    03:15 PM    00 hr 15 min
Letter to J. Donalds      D-555      08:00 AM    08:15 AM    00 hr 15 min
Phone call, Donalds       D-555      05:00 PM    05:15 PM    00 hr 15 min

                                     Total for D-555      --> 0.75 hr

Jackson contract          J-114      08:15 AM    09:45 AM    01 hr 30 min
Jackson contract          J-114      11:15 AM    12:45 PM    01 hr 30 min
Phone call, Jackson       J-114      03:15 PM    03:45 PM    00 hr 30 min

                                     Total for J-114      --> 3.50 hrs

Lunch meeting, Smith      S-205      01:00 PM    02:30 PM    01 hr 30 min

                                     Total for S-205      --> 1.50 hrs

Meeting with Wu           W-992      10:00 AM    11:15 AM    01 hr 15 min
Wu contract               W-992      03:45 PM    05:00 PM    01 hr 15 min
Wu contract               W-992      05:15 PM    07:15 PM    02 hr 00 min

                                     Total for W-992      --> 4.50 hrs

                                     *** Total Work Time ---> 10.25 hrs
```

Figure 10.5 The time sheet data from which the pie chart (Figure 10.4) was created

seven reference numbers with the greatest number of recorded work hours for the day.

Figure 10.5 shows a report produced by the *Workday* application for the same day pictured in Figure 10.4. Examining the report, you can confirm that four projects with different reference numbers were recorded for the day. The total work time displayed on the bottom line of the report matches the total figure given at the bottom of the pie chart. Furthermore, you can see that each of the four subtotal amounts appears to be correctly represented by the size of the corresponding wedge.

Next try creating a pie chart for an SLS file from the *Sales Week* application:

1. In the directory list box, double-click the root directory, represented as **c:**. This action closes the **WorkDay** subdirectory, and restores the full list of subdirectories on the C drive.

2. Scroll down to the **SalesWk** directory, where the SLS files from the *Sales Week* application are stored. Double-click the directory name to open the directory. As a result, the file list box displays all the SLS files in the directory.

3. Select a file name in the file list box. Double-click the file name. The *Pie Chart* application recognizes the double click as a short cut for two actions: selecting a file name and clicking the **Draw Chart** button. As a result of your double click, the pie chart for the SLS file appears at the right side of the dialog box, as shown in Figure 10.6.

This time the pie depicts an entire week's sales, and each wedge represents one day. The legend identifies the wedge pattern or wedge color for each day of the week, from Sunday to Saturday. The total sales amount for the week is displayed beneath the pie chart. Compare this chart with the bar graph created by the *Sales Week* application for the same week's sales (Figure 10.7). Clearly the two charts depict the same data set, but they focus on the data in different ways. While the bar graph shows the strength of each day's sales in relation to other days, the pie chart shows how each day relates to the whole week's sales.

If the *Pie Chart* program reads a *Sales Week* file containing fewer than seven sales figures—that is, if the sales amount is 0 for one or more days in the week—the resulting pie chart includes only those days for which sales

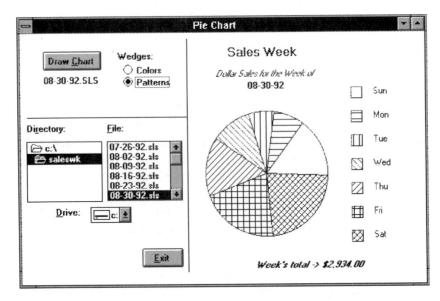

Figure 10.6 A pie chart created from an SLS file.

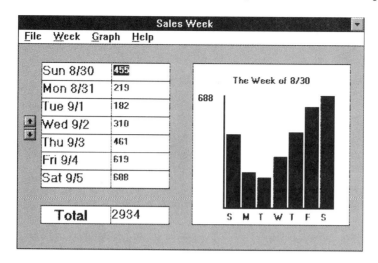

Figure 10.7 The weekly sales data from which the pie chart (Figure 10.6) was created.

are recorded. For example, Figure 10.8 shows a pie chart for a week that has only three days of sales data. The corresponding *Sales Week* bar graph appears in Figure 10.9.

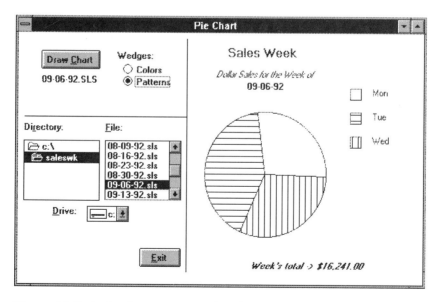

Figure 10.8 A pie chart representing three days of sales.

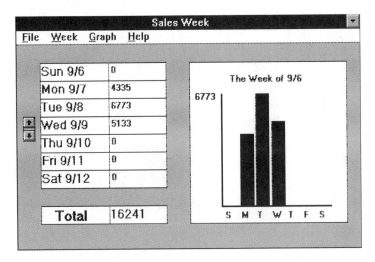

Figure 10.9 The bar graph representing three days of sales.

The *Pie Chart* program illustrates one approach you can use for integrating the operations of different Visual Basic applications: By designing programs that can recognize and read each other's data files, you can offer the user a variety of functions and operations to perform on shared data sets. Because *Workday* and *Sales Week* are related to *Pie Chart* in this way, you might want to organize the three applications as a program group in the Windows environment. For example, Figure 10.10 shows the application icons in their own group window. This group gives you convenient access to the three applications whenever you want to compare the data that they generate and display.

Figure 10.10 The icons for the three related applications

THE ELEMENTS OF THE *PIE CHART* APPLICATION

As you examine the controls, properties, and code of the *Pie Chart* program, you'll focus on the three file-system controls included in the application. In addition, *Pie Chart* has some good examples of the graphics methods associated with a picture box control. For one, it demonstrates the use of the **Circle** method for drawing the concentric wedges that make up a pie chart. The arithmetic algorithm for calculating the angles of wedges is also an interesting part of this program.

Controls and Properties

As you've seen, the application's single form, named **PieChart**, is divided into two parts. The left side of the form contains controls for selecting a file and for issuing the command to draw a chart. The right side of the form is reserved for the elements of the pie chart itself. When you first run the program, the right side is empty.

Most of the important properties for both the file-system controls and the picture box controls in this application are set at run time rather than at design time. Describing the form's status at design time is therefore relatively simple. Starting from the left side of the form, here are the controls and their distinctive design-time properties:

- The three file-system controls have **Name** settings of **DirectoryList**, **FileList**, and **DriveList**. Each of these three controls is paired with a nearby label that identifies its purpose.

- A pair of option buttons is organized as a control array named **Wedges**. The index numbers of the two buttons are 0 and 1, and the captions are **Colors** and **Patterns**. These controls allow the user to choose between colored and patterned wedges.

- Two command buttons have the **Name** settings of **DrawButton** and **ExitButton**. The user clicks the **DrawButton** control to request a pie chart for a selected file. Clicking the **ExitButton** control terminates the program performance.

- Finally, a label named **FileDisplay** is located immediately beneath the **DrawButton** control. This label, which initially has a blank caption, is where the program displays a usable file name that the user has selected from the file list.

The right side of the form contains picture boxes and labels, including two control arrays to represent the elements of the legend:

- The main picture box, in which the program ultimately draws the pie charts, is named **PiePicBox**. In addition to this **Name** setting, the picture box has two important design-time property definitions: A **BorderStyle** setting of **0-None** makes the box invisible until the program creates a drawing inside it. An **AutoRedraw** setting of **True** enables the application to redraw the graph whenever necessary.

- Three labels located above the main picture box have **Name** settings of **Title1**, **Title2**, and **Title3**. In addition, a label below the picture box is named **TotalLine**. All of these labels have blank **Caption** settings initially. Each label also has individual settings for the **FontSize**, **FontBold**, and **FontItalic** properties, as you can see by looking at the text that the program displays in these positions (Figures 10.4 and 10.6).

- Finally, an array of picture boxes named **Legend** and an array of labels named **LegLab** are arranged in adjacent columns at the right side of the frame. Each of these control arrays has seven elements, with **Index** settings from 0 to 6. Like **PiePicBox**, the **Legend** picture boxes have **BorderStyle** settings of **0-None** and **AutoRedraw** settings of **True**. The **LegLab** labels have blank caption settings, and **FontBold** settings of **False**.

Events

The program includes procedures for only a small number of events, most of them related to the file-system controls. As usual, a **Form_Load** event procedure performs initializations—in this case, defining the start-up settings for the drive, directory, and file list boxes, and establishing custom scales for the picture boxes. Subsequently, the program reacts to the following assortment of **Change**, **Click**, and **DblClick** events:

- **Change** events take place when the user makes new selections in the drive list box and the directory list box. The **DriveList_Change** and **DirectoryList_Change** procedures are therefore responsible for sending the user's drive and directory selections on to the file list box so that the appropriate list of files will appear. Thanks to the sophistication of the three file-system controls, this task requires only a few lines of code.

- A **Click** event takes place when the user selects a file in the file list box. The **FileList_Click** procedure examines the selected file name and determines whether it is a file that the program can work with—that is, a WKD or SLS file. If so, the procedure copies the file name to the **FileDisplay** label and enables the **Draw Chart** button.

- A **DblClick** event occurs if the user double-clicks a file name in the file list box. In this case, the program automatically makes a call to **FileList_Click**. If the selected file is usable, the **FileList_DblClick** procedure then goes on to force a call to the **DrawButton_Click** event procedure.

- Other **Click** events take place when the user clicks either of the application's two command buttons, labeled **Draw Chart** and **Exit**. The **DrawButton_Click** procedure begins by making a call to one of two general procedures that are in charge of reading data files. Then the **Click** procedure actually draws the pie chart. The **Exit-Button_Click** procedure terminates the program performance.

- Finally, the program recognizes a **Click** event when the user clicks either of the two option buttons, labeled **Colors** and **Labels**. The **Wedges_Click** procedure makes a call to **DrawButton_Click**, as long as the **DrawButton.Enabled** property setting is currently true. **DrawButton_Click**, in turn, reads the current settings of the option buttons to decide whether to fill the wedges with colors or with patterns.

Procedures and Methods

The code for the program appears in Listings 10.1 to 10.8. You'll concentrate first on the event procedures related to the three file-system controls (Listings 10.2 and 10.3). A large part of the program listing is taken up by two general procedures—named **ReadSalesFile** and **ReadTimeFile**—that read the data files and organize the data into convenient formats. After a brief overview of these two procedures, you'll examine the **DrawButton_Click** procedure (Listing 10.4), which illustrates the **Circle** method and other graphics tools.

File, Directory, and Drive Procedures

The **Form_Load** procedure (Listing 10.2) begins by initializing the settings for the program's three file-system controls, **DriveList**, **DirectoryList**, and **FileList**. This is done simply by assigning string values to their **Drive**, **Path**, and **Pattern** properties. First the program selects drive C:

```
DriveList.Drive = "C:"
```

The initial directory list path is the root directory of drive C:

```
DirectoryList.Path = DriveList.Drive + "\"
```

Then the program explicitly assigns this path to the **Path** property of the file list box:

```
FileList.Path = DirectoryList.Path
```

As a result, the file list box initially displays file names from the root directory of drive C.

At the beginning there is no reason to restrict the file list to any particular pattern of file names:

```
FileList.Pattern = "*.*"
```

However, until the user selects a file that the *Pie Chart* program can use, the **DrawButton** control is kept in a disabled state:

```
DrawButton.Enabled = False
```

By this simple mechanism, the program avoids trying to open and read any irrelevant files.

If the user makes a new selection in the drive list box, the program calls the **DriveList_Change** procedure. As a result of the **Change** event, Visual Basic automatically assigns the newly selected drive name to the control's **Drive** property. The **Change** procedure passes this change on to the directory list simply by assigning the new **Drive** setting to **Directory-List.Path**:

```
DirectoryList.Path = DriveList.Drive
```

Incidentally, this assignment results in an automatic **Change** event for the **DirectoryList** control. In other words, the **DirectoryList_Change** event procedure is called when the user makes a new selection either in the drive list box or the directory list box.

The **Change** event for the directory list results in a new setting for the control's **Path** property. The first task of **DirectoryList_Change** is therefore to pass this new setting on to the file list box:

```
FileList.Path = DirectoryList.Path
```

As a result, the file list box displays the files in the newly selected drive or directory.

If the user opens one of this program's two target directories—**WorkDay** or **SalesWk**—the **DirectoryList_Change** procedure restricts the file list to names with the appropriate extensions. First the procedure assigns the new directory name to the string variable **DName$**. Then the **Pattern** property of the file list box is adjusted according to the value of this variable:

```
If DName$ = "SALESWK" Then
   FileList.Pattern = "*.SLS"
ElseIf DName$ = "WORKDAY" Then
   FileList.Pattern = "*.WKD"
Else
   FileList.Pattern = "*.*"
End If
```

For the user's convenience, only SLS files appear in the file list when **SalesWk** is selected as the directory. Likewise, only WKD files appear for the **WorkDay** directory. For any other directory, the program makes no special restriction on the **Pattern** property.

Finally, a **Click** event takes place when the user selects a file in the file list box. (Actually, this event occurs for both mouse and keyboard selections: The user can click a file name with the mouse or press Alt+F to select the file list box and then use the up or down arrow keys to select a file name.) This event automatically changes the setting of the **FileName** property. In this case, the **FileList_Click** event examines the selected file name and determines whether the file is one that the *Pie Chart* program can use.

The first step in this task is to isolate the extension name of the current selection in the file list box:

```
Ext$ = UCase$(Right$(FileList.FileName, 3))
```

If the final three characters of this setting contain one of the two target extension names, this is a file the program can use:

```
If Ext$ = "SLS" Or Ext$ = "WKD" Then
```

In this case, the procedure copies the new **FileName** setting to the **Caption** property of the **FileDisplay** label and enables the **DrawButton** control:

```
FileDisplay.Caption = UCase$(FileList.FileName)
DrawButton.Enabled = True
```

The user can now click the **Draw Chart** command button to instruct the program to draw a pie chart for the currently selected file.

However, if the current **FileName** selection does not contain one of the two target extension names, the program keeps the **FileDisplay** label blank and the **DrawButton** control disabled:

```
FileDisplay.Caption = ""
DrawButton.Enabled = False
```

The program also recognizes a **DblClick** event for the **FileList** control. When the user double-clicks a file name in the list, the **FileList_Click** procedure first examines the file name and determines whether it is usable. If the **FileList_DblClick** procedure subsequently finds a file name displayed in the **FileDisplay** label position, the routine makes a call to the **DrawButton_Click** procedure:

```
If FileDisplay.Caption <> "" Then DrawButton_Click
```

As you'll see shortly, the **DrawButton_Click** procedure calls a procedure to read a data file and then draws the pie chart.

Procedures That Read Data Files

Once the user selects an appropriate file and clicks the **Draw Chart** button, the program opens the file and reads the data. But then the data has to be reorganized for use in the pie chart. This task involves specially designed data structures and calculations. Accordingly, the global module PIEGLOB.BAS (Listing 10.1) defines a record structure named **WedgeRec-Type**. It contains two fields, a single-precision numeric field named **Portion**, and a string field named **LegendStr**:

```
Type WedgeRecType
  Portion As Single
  LegendStr As String
End Type
```

An array of **WedgeRecType** records is then declared in the form-level declaration section of the **PieChart** form (also Listing 10.1):

```
Dim WedgeRecs(6) As WedgeRecType
```

This array is designed to store the information needed to draw a pie chart for either of the two file types. When the user clicks the **Draw Chart** button, a call to either **ReadSalesFile** or **ReadTimeFile** fills the array with data.

Each record in the array describes one of the wedges in the chart:

- The **Portion** field is a decimal value representing the percentage of the pie to be taken up by a given wedge.

- The **LegendStr** field contains the legend caption for the wedge.

Two other form-level variables provide additional information about the chart:

```
Dim WedgeCount As Integer
Dim Total As Double
```

WedgeCount is the number of wedges, from 0 to 7. For a file created by the *Sales Week* application, **WedgeCount** is 7 if there are sales recorded for each day of the week, or less than 7 if the sales figure is missing for one or more days. The **WedgeCount** for a *Workday* file depends upon the number of different reference numbers recorded in the file. The **Total** variable represents the sum of all the numeric data values that will be depicted in the pie chart—that is, the total dollar sales amount for an SLS file, or the total work hours recorded in a WKD file.

The **ReadSalesFile** and **ReadTimeFile** procedures (Listings 10.6 and 10.7) read their respective data files and assign values to **WedgeCount**, **Total**, and the **WedgeRecs** array. These form-level variables therefore become the means of passing information about the data file to the **DrawButton_Click** procedure.

The **ReadSalesFile** procedure has the relatively simple job of reading the seven daily sales amounts from an SLS file, calculating the total weekly sales, and assigning the **Portion** values to the **WedgeRecs** array. The variable **Count** keeps track of the number of nonzero daily sales amounts. The **Portion** for a given day is simply the ratio of the day's sales to the total sales for the week:

```
WedgeRecs(Count).Portion = SalesDay(i%) / WeekSales
```

The procedure also assigns day-of-the-week abbreviations to the **LegendStr** field of the **WedgeRecs** array.

The task of the **ReadTimeFile** procedure is somewhat more complex. The daily work records are stored in random-access files, and there is no fixed number of records in a file. The procedure opens a file, determines the number of records, and then reads all the records into a dynamic array named **WorkRecordList**. Then the procedure must accomplish a detailed sequence of steps:

1. Sort the **WorkRecordList** array by reference numbers and produce a count of the different reference numbers in the file. (These two tasks are performed by a call to the **SortWorkRecordList** function, shown in Listing 10.8.)

2. Copy the reference numbers and their subtotals into another dynamic array of records named **WorkTotals**.

3. Sort the **WorkTotals** array by the subtotal amounts. (This is done by a call to the **SortWorkTotals** procedure, also shown in Listing 10.8.) If there are more than seven reference numbers, select the top seven subtotals for the chart.

4. Calculate the **Portion** value for each subtotal. In this case, the **Portion** for a given reference number is the ratio of the subtotal to the total hours recorded for all the reference numbers.

5. Copy the reference numbers themselves to the **LegendStr** field of the **WedgeRecs** array.

When the **Portion** and **LegendStr** fields are available for each wedge, the program is ready to draw the pie chart.

Graphics Methods for Drawing a Pie Chart

One of the tasks of the **Form_Load** procedure is to establish convenient coordinate systems for the application's eight picture box controls. The program uses a Visual Basic method named **Scale** to define the coordinates of the upper-left and lower-right corners of each picture box. First the scale is set for the seven boxes of the **Legend** array and then for the **PiePicBox** control:

```
For i% = 0 To 6
   Legend(i%).Scale (-1, -1)-(1, 1)
Next i%
PiePicBox.Scale (-1, -1)-(1, 1)
```

Note that the center point of **PiePicBox** is $(0, 0)$ under this new coordinate system, and the width and height of the box both have a scaled value of 2. These characteristics prove particularly convenient when the time comes to draw the wedges of the pie chart.

It is possible to establish a coordinate system at design time rather than at run time by assigning settings to the **ScaleLeft, ScaleTop, ScaleWidth,** and **ScaleHeight** properties of a picture box. But using the **Scale** method is normally a simpler approach, especially in an application that has several picture boxes.

The **DrawButton_Click** event procedure (Listing 10.4) creates all the graphics and text displayed at the right side of the *Pie Chart* form. The procedure begins by assigning appropriate title strings to the **Caption** properties of the **Title1, Title2,** and **Title3** labels. Then it calls either **ReadSalesFile** or **ReadTimeFile** to read a data file and assign values to the **Portion** and **LegendStr** fields of the **WedgeRecs** array.

Before displaying a new chart and legend, the procedure clears away any previous graphics displays:

```
PiePicBox.Cls
For i% = 0 to 6
   Legend(i%).BackColor = QBColor(15)
```

```
   Legend(i%).Cls
   LegLab(i%).Caption = ""
Next i%
```

The **Cls** method clears the graphics from a picture box. Because a previous chart may have changed the **BackColor** setting for the **Legend** picture boxes, the program resets the color to white before clearing these boxes. By the way, the *Pie Chart* application uses Visual Basic's **QBColor** function to specify colors for the pie chart and the legend. The **QBColor** arguments and resulting color values appear in Table 10.1.

Next, a **For** loop draws the pie chart, wedge by wedge. The procedure uses three numeric variables to keep track of the wedge angles:

- **W1** is the starting angle of a given wedge, relative to the full sweep of the circle.

- **W2** is the ending angle.

- **Angle** is the actual angle measurement of the wedge—that is, the difference between **W1** and **W2**.

For the **Circle** method, angles are measured in *radians* rather than degrees. The full sweep of 360 degrees is equal to a radian measurement of 2π. (The *Pie Chart* application includes a function named **Pi** that calculates and returns the value of π. You can examine this function in Listing 10.5.)

The first step in drawing a given wedge is to calculate the angle measurement that will determine the size of the wedge:

```
For i% = 0 to WedgeCount - 1
  Angle = 2 * Pi() * WedgeRecs(i%).Portion
```

Multiplying the **Portion** field by the radian measurement of the full circle gives the angle measurement of the wedge. The next step is to calculate

Table 10.1 QBColor arguments and results

0	Black	8	Gray
1	Blue	9	Light Blue
2	Green	10	Light Green
3	Cyan	11	Light Cyan
4	Red	12	Light Red
5	Magenta	13	Light Magenta
6	Brown	14	Yellow
7	White	15	High-Intensity White

the starting angle, **W1**, and the ending angle, **W2**, of the wedge. The starting angle is equal to the ending angle of the previous wedge:

```
W1 = W2
```

And the ending angle is an offset of **Angle** radians from the starting angle:

```
W2 = W1 + Angle
```

The syntax of the **Circle** method for drawing wedges is:

```
Object.Circle (x, y), Radius, Color, -StartAngle, -EndAngle
```

The coordinate address *(x, y)* is the center of the circle. To make the **Circle** method draw the radius sides of the wedge, you must express *StartAngle* and *EndAngle* as negative radian measurements. (This has no effect on the actual angle of the wedge.) Here, then, is how the **DrawButton_Click** procedure draws each wedge:

```
PiePicBox.Circle (0, 0), .9, QBColor(0), -W1, -W2
```

Thanks to the custom scaling done in the **Form_Load** procedure, the center of the **PiePicBox** picture box is $(0, 0)$ and the shortest distance from the center to a side is 1. This statement gives the circle a radius of .9, almost touching the edge of the picture box. The outline of the wedge is drawn in black, represented by **QBColor(0)**. Finally, the negative values of **W1** and **W2** are presented as the starting and ending angles.

This formula works fine for all but the very first and the very last wedges of the pie. The **Circle** method can behave unpredictably if the *StartAngle* or *EndAngle* value is equal to 0 or 2π. Consequently, the program must instead use a small nonzero number or a value slightly decreased from 2π to represent this angle. For this purpose, the **DrawButton_Click** procedure defines a constant named **SmallDiff**:

```
Const SmallDiff = .000001
```

Before calling the **Circle** method to draw the first and last wedges, the procedure makes a small change in the value of **W1** or **W2**:

```
Select Case i%
  Case 0
    W1 = W1 + SmallDiff
  Case WedgeCount - 1
    W2 = W2 - SmallDiff
End Select
```

This small change results in properly drawn wedges for the pie.

There is one other contingency: If the data set happens to contain only one value—that is, one sales figure from an SLS file or one reference number from a WKD file—the "wedge" representing this value will consist of the entire circle. In this case the procedure calls the **Circle** method without supplying values for the *StartAngle* and *EndAngle* arguments:

```
PiePicBox.Circle (0, 0), .9, QBColor(0)
```

The **DrawButton_Click** procedure also takes care of filling the wedges and the legend boxes with colors or patterns. Visual Basic makes this task very easy, through the use of the following three picture box properties:

- The **FillStyle** property fills an enclosed shape with solid or patterned color.

- The **FillColor** property selects the color for the filled shape.

- The **BackColor** property selects the color for the background of a picture box.

To use these three properties successfully, you assign settings to them *before* drawing a shape. Settings for the **FillStyle** property range from 0 to 7, as shown in Table 10.2. The **FillColor** and **BackColor** properties accept color codes generated by either the **RGB** or **QBColor** function.

To decide between filling the wedges with color or patterns, the **DrawButton_Click** procedure reads the **Value** setting of **Wedges(0)**:

```
If Wedges(0).Value Then
```

If the value of this control element is true, the user has requested color wedges; if false, the user wants patterns. For a color-filled wedge, the program sets the **FillStyle** property to 0 (for a solid fill) and the **FillColor** property to a **QBColor** value from 8 to 15:

```
PiePicBox.FillStyle = 0
PiePicBox.FillColor = QBColor(i% + 8)
```

To display the same color in the corresponding legend box, the procedure simply sets the control's background color:

```
Legend(i%).BackColor = QBColor (i% + 8)
```

For a patterned wedge, the procedure selects a **FillStyle** setting from 1 to 7 and a **FillColor** setting of black:

```
PiePicBox.FillStyle = i% + 1
PiePicBox.FillColor = QBColor(0)
```

Table 10.2 FillStyle settings and results

0	Solid
1	Transparent
2	Horizontal Line
3	Vertical Line
4	Diagonal Line, down to right
5	Diagonal Line, down to left
6	Crossing Lines
7	Diagonal Crossing Lines

To display the same pattern in the corresponding legend box, the procedure sets the same property values, but then uses the **Line** method to draw a square slightly inside the perimeter of the picture box:

```
Legend(i%).FillStyle = i% + 1
Legend(i%).FillColor = QBColor(0)
Legend(i%).Line (-.9, -.9)-(.9, .9), QBColor(0), B
```

The current legend caption is stored as **WedgeRecs(i%).LegendStr**. To copy this value to the form, the procedure assigns the string to the **Caption** property of the corresponding **LegLab** label:

```
LegLab(i%).Caption = WedgeRecs(i%).LegendStr
```

When the pie chart is complete, the **DrawButton_Click** procedure prepares a total string and displays it as the **Caption** property of the **TotalLine** label.

SUMMARY: THE FILE-SYSTEM CONTROLS AND GRAPHICS

Visual Basic's three file-system controls are powerful tools to include in an application when you need to give the user access to files stored on disk. The drive and directory list boxes allow the user to select a new drive and directory during the process of searching for a file. The file list box then displays the files in the selected directory path.

Your program coordinates the activities of the three controls by reading and setting properties such as **Drive**, **Path**, **Pattern**, and **FileName**. However, your program is not responsible for building the lists displayed in the boxes. The controls read these lists directly from the operating system.

In short, the file-system controls are easy to incorporate into a program and require little code. But they offer the user complete access to files wherever they are stored on disk.

The properties and methods associated with picture boxes allow you to create graphic images during run time. For example, in this chapter you have seen how to accomplish the following tasks:

- Create a custom coordinate system for a picture box by calling the **Scale** method during run time.

- Select colors for the picture box by setting properties such as **Back-Color**, and using Visual Basic's **QBColor** function.

- Draw geometric shapes in a picture box using the **Circle** and **Line** methods. You can use the **FillStyle** and **FillColor** methods to fill these shapes with patterns or colors.

Listing 10.1 Module and form-level declarations for the **Pie Chart** program

```
' PieGlob.BAS
' Global Declarations for the
' Pie Chart Application

' Record type for wedge descriptions.

Type WedgeRecType
  Portion As Single      ' The decimal portion of a wedge.
  LegendStr As String    ' The caption of a legend entry.
End Type


' Record type for time-sheet files.

Type WorkRecordType
  DescriptField As String * 25  ' Description of job.
  IDField As String * 10        ' Reference number.
  StartField As Double          ' Starting time.
  FinishedField As Double       ' Ending time.
End Type


' Record type for time-sheet subtotals,
' organized by reference number.
```

(continued)

```
Type WorkTotalType
   IDField As String * 10   ' Reference number.
   TotalField As Double     ' Total hours for this job.
End Type

' End of Global Declarations for Pie Chart.


' Form-level declarations for PIECHART.FRM.

' Day-of-the-week string.
Const DayStr$ = "SunMonTueWedThuFriSat"

' Array of wedge-description records.
Dim WedgeRecs(6) As WedgeRecType

' The number of wedges in the current chart,
' and the total amount represented by the
' sum of the wedges.

Dim WedgeCount As Integer
Dim Total As Double

' Dynamic array of work records for
' reading a time-sheet file.

Dim WorkRecordList() As WorkRecordType

' Dynamic array of subtotal records
' for a time-sheet file.

Dim WorkTotals() As WorkTotalType

' End of form-level declarations for Pie Chart.
```

Listing 10.2 Form_Load, ExitButton_Click, and DriveList_Change

```
Sub Form_Load ()

   ' Initialize the drive, the path, and the pattern.

   DriveList.Drive = "C:"
```

```
   DirectoryList.Path = DriveList.Drive + "\"
   FileList.Path = DirectoryList.Path
   FileList.Pattern = "*.*"
   DrawButton.Enabled = False

   ' Customize the coordinate system for all the
   ' picture box controls--including the seven
   ' legend picture boxes, and the one picture box
   ' for the pie chart itself.

   For i% = 0 To 6
     Legend(i%).Scale (-1, -1)-(1, 1)
   Next i%
   PiePicBox.Scale (-1, -1)-(1, 1)

End Sub  ' Form_Load


Sub ExitButton_Click ()

   ' Terminate the program run.

   End

End Sub  ' ExitButton_Click


Sub DriveList_Change ()

   ' Record a change in the user's drive selection.

   ' Assign the new drive name to the Path property
   ' of the directory list box.

   DirectoryList.Path = DriveList.Drive

   ' Blank out the FileDisplay control, and
   ' disable the DrawButton command button.

   FileDisplay.Caption = ""
   DrawButton.Enabled = False

End Sub  ' DriveList_Change
```

Listing 10.3 Directory list and file list event procedures

```
Sub DirectoryList_Change ()

  ' Record the user's selections in the
  ' directory list box.

  Dim DName$  ' The current directory name.

  ' Copy the current path name to the Path
  ' property of the file list box.

  FileList.Path = DirectoryList.Path

  ' Blank out the FileDisplay control, and
  ' disable the DrawButton command button.

  FileDisplay.Caption = ""
  DrawButton.Enabled = False

  ' If the current directory is SALESWK or
  ' WORKDAY, establish an appropriate file-name
  ' pattern for the file list box.

  DName$ = UCase$(Right$(DirectoryList.Path, 7))
  If DName$ = "SALESWK" Then
    FileList.Pattern = "*.SLS"
  ElseIf DName$ = "WORKDAY" Then
    FileList.Pattern = "*.WKD"
  Else
    FileList.Pattern = "*.*"
  End If

End Sub  ' DirectoryList_Change


Sub FileList_Click ()

  ' Read the extension name of the user's selection
  ' from the file list box. If the extension is "SLS" or
  ' "WKD"--one of the two files that this application
  ' can work with--display the file name in the FileDisplay
  ' control, and activate the DrawButton command button.
```

```
   Ext$ = UCase$(Right$(FileList.FileName, 3))
   If Ext$ = "SLS" Or Ext$ = "WKD" Then
     FileDisplay.Caption = UCase$(FileList.FileName)
     DrawButton.Enabled = True
   Else
     FileDisplay.Caption = ""
     DrawButton.Enabled = False
   End If

End Sub  ' FileList_Click


Sub FileList_DblClick ()

  ' If a usable file has been selected from the
  ' file list box, accept a double-click as a command
  ' to create the pie chart.

  If FileDisplay.Caption <> "" Then DrawButton_Click

End Sub  ' FileList_DblClick
```

Listing 10.4 The **DrawButton_Click** procedure

```
Sub DrawButton_Click ()

  ' Draw the pie chart, from information stored in the
  ' form-level WedgeRecs array, and the form-level variables
  ' WedgeCount and Total.

  Const SmallDiff = .000001  ' Small delta value for
                             ' first and last wedge angles.

  Dim W1, W2, Angle  ' Wedge angle variables.
  Dim TtlStr$        ' The total line string.

  ' Determine whether this is an SLS or WKD file,
  ' and display the appropriate titles. Then
  ' call the procedure that opens and reads the file.

  If Right$(FileDisplay.Caption, 3) = "SLS" Then
```

(continued)

```
    Title1.Caption = "Sales Week"
    Title2.Caption = "Dollar Sales for the Week of"
    ReadSalesFile
ElseIf Right$(FileDisplay.Caption, 3) = "WKD" Then
    Title1.Caption = "Work Day"
    Title2.Caption = "Hours Worked, by Ref. #"
    ReadTimeFile
End If
Title3.Caption = Left$(FileDisplay.Caption, 8)

' Clear all the picture box controls.

PiePicBox.Cls
For i% = 0 To 6
    Legend(i%).BackColor = QBColor(15)
    Legend(i%).Cls
    LegLab(i%).Caption = ""
Next i%

W2 = 0
For i% = 0 To WedgeCount - 1

    ' Calculate the starting and ending
    ' angles for each wedge of the pie.

    Angle = 2 * Pi() * WedgeRecs(i%).Portion
    W1 = W2
    W2 = W1 + Angle

    ' Add or subtract the SmallDiff amount for
    ' the first and last wedges.

    Select Case i%
      Case 0
        W1 = W1 + SmallDiff
      Case WedgeCount - 1
        W2 = W2 - SmallDiff
    End Select

    ' Read the Wedges option buttons, and
    ' select a color or a pattern for the new wedge.
```

```
   If Wedges(0).Value Then
     PiePicBox.FillStyle = 0
     PiePicBox.FillColor = QBColor(i% + 8)
     Legend(i%).BackColor = QBColor(i% + 8)
   Else
     PiePicBox.FillStyle = i% + 1
     PiePicBox.FillColor = QBColor(0)
     Legend(i%).FillStyle = i% + 1
     Legend(i%).FillColor = QBColor(0)
     Legend(i%).Line (-.9, -.9)-(.9, .9), QBColor(0), B
   End If


   ' Display the legend caption.

   LegLab(i%).Caption = WedgeRecs(i%).LegendStr

   ' Draw the wedge (or the entire circle if
   ' there is only one data value).

   If WedgeCount > 1 Then
     PiePicBox.Circle (0, 0), .9, QBColor(0), -W1, -W2
   Else
     PiePicBox.Circle (0, 0), .9, QBColor(0)
   End If

 Next i%

 ' Display the total line at the bottom of the window.

 If Right$(FileDisplay.Caption, 3) = "SLS" Then
   TtlStr$ = "Week's total -> " + Format$(Total, "$##,###0.00")
 ElseIf Right$(FileDisplay.Caption, 3) = "WKD" Then
   TtlStr$ = "Day's total -> " + Format$(Total, "##0.00")
   If Total > 1 Then
     TtlStr$ = TtlStr$ + " hrs."
   Else
     TtlStr$ = TtlStr$ + " hr."
   End If
 End If
 TotalLine.Caption = TtlStr$

End Sub  ' DrawButton_Click
```

Listing 10.5 The **Pi** function and the **Wedges_Click** procedure

```
Function Pi ()

  ' Return the value of Pi
  ' as a double-precision number.

  Pi = 4# * Atn(1)

End Function  ' Pi


Sub Wedges_Click (Index As Integer)

  ' Redraw the pie chart when the user selects
  ' a new Wedge option button ("Colors" or "Patterns").

  If DrawButton.Enabled Then DrawButton_Click

End Sub  ' Wedges_Click
```

Listing 10.6 The **ReadSalesFile** procedure

```
Sub ReadSalesFile ()

  ' Read a weekly sales file, and arrange the data
  ' in the following form-level variables:

  '    -- The WedgeRecs contains the sales portion represented
  '       by each wedge, and the name of each legend entry.
  '    -- The WedgeCount variable gives the number of wedges
  '       (equal to the number of nonzero sales amounts).
  '    -- The Total variable gives the total weekly sales.

  ' The DrawButton_Click procedure creates the pie
  ' chart from the information stored in these variables.

  Dim SalesFile$        ' The name of the file.
  Static SalesDay(6)    ' The daily sales data.
  Dim WeekSales         ' The week's total sales.
  Dim Count As Integer  ' A temporary wedge count.
```

```
' Build the file name and open the file.
' (Weekly sales files, as created by the Sales Week
' application, are sequential-access files, with one
' numeric entry for each day of a given week.)

SalesFile$ = DirectoryList.Path + "\"
SalesFile$ = SalesFile$ + FileList.FileName
Open SalesFile$ For Input As #1

' Read the entire file.

WeekSales = 0
For i% = 0 To 6
  Input #1, SalesDay(i%)
  WeekSales = WeekSales + SalesDay(i%)
Next i%
Close #1

' Calculate the week's portion (WedgeRecs(i%).Portion)
' represented by each day of the week for which the sales
' figure is not zero.

Count = -1
For i% = 0 To 6
  If SalesDay(i%) <> 0 Then
    Count = Count + 1
    WedgeRecs(Count).Portion = SalesDay(i%) / WeekSales
    WedgeRecs(Count).LegendStr = Mid$(DayStr$, i% * 3 + 1, 3)
  End If
Next i%

WedgeCount = Count + 1
Total = WeekSales

End Sub   ' ReadSalesFile
```

Listing 10.7 The **ReadTimeFile** procedure

```
Sub ReadTimeFile ()

  ' Read a time-sheet file, and arrange the data
  ' in the following form-level variables:
```

(continued)

```
'    -- The WedgeRecs contains the portion of the day represented
'       by each wedge, and the name of each legend entry.
'    -- The WedgeCount variable gives the number of wedges:
'       in this case, the number of different reference numbers
'       in the time sheet. (The application includes a maximum
'       of seven entries in the pie chart.)
'    -- The Total variable gives the day's total hours worked.


' The DrawButton_Click procedure creates the pie
' chart from the information stored in these variables.


' A single work record variable.
Dim WorkRecord As WorkRecordType


' The file name, and the number of records in the file.
Dim WorkFileName As String, RecCount As Integer


' Reference number comparison variables.
Dim ThisRef As String, NextRef As String


' Reference number counters.
Dim RefIndex As Integer, RefCount As Integer, i%


' The subtotal for a given reference number.
Dim RefTot As Double

Dim T1 As Double, T2 As Double

' Create the file name, open the file, and count its records.

WorkFileName = DirectoryList.Path + "\" + FileList.FileName
Open WorkFileName For Random As #1 Len = Len(WorkRecord)
  RecCount = LOF(1) / Len(WorkRecord)

  ' Redimension the array of records accordingly, and read the file.

  ReDim WorkRecordList(RecCount)
  For i% = 1 To RecCount
    Get #1, i%, WorkRecordList(i%)
    If LTrim$(WorkRecordList(i%).IDField) = "" Then
      WorkRecordList(i%).IDField = "(no ref #)"
    End If
  Next i%
Close #1

' Sort the array by the reference numbers (IDField)
' and count the reference numbers.

RefCount = SortWorkRecordList(RecCount)

' Redimension the array of totals accordingly.
```

```
ReDim WorkTotals(RefCount)
RefTot = 0
RefIndex = 0

' Store the reference totals in the WorkTotals array.

For i% = 1 To RecCount
  T1 = WorkRecordList(i%).StartField
  T2 = WorkRecordList(i%).FinishedField

  If Not (T1 < 0 Or T2 < 0) Then
    RefTot = RefTot + (T2 - T1)
    If T1 > T2 Then RefTot = RefTot + 1
  End If

  ' If the reference number changes, record
  ' the total for this reference number.

  ThisRef = WorkRecordList(i%).IDField
  If i% <> RecCount Then
    NextRef = WorkRecordList(i% + 1).IDField
  Else
    NextRef = ""
  End If

  If ThisRef <> NextRef Then
    RefIndex = RefIndex + 1
    WorkTotals(RefIndex).IDField = ThisRef
    WorkTotals(RefIndex).TotalField = RefTot
    RefTot = 0
  End If
Next i%

' Sort the WorkTotals array by the subtotal amounts.

SortWorkTotals RefIndex

' If there are more than seven reference numbers,
' use the top seven--that is, the jobs with the
' greatest number of recorded work hours.

If RefIndex > 7 Then RefIndex = 7

' Find the total hours as a serial time value.

Total = 0
For i% = 1 To RefIndex
  Total = Total + WorkTotals(i%).TotalField
Next i%

' Compute the wedge portions, and record the legend captions.
```

(continued)

```
WedgeCount = RefIndex
For i% = 0 To RefIndex - 1
  If WorkTotals(i% + 1).TotalField > 0 Then
    WedgeRecs(i%).Portion = WorkTotals(i% + 1).TotalField / Total
    WedgeRecs(i%).LegendStr = WorkTotals(i% + 1).IDField
  Else

    ' Don't include a subtotal of zero.

    WedgeCount = WedgeCount - 1
  End If

Next i%

' Calculate the total time as a number of hours.

Total = Total * 24

End Sub  ' ReadTimeFile
```

Listing 10.8 The two sorting routines used in the *Pie Chart* program

```
Function SortWorkRecordList (NumRecs As Integer) As Integer

  ' Sort the work record array by the reference numbers (IDField),
  ' and return a count of the different reference numbers in the file.
  ' (Called from the ReadTimeFile procedure.)

  Dim i%, j%, CountTemp As Integer
  Dim TempWorkRec As WorkRecordType

  For i% = 1 To NumRecs - 1
    For j% = i% + 1 To NumRecs
      If WorkRecordList(i%).IDField > WorkRecordList(j%).IDField Then
        TempWorkRec = WorkRecordList(i%)
        WorkRecordList(i%) = WorkRecordList(j%)
        WorkRecordList(j%) = TempWorkRec
      End If
    Next j%
  Next i%

  ' Count the reference numbers.

  CountTemp = 1
  For i% = 1 To NumRecs - 1
    If WorkRecordList(i%).IDField <> WorkRecordList(i% + 1).IDField Then
      CountTemp = CountTemp + 1
    End If
  Next i%
```

```
  ' Return the number of different reference numbers.

  SortWorkRecordList = CountTemp

End Function   ' SortWorkRecordList



Sub SortWorkTotals (NumRefs As Integer)

  ' Sort the WorkTotals array by the subtotal amounts (TotalField).
  ' (Called from the ReadTimeFile procedure.)

  Dim TempTotRec As WorkTotalType
  Dim i%, j%

  For i% = 1 To NumRefs - 1
    For j% = i% + 1 To NumRefs
      If WorkTotals(i%).TotalField < WorkTotals(j%).TotalField Then
        TempTotRec = WorkTotals(i%)
        WorkTotals(i%) = WorkTotals(j%)
        WorkTotals(j%) = TempTotRec
      End If
    Next j%
  Next i%

End Sub   ' SortWorkTotals
```

11

Multiline Text Boxes: The Memo Printer Application

INTRODUCTION

Visual Basic supports *multiline* text boxes, in which the user can enter, view, and edit multiple lines of text. Inside an appropriately designed text box, the user can perform several basic text processing operations:

- Insert new lines of text, write over existing text, or delete text.
- Scroll vertically through the length of the text.
- Use standard keyboard operations to move the cursor to new locations inside the text: for example, Ctrl-Right Arrow or Ctrl-Left Arrow to move to the beginning of the next or previous word; Home or End to move to the beginning or end of the current line; and Ctrl-Home or Ctrl-End to move to the beginning or the end of the text box contents.
- Use the mouse or the keyboard to select and highlight any sequence of text. (On the keyboard, hold down the Shift key and press any combination of arrow keys to select a block of text.)
- Perform *copy* and *move* operations on a selection of text.
- Enter long lines of text in a text box that includes a horizontal scroll bar; or, alternatively, enter paragraphs of text with automatic *word wrap* in a text bar that does not have a horizontal scroll bar.

All these features are available automatically—without any extra programming on your part—once you design the text box itself appropriately. To create a multiline text box, you add a text box to a form and assign settings to several of its relevant properties at design time. Most obviously, you should establish large enough **Height** and **Width** settings to give the user space for entering and editing multiple lines of text. In addition, the following properties have special settings for a text processing application:

- The **Multiline** property setting is **True** for a mutliple-line text box. (The default setting is **False** for a single-line text box.)

- The **ScrollBars** property has four possible settings:

  0 - None
  1 - Horizontal
  2 - Vertical
  3 - Both

  In a multiline text box, the **2 - Vertical** setting provides a vertical scroll bar, enabling the user to move easily up and down the text. Word wrap takes place within the width of a multiline text box that *does not* include a horizontal scroll bar. By contrast, the **1 - Horizontal** setting and the **3 - Both** settings allow the user to enter long lines of text.

As always, the **Text** property represents the contents of a text box, whether the box is designed for single-line or multiple-line entries. For example, **MemoBox.Text** refers to the entire text in a multiline text box. In your program code, you can add new lines to such a text box by concatenating a string to the end of the current **Text** value. In this context, you may also want to concatenate an end-of-line marker, represented by a combination of the carriage-return character (**CHR$(13)**) and the line-feed character (**CHR$(10)**); for example:

```
MemoBox.Text = MemoBox.Text + NewLine$ + Chr$(13) + Chr$(10)
```

This chapter's sample project, called the *Memo Printer* application, illustrates techniques of multiple-line text processing. The application's main form includes a large text box in which you can write and edit an office memorandum directed to employees, colleagues, or co-workers. Listed above the memo box are the names of the people to whom you normally send memos. (You develop this list yourself when you first run the program, and you can revise the list whenever necessary.) To print copies of a particular memo, you simply click the names of the recipients—placing Xs in the corresponding check boxes—and then choose the program's print command. In effect, the *Memo Printer* carries out the equivalent of a print-merge operation, producing multiple personalized copies of a memo document.

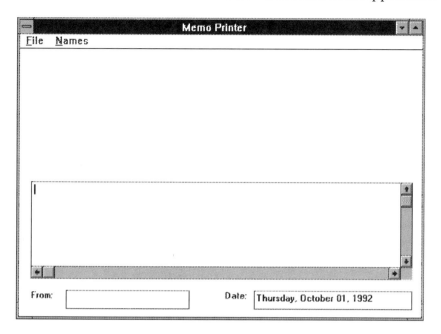

Figure 11.1 The startup form from the *Memo Printer* application

The *Memo Printer* project is stored on the exercise disk under the name MEMO.MAK. Open the project now and press the F5 key to run the program. The form shown in Figure 11.1 appears on the screen.

THE *MEMO PRINTER* APPLICATION

To set up the *Memo Printer* program for your own use, you begin by creating a list of names representing the people to whom you regularly send memos. You need to develop this list only once; the program saves your list on disk and automatically reads the list into the main dialog box when you next run the application. You may add new people to the list at any time—up to a maximum of 30 names; you may also delete names from the list.

For example, Figure 11.2 shows the *Memo Printer* form, complete with a list of imaginary names. Each name appears as the caption of a check box. You select the people who are to receive a copy of a given memo by clicking the corresponding check boxes.

As you can see in Figure 11.3, the application's **Names** menu gives you commands for building and using this list. To add a name to the list—or to begin building the list the first time you run the program—select the **Add a Name** command or press Ctrl+A. When you do, the program displays

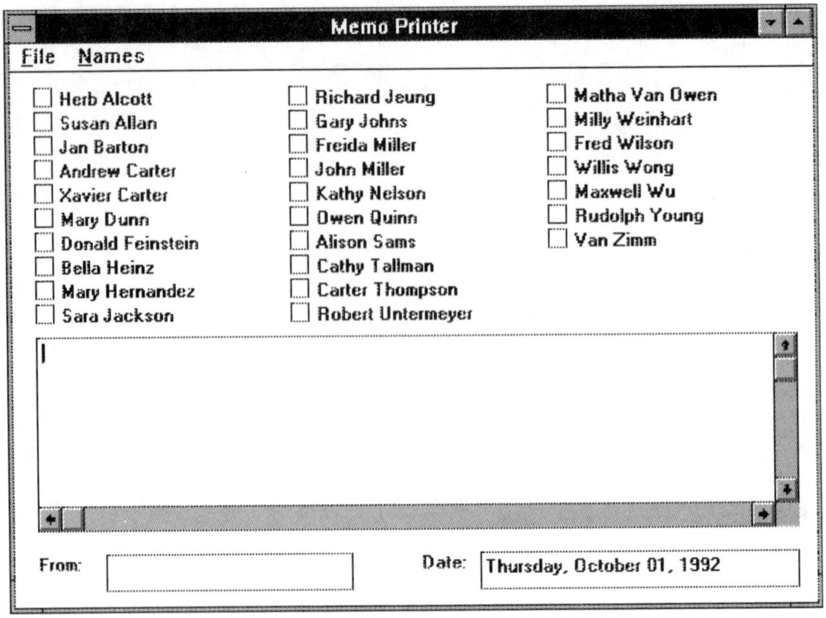

Figure 11.2 A list of names in the *Memo Printer* form

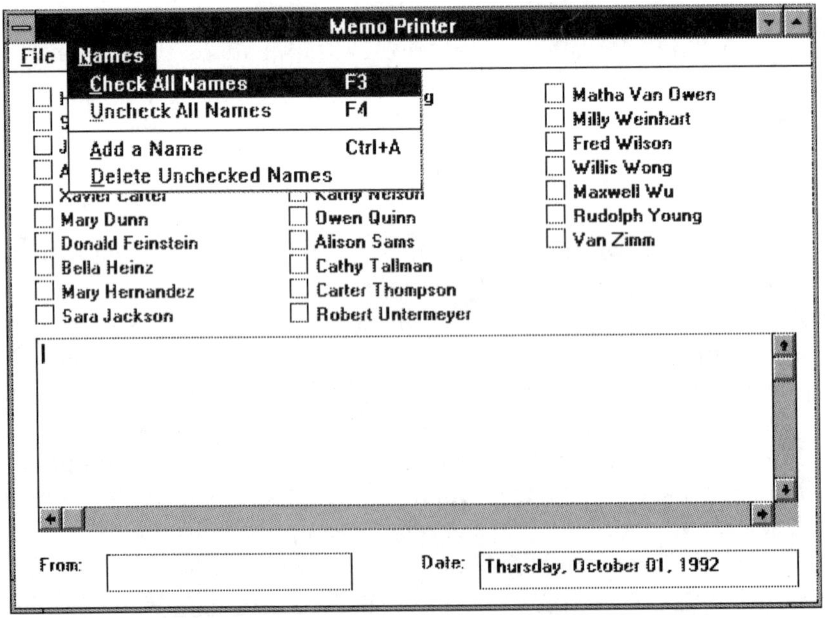

Figure 11.3 The **Names** menu

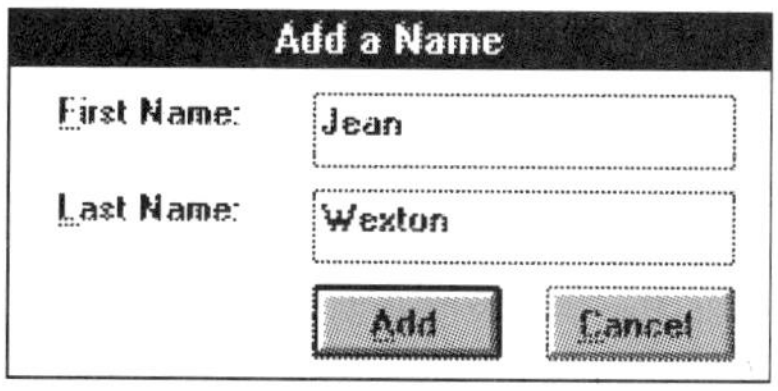

Figure 11.4 Adding a name to the *Memo Printer* form

a dialog box on the screen to elicit the first and last name of the person you want to include in the list (Figure 11.4). Each time you add a new name, the program alphabetizes the list and redisplays the names in the form. The list is saved on disk as MEMOLIST.TXT in the root directory of the C drive.

The **Check All Names** and **Uncheck All Names** commands in the **Names** menu give you quick ways to select or deselect names for printing memos. Press the F3 function key to check all the names if you want to print a copy of a memo for each person on your list. Or press F4 to uncheck all the names, and then click individual names with the mouse to select the people who will receive your memo (Figure 11.5).

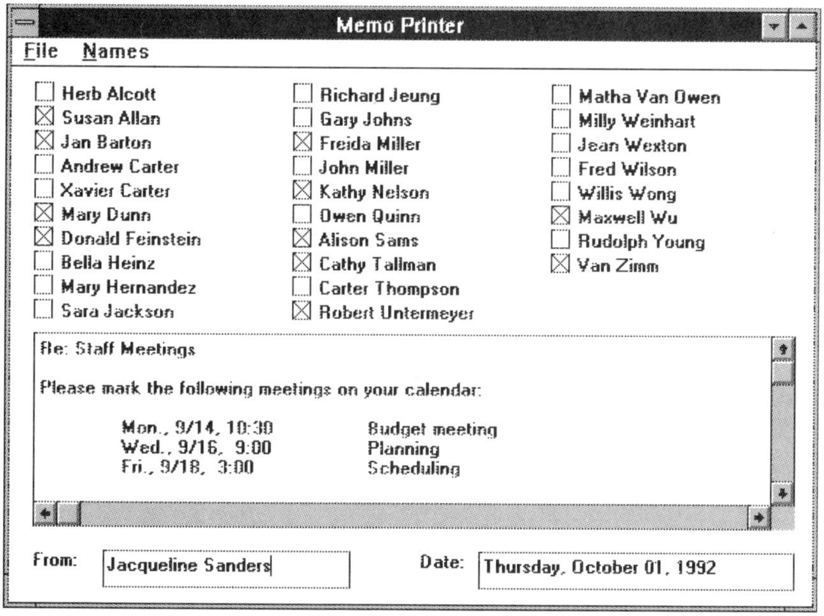

Figure 11.5 Selecting names for the memo

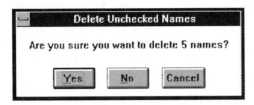

Figure 11.6 Deleting names from the list

The **Delete Unchecked Names** command deletes names from the list. To use this command, follow these steps:

1. Press F3 to check all the names in the list.

2. Use the mouse to uncheck the selected names that you want to delete from the list.

3. Pull down the **Names** menu and select the **Delete Unchecked Names** command.

Before deleting any names, the program displays a dialog box asking you to confirm that you want to go ahead with the deletions (Figure 11.6).

Once you have developed a list of names, the next step in using the *Memo Printer* application is to type the memo itself into the memo box or load a text file from disk as your memo document. The first three commands in the program's **File** menu (Figure 11.7) are designed to help you begin a memo. Choose the **Activate Memo Box** command (or simply press Ctrl+M at the keyboard) to move the focus to the memo text box. Or, choose **Erase Current Memo** (or press Ctrl+E) to erase any text currently displayed in the memo box and to activate the box. Once the flashing cursor is displayed inside the box, you can begin composing your memo. As you can see back in Figure 11.5, the memo box shows only several lines of your document at a time, but you can use the scroll bar or the PgUp and PgDn keys to scroll up and down the document. Because the memo box has both vertical and horizontal scroll bars, word wrap does not take place for long lines of text. As you type your memo, press the Enter key when you want to begin a new line.

Do not include a heading in the text of your memo. As you'll see shortly, the application automatically supplies relevant information—including *To:* and *From:* lines and the date—at the top of each printed memo.

If you have previously written a memo and saved it as a text file, you can load the memo directly into the memo box from disk. Choose the **Open Memo File** command from the **File** menu (or press Ctrl+O) and the input box shown in Figure 11.8 appears on the screen. Type the full name (and

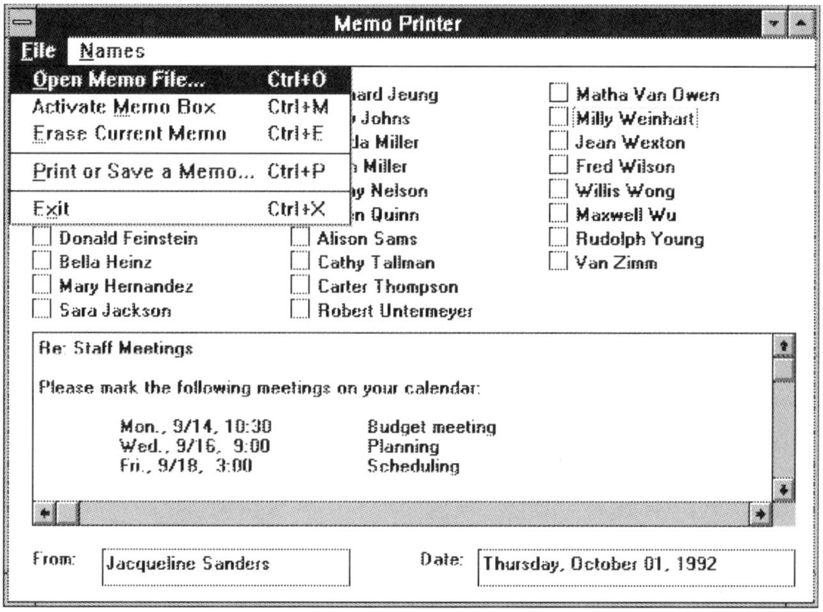

Figure 11.7 The **File** menu

path if necessary) of the text file you want to read; the program opens your file and copies the text into the memo box. (If the program does not find the file name you enter, an error message appears on the screen.)

Before you begin printing copies of your memo, enter your own name in the **From** text box. (When you later choose the File Exit command, the program saves the current **From** name in a text file called MEMO-FROM.TXT. In subsequent runs of the program, this name is read from

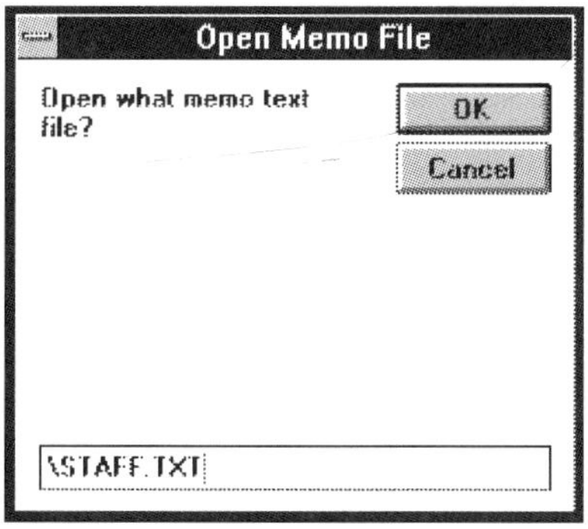

Figure 11.8 Opening a memo text file

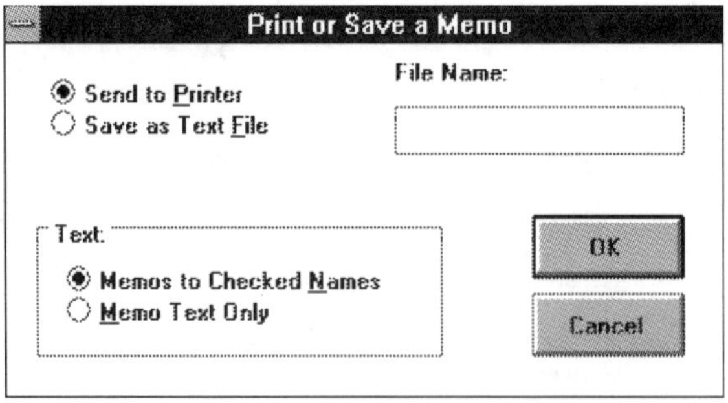

Figure 11.9 Printing the memos or saving them in a text file

disk into the **From** text box so that you don't have to retype your own name. You can, however, *change* the name in this box at any time.) The **Date** text box displays the current date by default, but you can change this entry too, if you want to print some other date at the top of your memos.

The **Print or Save a Memo** command in the **File** menu displays yet another dialog box on the screen (Figure 11.9) to elicit your instructions for an upcoming output operation. Most commonly, you'll simply click OK or press Enter to accept the default options on the dialog box; when you do so, the program begins printing one copy of the memo for each person whose name you have checked in the list. As you can see in the example shown in Figure 11.10, each copy of the memo includes the date, a *To:* line that gives the name of the recipient, and a *From:* line that gives your name. These three items of information are copied from your selections and entries on the main *Memo Printer* form. The remaining text of the memo comes directly from the lines you have typed into the memo box.

The **Print or Save a Memo** command also offers you several other options. First, you can select the **Save as Text File** option if you want to store the memos in a text file instead of printing them. This gives you the opportunity to revise the memos in your word processing program before you print them out. When you select this option, the program activates the **File Name** box. Enter a name for the file in which you want to save your memos and then click OK. If you enter an invalid file name or if your printer is not ready when you select the **Send to Printer** option, the program displays the error message shown in Figure 11.11.

Finally, the *Print or Save a Memo* dialog box allows you to specify what portion of the text will be sent to the printer or the text file. The default option, **Memos to Checked Names**, prints or saves a complete copy of the memo for each checked name in the list. The other available option, **Memo Text Only**, allows you to create a text file just for saving the current contents of the memo text box.

```
*** Memo ***

Sunday, October 1, 1992

To:    Susan Allan
From:  Jacqueline Sanders

Re: Staff Meetings

Please mark the following meetings on your calendar:

    Mon., 9/14, 10:30      Budget meeting
    Wed., 9/16,  9:00      Planning
    Fri., 9/18,  3:00      Scheduling

It is very important that you attend these meetings.

                    Thank you.


                      J.S.
```

Figure 11.10 A sample of a printed memo

In summary, here are the steps for using the *Memo Printer* application:

1. When you run the application for the first time, use the **Add a Name** command in the **Names** menu to develop a list of people to whom you regularly send memos. You need do this only once, because the application saves the list to disk and rereads it each time you run the program.

2. Type the text of your memo or choose the **Open Memo File** command from the **File** menu to read the memo from a text file stored on disk.

Figure 11.11 Error in printing or saving

3. If necessary, enter or edit the items displayed in the **From** and **Date** text boxes.

4. When you are ready to print a memo, click the names of the people to whom you want to send the memo.

5. Select the **Print or Save a Memo** command from the **File** menu and click OK. The program prints one copy of the memo for each name that is checked in the names list. (Alternatively, use this same command to save the memos or the memo text alone to a text file on disk.)

THE ELEMENTS OF THE *MEMO PRINTER* APPLICATION

The *Memo Printer* project consists of three forms and a code module, as shown in Figure 11.12. The startup form, which displays the list of names, the memo box, the **From** and **Date** boxes, and the program's menu bar, is named **MemoPrnt**. The two secondary forms, **MemoFile** and **MemoName**, are the dialog boxes for printing or saving a memo and for developing the name list. The module is **MEMOGLOB.BAS**.

The bulk of the application's code is devoted to three major tasks: managing the list of names that appears in the **MemoPrnt** form; performing input operations—most notably, reading memo files from disk; and performing output operations with the memos themselves—printing them or saving them to disk.

Controls, Menus, and Properties

The **MemoPrnt** form, shown in Figure 11.13, contains an array of check boxes, along with three text boxes:

- The check box array has a **Name** setting of **SendTo**, with individual **Index** settings from **1** to **30**. Initially the **Caption** settings are blank.

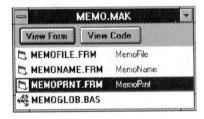

Figure 11.12 The MEMO.MAK project

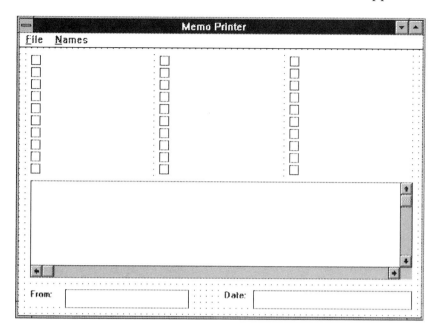

Figure 11.13 The **MemoPrnt** form

In addition, the program sets the **Visible** and **Enabled** settings to **False** for check boxes that are not in use—that is, when there are fewer than 30 names in the list. To fill in the captions, the program reads names from the MEMOLIST.TXT file on disk and changes **Visible** and **Enabled** to **True** for each check box that has a name caption.

- The memo box has a **Name** of **MemoText**, a **MultiLine** setting of **True**, and a **ScrollBars** setting of **3 - Both**.

- The remaining two text boxes have **Name** settings of **FromName** and **DateText**.

In addition to these controls, the **MemoPrnt** form has an important set of menus and menu commands. The Menu Design Window for the application appears in Figure 11.14. Because each of the menu commands has a corresponding **Click** procedure in the program's code, you'll need to be familiar with the **Name** settings defined for the menu:

- The five commands in the **File** menu have **Name** settings of **Open-Command** (for opening a memo file), **MemoCommand** (for activating the memo box), **ClearCommand** (for erasing the contents of the memo box), **PrintCommand** (for printing or saving a set of memos), and **ExitCommand** (for exiting from the program).

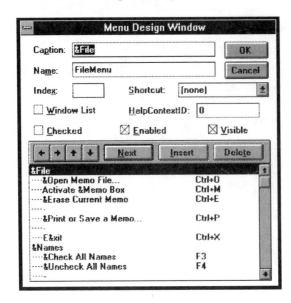

Figure 11.14 Menu Design Window for the MEMOPRINT form

- The four commands in the **Names** menu have **Name** settings of **CheckCommand** and **UnCheckCommand** (for checking or unchecking all of the names in the list and **AddCommand** and **DeleteCommand** (for adding or deleting names in the list).

The Data Files

The names of people who can receive copies of printed memos are stored on disk in a text file named MEMOLIST.TXT. Each line of this file contains a person's first name and last name; for example:

```
"Martha", "Van Owen"
"Jan", "Barton"
"Maxwell", "Wu"
"Milly", "Weinhart"
"John", "Miller"
```

The program appends lines of data to this file when the user adds a person to the name list. In contrast, when the user deletes a name, the program completely rewrites the file. The names list contains a maximum of 30 first and last names.

The program creates an additional text file, MEMOFROM.TXT, to store the current name in the **From** text box.

Events

The **Form_Load** procedure of the **MemoPrnt** form initializes the names list by calling a routine that reads the MEMOLIST.TXT data file. Subsequently, the program recognizes **Click** events for the menu commands and for the command buttons on the *Add a Name* and *Print or Save a Memo* dialog boxes.

When you run the program for the first time, you'll notice that certain menu commands are disabled—appearing in gray type in the menu lists—until you have created a names list. Specifically, the **Check All Names**, **UnCheck All Names**, and **Delete Unchecked Names** commands are dimmed until there are names in the list. Disabling these commands is a simple technique for avoiding inappropriate **Click** events during the program run.

Procedures and Methods

The declarations from the program's code module, **MEMOGLOB.BAS**, and the form-level declarations from the **MemoPrnt** form appear in Listing 11.1. The procedures from the **MemoPrnt** form are in Listings 11.2 through 11.9. Event procedures for the other two forms, **MemoFile** and **MemoName**, appear in Listings 11.10 and 11.11. The sections ahead give you a brief overview of the code, and then a more detailed look at the routines that perform input and output operations with the **MemoText** box.

Overview

The program's code module defines a structured data type for storing the list of names in memory. The **NameRec** structure has string fields to represent a recipient's first and last names:

```
Type NameRec
  FirstName As String
  LastName As String
End Type
```

The **MemoPrnt** form declares an array of records for the list. A constant declaration establishes the maximum length of the list:

```
CONST MaxListLen = 30
```

Then the static array structure is declared:

```
DIM NameList(MaxListLen) AS NameRec
```

The **Form_Load** procedure (Listing 11.2) initializes this array by calling the procedure that reads the list of names from its file on disk:

```
ReadMemoNames
```

The **ReadMemoNames** procedure (Listing 11.5) begins by setting the **Enabled** and **Visible** settings to **False** for the entire array of **SendTo** check boxes:

```
For i% = 1 TO MaxListLen
   SendTo(i%).Enabled = False
   SendTo(i%).Visible = False
Next i%
```

Then the procedure reads the MEMOLIST.TXT file if it exists. For each name in the list, the procedure displays and activates the corresponding check box and then copies the name to the **NameList** array:

```
SendTo(CurListLen).Enabled = True
SendTo(CurListLen).Visible = True
SendTo(CurListLen).Value = Unchecked

Input #1, NameList(CurListLen).FirstName
Input #1, NameList(CurListLen).LastName
```

After reading the entire list of names from the file, the procedure makes a call to **SortNameList** (Listing 11.6) to alphabetize the list by last and first names. Then each name appears on the form as the **Caption** property of one of the **SendTo** check boxes:

```
For i% = 1 TO CurListLen
   TempStr = RTrim$(NameList(i%).FirstName) + " " +
RTrim$(NameList(i%).LastName)
   SendTo(i%).Caption = TempStr
Next i%
```

If the list is at its maximum length, the program disables the **Add a Name** menu command:

```
If CurListLen = MaxListLen Then
   AddCommand.Enabled = False
Else
   AddCommand.Enabled = True
End If
```

The **AddCommand_Click** procedure (Listing 11.4) reads a new name entry from the **MemoName** form and adds the entry to the name list. The first step in this process is to display the **MemoName** form on the screen as a dialog box for eliciting the new entry:

```
MemoName.Show 1
```

Notice the use of the optional integer argument of the **Show** method. This argument represents the important *style* characteristic of the new form that appears on the screen:

```
FormName.Show style
```

Show accepts values of 0 or 1 for the *style* argument:

- With the default argument of 0, the newly displayed form is said to be *modeless.* As a result, the user can activate another form, even before completing the response to the newly displayed form.

- In contrast, an argument of 1 gives the newly displayed form a *modal* style. In effect, the new form takes control of the program. No events will be recognized on other forms until the user completes the input and/or closes the modal form.

When you design a form as a secondary dialog box, you will normally show the form in its modal style. This prevents the user from performing other actions until the new dialog box has received its required input response. The **MemoName** and **MemoFile** forms are both examples of modal-style dialog boxes.

When the user completes the input in the **MemoName** form, the **Add-Command_Click** procedure reads the input from the form and then appends the new name to the MEMOLIST.TXT file on disk:

```
Open NamesFile For Append As #1
  Write #1, First, Last
Close #1
```

Then the program calls a procedure named **UnloadAllNames** (Listing 11.4), which clears the current list of names from the **MemoPrnt** form. Finally, a call to **ReadMemoNames** alphabetizes and redisplays the list, including the new name that the user has just added.

The **DeleteCommand_Click** procedure (Listing 11.7) rewrites the MEMOLIST.TXT file, including only those names that are currently checked in the names list on screen:

```
If SendTo(i%).Value = Checked Then
  First = RTrim$(NameList(i%).FirstName)
  Last = RTrim$(NameList(i%).LastName)
  Write #1, First, Last
End If
```

Then, like **AddCommand_Click**, the delete procedure makes calls to **UnloadAllNames** and **ReadMemoNames** to display the new version of the names list on the **MemoPrnt** form.

Click procedures shown in Listing 11.2 are responsible for making selections in the list of names. For example, the **CheckCommand_Click** procedure puts an X in each **SendTo** check box:

```
For i% = 1 TO CurListLen
   SendTo(i%).Value = Checked
Next i%
```

Likewise, the **UnCheckCommand_Click** procedure loops through the entire list and removes all the Xs.

Text Processing

The **PrintCommand_Click** procedure (Listing 11.3) is called when the user selects the print command in the *Memo Printer* application's **File** menu. The procedure begins by establishing default settings on the **MemoFile** form, and then shows the form as a *modal*-style dialog box:

```
MemoFile.Show 1
```

As you can see in Figure 11.15, the **MemoFile** form has the following controls:

- An array of option buttons named **Dest**, representing the possible output destinations.

- A second array of option buttons named **WhatText**, giving the user a choice between two output options.

- A text box named **OutFileName** for accepting a file name from the user.

- Two command buttons, **CancelButton** and **OKButton**.

The **Dest** array has three elements, although only the first two are visible to the user: **Dest(0)** represents the print option; **Dest(1)** is the save option; and **Dest(2)** is a hidden option that the program selects if the user clicks the Cancel button. Because **Dest(2)** is available excusively for the program's internal use, the **Dest(2).Visible** and **Dest(2).Enabled** properties are both **False**. As you'll see shortly, **MemoFile** uses **Dest(2)** to instruct **MemoPrnt** to perform no output operation.

The user makes selections on the **MemoFile** dialog box and then clicks either **OK** or **Cancel**. Control of the program returns to the

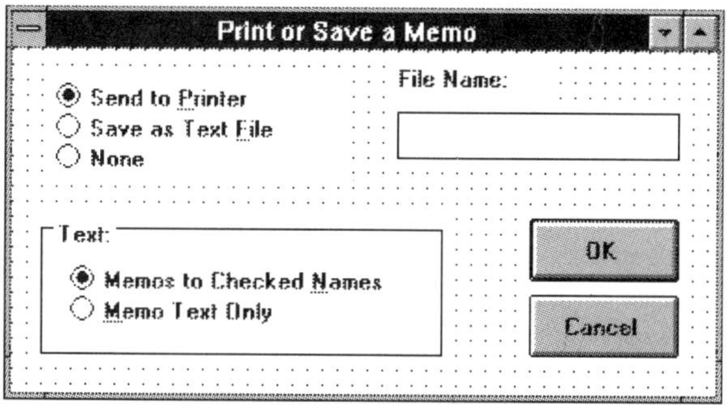

Figure 11.15 The MemoFile form in the design environment

PrintCommand_Click procedure in **MemoPrnt**. On regaining control, the procedure first reads the setting that the user has selected for the output destination—that is, the choice between sending the memos to the printer or saving them in a text file on disk. Here is how **MemoPrnt** reads the selection in the **Dest** array:

```
If MemoFile!Dest(0).Value Then
  OutName$ = "Prn"
Else
  If MemoFile!Dest(1).Value Then
    OutName$ = MemoFile!OutFileName.Text
  Else
    Exit Sub
  End If
End If
```

If the user has selected **Dest(0)**—that is, if the control's **Value** property is **True**—the procedure assigns the device name "Prn" to the string variable **OutName$**. For a selection of **Dest(1)**, this string variable receives the value that the user has entered into the file name text box, **MemoFile!OutFileName.Text**. But, if the user has clicked the **Cancel** button—and **Dest(2).Value** is true—the current performance of **PrintCommand_Click** is terminated:

```
Else
  Exit Sub
```

In Listing 11.10 you can see that the **CancelButton_Click** procedure in the **MemoFile** form takes care of setting the value of **Dest(2)** to **True** in response to a click of the Cancel button:

```
Dest(2).Value = True
```

Assuming the user has selected one of the two available output destinations, **PrintCommand_Click** opens the selected output device—the printer (**Prn**) or the named text file on disk:

```
Open OutName$ For Output As #1
```

Then the procedure examines the selection in the **MemoFile.WhatText** array:

```
If MemoFile!WhatText(0).Value Then
```

If the user has chosen to print (or save) all the personalized memos, the procedure uses a **For** loop to produce a memo for each checked name in the **SendTo** array:

```
For i% = 1 To CurListLen
  If SendTo(i%).Value = Checked Then
    Print #1, "*** Memo ***"
    Print #1,
    Print #1, DateText.Text
    Print #1,
    Print #1, "To:     "; SendTo(i%).Caption
    Print #1, "From:   "; FromName.Text
    Print #1,
    Print #1, MemoText.Text
    Print #1,
```

Alternatively, if the user has selected the **Memo Text Only** option, the contents of the **MemoText** box are sent alone as the output:

```
Else
  Print #1, MemoText.Text
End If
```

In either event, you can see that the **MemoText.Text** property represents the user's entire multiline entry in the memo box.

Finally, another interesting text operation takes place in the **Open-Command_Click** procedure (Listing 11.8). This event procedure is called when the user chooses the **Open Memo File** command from the **File** menu. The procedure begins by using Visual Basic's **InputBox$** function to display a simple dialog box on the screen:

```
prompt$ = "Open what memo text file?"
title$ = "Open Memo File"
FileName$ = INPUTBOX$(prompt$, title$)
```

If the user's **FileName$** entry is valid, the procedure opens the file and reads its contents line by line:

```
Open FileName$ For Input As #1
  Do While Not EOF(1)
    Line Input #1, inLine$
```

Each line in turn is concatenated to the end of **MemoText.Text**:

```
  MemoText.Text = MemoText.Text + inLine$ + CrLf$
Loop
```

The form-level string variable **CrLf$** represents the carriage-return and line-feed characters; its value is assigned in the **Form_Load** procedure:

```
CrLf$ = Chr$(13) + Chr$(10)
```

By inserting this combination of characters at the end of each concatenation, the program creates a multiline entry in the **MemoText** box.

SUMMARY: MULTILINE TEXT BOXES

By selecting appropriate settings for the **Height**, **Width**, **MultiLine** and **ScrollBar** properties, you can design a text box that serves as a multiline editing environment in a Visual Basic application. Conveniently, the essential editing operations are built into the text box without the need for any detailed text processing code. In addition, a program can access the entire contents of a multiline text box simply by referring to the control's **Text** property.

Listing 11.1 Module-level and **MemoPrnt** form-level declarations

```
' MEMO.MAK
' The Memo Printer Application
' Global Declarations (MEMOGLOB.BAS)

' Record type for name list.

Type NameRec
  FirstName As String  ' Person's first name.
  LastName As String   ' Person's last name.
End Type

' End of Global declarations.
```

(continued)

```
' The Memo Printer Application (MEMO.MAK)
' MEMOPRNT.FRM
' Declarations

' The file names for storing the two
' text files that the program creates
' and reads: NamesFile contains the list
' of people to whom memos can be sent, and
' FromFile contains the name of the person
' who is sending the memos.

Const NamesFile = "C:\MemoList.TXT"
Const FromFile = "C:\MemoFrom.TXT"

' The maximum number of "records" in
' the NamesFile list.

Const MaxListLen = 30

Const Checked = 1
Const Unchecked = 0

' Date format for the DateText box.

Const DateFormat$ = "DDDD, MMMM DD, YYYY"

' Array for storing the list of people.

Dim NameList(MaxListLen) As NameRec

' CurListLen is the number of people
' currently in the name list.

Dim CurListLen As Integer

' Carriage-return/Line-feed codes.

Dim CrLf$

' End of form-level declations
' for the MEMOPRNT form.
```

Listing 11.2 The **Form_Load** and **Click** procedures (**MemoPrnt**)

```
Sub Form_Load ()

  ' Initializations.

  ' Carriage-return/Line-feed.

  CrLf$ = Chr$(13) + Chr$(10)

  ' Display the current date.

  DateText.Text = Format$(Now, DateFormat$)

  ' Read and display the list of names

  ReadMemoNames

  ' Read the current FromFile if it exists.

  On Local Error GoTo NoFromName
    Open FromFile For Input As #1
      Input #1, InName$
      FromName.Text = InName$
    Close #1
  On Local Error GoTo 0

SkipFromName:
  Exit Sub

NoFromName:
Resume SkipFromName

End Sub   ' Form_Load


Sub CheckCommand_Click ()

  ' Place a check in all the check boxes
  ' in the list of names.

  Dim i%
```

(continued)

```
   For i% = 1 To CurListLen
     SendTo(i%).Value = Checked
   Next i%

End Sub   ' CheckCommand_Click

Sub ClearCommand_Click ()

  ' Clear the contents of the MemoText box.

  MemoText.Text = ""
  MemoText.SetFocus

End Sub   ' ClearCommand_Click


Sub ExitCommand_Click ()

  ' Terminate the program run.

  ' First save the current FromName entry.

  Open FromFile For Output As #1
    Write #1, FromName.Text
  Close #1

  End

End Sub   ' ExitCommand_Click


Sub MemoCommand_Click ()

  ' Move the focus to the MemoText box.

  MemoText.SetFocus

End Sub   ' MemoCommand_Click


Sub UnCheckCommand_Click ()

  ' Uncheck the entire list of names.
```

```
   Dim i%
   For i% = 1 To CurListLen
     SendTo(i%).Value = Unchecked
   Next i%

End Sub   ' UnCheckCommand_Click
```

Listing 11.3 The **PrintCommand_Click** procedure (**MemoPrnt**)

```
Sub PrintCommand_Click ()

  ' Print memos to the checked names in the list,
  ' or save the memos as a text file; alternatively,
  ' print or save the memo text alone.

  Dim i%, OutName$

  Const NextPage = 12

  ' Establish the initial settings in the
  ' MemoFile form.

  If CurListLen = 0 Then
    MemoFile!WhatText(1).Value = True
    MemoFile!WhatText(0).Enabled = False
  Else
    MemoFile!WhatText(0).Enabled = True
    MemoFile!WhatText(0).Value = True
  End If

  MemoFile!Dest(0).Value = True
  MemoFile!OutFileName.Text = ""

  ' Show the form, and give it the focus
  ' until the user responds.

  MemoFile.Show 1

  ' Read the option the user has selected
  ' for the destination of the text output.

  If MemoFile!Dest(0).Value Then
    OutName$ = "Prn"
  Else
    If MemoFile!Dest(1).Value Then
      OutName$ = MemoFile!OutFileName.Text
    Else
```

(continued)

```
      ' If the user clicked Cancel, exit from
      ' this routine. (In this case, the hidden
      ' MemoFile!Dest(2) option button has a
      ' Value setting of true.)

     Exit Sub
   End If
End If

On Local Error GoTo DeviceNotReady

' Open the file or the printer device for output.

Open OutName$ For Output As #1

' If the user has selected the first WhatText
' option, print or save the memos to the
' checked names in the list.

If MemoFile!WhatText(0).Value Then
  For i% = 1 To CurListLen
    If SendTo(i%).Value = Checked Then
      Print #1, "*** Memo ***"
      Print #1,
      Print #1, DateText.Text
      Print #1,
      Print #1, "To:    "; SendTo(i%).Caption
      Print #1, "From:  "; FromName.Text
      Print #1,
      Print #1, MemoText.Text
      Print #1,

      ' Issue a form-feed at the end of
      ' each memo if the memos are being
      ' printed, or a line of hyphens if
      ' the memos are being saved to disk.

      If OutName$ = "Prn" Then
        Print #1, Chr$(NextPage)
      Else
        Print #1, String$(65, "-")
      End If

    End If
  Next i%

' If the user has selected the second WhatText
' option, print or save only the text of the memo.

Else
  Print #1, MemoText.Text
End If
```

```
AbortPrint:
  Close #1

Exit Sub

DeviceNotReady:
  MsgBox "Check printer or file name and try again.", 0, "Device Error"
Resume AbortPrint

End Sub  ' PrintCommand_Click
```

Listing 11.4 AddCommand_Click and UnLoadAllNames (MemoPrnt)

```
Sub AddCommand_Click ()

  ' Add a person's name to the list of names.

  Dim First As String
  Dim Last As String

  ' Show the dialog box for eliciting a name.

  MemoName.Show 1

  ' Read the name, and then blank out the text
  ' boxes on the MemoName dialog box.

  First = LTrim$(RTrim$(MemoName!NewFirstName.Text))
  Last = LTrim$(RTrim$(MemoName!NewLastName.Text))
  MemoName!NewFirstName.Text = ""
  MemoName!NewLastName.Text = ""

  ' If the user entered a valid name, append
  ' it to the names file on disk.

  If First <> "" And Last <> "" Then
    Open NamesFile For Append As #1
      Write #1, First, Last
    Close #1

    ' Unload the current list, and
    ' reread the entire list.
```

(continued)

```
      UnLoadAllNames
      ReadMemoNames
   End If

End Sub   ' AddCommand_Click


Sub UnLoadAllNames ()

   ' Erase the check boxes in the
   ' SendTo control array.

   For i% = 1 To CurListLen
      SendTo(i%).Enabled = False
      SendTo(i%).Visible = False
      SendTo(i%).Caption = ""
   Next i%

End Sub   ' UnloadAllNames
```

Listing 11.5 The **ReadMemoNames** procedure (**MemoPrnt**)

```
Sub ReadMemoNames ()

   ' Read the file of names that will appear
   ' in this form's list.

   Dim TempStr As String
   Dim i%, NoFile As Integer

   CurListLen = 0
   NoFile = False

   For i% = 1 To MaxListLen
      SendTo(i%).Enabled = False
      SendTo(i%).Visible = False
   Next i%

   ' Attempt to open the file, but go to the
   ' error-handling routine if the file does
   ' not exist. (NoFile then becomes True.)
```

```
On Local Error GoTo NoNamesFile
  Open NamesFile For Input As #1
On Local Error GoTo 0

' If the file does not exist, there will
' be no names list in the form. Disable the
' menu commands that deal with the list, and
' exit from this procedure.

If NoFile Then
  DeleteCommand.Enabled = False
  CheckCommand.Enabled = False
  UnCheckCommand.Enabled = False
  Exit Sub
End If

' If the file does exist read it from beginning
' to end, or up to MaxListLen records.

Do While Not EOF(1) And CurListLen < MaxListLen
  CurListLen = CurListLen + 1

  SendTo(CurListLen).Enabled = True
  SendTo(CurListLen).Visible = True
  SendTo(CurListLen).Value = Unchecked

  ' Read the first name and the last name,
  ' and store them as a record in the
  ' NameList array.

  Input #1, NameList(CurListLen).FirstName
  Input #1, NameList(CurListLen).LastName

Loop
Close #1

' Alphabetize the list of names.

SortNameList

' Display the names as the caption properties
' of the check boxes.
```

(continued)

```
   For i% = 1 To CurListLen
      TempStr = RTrim$(NameList(i%).FirstName) + " " +
RTrim$(NameList(i%).LastName)
      SendTo(i%).Caption = TempStr
   Next i%

   ' If there are MaxListLen names in the list,
   ' disable the Add a Name menu command.

   If CurListLen = MaxListLen Then
      AddCommand.Enabled = False
   Else
      AddCommand.Enabled = True
   End If

   ' Now that there are names in the list,
   ' enable the appropriate menu commands.

   DeleteCommand.Enabled = True
   CheckCommand.Enabled = True
   UnCheckCommand.Enabled = True

   Exit Sub

' Error routine for a missing file.

NoNamesFile:
   NoFile = True
Resume Next

End Sub   ' ReadMemoNames
```

Listing 11.6 The **SortNameList** procedure (**MemoPrnt**)

```
Sub SortNameList ()

   ' Alphabetize the list of names.

   Dim i%, j%
   Dim FullName1 As String
   Dim FullName2 As String
   Dim TempNameRec As NameRec
```

```
   For i% = 1 To CurListLen - 1
     For j% = i% + 1 To CurListLen

        ' Sort by last name and then first name,
        ' to allow for identical last names in the list.

        FullName1 = UCase$(RTrim$(NameList(i%).LastName) + " " +
NameList(i%).FirstName)
        FullName2 = UCase$(RTrim$(NameList(j%).LastName) + " " +
NameList(j%).FirstName)
        If FullName1 > FullName2 Then
          TempNameRec = NameList(i%)
          NameList(i%) = NameList(j%)
          NameList(j%) = TempNameRec
        End If
     Next j%
   Next i%

End Sub  ' SortNameList
```

Listing 11.7 The **DeleteCommand_Click** procedure (**MemoPrnt**)

```
Sub DeleteCommand_Click ()

  ' Delete all the names in the list that are
  ' not currently checked.

  Const Yes = 6
  Dim i%, DelCount As Integer
  Dim Ans As Integer, Msg$
  Dim First As String, Last As String

  ' First count the unchecked names in the list.

  DelCount = 0
  For i% = 1 To CurListLen
    If SendTo(i%).Value = Unchecked Then DelCount = DelCount + 1
  Next i%

  ' If the count is greater than zero, give the
  ' user a chance to back out of the delete operation.
```

(continued)

```
If DelCount > 0 Then
  Msg$ = "Are you sure you want to delete"
  Msg$ = Msg$ + Str$(DelCount)
  If DelCount = 1 Then
    Msg$ = Msg$ + " name?"
  Else
    Msg$ = Msg$ + " names?"
  End If
  Ans = MsgBox(Msg$, 3, "Delete Unchecked Names")

  ' If the user confirms, go ahead with the
  ' delete operation.

  If Ans = Yes Then

    ' If the entire list is unchecked,
    ' simply delete the names file.

    If DelCount = CurListLen Then
      Kill NamesFile
    Else

      ' Otherwise, rewrite the checked names
      ' to a new version of the file.

      Open NamesFile For Output As #1
        For i% = 1 To CurListLen
          If SendTo(i%).Value = Checked Then
            First = RTrim$(NameList(i%).FirstName)
            Last = RTrim$(NameList(i%).LastName)
            Write #1, First, Last
          End If
        Next i%
      Close #1
    End If

    ' Unload the entire list of check boxes,
    ' and then reread the name list.

    UnLoadAllNames
    ReadMemoNames
  End If
Else
```

```
   ' Display an error message if the user hasn't
   ' unchecked any names before selecting the Delete command.

   Msg$ = "To delete a name, first uncheck it in the " + CrLf$
   Msg$ = Msg$ + "list and then select the Delete " + CrLf$
   Msg$ = Msg$ + "Unchecked Names command again."
   MsgBox Msg$, 64, "Delete Unchecked Names"
 End If

End Sub  ' DeleteCommand_Click
```

Listing 11.8 The **OpenCommand_Click** procedure (**MemoPrnt**)

```
Sub OpenCommand_Click ()

  ' Open a text file and display the
  ' file's contents in the MemoText box.

  Dim prompt$, title$, FileName$

  ' Display an input box to elicit the file name.

  prompt$ = "Open what memo text file?"
  title$ = "Open Memo File"
  FileName$ = InputBox$(prompt$, title$)

  ' If the user has entered a name,
  ' attempt to open the file.

  If RTrim$(FileName$) <> "" Then
    ClearCommand_Click
    On Local Error GoTo NoMemoFile

    ' Read the file line by line and append
    ' each line to the end of the MemoText box.

    Open FileName$ For Input As #1
      Do While Not EOF(1)
        Line Input #1, inLine$
        MemoText.Text = MemoText.Text + inLine$ + CrLf$
      Loop
```

(continued)

```
      Close #1
    End If

AbortOpen:
    Exit Sub

NoMemoFile:

    ' Display an error message if the file wasn't found.

    MsgBox "Can't find " + UCase$(FileName$) + ".", 0, "File Name"

Resume AbortOpen

End Sub   ' OpenCommand_Click
```

Listing 11.9 GotFocus and **LostFocus** procedures (**MemoPrnt**)

```
Sub DateText_GotFocus ()

    ' Highlight the contents of the DateText box.

    DateText.SelStart = 0
    DateText.SelLength = Len(DateText.Text)

End Sub   ' DateText_GotFocus


Sub DateText_LostFocus ()

    ' Validate a new date entry and redisplay
    ' the date in a standard date display format.

    Dim DateGood As Integer
    Dim CurDate&

    ' Attempt to convert the date string to
    ' a serial date. If the attempt fails,
    ' go to error-handling routine at BadDate.

    DateGood = True
```

```
   On Local Error GoTo BadDate
      CurDate& = DateValue(DateText.Text)
   On Local Error GoTo 0

   ' If new date is valid, display it;
   ' otherwise, display today's date.

   If DateGood Then
      DateText.Text = Format$(CurDate&, DateFormat$)
   Else
      DateText.Text = Format$(Now, DateFormat$)
   End If

   Exit Sub

BadDate:
   DateGood = False
Resume Next

End Sub   ' DateText_LostFocus


Sub FromName_GotFocus ()

   ' Highlight the current contents
   ' of the FromName box.

   FromName.SelStart = 0
   FromName.SelLength = Len(FromName.Text)

End Sub   ' FromName_GotFocus
```

Listing 11.10 Event procedures from the **MemoFile** form

```
' MEMOFILE.FRM
' The dialog box for printing or saving memos.


Sub CancelButton_Click ()

   ' If the user clicks Cancel, set the Value property
```

(continued)

```
    ' of the hidden Dest(2) option button to True.
    ' (This is a signal to MEMOPRNT.FRM to
    ' perform no output operation.)

    Dest(2).Value = True

    ' Close the dialog box.

    Hide

End Sub  ' CancelButton_Click


Sub Dest_Click (Index As Integer)

    ' Reset the OutFileName properties,
    ' depending on the Dest option that the
    ' user selects.

    If Index = 0 Then
      OutFileName.Enabled = False
      OutFileName.Text = ""
    Else
      OutFileName.Enabled = True
      OutFileName.SetFocus
    End If

End Sub  ' Dest_Click


Sub OKButton_Click ()

    ' Close the dialog box. (The PrintCommand_Click
    ' procedure reads the user's selections from
    ' MEMOFILE.FRM and performs the requested output.)

    Hide

End Sub  ' OKButton_Click
```

Listing 11.11 Event procedures from the **MemoName** form

```
' MEMONAME.FRM
' Dialog box for eliciting the first name
' and last name of a new person in the
' memo list.


Sub AddButton_Click ()

  ' Validate and accept the user's entries.

  ' Display an error message if both
  ' name entries are not present.

  If NewFirstName.Text = "" Or NewLastName.Text = "" Then
    Msg$ = "Enter a first name and a last name."
    MsgBox Msg$, 64, "Add a Name"
  Else
    NewFirstName.SetFocus

    ' Hide this form, returning control to
    ' the MEMOPRNT form.

    Hide
  End If

End Sub  ' AddButton_Click


Sub CancelButton_Click ()

  ' Respond to the user's cancel command.

  ' Blank out the two text boxes
  ' and reset the focus.

  NewFirstName.Text = ""
  NewLastName.Text = ""
  NewFirstName.SetFocus
```

(continued)

```
    ' Hide this form, returning control
    ' to the MEMOPRNT form.

    Hide

End Sub  ' CancelButton_Click
```

12

Drag-and-Drop Operations: The Program Summaries *Application*

INTRODUCTION

Windows applications often include objects you can drag from one place to another on the desktop to achieve particular results. In an application that uses dragging as a meaningful operation, here is how you move an object from one place to another with the mouse:

1. Position the mouse pointer over the object on the screen.
2. Hold down the mouse button, and move the mouse to a new position. The object on the screen moves along with the mouse pointer.
3. Release the mouse button at the screen position where you want to leave the object. This action is known as *dropping* the object.

The specific purpose of this familiar *drag-and-drop* operation is defined by the application itself. A program might expect you to drag one object to the location of a second screen object that represents a particular function or operation. In this context, the object you drag is known as the *source*, and the object where you drop the source is the *target*. For example, dragging an icon to a target object might represent an instruction to copy a document from one place to another or to merge one document with another.

Visual Basic defines properties, methods, and events for activating and recognizing drag-and-drop operations in an application. Two relevant control properties that you set either at design time or at run time are **DragMode** and **DragIcon**:

- The **DragMode** property has settings of **0-Manual** and **1-Automatic**. In the manual mode, your program uses a Visual Basic method named **Drag** to enable dragging. In the automatic mode, dragging is always available for the specified object.

- The **DragIcon** property identifies the icon that moves on the screen while an object is being dragged. By default, Visual Basic simply displays an empty box as the drag image, but you can redefine this image by choosing an icon for the **DragIcon** property. At design time you set the image for the **DragIcon** property by selecting an ICO file from Visual Basic's icon library, just as you can do for the **Picture** property of a picture box or the **Icon** property of a form. (There are also ways to assign an icon to the **DragIcon** property at run time, as you'll learn later in this chapter.)

An event called **DragDrop** is another important feature in an application that uses dragging. This event occurs when the user drags a source object to a target object and then releases the mouse button. Because the target control is the object of this event, the corresponding event procedure has the following name:

```
TargetObject_DragDrop
```

One of the values that Visual Basic automatically passes to this procedure is a control-type argument that identifies the source object. The code you write for the **DragDrop** event procedure therefore defines your program's specific reaction to the drag-and-drop operation.

This chapter's sample project, named the *Program Summaries* application, illustrates drag-and-drop operations. As its name suggests, this program provides summaries of all the major applications that you have worked with in this book. It is also a convenient launch for running the programs. *Program Summaries* displays the icon for each of this book's nine major programs, and offers you three options for any program you select. By dragging a program icon to a particular function box you can:

- Request a description of the program.

- Request a list of the Visual Basic features illustrated in the program.

- Start a performance of the program.

With its nine program icons and three options, this application potentially performs 27 different operations. This assortment could result in a confusing array of options if presented as command buttons or option buttons. Instead, the program displays a row of drag-and-drop icons, along with three picture boxes that recognize the **DragDrop** event. As you'll see, this combination of controls results in a clear set of options that are easy to select.

THE *PROGRAM SUMMARIES* APPLICATION

The project is stored on the exercise disk under the name PRO-GRAMS.MAK. Load the project now and press F5 to run it. Figure 12.1 shows the form you see on the desktop. The nine icons displayed in the upper half of the form represent the applications presented in Chapters 5 to 12. The three boxes in the lower half of the form—labeled **Description**, **Visual Basic Features**, and **Run**—represent the three functions of the *Program Summaries* application: describe a program, list the Visual Basic features of a program, or run a program. To select one of these functions for a given program, you drag the program icon and drop the icon into the box corresponding to the operation you want to perform.

For example, Figure 12.2 shows what happens when you drag the *Address File* icon down to the **Description** box. The image disappears from the row of program icons, and appears inside the **Description** box. More importantly, the program displays a new form on the desktop, giving a brief description of the *Address File* application.

While this new **Description** form is on the screen, the controls on the main *Program Summaries* form are inactive. After you read the description, click the **OK** button on the second form. The description disappears and you can once again drag any of the nine icons to any of the three function

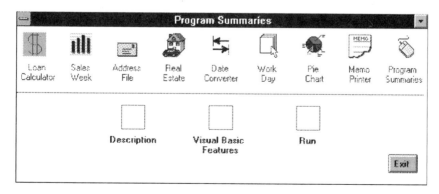

Figure 12.1 The *Program Summaries* Application

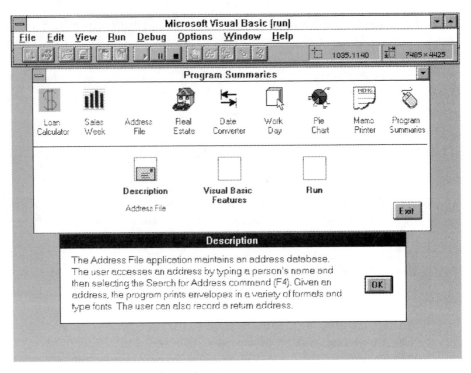

Figure 12.2 The description of a program

boxes. Figures 12.3 to 12.11 show the **Description** forms and the **Visual Basic Features** windows that the program displays for the nine programs. These summaries serve as an informal reference to the work you've done with Visual Basic in this book.

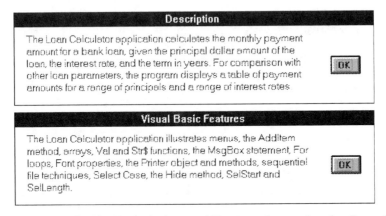

Figure 12.3 The **Description** and **Features** boxes for the *Loan Calculator* Application

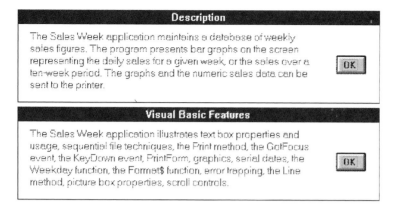

Figure 12.4 The **Description** and **Features** boxes for the *Sales Week* Application

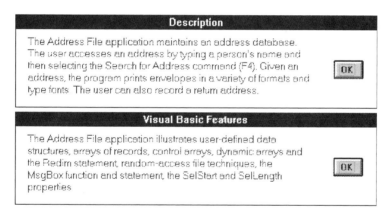

Figure 12.5 The **Description** and **Features** boxes for the *Address File* Application

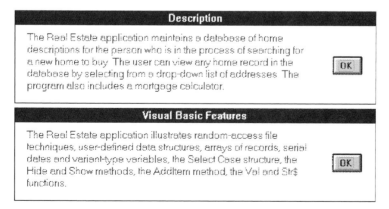

Figure 12.6 The **Description** and **Features** boxes for the *Real Estate* Application

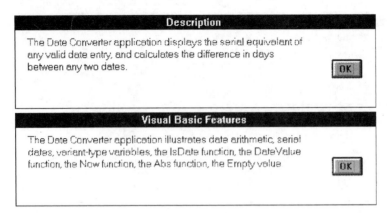

Figure 12.7 The **Description** and **Features** boxes for the *Date Converter* Application

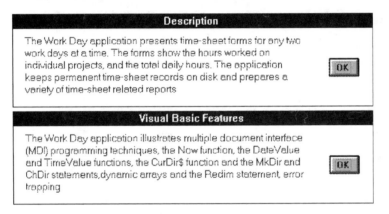

Figure 12.8 The **Description** and **Features** boxes for the *Workday* Application

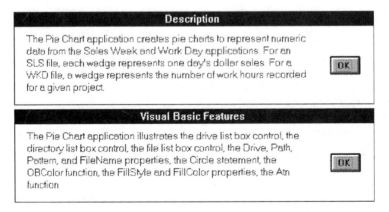

Figure 12.9 The **Description** and **Features** boxes for the *Pie Chart* Application

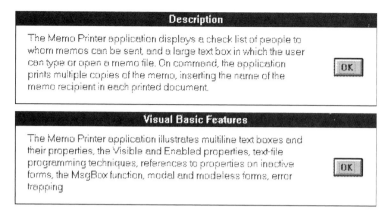

Figure 12.10 The **Description** and **Features** boxes for the *Memo Printer* Application

To run a program, the *Program Summaries* has to find the corresponding EXE file on disk in the Windows directory. Here are the names of the EXE files you need in order to take advantage of this feature:

```
LOAN.EXE
SALESWK.EXE
ADDRESS.EXE
REALEST.EXE
DATES.EXE
WORKDAY.EXE
PIE.EXE
MEMO.EXE
```

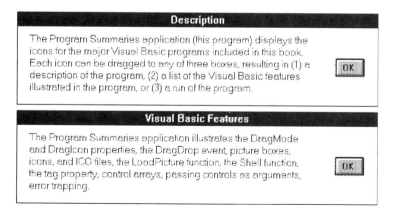

Figure 12.11 The **Description** and **Features** boxes for the *Program Summaries* Application

If you haven't yet created the EXE file for a particular application, load the program into Visual Basic and choose the **Make EXE File** from the **File** menu.

THE ELEMENTS OF THE *PROGRAM SUMMARIES* APPLICATION

The *Program Summaries* application consists of two forms, named **Prog-Summ** and **ProgDesc** (Figure 12.12). The **ProgSumm** form contains two arrays of picture box controls and two arrays of labels. The **ProgDesc** form has one large label and a command button. Much of the program's code is devoted to preparing the messages that appear on the **ProgDesc** form. But the most important event procedure, named **DestFunction_DragDrop**, is the one that defines the program's response to a **DragDrop** event. This is the procedure that you'll be concentrating on in this chapter.

Controls and Properties

The *Program Summaries* application relies on interaction between different control arrays to simplify the operations performed in code. The **Prog-Summ** form contains four control arrays: two arrays of picture boxes and two arrays of labels. Here are descriptions of these four arrays:

- An array of picture boxes named **ProgIcon** displays the nine program icons. The **Index** settings of these controls range from **1** to **9**. The design-time **Picture** properties are all icons. Eight of the nine icons come from Visual Basic's icon library, and one is a custom-made icon. Table 12.1 gives the file names for the nine icons. (Visual Basic's icon library is stored in the directory named VB\ICONS, which is in turn divided into several subdirectories.) The **DragMode** and **DragIcon** properties of these nine picture boxes are set at run time rather than at design time.

- An array of labels named **ProgName** displays the names of the nine applications. Like the **ProgIcon** array, these controls have **Index**

Figure 12.12 The PROGRAMS.MAK project

Table 12.1 The ICO file names of icons displayed in the *Program Summaries* application.

ProgIcon Index	Icon File Name
1	LOAN.ICO *(exercise disk)*
2	OFFICE\GRAPH08.ICO
3	MAIL\MAIL01A.ICO
4	MISC\HOUSE.ICO
5	COMPUTER\KEY06.ICO
6	DRAGDROP\DRAG3PG.ICO
7	OFFICE\GRAPH11.ICO
8	WRITING\NOTE08.ICO
9	COMPUTER\MOUSE02.ICO

settings ranging from **1** to **9**. All nine labels have **Alignment** settings of **2-Center** and **FontBold** settings of **False**.

- In the lower half of the **ProgSumm** form, the array of three bordered picture boxes is named **DestFunction**. These controls have **Index** settings ranging from **0** to **2**. Their **Picture** properties are set at run time when the user performs a drag-and-drop operation. (Immediately beneath each of these picture boxes is a label whose caption gives the program function represented by the box: **Description**, **Visual Basic Features**, and **Run**. These three labels are *not* part of a control array.)

- Finally, an array of three labels named **CopyName** is located at the bottom of the form. These labels have **Index** settings from **0** to **2**. They have no borders and blank **Caption** settings, and are therefore invisible at run time until the user performs a drag-and-drop operation. When an icon is dropped into one of the **DestFunction** boxes, the application displays the corresponding program name as the **Caption** property of the **CopyName** label.

The **ProgSumm** form also has one command button named **ExitButton**.

The **ProgDesc** form has two controls. The large label named **DescriptLabel** is where the program displays program descriptions and Visual Basic feature lists. The user clicks the command button named **DoneButton** to return to the main dialog box.

Procedures and Methods

The program's code appears in Listings 12.1 to 12.8. As usual, a **Form_Load** event procedure performs several important initializations in this application. Subsequently, the main action of the program is controlled by the **DragDrop** event procedure, along with **Click** procedures for the two command buttons.

Overview

The form-level declaration section for the **ProgSumm** form (Listing 12.1) includes **Dim** statements for three string arrays:

```
Dim Description(ProgCount) As String
Dim Features(ProgCount) As String
Dim ProgramNames(ProgCount) As String
```

In the **Descriptions** and **Features** arrays the program stores a description string and a list of program features for each of the nine programs. The **ProgramNames** array stores the names of the EXE files in which the compiled programs are stored on disk. The **Form_Load** procedure (Listing 12.2) initializes these three arrays by making calls to the three procedures designed to prepare the string values:

```
WriteDescriptions
ListProgramNames
ListFeatures
```

Form_Load also defines some important properties for the elements of the **ProgIcon** control array. Within a **For** loop, the procedure assigns settings to the **DragMode** and the **DragIcon** properties. First, the **DragMode** property for each element of **ProgIcon** is given a setting of **1**, representing the automatic drag mode:

```
For i% = 1 to ProgCount
  ProgIcon(i%).DragMode = 1
```

As a result, the user can perform drag-and-drop operations on all nine of the program icons. Then the procedure copies the design-time setting of each control's **Picture** property to the **DragIcon** property:

```
ProgIcon(i%).DragIcon = ProgIcon(i%).Picture
```

Thanks to this setting, each icon appears as a copy of its own image while it is dragged from one place to another. (Actually, you'll notice during run time that the drag icon is a black-and-white copy of the original full-color icon.)

Finally, the **Form_Load** procedure assigns settings to one additional property of each **ProgIcon** picture box—the **Tag** property. **Tag** is a property that you can use in any way you wish to store text information about a control. Unlike other properties, **Tag** has no effect on the actual behavior or appearance of a control. In effect, **Tag** is simply a storage place for information that your program might need about a particular control.

The **Form_Load** procedure stores each program's application name—copied from the **Caption** property of the corresponding **ProgName** label—as the value of the **Tag** property:

```
ProgIcon(i%).Tag = ProgName(i%).Caption
```

Recording this value now as a property of each **ProgIcon** control is a convenience later in the program, as you'll see when you examine the **DragDrop** event procedure.

Responding to the DragDrop Event

The **DestFunction_DragDrop** procedure (Listing 12.3) is called when the user drags any one of the nine program icons and drops it into one of the three **DestFunction** picture boxes. This event procedure receives several important arguments:

```
Sub DestFunction_DragDrop (Index As Integer, Source As Control,
                           X As Single, Y As Single)
```

Because **DestFunction** is a control array, the procedure's first argument is **Index**, representing the number of the target object in the drag-and-drop operation. The second argument, **Source**, is a control argument representing the icon that the user has selected to drag. There is no argument that specifies the index number of the source icon, but the procedure can read this number from the **Source.Index** property. The third and fourth arguments are **X** and **Y**, representing the address of the drop operation. These final two arguments are not used in this application.

The procedure's first step is to produce the visual illusion that the selected icon has moved from its original position at the top of the form down to the selected function box. To accomplish this, the program first copies the **Picture** property of the **Source** control to the **Picture** property of the selected **DestFunction** picture box:

```
DestFunction(Index).Picture = Source.Picture
```

This is another example of copying design-time icon selections to run-time property settings. The next step is simply to set the **Visible** property of the **Source** control to **False**:

```
Source.Visible = False
```

Notice that the program does not *remove* the source icon, but simply makes it temporarily invisible. Later the icon will reappear in its original position.

In addition to displaying the selected icon inside the target picture box, the form displays the corresponding application name as a label beneath the picture box. To accomplish this, the program copies the value of **Source.Tag** to the **Caption** property of the **CopyName** label:

```
CopyName(Index).Caption = Source.Tag
```

This is the first of several uses of the **Source.Tag** setting that was assigned in the **Form_Load** procedure.

The next action depends on which of the three **DestFunction** picture boxes the user has selected. A **Select Case** decision structure uses the **Index** argument as the selector value:

```
Select Case Index
```

If the user has requested a description or a list of Visual Basic features, the program moves its focus to the **ProgDesc** form. First the form's caption is changed to one of two titles:

```
ProgDesc.Caption = "Description"
```

or:

```
ProgDesc.Caption = "Visual Basic Features"
```

Then the program copies the appropriate text to the **Caption** property of the form's **DescriptLabel** control. This text comes either from the **Description** array:

```
ProgDesc!DescriptLabel.Caption = Description(Source.Index)
```

or from the **Features** array:

```
ProgDesc!DescriptLabel.Caption = Features(Source.Index)
```

Because these two assignments are made from within the **ProgSumm** form rather than the **ProgDesc** form, the procedure uses the extended notation for referring to a control property on another form:

```
FormName!ControlName.PropertyName
```

Also notice the use of **Source.Index** to select the correct text from the **Description** or **Features** array.

Finally, once the **ProgDesc** form contains the information the user has requested, a call to the **Show** method displays the form on the desktop:

```
ProgDesc.Show 1
```

The **Show** argument of **1** displays **ProgDesc** as a *modal* form. While **ProgDesc** has the focus, the **ProgSumm** controls are temporarily frozen in place.

If the user drops a program icon into the **Run** box, the **DragDrop** event procedure makes an attempt to initiate a run of the selected program. The Visual Basic function named **Shell** runs a Windows program. The syntax of the function call is:

```
Shell(ProgramName, ProgramWindow)
```

The first argument gives the name of an executable program file, along with the directory location if necessary. The second argument, which is optional, is an integer that specifies how the program window will appear on the desktop. **Shell** returns an integer that identifies the application in the Windows environment.

The **DestFunction_DragDrop** event procedure makes the following call to the **Shell** function:

```
ID = Shell(Path + ProgramNames(Source.Index), 7)
```

Path is a string constant defined in the form-level declaration section. (If you have copied the EXE program files to a directory other than C:\WINDOWS, you will have to revise the **Const** statement that defines the **Path** constant.) The EXE program names are stored in the string array named **ProgramNames**. A reference to **Source.Index** selects the correct program name from the array. The second **Shell** argument of **7** results in a minimized program window that does *not* have the focus.

As you might expect, the **Shell** function results in a run-time error if the program cannot be run for any reason—for example, if the executable file is not found, or if there is not enough memory to begin the performance. Anticipating this possibility, the **DragDrop** procedure sets up an error trap around the call to **Shell**:

```
On Error Goto BadStart
  ID = Shell(Path + ProgramNames(Source.Index), 7)
ON Error Goto 0
```

Figure 12.13 Error message displayed for an unsuccessful call to **Shell**

If the attempt to start the program fails, the error routine located at **BadStart** displays a brief error message on the desktop:

```
BadStart:
  MsgBox "Can't start program.", 48, Source.Tag
Resume Next
```

An example of this message appears in Figure 12.13.

If the user drags the *Program Summaries* application icon to the **Run** box, the program does not even attempt a call to the **Shell** function. Instead, a message appears on the desktop reminding the user that *Program Summaries* is already running.

When the action requested by the user's drag-and-drop operation has been completed, the program makes a call to a procedure named **RestoreIcons** (Listing 12.4) to restore the **ProgSumm** form back to its original appearance. This procedure begins by switching the **Visible** property back to **True** for the **ProgIcon** picture boxes—in effect, returning the source icon back to its place:

```
For i% = 1 to ProgCount
  ProgIcon(i%).Visible = True
Next i%
```

Because **RestoreIcons** does not know which icon was dragged, it switches **Visible** to **True** for all nine picture boxes.

Next the procedure removes the icon from the selected **DestFunction** picture box. This is done by a call to Visual Basic's **LoadPicture** function:

```
DestFunction(i%).Picture = LoadPicture()
```

The primary use of the **LoadPicture** function is just the opposite of its use here. Given a string argument containing the name of an ICO file on disk, the function *loads* the picture into an object:

```
LoadPicture(PictureFileName)
```

But without an argument, **LoadPicture** instead clears the current picture value from an object.

Finally, the **RestoreIcons** procedure blanks out the **Caption** property of the **CopyName** label:

```
CopyName(i%).Caption = ""
```

These assignments restore the original appearance of the **ProgSumm** form. The program is now ready for the next drag-and-drop operation.

SUMMARY: DRAG-AND-DROP OPERATIONS

Drag-and-drop is a typical Windows feature that you can support in your Visual Basic applications. To plan for a drag-and-drop operation, you use a combination of properties, methods, and event procedures:

1. Activate the drag mode for an object by assigning a setting of **1** to the **DragMode** property. The object that the user drags is known as the *source* in the drag-and-drop operation.

2. Select an icon that will appear on the screen during the drag operation. Assign this icon to the **DragIcon** property of the source object. At design time you select an ICO file from the directory box that Visual Basic displays on the screen. At run time you can use the **LoadPicture** function to assign an icon, or you can copy an icon from one property to another.

3. Write a **DragDrop** procedure for the *target* object. This procedure defines your program's specific reaction to the user's drag-and-drop operation.

Drag-and-drop operations give the user a dramatically visual way of making selections and issuing instructions, simplifying the user interface for an application that contains a complex array of options.

Listing 12.1 Declarations from the **ProgSumm** form

```
' PROGSUMM.FRM
' The main dialog box for
' the Program Summaries application.

' Form-level Declarations.

Const ProgCount = 9

' The path for locating programs.

Const Path = "C:\Windows\"

' The arrays of program descriptions.

Dim Description(ProgCount) As String
Dim Features(ProgCount) As String
Dim ProgramNames(ProgCount) As String

' End of form-level declarations
' for the PROGSUMM form.
```

Listing 12.2 The **Form_Load** procedure (**ProgSumm**)

```
Sub Form_Load ()

   ' Initialize the picture box properties and
   ' call the program-description procedures.

   For i% = 1 To ProgCount

      ' DragMode and DragIcon determine the
      ' icon-dragging behavior.

      ProgIcon(i%).DragMode = 1
      ProgIcon(i%).DragIcon = ProgIcon(i%).Picture
      ProgIcon(i%).Tag = ProgName(i%).Caption

   Next i%
```

```
    ' Call the three procedures that
    ' prepare program descriptions.

    WriteDescriptions
    ListProgramNames
    ListFeatures

End Sub  ' Form_Load
```

Listing 12.3 The **DestFunction_DragDrop** procedure

```
Sub DestFunction_DragDrop (Index As Integer, Source As Control, x
As Single, Y As Single)

  ' Respond to the user's action of dragging and dropping an icon.

  ' First copy the icon to the destination picture box, and
  ' temporarily set the Visible property of the source icon
  ' to false. Also, copy the program name to the label beneath
  ' the destination picture box.

  DestFunction(Index).Picture = Source.Picture
  Source.Visible = False
  CopyName(Index).Caption = Source.Tag

  ' Select an action, depending upon the destination box
  ' in which the user has dropped the icon.

  Select Case Index
    Case 0

      ' For the first destination box, display
      ' a description of the program.

      ProgDesc.Caption = "Description"
      ProgDesc!DescriptLabel.Caption = Description(Source.Index)
      ProgDesc.Show 1

    Case 1

      ' For the second destination box, display
      ' the list of Visual Basic features.
```

(continued)

```
        ProgDesc.Caption = "Visual Basic Features"
        ProgDesc!DescriptLabel.Caption = Features(Source.Index)
        ProgDesc.Show 1

    Case 2

        ' For the third destination box, attempt
        ' to run the program. If an error occurs
        ' display an error message on the screen.

        If Source.Index <> ProgCount Then
          On Error GoTo BadStart
            ID = Shell(Path + ProgramNames(Source.Index), 7)
          On Error GoTo 0
        Else

            ' This program is already running.

            MsgBox "This program.", 64, Source.Tag
        End If
  End Select

  ' Restore the original row of program icons.

  RestoreIcons
  Exit Sub

' Display an error message if an error
' occurs during the attempt to run a program.

BadStart:
  MsgBox "Can't start program.", 48, Source.Tag
Resume Next

End Sub   ' DestFunction_DragDrop
```

Listing 12.4 The **RestoreIcons** procedure

```
Sub RestoreIcons ()

  ' Move an icon from where it has been dropped,
  ' back to its place in the row of program icons.
```

```
  ' Restore the Visible property for all the icons.

  For i% = 1 To ProgCount
    ProgIcon(i%).Visible = True
  Next i%

  ' Remove the icon from the function box.

  For i% = 0 To 2
    DestFunction(i%).Picture = LoadPicture()
    CopyName(i%).Caption = ""
  Next i%

End Sub  ' RestoreIcons
```

Listing 12.5 The **ListProgramNames** and **ExitButton_Click** procedures

```
Sub ListProgramNames ()

  ' List the EXE program names, for running
  ' each program from the Shell function.

  ProgramNames(1) = "Loan"
  ProgramNames(2) = "SalesWk"
  ProgramNames(3) = "Address"
  ProgramNames(4) = "RealEst"
  ProgramNames(5) = "Dates"
  ProgramNames(6) = "WorkDay"
  ProgramNames(7) = "Pie"
  ProgramNames(8) = "Memo"
  ProgramNames(9) = "Programs"

End Sub  ' ListProgramNames


Sub ExitButton_Click ()

  ' Terminate the program performance.

  End

End Sub  ' ExitButton_Click
```

Listing 12.6 The **WriteDescriptions** procedure

```
Sub WriteDescriptions ()

  ' Prepare the program descriptions.

  Dim D As String

  D = "The Loan Calculator application calculates the monthly payment "
  D = D + "amount for a bank loan, given the principal dollar amount "
  D = D + "of the loan, the interest rate, and the term in years. "
  D = D + "For comparison with other loan parameters, the program "
  D = D + "displays a table of payment amounts for a range of "
  D = D + "principals and a range of interest rates."
  Description(1) = D

  D = "The Sales Week application maintains a database of weekly sales "
  D = D + "figures. The program presents bar graphs on the screen "
  D = D + "representing the daily sales for a given week, or the sales "
  D = D + "over a ten-week period. The graphs and the numeric sales "
  D = D + "data can be sent to the printer."
  Description(2) = D

  D = "The Address File application maintains an address database. "
  D = D + "The user accesses an address by typing a person's name "
  D = D + "and then selecting the Search for Address command (F4). "
  D = D + "Given an address, the program prints envelopes in a variety "
  D = D + "of formats and type fonts. The user can also record a "
  D = D + "return address. "
  Description(3) = D

  D = "The Real Estate application maintains a database of home "
  D = D + "descriptions for the person who is in the process of "
  D = D + "searching for a new home to buy. The user can view any "
  D = D + "home record in the database by selecting from a drop-down "
  D = D + "list of addresses. The program also includes a mortgage "
  D = D + "calculator."
  Description(4) = D

  D = "The Date Converter application displays the serial "
  D = D + "equivalant of any valid date entry, and calculates "
  D = D + "the difference in days between any two dates."
  Description(5) = D

  D = "The Work Day application presents time-sheet forms for any "
  D = D + "two work days at a time. The forms show the hours "
  D = D + "worked on individual projects, and the total daily hours. "
  D = D + "The application keeps permanent time-sheet records on disk "
  D = D + "and prepares a variety of time-sheet related reports."
  Description(6) = D

  D = "The Pie Chart application creates pie charts to represent "
```

```
    D = D + "numeric data from the Sales Week and Work Day applications. "
    D = D + "For an SLS file, each wedge represents one day's dollar "
    D = D + "sales. For a WKD file, a wedge represents the number of "
    D = D + "work hours recorded for a given project."
    Description(7) = D

    D = "The Memo Printer application displays a check list of people "
    D = D + "to whom memos can be sent, and a large text box in which "
    D = D + "the user can type or open a memo file. On command, the "
    D = D + "application prints multiple copies of the memo, inserting "
    D = D + "the name of the memo recipient in each printed document. "
    Description(8) = D

    D = "The Program Summaries application (this program) displays the "
    D = D + "icons for the major Visual Basic programs included in "
    D = D + "this book. Each icon can be dragged to any of three boxes, "
    D = D + "resulting in (1) a description of the program, (2) a list "
    D = D + "of the Visual Basic features illustrated in the program, "
    D = D + "or (3) a run of the program."
    Description(9) = D

End Sub   ' WriteDescriptions
```

Listing 12.7 The **ListFeatures** procedure

```
Sub ListFeatures ()

  ' List the Visual Basic features illustrated in
  ' each of the programs.

  Dim i%, F As String

  For i% = 1 To ProgCount
    Features(i%) = "The " + ProgName(i%).Caption
    Features(i%) = Features(i%) + " application illustrates "
  Next i%

  F = "menus, the AddItem method, arrays, Val and Str$ functions, "
  F = F + "the MsgBox statement, For loops, Font properties, "
  F = F + "the Printer object and methods, sequential file techniques, "
  F = F + "Select Case, the Hide method, SelStart and SelLength."
  Features(1) = Features(1) + F

  F = "text box properties and usage, sequential file techniques, "
  F = F + "the Print method, the GotFocus event, the KeyDown event, "
  F = F + "PrintForm, graphics, serial dates, the Weekday function, "
  F = F + "the Format$ function, error trapping, the Line method, "
  F = F + "picture box properties, scroll controls."
  Features(2) = Features(2) + F
```

(continued)

```
    F = "user-defined data structures, arrays of records, "
    F = F + "control arrays, dynamic arrays and the Redim "
    F = F + "statement, random-access file techniques, the MsgBox "
    F = F + "function and statement, the SelStart and SelLength "
    F = F + "properties."
    Features(3) = Features(3) + F

    F = "random-access file techniques, user-defined data structures, "
    F = F + "arrays of records, serial dates and variant-type "
    F = F + "variables, the Select Case structure, the Hide and "
    F = F + "Show methods, the AddItem method, the Val and Str$ "
    F = F + "functions."
    Features(4) = Features(4) + F

    F = "date arithmetic, serial dates, variant-type variables, "
    F = F + "the IsDate function, the DateValue function, "
    F = F + "the Now function, the Abs function, the Empty value. "
    Features(5) = Features(5) + F

    F = "multiple document interface (MDI) programming techniques, "
    F = F + "the Now function, the DateValue and TimeValue functions, "
    F = F + "the CurDir$ function and the MkDir and ChDir statements,"
    F = F + "dynamic arrays and the Redim statement, error trapping."
    Features(6) = Features(6) + F

    F = "the drive list box control, the directory list box control, "
    F = F + "the file list box control, the Drive, Path, Pattern, and "
    F = F + "FileName properties, the Circle statement, the QBColor "
    F = F + "function, the FillStyle and FillColor properties, "
    F = F + "the Atn function."
    Features(7) = Features(7) + F

    F = "multiline text boxes and their properties, the Visible and "
    F = F + "Enabled properties, text-file programming techniques, "
    F = F + "references to properties on inactive forms, "
    F = F + "the MsgBox function, modal and modeless forms, "
    F = F + "error trapping."
    Features(8) = Features(8) + F

    F = "the DragMode and DragIcon properties, the DragDrop event, "
    F = F + "picture boxes, icons, and ICO files, the LoadPicture "
    F = F + "function, the Shell function, the tag property, "
    F = F + "control arrays, passing controls as arguments, "
    F = F + "error trapping."
    Features(9) = Features(9) + F

End Sub  ' ListFeatures
```

Listing 12.8 The **DoneButton_Click** procedure (**ProgDesc** form)

```
' PROGDESC.FRM
' Displays program descriptions
' and lists of Visual Basic features.


Sub DoneButton_Click ()

  ' Return control to the PROGDESC form.

  DescriptLabel.Caption = ""
  Hide

End Sub   ' DoneButton_Click
```

Appendix

Using an Access Database in a Visual Basic 3.0 Application

Several of the major projects you've worked with in this book are, in effect, database applications: They manage collections of data on disk, and they give you specific tools for entering, organizing, updating, examining, presenting, and understanding the data. For example, the *Sales Week* program (Chapter 6) stores weekly sales data and creates bar graphs for comparing the sales in a given week or in a series of weeks. The *Real Estate* program (Chapter 8) maintains a database of residential property descriptions and allows you to examine any address record, one at a time. The *Workday* application (Chapter 9) stores daily work records in a time-sheet format and prints a variety of reports from the data.

All of these programs use standard Basic-language techniques for creating and updating sequential-access and random-access data files. In addition, some of the applications contain their own routines for performing common database tasks such as sorting and searching. Although this traditional approach to database programming remains eminently viable, Visual Basic 3.0 now offers you yet another way to develop database applications: You can establish a connection between a Visual Basic application and a database that you have developed in any one of several database management environments—including Microsoft Access, dBASE III or IV, FoxPro, Paradox, and BTrieve. Once the connection is made, you can use your own Visual Basic application as a convenient "front-end" form for viewing and revising existing records in the database and for appending new records.

Figure A.1 The data control

Remarkably, this new approach requires little or no programming. The key to creating a database connection is Visual Basic's new data control, identified in Figure A.1. By including a data control in a form and setting the control's relevant properties, you can efficiently identify the database that you want to connect to your application. You then designate other controls in the same form—such as text boxes, labels, and check boxes—as *bound* controls that will represent individual fields in the database.

Here is a preview of the major steps necessary for connecting a database to a Visual Basic 3.0 application:

1. Double-click the data control icon in the toolbar to add a data control to the current form. Use the mouse to resize the control and move it to the position where you want it to appear in the application.

2. While the data control is selected, activate the Properties window and enter settings for the following essential properties:

    *   The **Connect** property identifies the type of database you'll be working with (for example, dBASE IV or FoxPro 2.5). You do not need to set this property for a Microsoft Access database.

    *   The **DatabaseName** property gives the path and file name of the database you want to connect to your application.

    *   The **RecordSource** property identifies the database table to which your application will gain access.

- The **Name** property, as always, assigns a specific name to the control. You subsequently use this name to bind other controls in the form to the database.

- The **Caption** property is the text that appears inside the data control itself. You can use this property to supply a brief caption that will identify the database to which your application is connected.

3. Add other controls to the form to represent the fields of the database. These bound controls will display the actual information that the database contains. In the Standard Edition of Visual Basic 3.0, five types of controls can be bound to database fields: text boxes, check boxes, labels, picture boxes, and image controls.

4. For each control that you want to bind to a database field, set the following essential properties:

- The **DataSource** property setting is the name of the data control that represents the connected database.

- The **DataField** control is the name of the database field to which the control will be bound.

You accomplish all of these steps in the design mode, using the Toolbox and the Properties window. No programming is involved up to this point. When you complete these steps, you can run your application and immediately begin viewing individual records from the connected database, one record at a time.

To illustrate the process of connecting a database to a Visual Basic 3.0 application, this appendix presents a new version of the *Real Estate* project. Instead of creating its own data files on disk, this program will use a database developed in Microsoft Access. If Access is installed on your computer, you can begin your work by creating the database itself. (If you do not have Access, you can create the database in the Data Manager program that is supplied with Visual Basic. Choose the **Data Manager** command from the **Windows** menu to start the program.) Once the resulting MDB file is stored on disk, you'll establish a connection between the database and a new Visual Basic application.

THE REAL ESTATE DATABASE IN MICROSOFT ACCESS

Figure A.2 shows the window for an Access database named REALEST (saved on disk as REALEST.MDB). As you can see, the database contains one table, named Homes. The Homes table stores descriptions of individ-

Figure A.2 The REALEST database

ual residential properties that are currently on the market in a particular city. Figure A.3 shows the structure of the Homes table; it contains ten fields, for storing the address of a home, the asking price, the various characteristics of the home, the date the home was viewed, and the viewer's comments. You'll notice that these fields match the controls that appear in the original *Real Estate* application, as presented in Chapters 1 and 8. The ten fields belong to a variety of data types: Address and Comments are text fields; Asking Price is a currency field; Sq Feet, Bedrooms, and Bathrooms are numeric fields; Garage, Views, and Garden are Yes/No fields; and Date Viewed is a date field. The Address field is the table's primary key.

In an Access table, each row contains an individual record of information and each column represents one of the table's fields. For an example,

Field Name	Data Type	Description
Address	Text	Address of home viewed.
Asking Price	Currency	Current asking price of home.
Sq Feet	Number	Size of home in square feet.
Bedrooms	Number	Number of bedrooms in home.
Bathrooms	Number	Number of bathrooms in home.
Garage	Yes/No	Does home have a garage?
Views	Yes/No	Are there significant views from the home?
Garden	Yes/No	Does the home have a garden?
Date Viewed	Date/Time	Date when the home was viewed.
Comments	Text	Other information about the home.

Field Properties

Field Size	50
Format	
Caption	
Default Value	
Validation Rule	
Validation Text	
Indexed	Yes (No Duplicates)

A field name can be up to 64 characters long, including spaces. Press F1 for help on field names.

Figure A.3 The structure of the Homes table

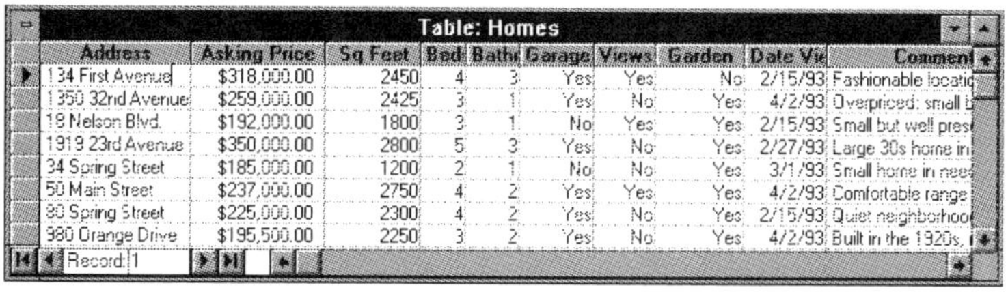

Table: Homes

Address	Asking Price	Sq Feet	Bed	Bath	Garage	Views	Garden	Date Vi	Comment
134 First Avenue	$318,000.00	2450	4	3	Yes	Yes	No	2/15/93	Fashionable locati
1350 32nd Avenue	$259,000.00	2425	3	1	Yes	No	Yes	4/2/93	Overpriced; small b
18 Nelson Blvd.	$192,000.00	1800	3	1	No	Yes	Yes	2/15/93	Small but well pres
1919 23rd Avenue	$350,000.00	2800	5	3	Yes	No	Yes	2/27/93	Large 30s home in
34 Spring Street	$185,000.00	1200	2	1	No	No	Yes	3/1/93	Small home in nee
50 Main Street	$237,000.00	2750	4	2	Yes	Yes	Yes	4/2/93	Comfortable range
80 Spring Street	$225,000.00	2300	4	2	Yes	No	Yes	2/15/93	Quiet neighborhoo
980 Orange Drive	$195,500.00	2250	3	2	Yes	No	Yes	4/2/93	Built in the 1920s,

Record: 1

Figure A.4 Sample records in the Homes table

Figure A.4 shows a few sample records in the Homes table. Notice that the entries in each field column all belong to a consistent data type.

Suppose you have developed this database in Microsoft Access and you now want to create a Visual Basic project that uses the information contained in the database. Although Microsoft Access itself supplies a variety of sophisticated programming tools, you may have your own reasons for prefering Visual Basic as an environment for developing a database application. Perhaps you are more familiar with Visual Basic, or you want to use some programming features that Access does not supply. Or you may have already designed several parts of a Visual Basic application that you now want to use with the Access database. Whatever your reasons, you'll find that you can quickly establish the connection between your Visual Basic application and the Access database.

A DATABASE APPLICATION

In the first stage of developing a Visual Basic application to use the Access REALEST database, you define the characteristics of a data control that will represent the database. If Access is running in the Windows environment, make sure that the REALEST database is closed. Then start a new Visual Basic project and follow these steps:

1. Double-click the data control in the Toolbox to add the control to the active form (Form1 of the new project). Inside the form itself, the new control initially consists of a horizontal arrangement of four buttons, labeled |◀, ◀, ▶, and ▶|, respectively. (See Figure A.5.)
2. Drag the control to the lower left corner of the form, and increase its dimensions to a width setting of 2175 and a height setting of 390. The new width setting reveals a caption area between the ◀ and ▶ buttons. The initial caption is Data1.
3. While the data control remains selected, activate the Properties window. Enter a new setting of **Homes** as the setting of the **Caption**

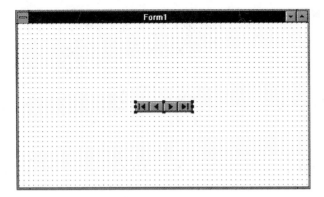

Figure A.5 The data control as it initially appears on a form

property. In the form, the control now appears as shown in Figure A.6.

4. Select the **DatabaseName** property. Then click the **...** button located at the right side of the Settings box in the Properties window. In response, Visual Basic opens the **DatabaseName** dialog box, designed for you to identify the location and name of the database that you want to connect to your application. In the Directories box, find the directory where the target database is stored; then, in the file list box, select the name of the target database, **realest.mdb**. (See Figure A.7.) Click **OK** to confirm this selection. Back in the Properties window, the path name and file name of the Access database now appear as the setting of the **DatabaseName** property.

5. Now scroll down to the property named **RecordSource** in the Properties window. Select this property and then click the down-arrow

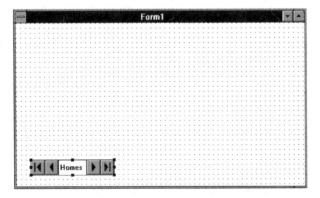

Figure A.6 Changing the dimensions and the caption of the data control

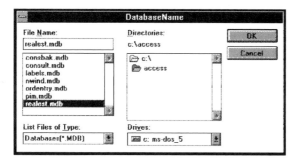

Figure A.7 Selecting an Access database to connect to the appliction

button at the right side of the Settings box. Because you have
designated REALEST.MDB as the connected database, Visual Basic
can now show you a drop-down list of the tables and queries contained in this database. As it happens, there is only one table in the
database, the table named Homes. (See Figure A.8.) Select this table
in the drop-down list, and Homes becomes the setting of the
RecordSource property.

6.   Finally, select the **Name** property in the Properties window and enter
HomeConnect as the name of the data control.

Now you are ready to begin adding other controls to the form and *binding*
them individually to fields in the Homes table. As a first experiment with
this procedure, follow these steps to create a text box for displaying the
Address field:

1.   Double-click the text box control in the Toolbox to add a new text
box control to the form. Drag the control to the upper-left corner
of the form, and adjust the control's dimensions to a width setting
of 2295 and a height setting of 375.

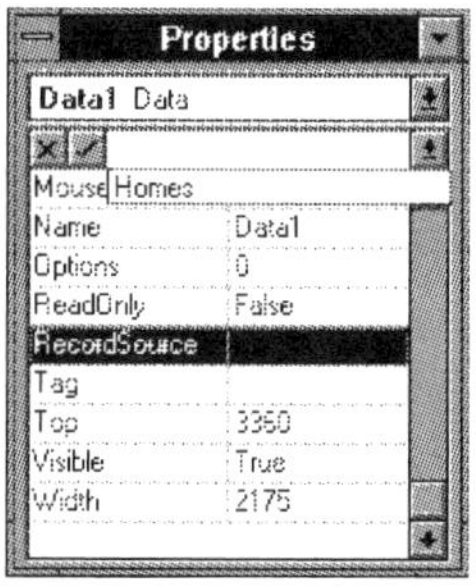

Figure A.8 Selecting a table as the **RecordSource** property setting

2.   While the text box control is still selected, activate the Properties window. Change the control's **Name** setting to **Address.** Then delete the default setting of the **Text** property, blanking out the current contents of the text box.

3.   Scroll up to the **DataSource** property. Click the down-arrow button at the right side of the Settings box; the resulting drop-down list contains the name of the form's data control, HomeConnect. Select this name as the setting for the **DataSource** property.

4.   Now select the **DataField** property, and once again click the down-arrow button at the right side of the Settings box. In response, Visual Basic displays a list of all the fields in the table that you have connected to this application, as shown in Figure A.9. Select Address in the list; this selection becomes the setting of the **DataField** property for the **Address** text box. In other words, the text box is now *bound* to the Address field in the Homes table.

Now you're ready to try running the appliction. Press F5 at the keyboard. When the performance begins, the Address text box initially displays the address entry from the first record of the Homes table. (See Figure A.10.) To scroll to other records in the table, you can use the four buttons in the data control, as follows:

- Click ▶ to move forward to the next address record in the table.

- Click ◀ to move to the previous record in the table.

- Click ▶| to move to the last record in the table.

- Click |◀ to move to the first record in the table.

Try clicking these buttons to see how your application allows you to view information from the connected database. Keep in mind that this data access is the result of the property settings you have established for the data

Figure A.9 Selecting a field for the **DataField** property

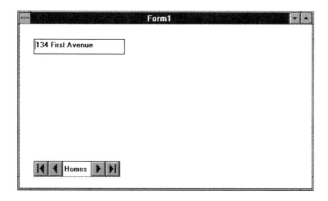

Figure A.10 Testing the database application early in its development

control and the text box; you have not yet written a single line of code in the application.

Choose **End** from the Visual Basic **Run** menu to stop the program performance. You can now continue developing your application by adding other bound controls to the form, to represent the remaining fields in the Homes database. Figure A.11 shows how the completed form might appear. Notice that the form now contains an assortment of text boxes, check boxes, and labels. The text boxes are bound to the text, currency, numeric, and date fields in the database, and the three check boxes are bound to the Yes/No fields. The labels in the form are unbound controls. Like the initial Address text box, each bound control has appropriate settings for the **DataSource** and **DataField** properties. When you run this application, the form shows a complete record from the Homes table, as in Figure A.12. As you've already seen, you can scroll through the records of the table by clicking the ◄, ◄, ►, and ►│ buttons in the data control.

You can use this form not only for *viewing* the records of the database table, but also for *revising* them. The steps for revising a record are simple:

1. Scroll to the record that you want to revise, and select the field containing the data you want to change.

2. Enter a new value for the field. (You can also revise the entries in any other fields of the same record.)

3. Click ◄, ◄, ►, and ►│ in the data control to scroll to a different record in the table. When you do so, the revision in the previously displayed record becomes permanent.

You may also want to use this Visual Basic application to add new records to the Homes table in the Access database. This is a database operation that requires some programming—but not much. As you'll see in the next

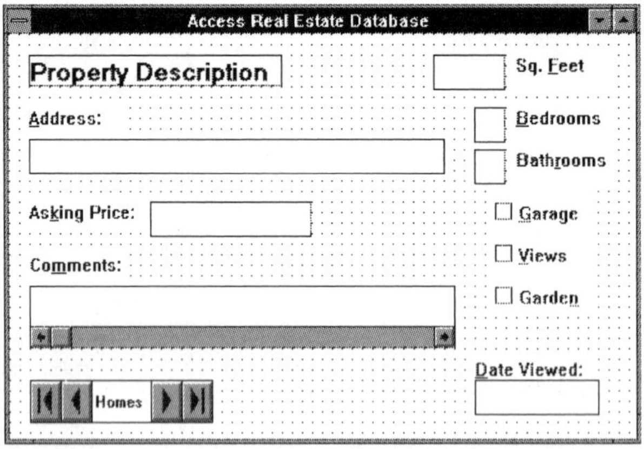

Figure A.11 The real estate application with additional bound controls

exercise, you can implement this operation by placing a command button in the form and writing a single line of code in the corresponding **Click** procedure. You'll also take this opportunity to add an **Exit** button to the form, for terminating the application:

1. In the design mode, double-click the command button tool twice in the Toolbox. Drag the two new controls to the bottom of the form, just to the right of the data control.

2. Select the first of the two buttons, and then activate the Properties window. Change the control's **Caption** property to **&New Home**, and then change the **Name** property to **NewRecButton**. This button will eventually allow you to add new records to the database.

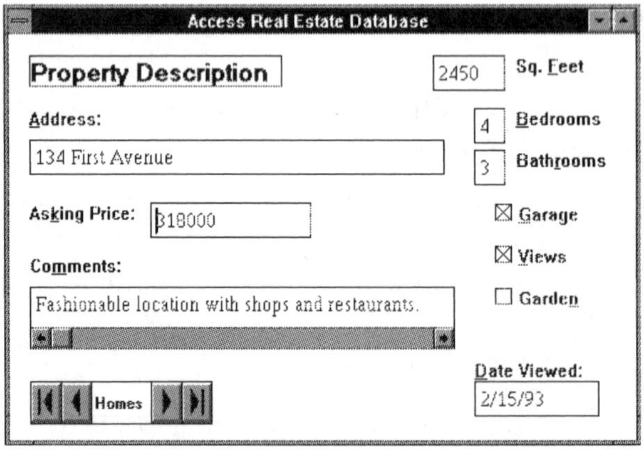

Figure A.12 Viewing a complete record from the Homes table

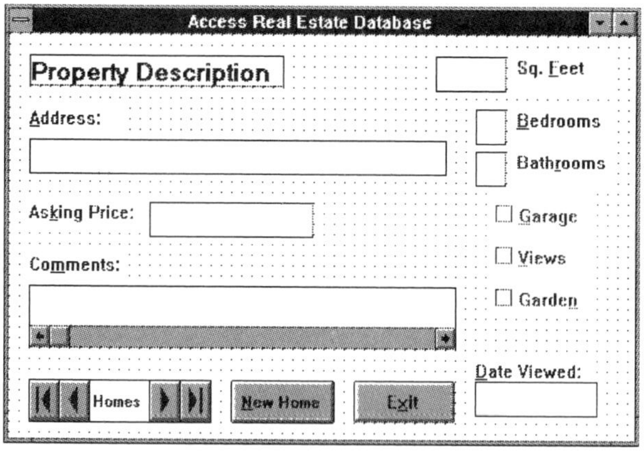

Figure A.13 Adding **New Home** and **Exit** buttons to the database application

3. Select the second button. Change the **Caption** property to **E&xit**, and the **Name** property to **ExitButton**. At this point in your work, the form appears as shown in Figure A.13.

4. Click the **View Code** button on the project window. In the code window, select **NewRecButton** in the **Object** box and **Click** in the **Proc** box. Enter one line of code into the **NewRecButton_Click** procedure, as follows:

```
Sub NewRecButton_Click ()
  HomeConnect.RecordSet.AddNew
End Sub
```

The **RecordSet** property of a data control represents the *dynaset* of records from the connected database. The **AddNew** method clears the bound controls in your application in preparation for adding a new record to the table. You'll see exactly how this method works shortly.

5. Still in the code window, select **ExitButton** in the **Object** box and **Click** in the **Proc** box. Enter one line of code into the **ExitButton_Click** procedure, as follows:

```
Sub ExitButton_Click ()
  End
End Sub
```

6. Close the code window and the form, and save your work.

You're now ready to try running the program. Press F5 at the keyboard. Once again, the form displays the entries from the first record in the

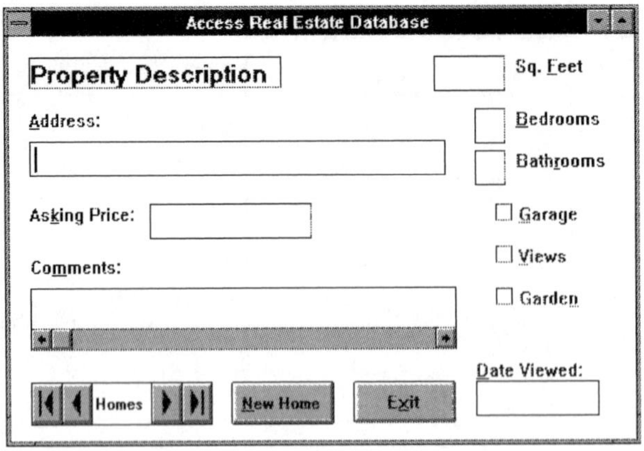

Figure A.14 Clearing the bound controls for a new record entry

database table. Try scrolling to other records if you wish, to make sure the application is still working as before. Then click the **New Home** button. In response, Visual Basic clears the information from all of the bound controls in the form, as shown in Figure A.14. You can now enter a new record: Type fields of information into the bound text boxes, and click any combination of options in the bound check boxes.

When you've finished the record entry, there are two ways to confirm the new record and add it to the table:

- Scroll to a different record in the table.

- Click **New Home** again to prepare for another new record.

After you take either one of these actions, the record becomes part of the table. On the other hand, if you click the **Exit** button to terminate the application—before confirming the new record—Visual Basic closes the database without adding the new record.

In summary, the data control and its associated database properties allow you to develop powerful database connections in just a few simple steps. Of course, once you have established this kind of connection, you can continue to expand your Visual Basic application in any number of directions. For example, in this version of the *Real Estate* application you might want to add features for calculating mortgages, just as in the original version of the program. All the powerful programming features of Visual Basic remain available to you, regardless of the source of data in your application.

Index